1983–84 Supplement
to the
Encyclopedia
of
Social Work

1983-84 Supplement

to the

Encyclopedia

of

Social Work

17th Edition

Encyclopedia Supplement Subcommittee

Scott Briar

Anne Minahan

Elaine Pinderhughes

Tony Tripodi

National Association of Social Workers
Silver Spring, Maryland

Library of Congress Cataloging in Publication Data
Main entry under title:

1983–84 supplement to the encyclopedia of social
  work, 17th edition.

  Includes index.
  1. Social service—United States—Yearbooks.
I. Briar, Scott, 1926-   . II. Encyclopedia of social
work. III. National Association of Social Workers.
HV91.A18 1983   361 '.003 '21   83–19507
ISBN 0–87101–122–0

Printed in U.S.A.

 3

PREFACE

This supplement to the *Encyclopedia of Social Work* represents a new departure for the NASW Publications Department. In the past, a new edition of the encyclopedia has been published every six or seven years. The most recent edition, the seventeenth, was published in 1977 and, following the pattern of the past, the plan had been to publish the eighteenth edition in 1984. However, several years ago, as the Publications Committee approached the decisions that would have initiated the long and difficult process required to produce the eighteenth edition, some questions arose.

One question was whether it was timely to publish the encyclopedia during a period when such extensive and pervasive changes were occurring in social work and social welfare in response to the initiatives of the Reagan Administration. Although similar questions may have been raised in the planning of previous editions, the present committee had a strong sense that unusually sweeping changes were currently occurring and that the magnitude and effects would be more clear and therefore more readily described if the eighteenth edition were delayed a few years.

Another loosely related question was why there had to be a six- or seven-year interval between editions of the encyclopedia. Why not make the interval longer, say ten years? Although the encyclopedia is, in the long run, fiscally self-supporting, each edition still represents a large and costly effort for the Publications Department and a substantial investment for purchasers. This question reflected the financial stringency of the time, but it was a natural question that deserved an answer.

In the discussion of these questions, an additional alternative was proposed, namely to publish regular supplements to the encyclopedia between editions. This proposal would make it possible to describe major new developments and changing trends without the need to rewrite or even revise those topics in which comparatively little change had occurred. This proposal also supported the suggestion to increase the interval between editions, because it addressed the concern that the encyclopedia would become too dated if it were published less frequently.

The outcome of these deliberations by the Publications Committee was a recommendation to the NASW Board of Directors, which the board accepted, to postpone publication of the eighteenth edition of the *Encyclopedia of Social Work* until 1987, to establish a regular ten-year schedule, and to publish this 1983–84 supplement to the seventeenth edition as the first in a regular series of full-length interim supplements.

The articles included in this supplement are focused on topics of two kinds. The first are topics that have emerged in the field since the seventeenth edition was published and thus describe new developments in the field. One example is the article "Computers." This subject was not covered in the 1977 encyclopedia. Even though computers were heavily used by some social workers before 1977, computers did not have a significant impact on the field until quite recently.

The second set of topics included in the supplement consists of those in which considerable change has occurred since publication of the 1977 encyclopedia. Two examples of such topics are the articles "Social Issues" and "Federal Social Welfare Programs."

One of the distinctive features of this supplement is its comprehensive section of statistical and demographic tables. Rather than merely updating the tables contained in the statistical supplement issued in 1980, this section represents an entirely new approach to the problem of surveying social and economic developments. There are more than twice as many tables as previously, and each table includes a statement summarizing the significance of the data it contains. It should be pointed out, however, that real or apparent statistical discrepancies may be found between the tables and the supplement's articles. Such conflict is not only inevitable when authors use differing source material and make individual interpretations of their sources, but it underscores the difficulties of research in the area of social services.

It is important to emphasize that this supplement is not comprehensive. Obviously, not all topics covered in the encyclopedia have been updated in this supplement, but only those—as explained previously—in which major changes have occurred in recent years. Nor was any effort made to use the supplement to respond to some of the criticisms of the seventeenth edition, such as the request for more biographies on people of color and other minority persons who were prominent in the history of social work. Finally, efforts were unsuccessfully made to obtain articles in some subjects, but time constraints forced us to go to press without them.

All these disclaimers aside, this supplement contains well-informed articles on important developments across a wide range of fields and topics in social work. As such, the Publications Committee and the Supplement Subcommittee believe this volume will be a valuable resource for users of the *Encyclopedia of Social Work.*

SCOTT BRIAR, *Chair*
NASW Publications Committee

Contributors

CHAUNCEY A. ALEXANDER, MSW
Former Executive Director, National Association of Social Workers, Silver Spring, Maryland; President, Alexander Associates, Huntington Beach, California

JIM BAUMOHL, MSW
Hotel Project Coordinator, Berkeley Support Services, Berkeley, California, and *Doctoral Candidate,* School of Social Welfare, University of California, Berkeley, California

RAYMOND M. BERGER, PH. D.
Associate Professor, School of Social Work, University of Illinois at Urbana-Champaign, Urbana, Illinois, and *Outpatient Clinician,* Champaign County Mental Health Center, Champaign, Illinois

MARTIN BLOOM, PH. D.
Professor, Virginia Commonwealth University, Richmond, Virginia

KATHARINE HOOPER BRIAR, DSW
Assistant Professor, School of Social Work, University of Washington, Seattle, Washington

SCOTT BRIAR, DSW
Dean, School of Social Work, University of Washington, Seattle, Washington

MARGUERITE J. DAVID, MSW
Lecturer and *Coordinator,* Project on Disability, School of Social Work, University of Washington, Seattle, Washington

DAVID FANSHEL, DSW
Professor, School of Social Work, Columbia University, New York, New York

LEON H. GINSBERG, PH. D.
Commissioner, West Virginia Department of Human Services, Charleston, West Virginia

JUNE GARY HOPPS, PH. D.
Dean and *Professor,* Graduate School of Social Work, Boston College, Chestnut Hill, Massachusetts

ALFRED J. KAHN, DSW
Professor, School of Social Work, Columbia University, New York, New York

ARTHUR J. KATZ, PH. D.
Executive Director, Council on Social Work Education, New York, New York

MARYANNE P. KEENAN, MSW
Doctoral Student, School of Hygiene and Public Health, Johns Hopkins University, Baltimore, Maryland; and *former Senior Staff Associate in Health Policy,* National Association of Social Workers, Silver Spring, Maryland

PAUL A. KURZMAN, PH. D.
Professor, Hunter College School of Social Work, City University of New York, New York City

GORDON MANSER, MSW
Volunteer, Belgrade Lakes, Maine

ELIZABETH MUTSCHLER, PH. D.
Assistant Professor, School of Social Work, University of Michigan, Ann Arbor, Michigan

RINO J. PATTI, DSW
Professor, School of Social Work, University of Washington, Seattle, Washington

WILLIAM J. REID, DSW
Professor, School of Social Welfare, State University of New York, Albany, New York

SUMNER M. ROSEN, PH. D.
Associate Professor, School of Social Work, Columbia University, New York, New York, and *Visiting Professor,* Department of Labor Education, Rutgers University, New Brunswick, New Jersey

BRENDA L. RUSSELL, MSW
Legislative Representative, Office of the Mayor, City of New York, Washington Office, Washington, D.C.

STEVEN P. SEGAL, PH. D.
Professor and *Director,* Mental Health and Social Welfare Research Group, School of Social Welfare, University of California, Berkeley, California

GEORGE R. SHARWELL, JD
Associate Professor, College of Social Work, University of South Carolina, Columbia, South Carolina

ROBERT J. TEARE, PH. D.
Professor of Social Work and *Director of Research,* School of Social Work, University of Alabama, Tuscaloosa, Alabama

RICHARD E. VERVILLE, JD
Washington Counsel, Council on Social Work Education, New York, New York

ANN WEICK, PH. D.
Associate Professor, School of Social Welfare, University of Kansas, Lawrence, Kansas

JAMES K. WHITTAKER, PH. D.
Fellow, Bush Institute for Child and Family Policy, and *Visiting Professor of Social Work,* University of North Carolina, Chapel Hill, North Carolina

Contents

Part Two   Statistical and Demographic Trends

Appendix

Part 1

CHILD WELFARE POLICY

Numerous changes that have occurred in governmental policies since the late 1970s have affected child welfare programs. Because the range of federal programs serving children is too broad to permit discussion here of all such policy changes and their implications, this article focuses on the main federal programs affecting child welfare provided under the Social Security Act: Aid to Families with Dependent Children (AFDC), Title XX Social Services Block Grant, and the Adoption Assistance and Child Welfare Act of 1980 (P.L. 96–272).

Before considering recent developments, it will be helpful to review briefly the history of primary child welfare programs. AFDC was created in 1935 as part of the Social Security Act to prevent the removal of children from their own homes because of financial deprivation. Almost 70 percent of AFDC recipients are destitute children who would be at risk of out-of-home placement without the small maintenance payment provided to their families. To insure the provision of necessary health care, Medicaid coverage is automatically provided to AFDC recipients. Although negative myths abound regarding AFDC, this program remains the primary preventive and family support program serving children.

Effective October 1, 1975, the Title XX Social Services program consolidated most service provisions under the Social Security Act into a block grant to the states and stipulated a federal funding level of $2.5 billion. Services, which were separated from income maintenance functions, were to be directed toward five goals: economic self-support; self-sufficiency; prevention and remedy of neglect, abuse, or exploitation of children or adults and preservation of families; prevention of inappropriate institutional care through community-based programs; and provision of institutional care where it appeared to be appropriate.

Establishing Federal Leadership

Prior to enactment of P.L. 96–272, the Adoption Assistance and Child Welfare Act, in 1980, overwhelming documentation presented to Congress had demonstrated that the state was not a good parent.[1] Some children were literally lost once they "temporarily" entered the system; many children stayed in foster care until they reached the age of majority.[2] In 1979 the Department of Health, Education, and Welfare testified before the Senate Finance Committee that approximately 500,000 to 502,000 children were in substitute care. This meant that no one knew exactly how many children were living in foster care!

Sufficient funding to serve children at risk was available only under the AFDC foster care program (AFDC-FC), thereby emphasizing foster care as the main alternative for children in need of services. Congressional concern was mounting regarding the high cost of maintaining children in out-of-home care. Yet, year after year Congress did not appropriate sufficient funds under the child welfare services program to provide alternatives to children and families at risk. In 1979 the federal share represented only 7 percent of the nearly $800 million expended on the child welfare services program, whereas the federal share of the AFDC-FC program represented approximately 50 percent. States did not have sufficient resources or financial incentive to reform the system.

Thoroughly convinced that foster care was overutilized because of a lack of alternative services, Congress, in P.L. 96–272, emphasized creating necessary protections and procedures for children and their families. The act mandated major reforms in child welfare programs through a painstakingly crafted, systematic restructuring of the child welfare system. Federal financial incentives were provided to induce states to conduct an inventory of all children in the child welfare services program in foster care over six months; implement statewide management information systems that would contain the current status and demographics of children in foster care; implement case review systems that included a six-month review and an eighteen-month dispositional hearing designed to achieve a placement in the least restrictive setting and in close proximity to home and to provide procedural safeguards for children, parents, and foster care providers; operate family reunification services programs; and implement preventive services programs. All states received an increase in federal child welfare service funds up to a certain level. Congress also emphasized increasing federal child welfare services funds by tying the requirements to the additional "incentive" revenues and mandating that specific protections be in place for a state to draw down the additional funds.

In this family-strengthening bill, Congress established the principle of permanency for all vulnerable children in America, children who in some cases had been in out-of-home placements for years. P.L. 96–272 specifically mandates preventing the unnecessary separation of children from their families, improves the quality of care and services to children and their parents, and encourages permanency through reuniting families or through adoption or other permanency-planning provisions. Most important, Congress put some teeth into these provisions by requiring (1) that the protections, procedures, and services be in place as a condition for receiving increased federal funds and (2) that, after sufficient time and resources were made available to the states, financial sanctions be imposed if the state had not implemented the child welfare reforms.

Title XX's place in child welfare. To support this new thrust toward strengthening families and providing permanency for children, P.L. 96–272 included amendments to the Title XX social services program. In fiscal year (FY) 1979, temporary provisions provided for a $2.9 billion Title XX ceiling, with $200 million earmarked for day care services. The 1980 amendments permanently changed the federal funding level to $2.7 billion in FY 1980, $2.9 billion in FY 1981, $3 billion in FY 1982, $3.1 billion in FY 1983, $3.2 billion in FY 1984, and $3.3 billion for FY 1985 and thereafter. States were required to provide one dollar for every three federal dollars they received, except for the day care earmark, which was 100 percent federal monies. The day care earmark was made permanent and converted to up to 8 percent of a state's Title XX allotment. A separate $16.1 billion entitlement was established for social services to the territories, and a temporary $75 million limit was placed on the separate Title XX social services personal training program.

Implementation of the Reforms

The systematic reforms and the increased federal funds under P.L. 96–272 and Title XX promised a new future for America's vulnerable children. Attention turned toward implementing the new provisions. Even before the proposed regulations were published, the Department of Health and Human Services (HHS) solicited public input through public meetings with concerned organizations and by soliciting written comments on issues of concern. Regional hearings across the country gathered information on the significant issues. Advocates felt strongly that the regulations must be clear and specific so all children, regardless of state of residence, would be assured full protection under the law. HHS believed that the proposed regulations were sensitive to state practice, yet specific enough to ensure consistency in interpretation and uniformity in implementation.[3]

The proposed regulations defined what exemplified the best professional practice in child welfare and included those provisions most essential to insure that the best interests of the child and family would be served. It also spelled out what constituted adequate compliance with the programmatic requirements, so that states had a standard to measure themselves against. For instance, the reunification services program designed to assist children to return home had to include day care services, homemaker or caretaker services, family or individual counseling for all children and families in need; and other services the state identified as necessary and appropriate, including respite care; parent education; self-help groups; mental health, alcohol, and drug abuse counseling; and vocational counseling or rehabilitation. The preplacement preventive services program included the services offered under the reunification services program plus twenty-four-hour emergency caretaker or homemaker services, crisis counseling, emergency shelters, access to available emergency financial assistance, respite care, and home-based services. State compliance with these requirements was to be determined by reports submitted to HHS and by on-site surveys of the implementation, conducted before awarding a state any additional incentive funds.

New Federalism and Deregulation

The change in administration ushered in a new philosophy regarding the federal government's role in the delivery of human services. An early initiative of the Reagan Administration was the establishment, on January 22, 1981, of the Task Force on Regulatory Relief, which on January 29, 1981 suspended all recently issued regulations under the Carter Administration. This action canceled proposed rules for P.L. 96-272, leaving those concerned about implementing the new law without any guidance or leadership from the federal government and causing a great deal of confusion in the states. Still, there was hope that the tremendous public input received could not be ignored and would result in detailed regulations.

The new Administration was on a fast track, however. On February 18, 1981, the White House released its agenda for the future—*America's New Beginning: A Program for Economic Recovery*.[4] This document contained the blueprint for a dramatic turnaround in public policy—massive increases for defense, dramatic tax cuts, regulatory "relief," and draconian cuts in human service programs. This major shift in budgetary priorities was dramatized by the president's proposal to repeal more than forty categorical health and social services programs and to consolidate them, with 25 percent less funding, into one or more block grants to the states. The assumption was that service reductions would not necessarily occur because block grants were less costly for the states to administer.

On March 10, 1981, a fully revised federal budget for fiscal year 1982 was transmitted to Congress. By April, the White House had refined its proposals and sent another document to Congress, outlining additional details on budget savings.[5] A Social Services Block Grant was proposed that would have reduced the federal funding from $5.25 billion to $3.8 billion and repealed Title XX Social Services; Title XX Day Care; Title XX Training; Child Welfare Services; Foster Care, Adoption Assistance; Child Abuse Services; Runaway and Homeless Youth Services; Services to the Developmentally Disabled; Office of Human Development Services salaries and expenses; Rehabilitation Services; and the Community Services Administration.

The Reagan Administration gained passage of its revised budget, which required certain congressional committees to reduce spending levels in programs under their jurisdiction through a process called reconciliation. The House Ways and Means Committee refused to alter the Adoption Assistance and Child Welfare Act or the Title XX program and developed alternative ways to reduce spending that would not impose as much harm on the beneficiaries. However, on the House floor, a substitute bill hastily drafted by conservatives and the Administration was enacted. This legislation, among other things, made extensive reductions in the AFDC program and created, with a 16 percent reduction in funding, a Social Services

Block Grant consisting of Title XX Social Services, Title XX Day Care, Title XX Training, Social Services to the Territories, Child Abuse Services, Runaway and Homeless Youth Services, and most of the titles of the Community Services Administration. Fortunately, P.L. 96-272 claimed staunch conservative supporters in the House and was spared the budget-cutting knife in the substitute budget.

In its version of the reconciliation bill, the Senate Finance Committee accepted the Administration's proposal to a degree. They adopted the Administration's Social Services Block Grant language and consolidated Title XX Social Services, Title XX Day Care, Title XX Training, Services to the Territories, Child Welfare Services, Child Welfare Training, Foster Care Services, and the new Adoption Assistance program. All these programs were to be funded at $2.6 billion, a 25 percent reduction.

When Congress finally passed the Omnibus Budget Reconciliation Act of 1981 (OBRA), fundamental policy changes were in place. The AFDC program underwent massive revamping through restricting eligibility and benefits; particularly penalized were the working poor families struggling to provide for their children with the assistance of a supplemental AFDC grant. The Title XX Social Services Block Grant contained only the program components of Title XX, such as day care, training, and services to the territories. However, children and families paid a high price to maintain the Adoption Assistance and Child Welfare Act intact; Title XX was reduced to $2.4 billion for FY 1982 (an amount $100 million lower than when the original program was created in 1975), $2.45 billion for FY 1983, $2.5 billion for FY 1984, $2.6 billion for FY 1985, and 2.7 billion for FY 1986 and thereafter.

Even though the enactment of OBRA on August 13, 1981, brought major policy shifts in human services that would be extremely difficult for public and private service providers to implement in a short time, the provisions of the law became effective on October 1, and implementing regulations in interim final form, which meant that they were effective immediately until final regulations were published, were issued in the *Federal Register* on October 1.[6] Conversely, regulations to implement the Adoption Assistance and Child Welfare Act passed more than a year earlier were still not forthcoming. It appeared that the Administration could move rapidly on the provisions it wanted and ignore those that were not in line with its philosophy.

In the Administration's zeal to eliminate the federal role in human services, it deleted the provisions in Title XX requiring the states to establish child care standards in line with those of national standard-setting organizations concerned with home care of children. It also altered the reference to federal day care standards for child care provided outside the home, replacing it with a reference to applicable state and local standards, which were nonexistent in some cases. In its haste, the Administration inadvertently applied foster care standards to the provision of day care, an error that was later rectified by an amendment.

Nineteen eighty-one was a fast-paced, phenomenal year for social policy, and the dust had not yet settled when the president brought forth fiscal year 1983 budget proposals in February 1982. Realizing that the child welfare act had strong support in Congress and was unlikely to be absorbed into another program, the Administration offered a small, separate child welfare block grant. Its rationale for eliminating P.L. 96-272 through the budget-cutting, block grant process was that, "Under the current system, states do not have the flexibility to direct their efforts to permanently place children rather than continue foster care arrangements."[7] This rationale totally contradicted the requirements of the law. The new block grant would have eliminated the individual entitlement program for AFDC foster children and special needs adoptive children, kept the child welfare services funding at low levels, and eliminated the child welfare training program designed to develop a competent cadre of specialized child welfare workers. The total authorization level for the block grant would have been only $380 million per year for fiscal years 1983 through 1985, after which the program would have had to be reauthorized or cease to exist. The proposed reduction for fiscal year 1983 would have been 47 percent below the anticipated funding levels for that year under the provisions of P.L. 96–272.

The Administration also proposed to reduce the FY 1983 funding for Title XX to $1.9 billion, which would have meant that more than $1.2 billion would have been cut from the program since 1981. Also, a zero budget was proposed for the Work Incentive program (WIN), which was designed to assist AFDC recipients to become employed through training and placement services and through support services such as day care. The Administration believed that such services could be provided under the Title XX program, which was already overburdened. A long list of further reductions for the AFDC program totaling $3.6 billion over three years was also requested by the Reagan Administration.

Congress was beginning to hesitate over making additional drastic reductions in human service programs and did not accept the changes proposed for P.L. 96–272, Title XX, or the WIN program. The list of cuts enacted in the AFDC program was whittled down to $405 million over three years. Child advocates learned the meaning of a "relative victory." Since the Reagan Administration had come to power, individuals concerned about children and families had been operating in a "damage control" mode. Proposals offered by the House Ways and Means Committee to restore some of the cuts were defeated in the end, but child advocates were at least given some hope for the future.

P.L. 92–272 implementation. Because the Reagan Administration believed that P.L. 92–272 should be replaced with a block grant, HHS implemented the legislation as if it were a block grant, refusing to issue regulations and utilizing a self-certification process with the states. Instead of requiring documentation and an on-site survey to assess the level of implementation before a state received additional incentive funds, the department allowed each state to interpret the law itself. In 1981 thirty-four states self-certified that they had met the necessary requirements.

Congress had grave concerns about the way the department was implementing P.L. 96–272, and on February 24, 1982, every member of the Ways and Means Subcommittee on Public Assistance and Unemployment Compensation sent a letter to the General Accounting Office, requesting that it investigate the matter. Child advocates and Congress alike applied as much pressure as possible to bring some accountability into the process. Without federal leadership and a real commitment to the law, states would find it extremely difficult to make child welfare reform a priority, particularly in light of the severe budget cuts they had sustained and the economic recession, which placed additional demands on the human service system.

In March 1982 HHS started to develop a voluntary postcertification review process to determine whether states had met the requirements of the law for 1981. Eighteen states volunteered to participate in such a program review in 1981. States became concerned that unknown criteria would be applied to their programs after the fact. A few states withdrew their certification, and other states were found in noncompliance. In sum, there was tremendous confusion among the states regarding what they should be doing; they were still operating without implementation regulations.

According to the national summary of the program reviews, less than one-third of the states encouraged the recruitment of professional staff with degrees in social work, and only two state merit systems required professional degrees.[8] Fourteen of the state agencies did not have workload standards. In county-administered programs, the state agency's role in influencing standards was unclear. In two states, workload standards were prohibited by law. The report concluded that there was no basis on which to determine that the states had sufficiently trained staff to perform some of the complex functions required to improve child welfare services and to place children appropriately. Virtually none of the states reviewed met the P.L. 96–272 requirements for the case review system. It was clear that training was needed at all levels for workers to be able to develop effective case review systems for children.

Most of the states had a policy statement regarding preventive services and provided some services. However, a comprehensive approach and systematic procedures to ensure that preventive services were available to children and their families were missing. In a significant number of the abuse and neglect cases, the investigation was not initiated within twenty-four hours. A trend reflected throughout the report was the need for the development of adequate resources and well-qualified staff to implement improvements in child welfare services.

Over two years after enactment, on July 15, 1982, final regulations covering the fiscal requirements for receipt of federal funds under the foster care and adoption assistance provisions of P.L. 96–272 were published in the *Federal Register*. At the same time, programmatic material was published as a second Notice of Proposed Rulemaking (NPRM) with a public comment period. The Department of Health and Human Services acknowledged in the narrative of the second NPRM that it received

> approximately 450 comments in addition to the testimony and discussion from the regional hearings . . . . Many comments supported detailed requirements and explicit regulatory expectations as essential to bring about the changes envisioned in the law. . . . Other respondents, including twenty-nine state agencies . . . objected to the numerous specific requirements in the December 31, 1980, NPRM.[9]

It was not until May 23, 1983, that the final programmatic regulations for P.L. 96–272 were issued by the department.[10] Respondents to the second NPRM had expressed strong support for public participation in numerous areas, including development of state plans, review of foster care and adoption assistance payment standards, and review of state foster care standards. The department declined to require public participation in these areas, choosing instead to limit the requirement to making the information available and encouraging each individual state to be responsible for bringing about the involvement of its citizenry.

Even though those commenting continued to support specific and detailed regulations, it appeared that the department ignored most of the comments it received because they did not fit into the administration's "states' rights" framework. An analysis of the regulations reveals a lack of assurances that the mandated reforms in the child welfare system would occur. Because the Administration was unsuccessful in obtaining repeal of the law, it attempted to emasculate it through the regulatory process. In dealing with the requirement for states to receive incentive funds, the regulations failed to specify even a minimum level of services that had to be provided. The final regulation merely parroted the law, allowing the states to determine for themselves what constituted reunification and preplacement preventive service programs.

Impact on quality. High rates of unemployment during a recession swell the population requiring some level of professional intervention. Reductions in the basic economic and social support programs increase the pressure on families struggling to maintain their equilibrium and contribute to the expanding need for professional services. When there is no increase in staff resources to meet such needs, the quality of service to clients is often compromised.

Private and Professional Standards

With the weakening of federal leadership in the provision of social services to children, private and professional organizations have become concerned over the possibility of the erosion of standards in this area. One result of this concern has been the formulation of new standards and the strengthening of existing guidelines.

In 1981, for example, the National Association of Social Workers published for the first time a set of standards prepared by a Task Force on Social Work Practice in Child Protection.[11] These standards included commitments to the concept of the family as a dynamic system, to the need for practitioners to seek new knowledge, to the importance of cooperation among professionals and agencies, and to the need to support legislative change.

The Child Welfare League of America (CWLA) has a policy of continually examining, revising, and updating its standards. The organization's Board Committee on Standards recently developed a new format that will allow its published standards to be updated more easily. In this new format, the standards will be published in separate volumes. The primary volume will consist of the generic standards for all services. This volume will be supplemented by unique and specific standards, including the revised standards for day care services and for supplying services to children and families in their own homes.[12]

Another important development related to standards was the incorporation in 1978 of the Council on Accreditation of Services for Families and Children. The council, which was established through the joint efforts of CWLA and the Family Service Association of America (FSAA), is not a standard-setting organization but deals only with accreditation based on compliance with standards set by other organizations. However, the council has developed provisions related to practice activities for which no standards have existed. These activities include services for refugees and the development of programs related to substance abuse. The council characterizes itself as the first national accrediting body that bases its requirements on a social service model as distinguished from a medical model.

Another national organization concerned with standards for child protective services is the National Humane Association, which published its most recent standards in 1977.[13] These consist of statements of philosophy, twelve operational standards, and eight steps of child protection.

Conclusion

Child welfare policy took a giant leap forward with the enactment of P.L. 96–272 in 1980, but the fundamental policy changes enacted by the Omnibus Budget Reconciliation Act of 1981 lowered both the statutory provisions and the funding levels that supported the child welfare reforms. As AFDC and Title XX were pared down, pressure increased on families and in turn on the child welfare system, further complicating implementation of the new child welfare protections.

Although Congress refused to enact most of the additional program reductions requested by the Reagan Administration, it did not make necessary restorations or provide the anticipated increases in the Child Welfare Services program. With the Administration weakening the system further through the regulatory process, states were placed in the position of dealing with major new requirements to implement without the necessary resources to retool their systems. Staff at all levels require training to enable them to make the complex decisions required and to understand the tenets of permanency-planning and family-based services.[14]

Private and professional social welfare organizations have formulated new standards in recent years and have strengthened existing guidelines, but such organizations have little or no ability to enforce compliance with their standards. It seems inevitable, therefore, that without federal leadership and adequate funding levels, child welfare reform will continue in a state of flux and that the quality of service provided to children in need will remain haphazard. The promise of a new future for children, which is contained in the Adoption Assistance and Child Welfare Act, is far from fulfilled.

BRENDA L. RUSSELL

Notes and References

1. U.S. Congress, *House Reports* No. 96–136 (Committee on Ways and Means), No. 96–136, Pt. 2 (Committee on Appropriations), and No. 96–900 (Committee of Conference); *Senate Report* No. 96–336 (Committee on Finance); *Congressional Record,* 125 (1979: Aug. 2, considered and passed House, Oct. 25 and 29, considered and passed Senate, amended), all 96th Cong., 1st sess.; and *Congressional Record,* June 13, 1980, House and Senate agreed to conference report, 96th Cong., 2nd sess.

2. Jane Knitzer, Mary Lee Allen, and Brenda McGowan, *Children Without Homes* (Washington, D.C.: Children's Defense Fund, 1978); and *Who Knows? Who Cares? Forgotten Children in Foster Care* (New York: National Commission on Children in Need of Parents, 1979).

3. *Federal Register*, Dec. 31, 1980.

4. The White House, *America's New Beginning: A Program for Economic Recovery* (Washington, D.C.: U.S. Government Printing Office, 1981).

5. *Fiscal Year 1982 Budget Revisions, Additional Details on Budget Savings* (Washington, D.C.: Executive Office of the President, Office of Management and Budget, 1981).

6. *Federal Register*, Oct. 1, 1981.

7. *Major Themes and Additional Budget Details, Fiscal Year 1983* (Washington, D.C.: Executive Office of the President, Office of Management and Budget, 1982).

8. "Child Welfare Services Program Reviews, FY 1981, National Summary" (Washington, D.C.: Children's Bureau, Administration for Children, Youth and Families, Office of Human Development Services, 1982). (Photocopied.)

9. *Federal Register,* July 15, 1982.

10. *Federal Register,* May 23, 1983.

11. *NASW Standards for Social Work Practice in Child Protection,* Policy Statement No. 8 (Washington, D.C.: National Association of Social Workers, 1981).

12. *Standards for Organization and Administration for All Child Welfare Services, Standards for Day Care Services, and Standards on Services for Children and Their Families in Their Own Homes,* (New York: Child Welfare League of America, all in press).

13. *Child Protective Service Standards* (Denver, Colo.: American Humane Association, 1977).

14. *The View from the Agency: Supervisors and Workers Look at In-Service Training for Child Welfare* (Ann Arbor, Michigan: National Child Welfare Training Center, University of Michigan School of Social Work, 1983).

COMPUTERS

Computers can be viewed as machines for storing and manipulating information. Their special advantages lie in their storage capacity and their speed, accuracy, and economy in processing large sets of data. The use of computers as efficient data and word processors has grown at a rapidly accelerating rate since the late seventies, and advances in computer technology and imaginative work in computer applications have begun to affect social service agencies in dramatic and substantive ways.

This article presents an overview of computer applications in social service organizations, providing a general orientation to the use of computer systems in social work administration, direct practice, and research.[1] First, it describes the major computer systems and types of information processing. It then discusses computer applications ranging from data management to recently developing decision-making functions in social work administration and direct practice. The final section of the article addresses issues of confidentiality and the need for safeguarding the access to computerized information. Several major themes appear throughout the article: the implications of such current trends as the move from centralized batch processing on large mainframe computers to interactive data processing on less expensive, smaller computers; the potential of computer technologies not only for providing greater efficiencies in routine tasks but also as powerful tools for professional decision making; and the need for social workers to understand the concepts and techniques of information processing and to become innovators and architects of change, able to keep emerging computer applications responsive to social work practice.

Computer Systems

The computer, the machine itself, and its various peripheral devices, such as the card reader and printer, are referred to as hardware. Three major types of computers can be distinguished: mainframe computers, minicomputers, and microcomputers. In the past most social service agencies relied on mainframe computers. Because of their prohibitive cost, mainframes were typically leased or bought by large, centralized organizations, such as statewide social service departments or universities. Minicomputers have gained prominence in the last decade because they are much cheaper than the mainframes but can still store and process the data of an agency system with more than eight hundred or a thousand clients. The microcomputer, or personal computer, has been available for commercial use only during the past six or seven years. It has become popular because of its relatively low cost ($3,000 to $7,000) and the rapid development of programs that enable the computer to perform a multiplicity of functions. The present restrictions on microcomputer applications in social service agencies are the limitations of the storage, or memory, available and the microcomputer's relatively slow speed in processing information. If an agency intends to record and process data for more than five hundred clients, a microcomputer may not have sufficient memory or speed to handle the entire database. The capacity of microcomputers will certainly increase in the coming years, and until it does, a solution is to link the microcomputer to a mainframe computer through telephone lines. These linkages permit data entered on the microcomputer to be stored and processed on the mainframe and also allow access to data files through the microcomputer terminal.

The computer performs its operations through a program, which is a set of specific instructions supplied by the user. These programs, referred to as software, provide the language to communicate instructions to the computer. Programs are either written by the user in relatively complex languages, such as FORTRAN, or marketed as standard "program packages" that can be used with relatively simple instructions. A widely known software package for mainframe computers is the Statistical Package for the Social Sciences (SPSS).[2] The capacity and range of software programs developed for microcomputers is escalating along with the growing popularity of these machines. A wide variety of software programs, costing from $50 to $1,000, are available for trivial computing activities, such as games, for fiscal management tasks, and for word processing and data management.

Information Processing

To be processed, information must be in a form that is acceptable to the computer. In word processing, text consisting of a combination of words and numbers, such as letters, client intake reports, and bills can be typed into and processed by the system. In data processing, the information acceptable to the computer must usually be in numerical form. When raw data are in nonnumerical form—for example, answers to open-ended questions—the data must be categorized and numbers assigned to each category. Frequently data originate in numerical form, such as the numbers of clients admitted or discharged each month. In either case, a codebook needs to be devised with instructions on how the raw data are to be reduced to numerical form and recorded for further processing.[3]

Batch processing and interactive on-line processing are the major types of information processing currently used. In the traditional, more time-consuming batch-processing mode, the coded numbers are punched on cards, each containing eighty columns of information. In addition to the data cards, control cards are punched, instructing the computer how to process the data. The entire set of cards, data cards and control cards, is fed into the computer by a card reader, which translates the punched cards into electronic signals and stores them for subsequent use. After the data are processed, the results are printed on a high-speed printing device at the location of the mainframe computer.[4]

The major disadvantage of batch processing is its turnaround time of up to one or two days. This results from delays in the delivery of the cards to the computing facility, from the user's limited access to the computer, and from delays in retrieval of the final printout. Also, errors in the control or data cards may require a rerun of the data set.

Technological advances that allow users to interact directly or on-line with the computer have had far-reaching effects on social service organizations; those advances have made computers immediately available for day-to-day tasks of decision makers. On-line terminals give direct access to data sets, and errors can be corrected and results obtained immediately. The typical terminal consists of a teletypewriter and a videoscreen, which are connected to the microcomputer and printer or, by telephone lines, to the mainframe computer. With most microcomputers, only one user at a time has access to the computer, whereas several users can have simultaneous access to a minicomputer, and scores of users can interact with a mainframe computer at the same time. Results can either be displayed on the videoscreen or printed out.

The next sections of this article describe the potential applications in social service agencies of these three computer systems —the mainframe computer, minicomputer, and microcomputer—in five major categories: data management, decision applications, database management systems, research, and word processing.

Data Management

Early computer applications in social service agencies used the computer's ability to store, process, retrieve, and analyze large amounts of data regarding client characteristics and the costs and outcomes of social services. During the sixties and seventies, Title XX and other federal programs that provided reimbursement for the costs of social services required documentation of who was doing what for whom, when, where, for what reasons, at what cost, and with what results. Other federal and state regulations required studies of program effectiveness and mandated participation in Professional Standard Review Organizations (PSROs). These heavy demands on social service organizations for specific information led to the implementation of computer-assisted Management Information Systems (MIS). MIS is a management tool that systematically collects information through input documents, accumulates these data in organized data files, and processes and summarizes various aspects of the data in periodic or special reports.[5]

The MISs initially used in social service agencies were not designed as comprehensive data systems but were tailored to relatively specific, well-defined agency management purposes. One kind of MIS involved non–client-oriented information systems, such as systems for accounting and budgeting and for inventory, personnel, and property management. Client-oriented MISs managed information about the demographic characteristics of clients, the types of problems they had, and when and by whom services were provided. Depending on the size of the data base, mainframes, minicomputers, or microcomputers are used to store, process, update, and prepare the required information in an efficient manner.[6]

Fanshel has reported an example of a data management system in child welfare.[7] A computerized information system was developed for meeting the information needs of agencies providing foster care services for 28,000 children in New York City. The information routinely collected by the agency about characteristics, service delivery, outcomes, costs, and personnel activities was computerized. The objective was to provide the information needed for management and service delivery tasks in an efficient and cost-effective manner that reduced paperwork and eliminated redundant information. The data management system generated, for example, summary profile reports providing demographic information about foster children and foster parents. These summary reports can be used in numerous ways for program analysis, planning of services, and delivery and allocation of resources.

Computer applications in data management and decision making are not mutually exclusive, but can be seen on a continuum. As will be shown in the next section, decision applications are often based on data generated by data management procedures.

Decision Applications

Social work professionals usually accept the role of computers as efficient data processors, but the use of computer-assisted decision support systems to help administrators and direct service practitioners with their day-to-day tasks has received attention only during the last few years. Decision support systems (DSS) in human services are computer-based aids for decision-making tasks at policy, administrative, and service provision levels. Examples of decision support functions are data access or information retrieval; selective inquiry and summarizing of data; data analysis; modeling methods; and computerized simulation models. The development of decision support systems requires computing and data management capabilities, a data base, and a thorough analysis and understanding of the nature of the decisions to be supported.[8] Two examples of administrative decision making and two examples of decision making in direct practice illustrate computer-supported decision applications in social work practice.

Administrative decision making. Pointing to decision makers' underutilization of available information, Schoech states that the "data and information generated by an organization are considered a resource which, if not captured and managed, results in a costly opportunity loss for the organization."[9] Such a resource is the data routinely collected, quantified, and computerized by most agencies, such as client characteristics, services provided, staff activities, and service costs. Frequently this information is utilized only for fiscal management or for generating periodic reports.

The task of administrators in human service organizations is to acquire and use resources to create effective human services at a minimum cost. Administrators' decisions are often based on their own and their peers' experience or on educated guesswork using pencil and notepaper.[10] Many decision makers are not aware that there are readily available methods for submitting their ideas and tentative plans to more systematic reasoning. One modeling method for moving data from an operational to a strategic level is embodied in a software program called VisiCalc, which is widely used on microcomputers. VisiCalc provides a spreadsheet, which is displayed on the videoscreen. Along the vertical dimension of the spreadsheet are listed, for example, the expenditures of each line item of the budget, such as personnel, fringe benefits, equipment, and travel expenses. Displayed horizontally are the different cost centers of the agency, such as intake, residential program, outpatient program, and aftercare, and the proportion of each line item allocated to each cost center.

To apply this modeling method, administrators must be able to rephrase the issues and questions related to the decision in quantitative, calculable terms with finite alternatives. They can then use a modeling program to ask a series of "WHAT IF" questions. If, for instance, the agency had to generate alternatives for enforced budget cuts, the computer might be asked: WHAT would happen IF the workforce were decreased by X positions but it continued to serve the same number of clients? WHAT would be the consequences in terms of staff-client contact hours, client waiting times, service unit costs, support staff requirements, and so on? If the agency were planning to add a new service modality in the out-patient program without increasing the total number of staff positions, the computer could be asked to analyze the data from another angle: WHAT IF the staff-client contact hours in the outpatient program were increased by X hours? WHAT would be the effects on staff-client ratios and service unit costs in other cost centers?

The modeling program provides immediate answers to these questions. When one figure on the spreadsheet is changed (for example, the number of staff positions), VisiCalc automatically adjusts all related figures and displays this on the videoscreen —fringe benefits, staff-client ratios, service unit cost, and so on. Such modeling programs are powerful tools that structure the logical operations to be performed on the available data and allow the decision maker to permutate estimations systematically to approximate optimal or preferred relationships between the measures of interest.

Another use of computers in administrative decision making illustrates the application of a computerized simulation model. "Simulation" means to imitate the conditions and processes of the real system and to predict how that system might react to certain changes. Simulations combine probability theory with a formalized modeling approach to estimate, for example, what percentage of the elderly in a community will use nursing homes during the next ten years, given certain characteristics of this population and the expected resources during that period. In other words, a simulation model shows how a particular system works under specific conditions.

Eisele and Kleindorfer describe how local agencies on aging benefited from the implementation of a computerized simulation model.[11] The agencies were interested in estimating the future use and costs of their services. Rates of future use and costs are variables that are not under the control of the agency and are referred to as exogenous variables. Financial and personnel resources are under the control of the agency and can be specified in a model. Other variables included in the Eisele and Kleindorfer model were expected numbers of elderly in the community based on U.S. census data and agency data regarding current services and costs of services to the aged. Using the probability functions of the model, the investigators were able to generate critical information for short-term forecasting and decision making related to expected service costs and rates of use. Both examples illustrate how modeling methods require that the decision maker thoroughly understand the issues and be able to transpose the questions into quantitative data and arithmetic or logical operations that the computer can perform on the data.

Direct-practice decision making. The application of computers to direct practice has lagged behind fiscal and administrative uses. Among the reasons for delays in the development and implementation of clinical applications were (1) that early programs were too time consuming to prepare and often operated only in the batch mode, (2) that the standardization necessary for a client data system was hard to achieve because of the differences in the way different practitioners treat and evaluate clients with similar problems, and (3) that the issues that arise at the person-machine interface when clients or practitioners interacted with the computer contained too many problems. Today a substantial and growing literature addresses the issues of person-machine interaction and describes how computers are resisted, considered, evaluated, and integrated into clinical practice.[12]

Direct client-computer interviews were among the earliest applications of computing in clinical practice. The development of interactive computing and better programming languages has contributed to innovative applications in client interviewing. Greist and his colleagues, for example, developed several programs in which the client sits before a microcomputer terminal and completes an intake interview.[13] Other programs were developed for emergency room clients and for administering standardized questionnaires to clients.[14] The client reads a question on the videoscreen, such as "What is your last name?" or "Please indicate which of the following problem areas are of concern to you," types the answer on the key-board, and enters it into the computer. Recently developed software can produce text as a function of the data entered by the client.[15] For example, if the client completes an intake interview on a microcomputer terminal, the computer can then generate an intake summary based entirely on the information provided by the client. Clinicians who use computer interviews report that, with few exceptions, clients find computer interviews acceptable and often prefer to give information to a computer rather than to a therapist. This preference for a nonhuman interviewer seems particularly strong when the subject matter is sensitive. With the exception of some clients with manic or antisocial personality disorders, the data clients provide computers are at least as reliable and valid as those provided to clinicians, and the data obtained by computers are far more complete.[16] The second example in direct-practice decision making is an integrated clinical and financial information system in a community mental health center in Texas, described by Newkham and Bawcom.[17] The center provides a wide variety of services through fifteen service locations in a six-county region. Annually, 5,000 persons are screened and 2,700 persons are served in one or more of the programs.

A key management principle in the successful development of this system was to compile available data in ways that have meaning to staff members and can communicate knowledge for effective decision making. The system's objectives were to (1) document the flow of clients and the provision of services, (2) give immediate feedback to direct service providers and keep records current, (3) meet internal and external reporting needs for data on clients and services, (4) meet financial reporting requirements for funding sources and provide an audit "trail" for fiscal review, (5) provide summary information for client and system management, and (6) lend itself to cost outcome analysis. Although these objectives include financial and administrative decision applications, only examples of direct service decision making are described here.

One requirement of the computerized information system was to convert the previously used nonstandardized recording system into a problem-oriented record (POR) system. A POR committee, including direct service practitioners, designed a Direct Service Record (DSR) form that captured specific client data at each major treatment juncture. On a single sheet, the DSR provides a preprinted visual array of data including the client's problems, case objectives and status, and individual treatment modalities (medication, initial and current level of functioning, and future service plans). Following each service contact, the practitioner records the services provided, the time involved, and billing information. Scales indicating the client's level of functioning are completed at intake, at subsequent intervals of ninety days, at major treatment junctures, and at discharge.

All workers regularly receive summary reports for each of their clients. This information facilitates direct service decision making in a number of ways. In treatment planning, it provides a communication tool specifying how healthy or dysfunctional a client is at any given time; it helps the practitioner obtain a measure of the client's change in independent functioning over the course of treatment, and it serves as an instrument to measure the effectiveness of treatment and the cost improvement or maintenance.

The case summary report also has been useful in tracking case management functions and in establishing responsibility for treatment. For example, when a worker plans to leave the agency, a list is produced specifying clients for whom a disposition must be made prior to the worker's departure. A unique feature of the computerized information system is its ability to remind a worker of any planned service event. An event can be planned for up to a year in advance by coding in the date and activity. The computer will print a reminder on the specified date. This capability has been used to notify practitioners on a daily basis of case assignments, scheduled treatment appointments, ninety-day reviews, and fee reassessment follow-ups. It has been found particularly helpful by busy staffs managing large numbers of clients.

After a three-year implementation phase, this information system has enhanced client treatment, has improved clinical and fiscal accountability, and has become an indispensable tool for supporting the quality of care provided by the staff of this community mental health center.

In settings where workers are learning to use sophisticated decision support systems, the boundaries between the direct service, administrative, educational, and research applications of computers are beginning to disappear. Work is underway, particularly in mental health and medical settings, to create database management systems that can serve multiple functions: billing, accounting, personnel record keeping, administrative planning, assessing, monitoring, and evaluating service delivery.

Database Management Systems

As described earlier, most management or client information systems in social service agencies have been developed for specific areas, such as for fiscal management only, for purposes of program evaluation, or for a specific research project. In time, however, the widespread application of computers in social service agencies will foster agreement about what basic data sets should consist of and lead to the development of comprehensive database management systems. A database management system consists of sets of logically related data files, or databases and an associated grouping of software necessary to store, manage, and retrieve data from the database. Efforts to develop comprehensive database systems are occurring in mental health and in medical settings. The National Institute of Mental Health, for example, is supporting the development of a minicomputer management information system for a prototype community mental health program as a trial of the common data set approach.

The database thus consists of interrelated subsets for purposes of planning, quality assurance, clinical accountability, case management, and financial and personnel management.[18] Other mental health facilities have gone ahead and developed their own stand-alone information systems.[19] (Stand-alone systems are those that can receive, store, and analyze data and produce output without being connected to another computer.)

Some of the most modern information systems can be found in medical settings. They have at their core a database management system that permits clinicians, administrators, researchers, and educators to track patients and their progress, follow a course of treatment, keep a service history, analyze staff or trainees' activities, record fees, monitor costs, and keep inventories. The most sophisticated of these database management systems incorporate a dictionary-driven concept in which the computer is programmed to ask a series of questions about the data which, once answered, establish the "dictionary." The dictionary "drives" all other programs in that it can enter new data, edit existing data, search for the characteristics of patient groups, and generate periodic reports and statistics. Whenever new data are added to one of the subsets, the dictionary drives any required changes in all other subsets of the data system.[20] Such a constantly updated, comprehensive database management system reduces the need for manually operated patient files, and it provides on-line information for the planning and decision making of administrators, clinicians, and researchers. The outcomes of experiments with comprehensive database management systems will be of considerable importance to social service agencies interested in a common data set approach.

Research

The computer has become an indispensable tool for research in the social sciences; it provides simple and rapid access to the researcher's data and makes available a wide variety of data analysis procedures. Rather than writing their own programs, researchers frequently use packaged computer programs, such as the SPSS, to execute a sequence of analyses on data previously entered into the computer.[21] For example, the researcher might use the earlier cited Child Welfare Information System developed by Fanshel to explore what variables best predict the type of discharge in foster care, that is, whether children are returned to their parents, to residential care, or to their own responsibility.[22] As a first step, the researcher would use descriptive statistics and cross-tabulations to list the frequencies and percentages of the type of problem, the age of children at placement, the length of foster care, and the type of discharge. In a second round of analyses, the researcher might apply a series of regression analyses to explore which of the independent variables (type of problem, age at placement, length of care) are the best predictors of discharge.

As Nie and associates point out, it is important for the researcher to have developed some carefully derived theoretical or empirical expectations about the relationship between specific independent variables and the dependent variable—in the case of the foster care analysis, the type of discharge.[23] Otherwise, because modern computing packages make it so easy to produce large amounts of data, the researcher might be tempted to go on a "grand fishing expedition" and examine large numbers of potential independent variables in relation to the dependent variable. By the mere laws of probability, the researcher is bound to have some statistically significant findings. The general rule is that users should not attempt to apply a statistical procedure unless they understand both the appropriate procedure for the type of data they are analyzing and also the meaning of the statistics produced.

Word Processing

A widespread use of computers today is word processing. The three principal functions of word processing systems are (1) text entry and screen editing, (2) formatting, and (3) printing. The text is entered on a teletypewriter and displayed on a video-screen. Individual lines are corrected and edited on the screen after they are entered. The second function is the actual text processing or formatting. This transforms the raw text, which usually consists of a series of lines, into paragraphs, headings, and pages and generates the associated commands required by the printing device. The results, such as form letters, reports, and lengthy papers, are printed either on printers attached by cable to a minicomputer or microcomputer or on a high-speed printer at a central computing facility.

Many offices in social service agencies are already using highly sophisticated stand-alone word processing systems. Of specific interest to practitioners are recent developments that facilitate the integration of data management and word processing programs.[24] The integrated mode is used, for example, to print client intake reports or closing summaries for client files or to supply funding agencies with periodic reports containing tables of numbers and statistics accompanied by commentaries explaining the meaning of each table. It is likely that word processing systems will increasingly replace the traditional typewriter.

Confidentiality of Computerized Information

Data collected in social service agencies frequently involve highly confidential information. In an earlier review of computer technology in social work, Boyd, Hylton, and Price concluded that the very existence of computerized information posed a serious threat to the privacy of client information.[25] When Feldstone conducted a survey of attitudes toward information systems and computers in the human services, he found that administrators viewed computerization more favorably than did supervisors and that a major concern of line workers was the perceived threat to the confidentiality of client data.[26]

Professionals need to know that the computerization of client information need not compromise the ethic of confidentiality. Explicit guidelines and safeguards to prevent unauthorized access to client data can be developed. Typically this is accomplished by using client code numbers instead of their names or social security numbers. Hierarchical access codes are then assigned to each qualified user of the data system. This allows a user with a given access code to receive only certain types of information about specific cases in the system; anyone who has not been assigned a current access code cannot enter the system at all.

Although unauthorized access to specific data sets in the agency can be controlled, a larger issue is the potential abuse of human services information for nonprofessional or political reasons. As Schoech points out, well-managed information is powerful.[27] Information management adds power to the information collected and to the people in charge of this information. Accordingly, mechanisms must be established to plan for and control the power shifts that might develop from the implementation of information systems. For example, it is necessary to determine who will have access to what kinds of data within the hierarchy of an organization.

Because modern computing technology makes it easy to process and record large amounts of data, the potential for an abuse of this information and of the power associated with it is also multiplied and needs to be monitored carefully. In applying computer technology as an integral part of their practice, social work professionals need to become knowledgeable about safeguards to prevent misuse of and unauthorized access to client data.

Conclusion

The conclusion Boyd, Hylton, and Price reached in 1978 still seems to be true today: although computers are being used to facilitate routine administrative tasks in social service agencies, their potential for assisting in uniquely professional decision making remains largely unrecognized.[28] Today social service agencies use data management and word processing programs primarily for fiscal management, accounting, program evaluation, record keeping, and clerical tasks.

However, an increasing number of professionals and social service agencies are becoming aware of the technological advances occurring in computer applications. The move from large mainframe computers to interactive information processing with less expensive computers makes this technology accessible even to small agencies. More flexible programming techniques coupled with the availability of online terminals allow social workers to use this technology for their decision making. With modern computer systems, professionals can create, manipulate, and modify data files quickly and easily without needing the extensive resources in programming skills and time that were required in the past.

Nevertheless, if social workers are to participate in the rapid development of information processing technology, students and experienced practitioners need to be trained accordingly. An adequate orientation of professionals to information processing, data management procedures, and computer applications is essential to their acceptance and adoption of information processing techniques.

To summarize, the central notion behind the development of computerized information systems is that they yield sets of data that can be converted into information. This information can aid administrators and practitioners in their decision making, thereby enhancing the provision of social services. Unquestionably, computers can receive, store, process, and retrieve more data faster and with greater accuracy than manual systems, but users also need to be aware of the limitations of an information processing system. For example, information technology does not provide a quick cure for the ills of an organization. Dery explored the problems associated with the adoption of a generalized database man-

agement system on a statewide level in California.[29] He found that regardless of how much data are available or how quickly they are processed, access to information —who gets what data and for what purpose—is still determined by power plays in the bureaucratic hierarchy. The potential of information technology cannot be realized independently of the context in which it is used, but if applied knowledgeably and judiciously, it can become a powerful tool in the planning and delivery of social services.

ELIZABETH MUTSCHLER

Notes and References

1. The author thanks Robert D. Vinter for his comments on an earlier draft of this article and for his help with the section on applications in administrative decision making.

2. N. Nie et al., *SPSS: Statistical Package for the Social Sciences* (2d ed.; New York: McGraw-Hill Book Co., 1975).

3. For more extensive discussions of computer systems and the preparation of data for processing, see Duncan Lindsey, "Data Analysis with the Computer," in Richard M. Grinnell, Jr., ed., *Social Work Research and Evaluation* (Itasca, Ill.: F. E. Peacock Publishers, 1981), pp. 530–552; Joseph B. Sidowski, J. H. Johnson, and T. A. Williams, eds., *Technology in Mental Health Care Delivery Systems* (Norwood, N.J.: Ablex Publishing Corporation, 1980); and William J. Reid, "Applications of Computer Technology," in Norman A. Polansky, ed., *Social Work Research* (Chicago: University of Chicago Press, 1975), pp. 229–253.

4. Reid, "Applications of Computer Technology."

5. James L. Hedlund and Cecil R. Wurster, "Computer Applications in Mental Health Management," in Bruce I. Blum, ed., *Proceedings: The Sixth Annual Symposium on Computer Applications in Medical Care* (Washington, D.C.: Institute of Electrical and Electronics Engineers, 1982), pp. 366–370.

6. For more detailed discussions of MIS applications in human services, see Dick J. Schoech, *Computer Use in Human Services: A Guide to Information Management* (New York: Human Sciences Press, 1982); David Dery, *Computers in Welfare* (Beverly Hills, Calif.: Sage

Publications, 1981); and Simon Slavin, "Editor's Introduction," *Administration in Social Work*, 5 (Fall/Winter 1981), pp. 1–3.

7. David Fanshel, "Computerized Information Systems and Foster Care: The New York City Experience with CWIS," *Children Today*, 44 (November-December 1976), pp. 14–18.

8. Peter R. Keen and Michael Scott-Morton, *Decision Support Systems: An Organizational Perspective* (Reading, Mass.: Addison-Wesley Publishing Co., 1978).

9. Schoech, *Computer Use in Human Services*, p. 37.

10. Peter H. Rossi and Howard E. Freeman, *Evaluation: A Systematic Approach* (Beverly Hills, Calif.: Sage Publications, 1982).

11. Frederick R. Eisele and George B. Kleindorfer, "Forecasting for Social Services: A Model for Area Agencies on Aging," *Administration in Social Work*, 2 (Winter 1978), pp. 401–410.

12. See, for example, J. R. Faulkner et al., "EPIC: Information Management for Mental Health Clinicians, Administrators and Researchers," in Jeffrey L. Crawford, S. Vitale, and J. Robinson, eds., *Computer Applications in Mental Health* (Cambridge, Mass.: Ballinger Publishing Co., 1980); and J. H. Johnson et al., "Organizational Preparedness for Change: Staff Acceptance of an On-Line Computer-Assisted Assessment System," *Behavior Research Methods*, 10 (1978), pp. 186–190.

13. John H. Greist, L. J. Van Cura, and N. P. Kneppreth, "A Computer Interview for Emergency Room Patients," *Comparative Biomedical Research*, 6 (1973), pp. 247–253.

14. Greist, Van Cura, and Kneppreth, "A Computer Interview for Emergency Room Patients"; and A. C. Carr et al., "Direct Assessment of Depression by Microcomputer: A Feasibility Study," *Acta Psychiatry Scandinavia*, 64 (1981), pp. 415–422.

15. Ruth E. Dayhoff, ed., "Stretching Microcomputer Power with ANS MUMPS," *MUMPS User Group Quarterly*, 10 (November 1980), pp. 13–21.

16. John H. Greist et al., "Clinical Computer Applications in Mental Health," in Blum, *Proceedings: The Sixth Annual Symposium on Computer Applications in Medical Care*, pp. 356–365; and E. B. Cole, J. H. Johnson, and T. A. Williams, "When Psychiatric Patients Interact with Computer Terminals: Problems and Solutions," *Behavior Research Methods and Instrumentation*, 8 (1976), pp. 92–94.

17. Jim Newkham and Leon Bawcom, "Computerizing an Integrated Clinical and Financial Record System in a CMHC: A Pilot Project," *Administration in Social Work*, 5 (Fall/Winter 1981), pp. 97–111.

18. Cecil R. Wurster and J. D. Goodwin, "NIMH Prototype Management Information System for Community Mental Health Centers," in J. T. O'Neill, ed., *Proceedings of the Fourth Annual Symposium on Computer Applications in Medical Care* (New York: Institute of Electrical and Electronics Engineers, 1980).

19. J. E. Mezzich, J. T. Dow, and G. A. Coffman, "Developing an Efficient Clinical Information System for a Comprehensive Psychiatric Institute: Principles, Design, and Organization," *Behavior Research Methods and Instrumentation*, 13 (1981), pp. 459–463; John H. Greist et al., "Computer Applications in Psychiatry at the University of Wisconsin: Current Status," *Current Concepts in Psychiatry*, 3 (1977), pp. 13–16; and I. Sletten, G. Ulett, and H. Altman, "The Missouri Standard System of Psychiatry," *Archive of General Psychiatry*, 23 (1970), pp. 73–79.

20. Greist et al., "Clinical Computer Applications in Mental Health."

21. Nie et al., *SPSS*.

22. Fanshel, "Computerized Information Systems and Foster Care."

23. Nie et al., *SPSS*, p. 14.

24. Dayhoff, "Stretching Microcomputer Power with ANS MUMPS."

25. Lawrence H. Boyd, John H. Hylton, and Steven Price, "Computers in Social Work Practice: A Review," *Social Work*, 23 (September 1978), pp. 368–371.

26. Ch. E. Feldstone, *Attitudinal Survey Instrument: Test Data, Analysis, and Instructions* (Cincinnati, Ohio: Information Systems Center, 1973).

27. Schoech, *Computer Use in Human Services*.

28. Boyd, Hylton, and Price, "Computers in Social Work Practice."

29. Dery, *Computers in Welfare*.

DEINSTITUTIONALIZATION

Since the early 1950s, national policy has gradually come to reflect the search for an alternative to institutional care and control as the preferred solution to social problems. Deinstitutionalization, as the policy has come to be known, developed differently with respect to the various populations traditionally subject to care and control in large institutions: for example, the aged, children, the mentally ill, the developmentally disabled, and criminal offenders. Still, as it pertains to each of these groups, the term "deinstitutionalization" is best defined in the language of a 1977 General Accounting Office (GAO) report:

> The process of (1) preventing both unnecessary admission to and retention in institutions; (2) finding and developing appropriate alternatives in the community for housing, treatment, training, education, and rehabilitation of [persons] who do not need to be in institutions; and (3) improving conditions, care, and treatment for those who need to have institutional care. This approach is based on the principle that. . . persons are entitled to live in the least restrictive environment necessary and lead lives as normally and independently as they can.[1]

Although this definition reflects the broad aims of the policy of deinstitutionalization, the most discernible consequence of the policy has been the reduction of the average daily census of the large institutions that house the various problem populations.

Deinstitutionalization did not come about for any single reason. The following influences combined to make deinstitutionalization seem attractive and feasible: (1) the documented negative effects of institutionalization, particularly the syndrome of apathy and passive compliance known as institutional dependency, (2) the growing costs of institutional care relative to its alternatives, (3) advances in social, psychological, and medical sciences that were thought to make the confinement and isolation functions of the institution obsolete,

(4) the development of a broad-based civil rights movement that in its assault on status discrimination emphasized the protection of the individual's rights to full citizenship and due process and, as a corollary, the necessity to approach care and treatment in the least restrictive manner, and (5) the development of an extensive system of public aid that allowed the replacement of the in-kind room-and-board maintenance system of the institution with a system of cash grants. This last development, in particular, created a state-subsidized market for the local provision of care by the private sector.

A unique political coalition that spanned the political spectrum supported all these trends. Conservatives viewed the reduction of the institutionalized population as a means of saving money; liberals supported professional groups who saw deinstitutionalization as the most humane and effective approach to the organization of care. Political opposition to deinstitutionalization came almost entirely from groups, such as the Civil Service Employees Union, who were viewed as interested only in maintaining their jobs in state institutions. Without organized political opposition and with many groups seeing it as a means to achieving their ends, deinstitutionalization proceeded.

GAO's definition of deinstitutionalization, especially its three components, provides a structure by which to review the progress of deinstitutionalization and its effects on the populations involved. However, to understand the general process, it will be useful to reorder the three elements of the GAO definition and consider them in the following sequence: (1) the goal of improving the care and treatment of those who need institutional care, (2) the need for preventing both unnecessary admissions and undue retentions, and (3) the process of finding and developing appropriate alternatives in the community for housing, treating, training, educating, and rehabilitating persons who do not need to be placed in institutions.

Efforts to improve institutional conditions have usually been tied to increasing the cost of institutional care. The courts, in their various right-to-treatment decisions in the fields of mental health, child welfare, and developmental disability, specified the types of treatment to which involuntarily detained patients have a right and the types of treatment they may refuse. The courts have also specified patient-to-staff ratios and defined parameters of overcrowding.[2] The expense of carrying out these orders has often prompted institutional officials to reduce the numbers of patients or inmates rather than increase staff or construct new facilities. In California, for example, the majority of correctional institutions are one hundred years old. Building new institutions costs anywhere from $20,000 to $30,000 per cell. In addition, it may cost up to $20,000 a year to maintain a single offender in a correctional institution.[3] The large institution has become a costly dinosaur.

The major objectives of the deinstitutionalization movement have been to prevent unnecessary admissions to institutions and to reduce the rates and times of retention. The relationship between these goals and the development of appropriate community-based alternatives are best explored with respect to the groups affected.

The Mentally Ill

In 1950, the major site of institutionalization was the state mental hospital. These are the institutions that have been most affected by the deinstitutionalization movement. The census of state hospitals plummeted 55 percent between 1955 and 1973 from a high of 558,922 in 1955 to 248,518 in 1973. In 1980, the census stood at 245,029. Although the resident population fell drastically, admissions to state and county mental hospitals increased between 1950 and 1970, finally leveling off after 1970. In 1950 there were 152,286 admissions to state and county mental hospitals,

a ratio of .297 admissions for every resident (512,501). By contrast, in 1970 there were 348,511 admissions and 337,619 residents for a ratio of 1.14 admissions per resident. By 1974, this ratio had increased to 1.74.[4] Thus, in the mental health field, deinstitutionalization brought about a "revolving door" pattern, with high admission rates but short periods of retention.

Justification for this activity came from several points of view. Studies were unable to demonstrate the effectiveness of long-term treatment in mental institutions. Studies that compared hospital treatment to community treatment without hospitalization but with psychoactive medications supported the community-based approach. After their clinical trials, the first major psychoactive medications were presented to the public as a means for the control of mental health symptomatology and thus as a justification for trusting patients outside the confines of a mental institution. Patients were to use the hospital occasionally simply to have their medications adjusted.

Perhaps the major contributor to the reduction of the patient population of state mental hospitals was the 1962 decision of the federal Department of Health, Education, and Welfare (HEW) to revise its policies to allow federal matching funds to be used by state public assistance programs for the support of persons released from mental hospitals. The HEW reinterpretation made categorical aid available to former mental patients through the Aid to the Totally Disabled program, which is now part of the Supplemental Security program established by the Social Security Act. By providing for the maintenance of mental patients in local communities, HEW thus substituted cash assistance for institutional confinement and simultaneously provided the economic stimulus for the development of community-based residential care.

The broad-based civil rights movement put the final nail in the coffin of long-term hospitalization. With the elimination of indefinite commitment to state mental hospitals and the restriction of involuntary detention to brief periods, long-term residence in mental hospitals was effectively stopped. In some part as a reflection of deinstitutionalization, outpatient services increased from 2.3 episodes per thousand population in 1955 to 21.9 in 1975. (In 1979, this figure was 20.6.) However, a substantial proportion of this increase is attributable to the tendency of community mental health centers to make outpatient services more widely available to individuals without major mental disorders.

Unfortunately, the political coalition that engineered the demise of state mental institutions did not survive to foster the development of alternative care. Most individuals requiring supportive living arrangements were simply returned to the community to live on their own or with their families. A significant proportion, between 10 and 30 percent, went to live in alternative institutions or sheltered living arrangements; the latter included foster or family care homes, board and care homes, supervised hotels, and halfway houses.[5] A large proportion of these supervised living arrangements were, in many respects, similar in character to the large mental institutions, but were smaller entities that were locally and privately operated.

The Developmentally Disabled

The deinstitutionalization of the developmentally disabled occurred largely because they were maintained in the same institutions as the mentally ill. In 1950, traditional state and county mental hospitals housed 48,000 developmentally disabled residents; this was 27 percent of all developmentally disabled residents of public institutions. By 1974, the number had decreased to 20,000, or only 10 percent of developmentally disabled residents in such institutions. Thus, there was a 58 percent decline in the developmentally disabled population of state and county mental institutions. Corresponding to this decline, however, was an increase in the resident population of facilities specializing in services to the developmentally disabled.

Between 1950 and 1967, the population rose from 176,000 to 193,000. At this point, the population peaked and declined to 152,000 in 1979.[6] Figures from a different source indicate the continuing decline in this population to 140,043 in 1981 and 132,235 in 1982.[7]

The deinstitutionalization of the developmentally disabled, like that of the mentally ill, was prodded by the U.S. Supreme Court. Landmark decisions included *White* v. *Stickney*, relating to the right to treatment, and decisions requiring that the developmentally disabled be assigned to the least restrictive environments possible. New technologies, advanced communications, and the concept of normalization—the treatment of people in the environment most closely approximating a normal situation—combined with the increasing cost associated with improving institutions to accelerate the movement of the developmentally disabled into the community.

Like the mentally ill, most of these individuals have gone to live with their families or on their own. Yet, a significant proportion are housed in small community-based facilities, foster homes, and board and care homes; and others are in large-group homes that begin to approximate the formal character of the large institution.

Corrections

The scale of community programs for offenders is now greater than at any time in history. In 1977, over a million persons, including 200,000 adults, received probation services in the United States. At least twenty-eight states offered some form of community residential program for adult felons, and the U.S. Bureau of Prisons began fourteen such programs between 1965 and 1973. By 1977, forty-two states were operating furlough programs. As many as 40,000 offenders enter halfway houses each year.[8]

The use of community programs to reduce prison populations is now a central characteristic of the criminal justice system in the United States. Nevertheless, the national prison census has continued to grow, spawning controversial measures to finance the construction of new county jails and state prisons. Although the federal prison census increased but slightly between 1970 and 1981 (from 20,038 to 22,169), the state prison census grew from 176,391 in 1970 to 330,998 in 1981. Indeed, the proportion of the U.S. population imprisoned at the end of the year and under maximum sentence of more than one year rose by 58 percent between 1970 and 1981, primarily through the growth of the state prison population. This trend reflects, in part, the implementation of stronger penalties for some crimes, but also the maturation of the postwar "baby boom" generation, a huge birth cohort now passing through the young adult period during which the highest arrest rate traditionally prevails. Thus, although alternatives to correctional institutionalization have proliferated, the pressure on the correctional system to confine large numbers of people has increased dramatically.

Dependent and Neglected Children

The shift of dependent and neglected youths to community-based foster homes dates back to the early part of the twentieth century and represents the earliest departure from the institution. Although, for demographic reasons similar to those described for offenders, the actual number of youths in institutions has increased, the rate at which youths under 18 were housed in child welfare institutions decreased by 48 percent between 1933 and 1973.[9] Furthermore, the roles of child welfare institutions have changed; rather than serving the general functions of the children's home, they are now concerned primarily with special problems. Many of these institutions have become treatment centers for emotionally disturbed children. Although national data for 1970, 1971, and 1973 indicate a 10 percent reduction in the number of dependent and neglected children living in child welfare institutions, they also show a corresponding increase in the number of chil-

dren classified as emotionally disturbed. Recent trends in the deinstitutionalization of juvenile status offenders in California show a similar tendency toward "relabeling" and confinement in specialized child welfare institutions or mental health facilities.[10]

The Aged

From the early 1900s to the present, there has been a steady increase in the institutionalization of the aged in the United States. The population of the elderly residing in institutions and group quarters of one type or another increased 267 percent between 1910 and 1970. In 1940, the United States census showed that the institutionalized aged population was 4.1 percent of the total aged population: 40.5 percent were in group quarters, including hotels, boarding houses, and the like; 33 percent were in homes for the aged, infirm, and needy, such as nursing homes and personal care and residential homes; and 23 percent lived in mental institutions.[11]

Between 1960 and 1970, however, there was a 55 percent decrease in the proportion of the aged living in mental institutions, a 41 percent decrease in aged residents of noninstitutional group quarters, and a 45 percent increase in the proportion of the aged living in nursing homes and sheltered-care homes. Thus, by 1970, 1.1 million elderly were living in institutions, of whom 72 percent were residing in nursing homes, only 12 percent were in group quarters, and 10 percent were in mental institutions. By 1970, the total proportion of the elderly living in institutions had risen to 5.5 percent. This increase is explained by the growth of the nursing home industry and the corresponding decrease in the proportion of the elderly living in group quarters.[12] It is projected that the 1977 population of 1.3 million in nursing homes will grow to 1.95 million by the year 2000 and to 2.95 million by the year 2030.[13]

Three major federal programs have had a direct impact on the private nursing home and residential care industry: the Social Security Act of 1935, Medicare, and Medicaid. The Social Security Act provided funds to retired elderly persons so that they could live by themselves or purchase boarding home care.

By the late 1950s, shortages of beds in general hospitals created pressure to move chronic patients into nursing homes to make room for acute cases. In 1965, the Medicare and Medicaid legislation dramatically influenced institutional care for the aged. From its inception, Medicare has been oriented toward acute care services, providing, in 1979, 74 percent of the dollars taken in by hospitals and only 1 percent of those received by nursing homes. For those with long-term chronic illness requiring nursing home care, services are primarily available through federal and state Medicaid programs designed for the indigent. In 1979, federal and state programs paid for 57 percent of all nursing home care, thus providing a major resource for the private nursing home industry.[14]

The aged are a unique population in that deinstitutionalization has come in only one sector—their movement out of the mental hospital. Often, however, the aged were moved directly out of the hospital and into the nursing home. In many cases they were not moved at all: the names of buildings were changed, and the population stayed in place. It is estimated that 80 percent of those 65 years of age and older who live in nursing and personal care homes have some degree of mental impairment.[15] The large-scale and institutional character of the present-day nursing homes has created pressure for the deinstitutionalization of the aged from the nursing home toward more home-based situations. This pressure results primarily from the extensive costs of Medicare and Medicaid.

Evaluating Trends

At its best, deinstitutionalization has lived up to its lofty aims to promote local care that is more humane and effective than previous efforts based in large institutions. At its worst, deinstitutionalization has resulted in the forced homelessness of the former residents of state institutions and in the accumulation of individuals in community-based facilities that are no better than their antecedents.

The problems of deinstitutionalization derive not so much from the concept as from its naive implementation. The array of community-based services necessary to the support of true community care could not possibly come cheaply, and yet, as inflation became a severe problem in the 1970s, the bipartisan political coalition that had forged the deinstitutionalization movement fell apart. The fiscal retrenchment of government has left community care ominously incomplete, and the fate of a noble idea may hinge on a poorly designed experiment woefully short of resources.

As a result, many residential elements of community care have abandoned the "small is beautiful" philosophy that provided a marked contrast to the operations of the large institution. Capitalizing on economies of scale, many nursing homes, group homes, and similar accommodations for various populations have come to resemble community-based versions of the institutions they were intended to replace. The term "transinstitutionalism" has been coined to describe this lateral movement of individuals from one dominant institutional form to another.

There is ample evidence that deinstitutionalization can work well. However, insofar as it demands both the improvement of any large institutions that may be necessary and the provision of community-based care, it remains the expensive creation of a frugal era.

STEVEN P. SEGAL
JIM BAUMOHL

Notes and References

1. *Returning the Mentally Disabled to the Community: Government Needs to Do More* (Washington, D.C.: General Accounting Office, January 1977).

2. Donaldson v. O'Connor, 493 F.2d 507 (5th Cir. 1974); cert. granted 95S. Ct. 171; Wyatt v. Stickney, 493 F. Supp. 521, 522 (1972); Bartley v. Kremens, 402 F. Supp. 1039 (E.D. Pa. 1975).

3. Louis P. Carney, *Corrections and the Community* (Englewood Cliffs, N.J.: Prentice-Hall, 1977).

4. Morton Kramer, *Psychiatric Services and the Changing Institutional Scene, 1950-1985,* "Analytical and Special Study Reports," National Institute of Mental Health, Series B, No. 12 (Washington, D.C.: U.S. Government Printing Office, 1977).

5. Steven P. Segal and Uri Aviram, *The Mentally Ill in Community-Based Sheltered-Care* (New York: John Wiley & Sons, 1978).

6. Paul Lerman, *Deinstitutionalization* (New Brunswick, N.J.: Rutgers University Press, 1982), p. 66.

7. Lisa L. Rotegard and Robert H. Bruininks, *Mentally Retarded People in State Operated Residential Facilities: Years Ending June 30, 1981 and 1982* (Minneapolis: Center for Residential and Community Services, Department of Educational Psychology, University of Minnesota, April 1983).

8. John Hylton, *Reintegrating the Offender* (Washington, D.C.: University Press of America, 1981).

9. Lerman, *Deinstitutionalization*, p. 24.

10. Katherine T. Van Dusen, "Net Widening and Relabeling," *American Behavioral Scientist,* 24 (July-August 1981), pp. 801-810.

11. Carroll L. Estes and Charlene A. Harrington, "Fiscal Crisis, Deinstitutionalization and the Elderly," *American Behavioral Scientist,* 24 (July-August 1981), pp. 811-826.

12. Ibid., p. 815.

13. U.S. Senate Special Committee on Aging, *Developments in Aging, 1981,* vol. 1 (Washington, D.C.: U.S. Government Printing Office, 1982), pp. 354.

14. Estes and Harrington, "Fiscal Crisis, Deinstitutionalization and the Elderly," pp. 816-817; and Robert M. Gibson, "National Health Expenditures, 1979," *Health Care Financing Review,* 2 (summer 1980), pp. 1-36.

15. U.S. Senate Special Committee on Aging, *Developments in Aging, 1981,* vol. 2, p. 159.

DISABILITIES

The disability and rehabilitation arena has undergone rapid evolution in recent years, and change and refinement have also affected the nomenclature of the field. Although precise definitions are needed in describing the social, political, and professional changes that are altering the lives of persons with disabilities, differing approaches to the terminology still exist. In this article, the words "disability," "functional limitation," and "handicap" are used in the following ways:

• A *disability* is a medically diagnosed long-term or chronic condition involving a physiological, anatomical, mental, or emotional impairment resulting from a disease or illness, an inherited or congenital defect, or a trauma or other insult (including environmental) to mind or body.

• A *functional limitation* involves a hindrance or negative effect in the performance of tasks or major life activities, such as restrictions in the activities of a person with epilepsy because of the danger of unexpected unconciousness.

• A *handicap* is a disadvantage, interference, or barrier to performance, opportunity, or fulfillment in any desired role in life. Imposed by limitations in function or other problems associated with disabilities or personal characteristics, handicaps must be understood in the context of the individual's environment or role. For example, an arc welder would be vocationally handicapped by epilepsy if it imposed certain activity restrictions that affected performance in that job.[1]

These definitions are arbitrary, but they provide a constructive framework for separating the medical factors (disability) from the social or environmental factors (functional limitation and handicap). The words "handicap" and "disability" are frequently used interchangeably, and federal legislation uses "handicap" to cover both medical and environmental factors, but the distinctions outlined here will be maintained throughout this article.

Demographics

Because the definitions, population samples, and research methodologies vary from study to study, it is difficult to determine how many citizens with disabilities there are in the United States and the extent of the social and financial consequences of disabilities. The most comprehensive studies presently available are from the Health Interview Survey, sponsored in 1979 by the National Center for Health Statistics, and the Survey of Income and Education, conducted in 1976 by the Census Bureau.[2]

The Health Interview Survey concluded that in 1979, the latest year for which fully tabulated results are available, approximately 31.5 million Americans, or 14.6 percent of the noninstitutionalized population, are limited in some way by a chronic health condition. The severely disabled—persons unable to carry on some major life activity such as attending school, housekeeping, or working—constitute 3.7 percent of the population, or 7.9 million individuals. The Health Interview Survey further indicates that disability increases with age: Among individuals 16 years and younger, 3.9 percent are disabled; among those 17 to 44, 8.8 percent are disabled; of those 45 to 64, 24.1 percent are disabled; and 46 percent of those 65 years and older are disabled.

The Survey of Income and Education found that black citizens are significantly more likely to be disabled than white citizens, 17.6 percent versus 13.7 percent. The lowest rate of disability (10.6 percent) was found among those identified as Hispanic. The study discovered an inverse relationship between the prevalence of disability and the level of education. With the federal poverty line used as the income measure, poor persons between 18 and 64 were much more likely to be disabled than the nonpoor working-age population, 28.7 percent compared to 11.8 percent. Regional variation in the prevalence of disability also exists: When those over the age of 3 are the basis for the calculations, New England is at the low end of the spectrum with 12.6 percent, and the East South Central region at the high end with 18.3 percent.

Cause and effect relationships among these variables have not been established, but they certainly warrant exploration if for no other reason than that the number of citizens with disabilities continues to increase. Some researchers have concluded from the Health Interview Survey that the number of Americans with chronic limitations on their activity increased 37.3 percent between 1966 and 1976, whereas the general population increased by only 10 percent.[3] This conclusion can be attributed to many factors, including better research methodologies, increases in the population of the elderly, improved techniques of medical intervention, easier access to medical care, and a dramatic increase in the number of children with disabilities surviving the birth process.[4]

Societal Perceptions

The first known person with a disability was a Neanderthal man, now called Shandar I, who lived approximately 45,000 years ago. From those early years to the present, societal perceptions of the individuals who are born with or acquire disabilities have varied from culture to culture and time to time. American society has followed the patterns of Western society in general. Disability has been viewed as an aberration; the underlying belief has been that the individual must be guilty of some wrongdoing or at least possessed by some type of evil spirit. This attitude may sound archaic in the twentieth century, but it still exists in subtle ways. Why else are young children often pulled aside by a parent when the child attempts to talk with a person who has an obvious physical disability?

Beginning around the turn of the century, in the era of social idealism, the concept of benevolent care and institutionalization emerged and was gradually accepted. These views are still prevalent, particularly in relation to the most severely disabled. World War II marked a shift in attitudes and services for persons with disabilities. During that conflict, medical care improved dramatically and led to a large number of severely disabled adults returning to American shores. Physical rehabilitation, achieved through advanced medical care and the utilization of allied health professionals, emerged as a new perspective on disability. The focus shifted from the static variable (disability) to the dynamic variable (functional limitations). With the introduction of the rehabilitation and restoration model, the functional limitations associated with disabilities were reduced, and the life expectancy for this expanding segment of the population was increased.

The late 1960s and early 1970s produced a turning point in the evolution of attitudes toward disability. During those years, persons with disabilities and some rehabilitation professionals began advocating a view of disability that emphasized the disabled person's right of access to full social functioning. Turner defines such a perspective as the birth of a social movement:

A significant social movement becomes possible when there is a revision in the manner in which a substantial group of people, looking at some misfortune, see it no longer as a misfortune warranting charitable consideration but as an injustice which is intolerable in society.[5]

In this case, the new paradigm emphasized independent living for disabled individuals, and the social movement it inspired is sometimes referred to as the independent-living movement.

The independent-living paradigm is critical to understanding the dramatic changes that have occurred in federal legislation and the service delivery system relating to persons with disabilities. For adherents of the independent-living model, the major obstacles faced by persons with disabilities are not related necessarily to the disability

TABLE 1. DIFFERENCES BETWEEN THE REHABILITATION/MEDICAL AND INDEPENDENT-LIVING
PARADIGMS OF DISABILITIES

Area	Rehabilitation/Medical Paradigm	Independent-Living Paradigm
Definition of problem	Physical impairment or lack of vocational skill	Dependence on professionals, relatives, and so on
Locus of problem	In the individual	In the environment and the rehabilitation process
Solution to problem	Professional intervention by physician and allied health professionals	Peer counseling, advocacy, self-help, consumer control, removal of barriers
Social role	Patient/client	Consumer
Who controls	Professional	Consumer
Desired outcome	Maximum physical functioning, gainful employment	Independent living, regardless of vocational or functional status

Source: Gerben DeJong, "Independent Living: From Social Movement to Analytic Paradigm,"
Archives of Physical Medicine and Rehabilitation, 60 (October 1979), pp. 435–446.

or the functional limitations, but rather reside in the handicaps imposed by society's attitudes and the denial of access to basic rights and services. This model states that the abilities and social status assigned to "able" persons in the society should also be extended to disabled persons and should be implicit in all interactions with them. DeJong has outlined six areas in which the rehabilitation/medical paradigm contrasts with the independent-living paradigm (see Table 1).

Independent living has developed concurrently with other, complementary social movements, such as those addressing civil rights, consumerism, demedicalization, self-help, and deinstitutionalization. These movements share common values and assumptions, yet each stems from a different social dilemma. The independent-living movement is distinguished by its constituency and by the manner in which it has influenced the legislation and programs that concern rehabilitation.[6]

Landmark Federal Legislation

In 1968, the U.S. Congress commenced a gradual shift in disability-related legislation

and thus ushered in a new era in public policy toward citizens with disabilities. Prior to that year, the focus had primarily been on direct services for personal adjustment, medical maintenance, and employment. In a policy trend that continued until 1980, the hallmark of the new, expanded legislation was that it addressed environmental issues and program accessibility. The major pieces of legislation were as follows:

The Architectural Barriers Act. This act (P.L. 90–480), passed in 1968, requires all buildings built with federal funds or leased by the federal government be made accessible to persons with disabilities. A Compliance Board was established in 1973 to enforce the provisions of this act. Many states followed by enacting similar legislation for their jurisdictions. The resulting ramps and architectural symbol-of-access signs are the most publicly visible effects to have grown out of the independent-living movement.

The Developmental Disabilities Services Facilities and Construction Act. This 1970 act (P.L. 91–517) provided expansive responsibility to states for planning and implementing a comprehensive program of services for developmentally disabled children and adults.

The Rehabilitation Act. This 1973 bill is a pivotal piece of legislation for all persons with disabilities. Section 504 of this act (P.L. 93–112) is a one-sentence statement prohibiting discrimination against "otherwise qualified handicapped individuals . . . under any program or activity receiving federal financial assistance." Sections 501 and 503 mandate affirmative action in federal and federal contract employment. Section 502 established the Architectural and Transportation Barriers Compliance Board. The entire act places strong emphasis on expanding vocational rehabilitation services to the more severely disabled by giving them priority in receiving services. Independent-living, nonvocational programs were mentioned in this act; they were not funded, however.

The Developmental Disabilities Assistance and Bill of Rights Act. Passed in 1975, this bill (P.L. 94–103) established protection and advocacy systems for developmentally disabled persons. In addition, it established representative councils in each state that receive funds for developmental disability programs.

The Education for All Handicapped Children Act. This 1975 act (P.L. 94–142) ensures a free, appropriate education for children with disabilities and mandates that such education be provided in the least restrictive setting possible.

Amendments to the Rehabilitation Act of 1973. These 1978 amendments (P.L. 95–602) established independent living as a priority for state vocational rehabilitation programs and provided funding for independent-living centers.

The Social Security Disability Amendments of 1980. This legislative update (P.L. 96–265) removed certain disincentives

to employment by allowing disabled individuals a longer trial period for work and the deduction of certain nonvocational expenses in calculating income benefits.

Two of these acts, the Education for All Handicapped Children Act of 1975 and the 1973 Rehabilitation Act, had a significant impact on the lives of individuals with disabilities and the service delivery systems that assist all citizens. P.L. 94–142 and regulations adopted in 1977 to implement the law provide that all children with disabilities, regardless of their disability or its severity, are entitled to receive a free education, preferably in the home community. The regulations further stipulate that parents must be involved with their child's individual educational plan. In addition, supportive therapies, including student and parent counseling, must be available to these students. For many children and their families, the school system can now supply the tools for reducing functional limitations and financial hardship. Nondisabled students are the beneficiaries of increased social contact with children who are disabled and of heightened awareness of the effects of disabilities.[7]

For children and adults, Section 504 of the 1973 Rehabilitation Act, the "Civil Rights Act of the Disabled," has guaranteed the rights of full citizenship and participation in American society. Discrimination against persons with disabilities has not disappeared entirely, but individuals now have legal recourse when it occurs. Freedom of choice is the major achievement of Section 504. It guarantees that reasonable accommodation and access must be provided by service agencies, medical facilities, businesses, institutions of higher education, transportation systems, and landlords. Disabled consumers now have the right to choose from a variety of alternatives, and this is the first step toward independent living.

The passage of P.L. 94–142 and Section 504, like all other civil rights legislation, does not produce immediate solutions to complex social problems. The implementation of these laws is dictated by federal regulations, and these regulations are subject to interpretation and alteration. The formulation of Section 504 regulations was not begun until five years after the passage of the 1973 Rehabilitation Act, and the regulations still were not completed in 1983. Despite the slowness of the regulatory process, many positive advances have been made, particularly in the area of human services.

Services

Hospitals, extended care facilities, specialized schools and institutions, and intermediate care facilities are providing improved health and support services to the most severely impaired individuals. In recent years, community-based programs, especially home health care, have greatly increased. This increase is a natural outgrowth of the deinstitutionalization trend and the independent-living movement; both emphasize community living, with support, for the less severely disabled as a viable alternative to highly specialized professional care.

Agencies and programs not specifically designed for persons with disabilities are now offering to provide reasonable access or accommodation for disabled individuals who choose to live and function in communities. Public social agencies, community mental health centers, private therapy offices, sexual assault centers, and adoption agencies are but a few examples of the settings where persons with disabilities may choose to seek services. Many of these settings are finding innovative ways to expand or modify their programs to serve this clientele. In many cases, outreach to and recruitment of persons with disabilities is attracting additional clients and potential employees.

The 1978 amendments to the Rehabilitation Act of 1973 authorized federal funding for the establishment and operation of a new service delivery system, called independent-living centers. By 1983, there were approximately one-hundred and fifty independent-living centers in the United States. These centers have been funded via federal grants to state vocational rehabilitation agencies or, in some cases, by other public agencies or private organizations. Consumer participation in organizing and managing the centers is a key element. The stated mission of the independent-living centers is to "offer services which enable severely disabled individuals to live more independently in family and community or to secure and maintain employment."[8] These centers can serve any disabled person, whereas traditional vocational rehabilitation programs can serve only clients who have a reasonable expectation of becoming gainfully employed.

Independent-living centers provide a wide range of services: (1) peer counseling, (2) information and referral, (3) advocacy, (4) in-home attendant care, (5) housing and transportation, (6) health maintenance, (7) social and recreational activities, and (8) arrangements for group living. A center does not necessarily have all services on the premises but should be able to coordinate the provision of a combination of services, some of which may be provided elsewhere. State vocational rehabilitation agencies should be able to supply detailed information about independent-living centers that are found in a particular state or commonwealth.

Social Work Practice

The increasing population of persons with disabilities, the shift in societal attitudes toward an emphasis on independent living, and the changes in the legislative foundations of service delivery all affect social work practice. If current demographic trends continue, it can be predicted that, in the near future, disability will touch the lives of nearly every American family at some time during the life cycle. Knowledge about and sensitivity to disability-related issues are thus increasingly crucial to effective social work practice.

The emergence of the independent-living movement poses some new opportunities for the social work profession. The philosophical base of independent living and the social work tenet of client self-determination are highly compatible. The challenge facing the profession is this: How can the profession collaborate with the independent-living movement and adapt to the rapidly changing environment of persons with disabilities?

Social work services for persons with disabilities and social work education have traditionally focused on the health care system. This approach was a logical outgrowth of the fact that the health care system was a major point of access to the services needed by persons with disabilities. The health care system still fills that role, but if the trends toward community integration and demedicalization continue, social workers in health care settings will one day have the task of working with the most severely disabled individuals and the multiply disabled. Practitioners with nonmedical orientations, such as school social workers, will be thrust into the role that traditionally has belonged to the rehabilitation social worker. These transitions will be aided by several developments, namely, that medical, surgical, and technological advances are decreasing the extent of functional limitations, that persons with disabilities are living longer, and that there are many more options available. The psychological devastation formerly associated with the word "disability" is no longer warranted. It is no longer true, as it was thirty or forty years ago, that the diagnosis of a disability means an automatic reduction to a second-class or third-class status.

Social work administrators, managers, planners, and researchers have an opportunity to evaluate the effects of the independent-living movement and, at the same time, to create and provide programs to meet the evolving needs of this newly empowered group of citizens. In responding to and working with the independent-living movement, the social work profession needs to remember three critical facts: disabilities can sometimes be prevented, but they cannot be eliminated; functional limitations can be reduced; and handicaps can be eradicated. Social workers not only have the skills necessary to assist in the prevention of disabilities and in the reduction of functional limitations, but they also have the professional expertise to establish a leadership role in the eradication of handicaps.

MARGUERITE J. DAVID

Notes and References

1. Gerben DeJong, "Independent Living: From Social Movement to Analytic Paradigm," *Archives of Physical Medicine and Rehabilitation,* 60 (October 1979), pp. 435–446.

2. *Health Interview Survey* (Washington, D.C.: U.S. Department of Health & Human Services, National Center for Health Statistics, published intermittently beginning in 1961, with the most recent being issued in 1981); and *Current Population Report P-60, No. 110* (Washington, D.C.: U.S. Department of Commerce, Bureau of the Census, March 1978).

3. Gerben DeJong and Raymond Lifchez, "Physical Disability and Public Policy," *Scientific American,* 248 (June 1983), pp. 40–49.

4. Ibid.; and "Birth Defects Have Doubled in Twenty-five Years," *Seattle Times,* July 17, 1983, p. 1.

5. R. Turner, "The Theme of Contemporary Social Movements," *British Journal of Sociology,* December 20, 1969, p. 321.

6. DeJong, "Independent Living."

7. Richard Weatherley, "PL 94–142: The Education for All Handicapped Children Act of 1975," in *Federal Legislation and the School Social Worker* (Washington, D.C.: National Association of Social Workers, 1978), pp. 38–44.

8. George Wright, *Total Rehabilitation* (Boston: Little, Brown & Co., 1980).

FEDERAL SOCIAL WELFARE PROGRAMS: RECENT TRENDS

The early 1980s witnessed the most significant changes in federal social welfare policy and programs since federal participation in human services began in the 1930s. The most politically conservative American president of modern times, Ronald Reagan, was elected on a platform that he had espoused for nearly two decades—to reduce the U.S. government's role in social services for citizens, to reduce taxes, and to concentrate on building a strong military defense. His election was the major force in what may be described as a counterrevolution in social welfare policy.

Although many Americans believed that the consensus supporting programs such as social security, services for the aging, and income maintenance was an unbreakable, permanent fixture of American government, a significant minority believed that the Roosevelt New Deal and all the social programs that followed it were contrary to the best interests of the nation and its citizens. Even in the 1960s—when presidents John F. Kennedy and Lyndon B. Johnson supported expansion of existing services and initiated new programs such as Head Start, the Peace Corps, Vista, and community action—the Republican party nominated as its 1964 presidential candidate Senator Barry Goldwater who, along with his supporters, campaigned on a plan to dismantle many of the federally supported social programs. His convictions and his strategies for turning those convictions into policies were spelled out in 1960 in his book, *The Conscience of a Conservative.*[1]

When Goldwater's bid for the presidency was decisively defeated by Johnson, most observers concluded that the people wanted to maintain the social welfare programs that had become a major part of American life.[2] Several important changes resulted from the Goldwater campaign, however, among them the emergence of Ronald Reagan as a key spokesman for American conservative ideology. Reagan's 1964 speech on Goldwater's behalf was nationally televised. His articulate, persuasive approach to American government was a campaign highlight. Reagan went on to become governor of California, a nationally syndicated radio commentator, the clear leader of the Republican party's conservative wing, and, in 1980, the first avowed conservative to be elected president since 1928.

It was President Reagan's intention to break the pattern of maintaining and expanding social welfare programs, which had been the policy of Democratic and Republican presidents alike since the New Deal. With Reagan's inauguration, all social welfare programs were called into question. In pursuit of a popular American theme of the 1960s and 1970s, President Reagan also joined with a large and vocal minority of Americans in demanding changes in such fundamental social welfare programs as Aid to Families with Dependent Children (AFDC) and food stamps.

Echoing another popular theme of the era, which the United States president he defeated, Jimmy Carter, had also used, Reagan "ran against" U.S. government employees, many of whom planned and managed social welfare programs. He proposed measures that would reduce their numbers, dilute their influence, and dispose of them as an influential factor in American life.

President Reagan's appointees were committed to his program of reducing human services programs. Assistant Secretary of the Department of Health and Human Services Dorcas Hardy said in 1982 that she was "determined to break up the 'iron triangle' of special-interest groups, members of Congress, and sympathetic civil servants that once pressed insistently for expensive social programs."[3] Activities such as legal services for low-income people, advocacy for the disabled and the aged, and mandatory planning to improve health care services and lower costs were targeted for elimination, merged into more general "block grants," or reduced in other ways.

New Federalism

Involvement in human services to disadvantaged and disabled people had long been a central part of the federal government's efforts. The Reagan Administration's approach, which they called the "New Federalism," seemed an attempt to eliminate some federal domestic programs, to reduce the scope of others, and to let lower levels of government, particularly states, operate these programs if they chose to do so.

Some services were to be "turned back" to state and local governments, and the federal government was to be reduced in size and scope. Taxes would be reduced so the economy could grow stronger, making welfare services unnecessary except for the few "truly needy." Government would be removed from the backs of American citizens who, President Reagan believed, were overtaxed, overregulated, and provided with services they did not need by people, including many social workers, whose primary stake in these programs was often their own jobs.

In essence, the Reagan program of 1981 was the most sweeping collection of proposed changes in federal domestic policy in nearly fifty years. Had it all been implemented, the United States would have become a markedly different nation. But the American separation of powers into executive, legislative, and judicial branches tempered, as it often does, the initiatives of the president. Many of the programs the president hoped to terminate were continued by congressional action. Many of the programs the Administration wanted combined into "block grants" were left separate. Federal requirements were maintained concerning whom the programs would serve and how.

Congress's refusal to accept all the executive branch recommendations, some court decisions that required the continuation of services that might otherwise have been reduced or eliminated, and severe economic declines not unlike those of the 1930s that originally gave rise to these programs worked against the Reagan proposals. By the fall of 1981, when the New Federalism would have begun to change the scope of American domestic programs, social programs had been changed much less than the Reagan Administration had originally proposed.

President Reagan's convictions were the most visible source of reduced federal commitment to and support for social programs, but they were not the only source. For several years, governmental and private agencies that studied the growth of federal social welfare programs had voiced concern that the growth of social spending was unwarranted and even out of control.[4] Public opinion polls, which had become indispensable tools for seekers of public office, tended to reflect voter hostility to "welfare" programs.[5] Many members of Congress and federal and state officials became wary of continuing social programs as they were.

So a number of forces—a president who opposed federal participation in social welfare services, budget planners who were concerned about the growth of social welfare services, citizen hostility to some welfare clients, and the fears of elected officials—all came together to end the steady growth in social welfare spending that had been a fact of American government for nearly half a century. Although the changes discussed in this article are described as initiatives of the Reagan Administration, they were all enacted by Congress as part of the 1981 Omnibus Budget Reconciliation Act, with the involvement of many groups inside and outside government.[6]

In outlining the changes in federal policies and programs that occurred when the Reagan Administration attempted to introduce its New Federalism, this article first describes the Administration's modifications in the two major instruments of social welfare provision established by Democratic administrations—the social security program and the various Great Society programs. The article then examines the block grant system and other administrative mechanisms used to implement these changes and the effect they had on relations between the federal government and the states.

It should be recalled throughout that, despite the widespread tendency to discuss all social welfare programs and domestic spending as if they were the same, there are major distinctions among the federal programs. The basic social welfare programs for disadvantaged people (Aid to Families with Dependent Children, Medicaid, food stamps, Supplemental Security Income, and social services) constitute less than 7 percent of all federal spending. The bulk of domestic spending, which is 51 percent of the total federal budget, is composed of entitlement programs such as social security, veterans benefits, and military and other federal pensions.[7]

Changes in Social Security

Of all the proposed changes of the Reagan Administration, none were more universally debated and few were as great a cause of concern as modifications in the social security program. In 1983, 36 million Americans were beneficiaries of social security. Most of those beneficiaries are disabled and aged individuals and couples, who are among the most politically active citizens of the United States. Virtually everyone else pays social security taxes and is either a potential beneficiary of the program or has a relative who is. Therefore, most Americans are not only interested in but are directly involved in social security in one way or another.

A supposed crisis in social security financing has been an issue for many years. Ronald Reagan began publicly questioning the program's solvency and validity in the 1960s.[8] The strict conservative position on social security is that it might be better as a fully or at least partially voluntary program. However, most experts on social security view it simply as a massive public insurance program in which participants pay premiums and receive benefits if they happen to be affected by one of the conditions covered, such as disability, retirement, or the early death of the breadwinner. The crisis of the 1980s in social security resulted from what the National Commission on Social Security Reform called a "continuing deterioration of the financial position of the Old-Age and Survivors' Insurance Trust Fund, the inability of the president and the Congress to agree to a solution, and the concern about eroding public confidence in the social security system."[9] The commission was composed of fifteen members, eight of whom were Republicans and seven Democrats. Five were selected by the president, five by the Senate majority leader, and five by the Speaker of the House of Representatives, all chosen on a bipartisan basis.

The problems in financing social security resulted from earlier liberalizations in the program that created a potential crisis when combined in the seventies and eighties with certain weaknesses of the U.S. economy. For example, social security payments began to be "indexed" in line with the Consumer Price Index, which meant social security benefits would increase each six months in proportion to increases in the costs of goods and services. The adjustment seemed reasonable at the time because the goal was to remove the level of social security benefits from politics. Before indexing, Congress was often pressured into courting the support of beneficiaries, particularly the elderly, by increasing benefits periodically; benefit levels were a major political issue each election year. The indexing system also seemed workable because, for most of the history of the American economy, increases in the cost of living followed increases in wages and salaries. Increased wages and salaries led to higher premiums from employers and employees, who pay the social security taxes. Therefore, there should have been ample opportunity for money to flow into the social security system in time to pay the increased, indexed benefits to beneficiaries.

However, in the 1970s and the 1980s, the cost of living, for the first time since statistics were collected, began to rise more rapidly than wages and salaries, which put the program's resources and payment levels out of adjustment. Of equal significance, the numbers of people retiring and living for many retirement years were proportionately larger in the 1970s and 1980s than the numbers entering the work force.

The national commission concluded that in the 1990s and early 2000s, social security income would exceed outgo. Although social security had the potential to adjust itself by borrowing in the 1980s and repaying the loans in the first two decades of the next century, the national commission also concluded that during a longer period—through 2056—social security would be in overall financial difficulty.

The commission's recommendations were the basis for changes in social security passed by Congress and signed into law by President Reagan in 1983. Among the provisions enacted were the following:

1. A plan to reduce the long-range deficit in social security to zero. That is, social security should become completely self-sustaining, with no borrowing, no deficits, and completely balanced collections and benefits.

2. The Old-Age, Survivors, Disability, and Health Insurance (OASDHI) program, which is the basic social security program, becomes mandatory on January 1, 1984, for all new civilian employees of the federal government and all employees of nonprofit organizations. These extensions insure the coverage of new federal employees and nonprofit organization employees by Medicare as well as OASDHI.

3. Beginning in 1984, up to half of OASDHI benefits are to be considered as taxable income for individuals who earn $25,000 or more and for couples who earn $32,000 or more.

4. Cost-of-living adjustments, beginning in 1983, became applicable for the January rather than the July checks. The delay was to save almost $40 billion through 1989.

5. There were changes in the OASDHI tax schedule. By 1990, rates would increase to a maximum of 7.65 percent each for the employer and the employee. Self-employed

persons would pay the equivalent of the combined rate for employees and employers for a single employee. In addition, the maximum taxable wage base would increase from $32,400 in 1983 to $57,000 in 1990.

6. The age for receiving full retirement benefits will gradually rise from 65 to 67 during the period from 2005 through 2027. There will also be greater advantages for those who postpone their retirement than there were before the changes.

7. Prospective payments to hospitals were instituted for Medicare as a means of holding down costs. Prospective payments allow the government to specify how much will be paid for a service such as hospitalization over a period of time such as a succeeding year. Without prospective payments, hospitals and other providers were able to charge for the "cost" of their care, and Medicare costs were essentially uncontrollable.[10]

Other changes. Prior to the commission's appointment, some other changes were made in the social security program. For example, burial benefits were eliminated for all but surviving spouses; children were declared ineligible to collect burial benefits for their deceased parents' funerals; and benefits for college student survivors of social security recipients were also phased out. An attempt to eliminate the minimum social security payment of $153.10 a month was proposed by the Reagan Administration but rescinded.

Administrative mechanisms were also used to reduce the social security program. Most significant of all the administrative actions was the reevaluation of the cases of many social security disability recipients, which was called for by Congress but zealously enforced by the Reagan Administration. By 1983, more than 212,000 disability recipients had been removed from social security benefit status; approximately two-thirds were later reinstated on appeal.[11] Of course, disability is the most flexible criterion for determining eligibility. Strict factors, such as date of birth, determine retirement benefits; death determines survivor benefits; and blindness, which is measurable and more readily defined than other physical handicaps, determines eligibility by reason of visual handicaps. Disability, however, is a more complex criterion. Degrees of injury, degrees of disability, and the permanency of the disability are all factors subject to medical judgments, which are, in some ways, subjective.

This disability redetermination became an item of controversy in the early 1980s. People who believed themselves to be clearly unable to work were told that they were able to do so. The press reported on victims of heart disease and other handicapping conditions who had received social security benefits for years but were eliminated from the program. Many found themselves without skills for employment or resources to support themselves apart from social security. In 1983, the statutes were temporarily changed to continue benefits while these cases were being appealed.

Key to solvency. A major problem of the social security program was the lack of confidence in it among younger people. Clearly, if young wage earners lack confidence in social security, they may attempt to have the program changed so they can withdraw from it. Such a step could, of course, lead to the demise of the program, which depends on broad participation for its solvency. So it is important to supporters of the program not only that beneficiaries receive payments, but that those who pay for it are also confident that social security will someday benefit them.

Great Society Programs

The most significant of the changes proposed by the Reagan Administration in 1981 were in the area of the Great Society programs that were included in the Economic Opportunity Act of 1965—the so-called poverty program. These programs were designed to eradicate poverty in the United States. Their emphasis was on a combination of education, training, and legal services to insure that the disadvantaged received the benefits to which they were entitled and on community action to help low-income people achieve political and social objectives that would eliminate their poverty.

From their inception, the Great Society poverty programs had a spotty history. Some were popular with large portions of the American public, but others were a source of friction.

Head Start and the Job Corps. By the 1980s, Head Start, a program to help preschool children develop their skills, had achieved wide acceptance from the American public. President Reagan and most members of Congress insisted that Head Start would remain a federally funded program, with no reductions.

The Job Corps, although initially slated for reduction, was championed by many members of Congress, including some Reagan allies, such as Republican Senator Orrin Hatch of Utah.[12] The Job Corps, too, was maintained and expanded.

In their early days, both Head Start and the Job Corps had been criticized for excessive costs, duplication of existing resources and services, and an overemphasis on serving children from disadvantaged, minority families. The negative reaction had been overcome, however, and by 1980, the fifteenth anniversary of the programs, both were well regarded and, in many ways, were regarded as untouchable even by the officials who were most hostile to federal involvement in social programs.

Legal services programs. Legal services for the poor, funded through the Legal Services Corporation, did not fare as well. Local legal agencies had filed suits against officials and had taken on unpopular, well-publicized causes, such as attempting to secure the rights of homosexuals. Some believed the legal services were more oriented to social change than legal help. However, the legal services programs, which were individually operated by the states and by private organizations, largely handled routine legal problems for low-income people, such as divorces, property transactions, and consumer complaints. In 1981 the legal services funding was reduced by 25 percent from $321 million to $292 million, but the programs of the Legal Services Corporation continued.

Community action programs. These programs were treated somewhat differently. Their agencies, which were originally local and regional corporations funded with grants from the federal government, attempted to help the poor secure their rights through organizations that were under their own control. Many community action agencies focused on social services, sponsoring Head Start programs and day care centers, operating youth services and employment programs, organizing food banks, and otherwise carrying out traditional social welfare and economic assistance programs.

Other agencies concentrated on organizing the poor to protest against governmental policies that appeared to work against the poor and their needs. Groups of low-income people objected to school locations, unequal employment practices, and discrimination against minority groups. For these reasons, community action programs had a varied reaction from the public; many people opposed the social changes these programs sought.

The original plan of the Reagan Administration was to put the community action program funds into a social services block grant, which would allow the states receiving grants to use community action funds for other purposes. However, Congress maintained community action as a separate program through the community services block grant. The funds were reduced by 20 percent in 1981, but most community action programs were continued. In his budget proposal for the 1984 fiscal year, the president recommended terminating the funds for the community services block grant.[13]

It is likely that those who wanted to eliminate or make major reductions in these Great Society poverty programs mis-understood the depth of support for such programs as legal services and community action. Over the sixteen years of these programs' existence, thousands of American citizens had received their services, were employed in the programs, or were members of their boards. These citizens' concerns and their protests to Congress led to the continuation of most poverty programs despite the hostility toward them from some quarters.

Training. Professional training programs for social workers expanded dramatically in the 1960s as part of the hope that better-trained professionals could help disadvantaged people overcome their problems. Extensive training was required for state child welfare programs; there were expansions of training in the area of mental health; and special training programs were developed for undergraduate social work education. In addition, social work training in rehabilitation was also expanded during the 1960s. These programs were also reduced in the early 1980s.

Federal-State Relations

At the heart of the changes the Reagan Administration sought in social welfare programs was its fundamental disagreement with the prevailing trends in federal-state relations during the preceding half century, particularly with the vast expansion of federal involvement in social services during that period. Since the depression of the 1930s and the Social Security Act in 1935, which that Great Depression motivated, the federal government has been intimately involved with state governments in the operation of social welfare programs. These programs expanded steadily from 1935 until the 1980s. Throughout that period federal policy had the largest single role in shaping public social welfare programs and innovations, and the federal government was the single most important factor in the delivery of social services.

There are several historical reasons for federal involvement in social services:

• The U.S. Congress and presidents since Franklin Delano Roosevelt have promoted the development of human services by providing federal financial participation for state-operated social and economic assistance programs. This participation began when millions were unemployed during the 1930s depression. Although a few programs such as food stamps are required nationally, the federal government persuades the states to participate in most services by offering them funds to use for social welfare programs operated under federal standards.

• The nature of federal financing is such that it can expand to meet the needs of citizens for social services in bad as well as good economic times. Almost all states have constitutional requirements that forbid their borrowing money or otherwise exceeding their annual revenues. The federal government has no such limit. The federal government "creates" money by borrowing and by selling federal securities to individuals and financial institutions. The federal government also has the capacity, through the Federal Reserve system, to contract and expand the money supply. States, of course, have no such power. Therefore, the federal government is able to assume responsibility for programs that have elastic requirements and changing demands.

• Some federal programs result from politics. Members of Congress often campaign on platforms to continue or expand social services. Elected officials are also sensitive to the demands for services from various interest groups, such as the aging, advocates for the developmentally disabled, and low-income citizens. Programs of assistance and service are enacted as one means of responding to these demands. Social workers are among the most important and articulate of the interest groups that press for federal programs.

• The federal government participates in some programs to achieve specific national objectives. This is particularly true in some areas of the National Institutes of Health, through which the federal government provides funds for research on specialized health and mental health problems, for new forms of treatment, and for care for people who might not be able to obtain adequate treatment for their physical or mental problems in their own states and communities.

Conservative critique. Conflict over federal participation in state social welfare programs is not new. Political conservatives have traditionally rejected the idea that social programs are a responsibility of the United States government. They believe these programs are a responsibility of local and state governments or private, voluntary organizations and see social services as changing the federal government into a direct service organization. The federal government should be limited, they suggest, to foreign relations, national defense, and the operation of the money system.[14] That is the essential philosophy of the conservative wing of the Republican party, which President Ronald Reagan has supported throughout the extent of his political career.

Assistant Secretary of the Department of Health and Human Services Dorcas Hardy said in March of 1983 that the Office of Human Development Services, which she heads, had four major objectives: (1) to provide selected national services, (2) to promote social and economic development by targeting resources to reduce dependency, (3) to increase the control of state and local governments and promote the participation of the voluntary sector in the delivery of human services, and (4) to use cost-effective methods of management and service delivery.[15] The *Wall Street Journal* called such efforts to change the federal system "Reaganizing," which they described as a process involving "the transformation of departments and agencies by appointed officials devoted to President Reagan's vow to 'curb the size and influence of the federal establishment.'"[16]

Federal Supervision. Over the years, federal officials have recognized the need to exercise authority and supervision over state social welfare programs to insure both high-quality services and the proper expenditure of federal funds. The forms of federal control and supervision have varied over the years, alternating between detailed efforts to control programs and efforts to give the states maximum flexibility. At the start of the Reagan Administration there was a turning away from intensive federal supervision of many state programs, an elimination of federal regulations governing some of those programs, and a reduction in the federal staff employed to monitor and otherwise supervise federal-state programs. Partly as a result of these changes, employment in the Department of Health and Human Services dropped from 163,883 people in 1979 to 149,416 in 1983.[17]

Block Grants

The Reagan Administration's plans for revising the structure of federal-state relations in the 1980s included several key ideas. One was the development of "block grants" to replace many of the individual social welfare programs that were organized, funded, and monitored by the federal government. Under the block grant concept, funds would be given to the states with only brief, broad outlines of how they were to be used. No longer would there be detailed state plans requiring the approval of the federal officials. A few pages would suffice. General instructions would supersede the volumes of guidelines and details in the *Federal Register* and other government documents regulating the expenditure of federal funds. Federal accountants would not audit state-operated, federally funded programs. Instead, state governments would contract with accountants of their choosing to audit the block grants. The audits would be on file and available for federal inspectors who might want to see them.[18]

The president and his advisors believed block grants had a number of administrative, economic, and political advantages. If, for example, a large number of programs

were combined into a single block, the positions of many of the federal employees who administered the individual programs could be eliminated. In addition, the federal government would be able to sidestep debates about the merits of specific programs if all the money went to the states with just a few guidelines. Does the state want a special program to identify and treat family members who abuse and neglect their children? Fine—the state may use part of its social services block grant funds to carry out such a program. Does the state want to use community action agencies to organize low-income people to seek better public services, transportation, and schools? If so, community action programs can be funded out of a social services block grant.

This approach also meant that many federal officials, who had almost become pariahs in the minds of local and state officials because of their insistence that state governments follow their rules and regulations, would be out of work. No bureaucrats in distant Washington should determine state needs, the Reagan Administration believed. Federal financing would provide some of the money, but local experts would decide how best to spend it on the state's problems. Because states and localities would make the decisions and operate the programs, the federal government would thus be able to reduce its payroll and use the money saved for other activities or to reduce the chronic, growing federal deficit. The states would save money on their reports to the federal government, in their record keeping, and in many other ways.

Therefore, early in 1981 the Reagan Administration proposed that literally dozens of programs once categorical in nature, each with its own guidelines, forms, funding streams, and federal staff, be consolidated into four block grants—one for social services; one for community development, which was continued by the Reagan administration after being established by previous administrations; one for health services; and one that would encompass mental health services, energy and emergency assistance, and elementary and secondary education.[19] These block grants were proposed, moreover, with Administration recommendations that federal funds be reduced 20 percent compared to the previous year's funding levels for separate programs. State governments would save sufficient money through the reduced reporting and monitoring requirements to make up for the lost funds, federal officials reasoned.

Criticisms of block grants. These arguments had other sides to them, particularly for those who had long fought for social welfare programs. Some of the objections were embodied in the following arguments:

• The separate programs to be combined into blocks each represented hard-won victories for special constituencies—handicapped children, the developmentally disabled, victims of mental illness, and many others. The states might choose to neglect those special groups.

• The blocking of programs, which blurred the reasons for specific services, and the 20-percent reduction in funding sounded suspiciously like Senator Barry Goldwater's proposals in 1960. He wrote that the best means for removing the federal government from such "inappropriate" activities as social welfare programs would be to cut the funding a percentage each year until all federal participation in social welfare programs was eliminated.[20] This similarity led some to believe the block grants were only a first step in ending federal participation in social welfare.

• What the states saved in administering services through the block grants would not total 20 percent. The savings would be 10 percent or less, most states believed. The deep 20-percent reductions in funding would reduce not only the administrative costs, but the services themselves.

• Block grants could lead to the elimination of some controversial programs. Would state and local governments reserve block grant funds that could be spent on popular services—such as group care for children, aid to the aged, and mental health—for such controversial programs as advocacy for the mentally disabled, community action, and legal services for the poor?

Responses. Various groups reacted differently to the block grants, with most basing their thinking on their own best interests. For example, most governors and other state officials applauded the flexibility block grants gave them to pursue their own priorities, but state officials opposed the fiscal reductions that came with the block grants. Groups advocating for unpopular causes disliked the flexibility of the block grants; they feared that their constituents would be overlooked in the decision-making process.

The president's original proposal for the creation of four block grants was modified by Congress, which created nine instead, each combining many fewer programs than the president had originally proposed. The nine block grants established in 1981 were alcohol, drug abuse, and mental health; primary care; health prevention and health services; maternal and child health; social services; elementary and secondary education; community development; community services; and low-income energy assistance.[21]

Local fund replacement. One of the Administration's assumptions about block grants was that some funding reductions would be replaced by appropriations from state governments or contributions from foundations and other voluntary organizations. Although the replacement funds did not equal the lost funds, the reductions in many states were smaller than expected because legislatures and voluntary providers filled some of the financial gaps.

Many programs that had been slated to be included in the blocks were left separate. Community action, which was to have been part of the social services block grant, became its own community services block grant. Developmental disabilities and vocational rehabilitation were also left independent of the social services block grant. Program after program with strong constituencies managed to maintain their categorical, targeted, independent status in the federal government, even though funding for most services was reduced.

In 1983, the Reagan Administration again proposed new combinations of programs into block grants and submitted the necessary legislation to Congress. Among the proposed changes was a state fiscal assistance block grant to be funded through a trust fund in the Treasury Department; it would include low-income home energy assistance; social services; community services; alcohol, drug abuse, and mental health services; primary care; maternal and child health services; community development; and several other programs. In all, seventeen federal grant programs would be eliminated, and both the tax resources to fund them and the authority to administer them would become the responsibilities of the states. A local fiscal assistance block grant, which was to include community development and general revenue sharing funds, was proposed for local governments.[22]

Swaps and Turnbacks

President Reagan's New Federalism also included a plan, first proposed in 1982, to transfer many federal programs to the states. As originally proposed, the "turnback" of federal programs to the states, which was also called a swap, would have put total responsibility for AFDC and food stamps in the hands of the states. The federal government would operate and fully fund the Medicaid and Medicare programs. In addition, dozens of other federal assistance programs would be "given" to the states.[23]

Throughout 1982 and into early 1983, the federal government and the states, through the National Governors' Association, negotiated over the president's proposals for turning back and swapping programs, but the president did not introduce the legislation necessary to achieve those changes. The fiscal assistance block grants

mentioned earlier were to be the means for implementing the turnback of programs to the state.

For most states, the specific changes proposed by the president would have been much more costly than the status quo. For example, the combined Food Stamp and AFDC expenditures, which were largely federally financed, totaled more than most states' expenditures for Medicaid.

There were also doubts about the wisdom of making AFDC a state program because the needs it met were tied so closely to the national economy. Unemployment and economic disadvantages are only minimally under the control of the states. The largest influence on employment, poverty, and wealth is national policy. States experiencing severe economic problems—as Michigan did in the early 1980s because of the decline of the automobile industry—would be in greater need of help for their unemployed and disadvantaged citizens than other states, but because of lost revenues resulting from their economic conditions, they would be less capable of meeting those needs than other states.

There were proposals for a federal trust fund to back up state governments that found themselves in desperate financial conditions. However, most states believed that the federal-state partnership in programs such as AFDC, food stamps, and Medicaid made better fiscal and social sense than any turnback or swap of programs.

Changes in AFDC

There have been other major changes in federal-state relations. The AFDC program, for example, is still run under strict federal guidelines, and those guidelines were made even more stringent in the 1981 Omnibus Budget Reconciliation Act. Among the most significant of the changes made in AFDC through the 1981 Omnibus Budget Reconciliation Act were the following:

1. Establishing a cap on eligibility for families at 150 percent of the state needs standard.

2. Changing the amount of earnings AFDC families were allowed to keep without their grants being reduced. After four months of receiving benefits, families would lose the total amount of their earnings from their grants. Before the changes, they were allowed to retain the first $30 of monthly earnings and one-third of the remainder indefinitely.

3. Standardizing work expenses at $75 a month and establishing a limit on child care expenses of $161 a month.

4. Counting income of all minor children in the AFDC unit.

5. Requiring retrospective budgeting and monthly reporting by all recipient families.

6. Counting the income of stepparents as if it were available to children in the family.

7. Terminating eligibility for children over 18 even when they were full-time students. States had previously been able to continue assistance for children who were full-time students until they were 21.

8. Reducing allowable resources from $2,000 a month to $1,000 a month.

9. Eliminating benefits to pregnant women during the first six months of their pregnancies.

10. Prohibiting aid to strikers.

11. Counting lump sum payments such as inheritances or disability payments as income.

12. Allowing states to establish "work fare." (In 1983, proposals were made to require workfare in all states so that clients would work off their grants in public service and other jobs.)

13. Eliminating AFDC for mothers whose husbands are in the military.[24]

These tightened eligibility requirements eliminated thousands of families from the program. The new rules eliminating the $30 disregard on earnings changed reforms made during the Kennedy Administration. The disregard had been adopted so AFDC parents could hold part-time jobs, maintain work habits and skills, and, ultimately, pull themselves out of poverty through employment. The disregard was also designed to enable school-age children to have part-time jobs, paper routes, and other employment so they would be able to contribute to the family's income and also develop work skills. The Reagan Administration determined that the disregard had not increased the number of AFDC family members who were employed and, therefore, saw no need to leave it a permanent feature of the AFDC program.

The Reagan Administration's approach to AFDC was directly contrary to that of other recent Democratic and Republican administrations. Richard M. Nixon had proposed the Family Assistance Plan, which would have federalized AFDC and standardized payments throughout the United States. President Carter proposed the Better Jobs and Income Program, which resembled the Nixon proposal.[25]

President Reagan preferred that the entire program become state operated and state funded. The Reagan Administration also changed AFDC by allowing states to require recipients to work for their benefits, and it proposed mandatory "workfare" for many AFDC clients.[26]

However, in 1982, the former secretaries of Health, Education, and Welfare of all the presidencies from Dwight D. Eisenhower in the 1950s through Jimmy Carter in the 1970s and 1980s recommended that the AFDC program be federalized and nationalized to benefit clients, to simplify the administration of AFDC, and to avoid some of the inequities created by the Reagan Administration's operation of AFDC.[27] The former secretaries said that AFDC, with its new eligibility requirements, encouraged families to break up, encouraged teenage pregnancies, provided a disincentive rather than an incentive to work, discouraged thrift and savings, and was too bureaucratic and too costly.

Other Federal Cutbacks

Aging. The appropriations and programs provided under the Older Americans Act were left separate from the block grants proposed by the Reagan Administration, but the growth in funds for aging programs was reduced nonetheless. Aging programs throughout the United States benefit from purchase of service contracts under Title XX of the Social Security Act, and when the funds appropriated to Title XX were incorporated into the social services block grant, the aggregate funds were reduced. That reduced services to older adults in many parts of the nation.

The direct funding under the Older Americans Act was reduced in 1981 and 1982.[28] The 1984 budget request sought further cuts in funding for aging programs.

Health and mental health services. The block grants for alcohol, drug abuse, and mental health, primary care, preventive health services, and maternal and child health have been treated in much the same manner as all other block grants. The net effect has been a reduction in health and mental health funding throughout the United States.[29]

Rigid federal audits. Because many of the initiatives of the federal government in the 1980s were based on the need to reduce federal spending, program changes were not the only means used to effect those savings. For example, there was a notable increase in the rigidity of federal audits of state programs. During the Reagan Administration many state governments discovered, years after expenditures were made for social services, training, and other partially federally financed activities, that federal auditors took a more conservative position on what had been allowable for federal financial participation than the states were originally told was allowable. Many audits were appealed to the Federal Grants Appeals Board.

Quality control. In addition, greater attention was given to the issue of "quality control" in the food stamp, Medicaid, and AFDC programs. Quality control is a system used to determine the effect of errors made by state agencies, recipients, and providers of medical services in carrying out federally funded programs. Under federal guidance, the states periodically develop and evaluate a scientifically selected sample; the result is a statistical measure of the degree to which ineligible people received assistance or to which eligible people received too much or too little help.

Congress and the executive branch promoted quality control as a means for holding down the widely assumed growth in welfare fraud and abuse. Congress ordered that states be "sanctioned" by having their allocations of federal monies reduced if their errors were too high. The penalty, Congress assumed, would require the states to bring their error rates into line with federal standards.

Dozens of states have been threatened with fiscal penalties for having error rates that are too high. As of mid 1983, however, no state had been financially penalized in any program for excessive errors. Some states have received financial rewards for effectively holding down errors in the food stamp program.

Retreat from planning. Prior to 1982, the federal government encouraged and paid for planning for human services. Planning innovations were among the most significant of all legislation passed and implemented in the 1960s and 1970s. Much of what had been done under the rubric of planning was the development of state plans to conform to federal regulations and procedures, which were published in documents such as the *Federal Register*. Funds were provided to the states based on their satisfactory completion of plans for each program—social services, food stamps, AFDC, Medicaid, energy assistance, and all other services. The Reagan Administration questioned the need for these detailed plans, and it reduced the number of regulations and planning requirements, emphasizing, instead, greater state flexibility.

Perhaps most significant of the changes in planning was the near elimination of funding for the Health Systems Agency program, which had been developed in the 1970s as a means for holding down the rapidly increasing costs in health care. Under this program, a network of groups, including professional health care providers and consumers, screened applications for health care expansion and approved or disapproved them on the basis of need and their impact on the health care system in their states and localities. The 1981 Omnibus Budget Reconciliation Act eliminated much of the funding for such health-planning activities.

Co-payments under Medicaid. Few programs were neglected in the Reagan Administration's proposals for modifications in the relationship between the federal and state governments. For example, a whole series of new co-payments by patients was recommended for the Medicaid program. However, Congress actually reduced the states' ability to require patients to pay for some of their own care.

Child support collections. The Administration also recommended major changes in the Title IV-D program, which requires states to collect child support payments from absent fathers of children who receive aid under the AFDC program. The Administration sought to have the states pay for the Child Support Enforcement program out of receipts from their own child support collections. However, Congress made only minor modifications in the federal support formula for child support enforcement.

Conclusion

During the Reagan Administration and the ninety-eighth Congress, the relationship between state and federal governments on matters of social welfare changed more than at any other time since social welfare programs began in the 1930s. In some ways, block grants gave states greater opportunities to develop and carry out their own programs of social welfare; in other ways, states were held more accountable to federal officials and federal guidelines because of changes in AFDC program regulations and more rigid audits and quality control.

The early 1980s were thus an era of significant tension between the federal and state governments over social welfare programs. President Reagan's desire to transfer full responsibility for programs such as food stamps and AFDC to the states and to reduce funding for such programs were matters of controversy between the president and most governors.

Except for the changes in AFDC, which primarily affected clients, and the block grants, which affected some programs, the changes actually implemented during the first three years of the Reagan Administration's New Federalism were relatively few and had less impact on state governments or those they served than was anticipated. The basic funding formulas for AFDC, food stamps, and Medicaid were not changed; in more cases than not, federal responsibility for programs was maintained; and the number of people receiving assistance through federal-state programs was not significantly reduced. In fact, the weak U.S. economy of the early 1980s made more people eligible for social welfare services than had been in the past. Most of the changes were in the quality and tone of the relationships between federal and state officials, and the threats of change by the federal government were more profound than the changes themselves.

Despite his clear philosophical position on issues, President Reagan showed himself to be, above all, a talented politician who was willing to compromise when he had to. Those who had observed his California governorship were not surprised, because he had compromised there as well.[30] The Emergency Jobs and Humanitarian Aid Bill, a $4.6 billion package that he signed to provide employment through public works projects, contained over a billion dollars for human services. These services included the social services block grant, the Job Corps, weatherization programs, community action activities, and many of the other domestic programs that had been criticized and reduced in the first years of the Reagan Administration.[31]

LEON H. GINSBERG

Notes and References

1. Barry Goldwater, *The Conscience of a Conservative* (Shepherdsville, Ky.: Victor Publishing Co., 1960).
2. *The 1983 World Almanac and Book of Facts* (New York: Newspaper Enterprise Association, 1982) p. 298. In the 1964 election, Johnson carried forty-four states and the District of Columbia; Goldwater carried six states.
3. Burt Schorr and Andy Pafztor, "In Command: Reaganites Make Sure That the Bureaucracy Toes the Line on Policy," *Wall Street Journal*, February 10, 1982, p. 1.
4. For a description of the unchecked growth in social spending that concerned many private research organizations and members of both parties in Congress, see Martha Derthick, *Uncontrollable Spending for Social Services Grants* (Washington, D.C.: Brookings Institution, 1975).
5. Leon H. Ginsberg, "Changing Public Attitudes about Public Welfare Clients and Services Through Research," *Policy Studies Journal* (March 1982), pp. 581–591. See also Martha N. Ozawa, *Income Maintenance and Work Incentives* (New York: Praeger Publishers, 1982).
6. P.L. 97-35, H.R. 3982/S1377.
7. "Setting the Record Straight," *Washington Report*, 18 (February 1983), pp. 1–2, issued by the American Public Welfare Association.
8. Bill Boyarsky, *The Rise of Ronald Reagan* (New York: Random House, 1968).
9. *Report of the National Commission on Social Security Reform* (Washington, D.C.: U.S. Government Printing Office, 1982), p. 1.
10. James M. Hildreth, Roberta A. Barr, and Richard L. DeLouise, "Social Security Rescue —What It Means to You," *U.S. News and World Report*, April 4, 1983, pp. 23–25.
11. Social Legislation Information Service. "Congress Passes Legislation to Amend Disability Review," *Washington Social Legislation Bulletin*, January 10, 1983, p. 2. See also Ozawa, *Income Maintenance and Work Incentives*.
12. *Congressional Record*, February 25, 1981, S-1600.
13. *Washington Report*, 18 (March 1983), pp. 1–3, issued by the American Public Welfare Association.
14. Leon H. Ginsberg, "Human Services in the 1980s: The Ethical Debate," *Centerboard* (Spring 1983), pp. 30–32.
15. Dorcas Hardy, untitled keynote speech presented at a national conference on "Informa-

tion for Decisionmaking: Challenges and Opportunities" sponsored by the Department of Health and Human Services and the University of Southern California, San Diego, Calif., March 21, 1983.
16. Schorr and Andy, "In Command."
17. Telephone conversation with Don Moore, Director of the Systems Support Division of the Employees Systems Center, Office of the Assistant Secretary for Personnel Administration, U.S. Department of Health and Human Services, Washington, D.C., February 25, 1983.
18. Timothy J. Conlan, "Back in Vogue: The Politics of Block Grant Legislation," *Intergovernmental Perspective*, 7 (Spring 1981).
19. Ibid.
20. Goldwater, *The Conscience of a Conservative*.
21. R. Larry Beckett, Phil Favero, and Anthony Ferrise, *Our Changing Federal System: The Block Grants of 1981* (Morgantown, W. Va.: Cooperative Extension Service, West Virginia University Center for Extension and Continuing Education, January 1982).
22. *New Directions in Funding: Special Reports* (Arlington, Va.: Government Information Services, March 1983).
23. Leon H. Ginsberg, *The Practice of Social Work in Public Welfare* (New York: Free Press, 1983).
24. *Effects of Federal AFDC Policy Changes: A Study of a Federal-State "Partnership"* (Washington, D.C.: Center for the Study of Social Policy, 1983).
25. Ginsberg, *The Practice of Social Work in Public Welfare*, pp. 9 and 39.
26. "Statement by Richard S. Schweiker, Secretary of Health and Human Services," *HHS News*, January 31, 1983, p. 3.
27. *The Wingspread Journal*, Special Report on Welfare Policy in the United States (Racine, Wis. Johnson Foundation, 1982). See also Ozawa, *Income Maintenance and Work Incentives*.
28. P.L. 97035, H.R. 3982/S1377.
29. *Washington Report*, 18 (March 1983), pp. 1–3, issued by the American Public Welfare Association.
30. Alistair Cooke, Book Review, *The New Yorker*, March 14, 1983, pp. 148–156.
31. "Emergency Jobs and Humanitarian Aid Legislation (P.L. 98–8) Passes," Memorandum W-3 (Washington, D.C.: April 7, 1983), p. 1.

FINANCING SOCIAL WELFARE

Social welfare programs are financed through appropriations from general tax revenues and through payroll taxes and trust funds. Programs financed by payroll taxes and trust funds include social security old age and disability insurance payments, the hospital insurance trust fund under Medicare, and entitlement and discretionary programs. Entitlement programs vest individuals with specific rights to certain benefits and to automatic payments of those benefits. Under discretionary programs, individuals have no legal right to specific benefits but rather have eligibility for programs whose benefits vary depending on the amounts of money actually appropriated each year. Entitlement programs include old age and disability insurance, Medicare, Medicaid, Aid to Families with Dependent Children (AFDC), Supplemental Security Income (SSI) maintenance programs, and the food stamp program. The discretionary programs include the mental health services block grant program, the maternal and child health block grant program, rehabilitation services, Title XX social services, and child welfare services.

The analysis of budget trends presented in this article is essentially limited to the Department of Health and Human Services (HHS) budget because that budget is entirely devoted to social welfare programs and can be traced systematically over the four years from fiscal year (FY) 1980 through FY 1983. President Reagan's budget proposal for FY 1984 is used as the fifth year. Although the trend in recent years has been for Congress to authorize expenditures beyond the president's proposed budget, the change is small enough each year so that it does not affect the trend analysis applied to FY 1984.

HHS Budget Trends

Figures 1 and 2 graphically demonstrate a number of significant principles related to the financing of public social welfare programs. First, despite the criticism voiced in various forums regarding cuts in domestic programs, Figure 1 shows that the total budget for the Department of Health and Human Services has actually been growing not only during the past twenty-four years, but even since 1980. There is even growth in the president's budget for FY 1984. The rate of growth per year has been declining, however, as is demonstrated by Figure 2. The first budget of the Reagan Administration was for the fiscal year running from October 1, 1981, through September 30, 1982; the budget for FY 1980, which ran from October 1, 1980, through September 30, 1981, was originated by the Carter Administration but was substantially modified and effectively became a Reagan Administration budget. Thus, it is clear that the decline in the rate of growth of the HHS budget began with the Reagan Administration.

During the Carter Administration, which included the years shown on Figure 2 as 1978–79 and 1979–80, growth rates were increasing in the range of 10 to 16 percent a year. During the Reagan years, the growth rates fell to 10 percent and as low as approximately 5 percent.

It is important to put this trend into an economically realistic framework, however, and that involves determining what the real growth rates of the social welfare budget for social welfare programs had real growth of 3 to 4 percent. The adoption of the president's budget for FY 1984 (1983–84 in Figure 2) would result in a no-growth budget for the year because the inflation rate of 4.5 to 5 percent would nullify the 5 percent rate of budgetary growth. In FY 1981–82, the real growth was 2 to 3 percent because there was about a 7 percent inflation rate that year. The inflation rates during the Carter Administration years kept the real growth in the budget to 3 to 4 percent. Overall, the rate of growth in real terms during the Carter years was probably slightly more than during the

FIG. 1. DISCRETIONARY AND ENTITLEMENT PROGRAMS OF THE DEPARTMENT OF
HEALTH AND HUMAN SERVICES

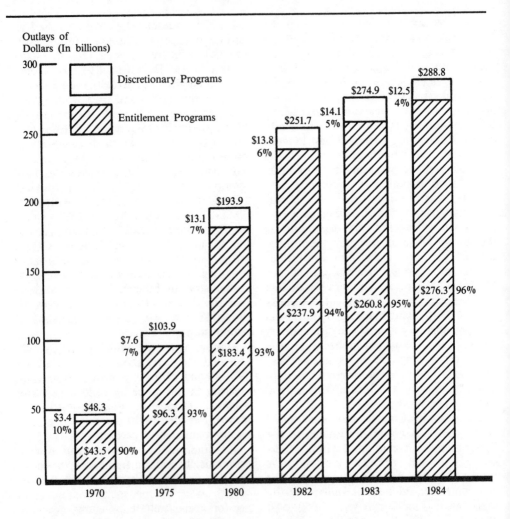

Source: Department of Health and Human Services, January 31, 1983

first two Reagan years and certainly more than the lack of real growth likely with the proposed 1984 budget. The differences, however, are nowhere near as dramatic as one might assume from the treatment of the issue in the press.

It should be noted that the inflation rate for health care has been 3 to 4 percent more than the general inflation rate. Because a large portion of the HHS budget is involved with Medicare and Medicaid,

the real growth in any of these years is probably somewhat less than has been estimated here. The Medicare and Medicaid programs make up almost 30 percent of the HHS budget. The high inflation rate for health care meant that those programs experienced little if any real growth in any of the years just discussed.

The point is that once this high rate of inflation for health care is factored in the real growth rate in social welfare, spending

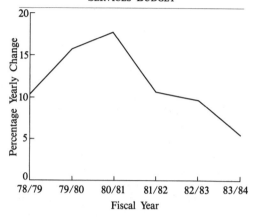

Source: Department of Health and Human Services, January 31, 1983

is seen to have declined slightly since FY 1979 and dramatically, about 3 or 4 percent, since FY 1981. The Reagan proposal for FY 1984 provided for no real growth, but the congressional budget was expected to include enough additional funds to allow some real growth.

An important factor in the financing of public social welfare programs is the large share of the total HHS budget that is consumed by the entitlement programs, especially by social security old age and disability payments, Medicare, and Medicaid. The AFDC and SSI entitlement programs make up only about 5 percent of the total entitlement budget—$11 to $12 billion in the HHS 1983 entitlement budget of about $260 billion. The old-age retirement and disability insurance programs, Medicare, and Medicaid constitute 95 percent of the entitlement programs and about 90 percent of the total budget of the Department of Health and Human Services.

As Figure 1 indicates, the share of the total HHS budget consumed by the entitlement programs has always been high, and the trend is clearly toward the entitlement programs taking a greater and greater share. In FY 1970 discretionary, nonentitlement programs represented 10 percent of the total HHS budget, and in FY 1984 those same programs represented only about 4 percent. This means that the relative share of the HHS budget that goes to discretionary programs decreased by 50 percent in the period between FYs 1970 and 1984.

It should be noted that the data regarding the total HHS budget have been corrected for the fact that the Department of Education (DOE) obtained a separate budget after FY 1978. All DOE programs are essentially discretionary. In FY 1983 the DOE budget was approximately $13 billion, about the same as the total HHS budget for discretionary programs. If the Department of Education were back in the Department of Health and Human Services, 90 percent of the total budget of that conglomerate agency would still be for entitlement programs.

The reason the entitlement programs consume such large portions of the HHS budgets is that large numbers of people are entitled to the benefits. All aged and disabled people who are entitled to social security payments are also entitled to receive Medicare benefits. Thus, some twenty-nine million people are eligible for Medicare coverage at a cost of approximately $60 billion. If all people who met the income eligibility test for Title XX social services were entitled to those services with benefits the annual dollar equivalent of Medicare benefits, the Title XX social service program would most likely cost much more than the Medicare program. Although it is unlikely that individual benefits under the social service program would ever equal those for health care, the number of eligible individuals is substantially greater than the twenty-nine million covered by Medicare because individuals are eligible for certain Title XX services with incomes that approximate the median income in their state. The reason the entitlement programs consume such a large percentage of the HHS budget is that there is only so much money to go around, particularly in the period of fiscal austerity that began in the mid or late 1970s.

Effects of Austerity

Social service programs are usually defined under Title XX of the Social Security Act and include social services to all people with low incomes; child welfare services; certain services to the aged; rehabilitation services; Head Start; alcohol, drug abuse, and mental health services; and a few of the Public Health Service Act health service programs. Medicare and Medicaid are considered health care programs rather than social service programs. Medicaid finances some programs that are similar to Title XX social services, but those programs are a small part of the total Medicaid budget. By far the largest part of the Medicaid budget goes to support intermediate care facilities and nursing home services. For this analysis, however, none of the Medicaid programs are considered social services.

After FY 1980, social service programs experienced dramatic reductions. The FY 1984 HHS budget recommended by President Reagan represented a $600 million loss from the FY 1980 budget recommended and managed by the Carter Adminstration. This analysis counts all discretionary programs as social service programs, which is a fairly accurate characterization because the only major non–social service program in that category is the National Institute of Health (NIH) budget of $4 billion. That budget increased substantially year by year, which means that the actual decrease in the service programs has been greater than $600 million. The FY 1983 budget for service programs in the discretionary area, excluding the NIH research activity, showed almost no increase. The total increase between 1980 and 1983 of $1 billion was more than made up for by the increases in the NIH research budget during that period, and because the inflation rate during those years averaged at least 8 percent, the service programs really lost about 8 percent a year. The social service programs thus lost at least one-third of their real purchasing power between FY 1980 and FY 1983. It was the reduction in these programs that caused the real pinches on services to be felt in various communities around the country.

Structural Changes

Beginning in 1981, a number of major structural changes accompanied the reductions in financing. These structural changes took the form of block grant legislation enacted in 1981 with regard to Title XX of the Social Security Act; alcoholism, drug abuse and mental health services; maternal and child health services: preventive health services; and community service programs, the successor to the community action and related programs of the Office of Economic Opportunity. The block grant legislation gave greater flexibility to state governments in administering the federal financing of these activities. In mental health programs in particular, this was a major change from days in which community mental health centers could operate with little involvement of the state mental health agencies.

None of these approaches involve pure block grants in the sense of leaving states with total discretion. Each grant was targeted at a particular area of activity, such as mental health or maternal and child health. In this sense the targeting was no different from the targeting done in the rehabilitation services program, which is not a block grant. However, the Rehabilitation Act provided many more requirements and directions with respect to the management of the federal funds by the state vocational rehabilitation agencies.

The block grant statutes also created ceilings on appropriations. This was not a major change because most of these programs had appropriations ceilings prior to the enactment of the block grant statutes in 1981. The major change was that the new ceilings were at levels equal to or below the 1980 service levels for these programs. Thus, because of inflation, the block grant statutes restricted the appropriations to levels that represented cuts.

These structural changes are important

for two reasons. First, as just described, the block grant legislation largely shaped service programs and their budgets. Second, proponents of block grants argued that because the block system would promote administrative efficiencies and allow more rational resource allocation by state governments, the cuts imposed by the appropriations ceilings were not really cuts—that because state governments would not be heavily regulated and would have much more discretion with respect to budget allocations, they would actually be able to purchase more services with less money.

This argument is countered by a number of significant factors. First, states must still comply with a fair number of regulatory requirements, and even the state governments admit that they are not saving much money with respect to the administrative costs of operating these programs. The money they are saving is by no means making up for the fact that the appropriations have either been reduced or, at a minimum, have not risen to keep pace with inflation rates, which have been between 5 percent and 10 or 12 percent. Second, the reallocation of resources achieved by state governments under these block grants is believed by most observers to be small. Because the funding at the state level has essentially been held even or reduced and because there were prior commitments to a number of local programs, the real discretion available to state governments has been limited.

Research Funding

The research budget for the Department of Health and Human Services is largely represented by two programs: the National Institutes of Health (NIH) and the Alcoholism, Drug Abuse, and Mental Health Administration (ADAMHA). The NIH and the ADAMHA research budgets increased substantially after FY 1979. Between FYs 1982 and 1983, a period in which discretionary funding generally increased by only $300 million, the NIH and ADAMHA research budgets increased by about $450 million,

which represented increases of 10 to 12 percent. At the same time, allocations for research involving health services, social services, and child welfare and aging services stayed level. The dramatic increases in the NIH and ADAMHA budgets financed research related to the causes of diseases and mental health problems and specific treatment methods. The FY 1984 budgets for NIH and ADAMHA research were expected to have similar increases.

It should be noted that the 5 to 6 percent real growth in the financing of NIH and ADAMHA research came largely at the insistence of Congress. The Reagan Administration's proposal for the NIH budget for FY 1983 called for only about 3 percent increase—one point less than the inflation rate. Congress provided the 10 percent increase over the fiscal 1982 budget, representing a 4 to 5 percent real growth rate.

This phenomenon can be explained largely on political grounds. Congress has been supportive of NIH research over the years. That support has been justified by arguments about the cost effectiveness of the NIH budget, but those same arguments apply to service programs with equal validity. For every dollar spent, the NIH budget returns approximately $13 in savings through reduced hospital care and disability payments. The budgets of the Center for Disease Control health services, rehabilitation services, and protective services for children can probably be shown to have been equally cost effective.

Nevertheless, the Reagan Administration did not treat NIH research activity with the same generosity that it treated the research programs of the National Aeronautics and Space Administration, the National Science Foundation, the Department of Defense, and the Department of Transportation. The Reagan Administration budget for FY 1984 proposed funding for research and development activities that amounted to a 17 percent increase over fiscal 1983, but the increase proposed for the NIH budget came to only 1.8 percent. Congress was expected to make that increase 7 to 10 percent, however.

The Administration requested increases of 10 to 15 percent for ADAMHA research in the areas of mental health, drug abuse, and alcoholism, which were comparable to the ADAMHA increases requested for FY 1983 and granted by Congress. Although most of the ADAMHA research focuses on the basic sciences, a substantial amount of it is in the social sciences. The explanation for the Reagan Administration's support of ADAMHA research compared to its neglect of NIH research also appeared to be political. The same extraordinary research breakthroughs in the neurosciences that affect the mental health research of ADAMHA are also relevent to NIH research. The cost-effectiveness arguments of research investments at NIH and ADAMHA are thus similar. The Reagan Administration probably assumes that Congress will add substantially to the NIH budget and that therefore it does not have to.

Professional Education and Training

The smallest part of the so-called discretionary HHS budget has always been professional education and training. In the early 1980s that part became so small as to be almost invisible. Support for clinical training programs in the fields of mental health, drug abuse, and alcoholism dwindled from approximately $100 million in FY 1978 to $20 million in FY 1983. In the same period, funds for child welfare training dwindled from approximately $9 million to approximately $4 million.

The Reagan Administration proposal for FY 1984 threatened to end both programs entirely. Training in the health area through programs administered by the Health Resources Administration was also reduced enormously. Nurse Training Act budgets declined from approximately $100 million in fiscal 1978 to about $30 million in fiscal 1983. The only programs of support for professional education that increased after 1980 were the student loan programs administered by the Department of Education. The loans available under these programs were not substantial enough to cover the complete cost of professional education, and the obligations they would impose on students attempting to enter the professions were too great for many to incur.

Some of the block grant programs such as the Title XX social services block grant and the mental health block grant, have statutory mandates to support professional training, but they do not. As noted earlier, the dollars in those programs declined dramatically in the early 1980s, and the first priority for a state social service organizational health agency had to be the meeting of service demands.

In 1983 the total amount of federal money spent on social work training was at most $20 million, which included money spent by state welfare agencies on the training of welfare employees. Each year in the late 1970s, federal programs provided about $90 million for the training of professional social workers. The president's budget for FY 1984 proposed no support whatsoever except $5 to $8 million that would be available to state AFDC and social service agencies to spend on training.

RICHARD E. VERVILLE

HEALTH CARE REGULATIONS AND STANDARDS

Social work in health care is a growing field of practice. Long established in some health settings, especially in acute-care hospitals, social workers are currently both forging new roles for themselves in areas of practice that previously received limited attention and returning to traditional settings in an expanded capacity. In hospitals, social workers staff services as diverse as maternity units and emergency rooms and are increasingly employed in hospice programs, in nursing homes and related services to the aged, and in community health centers. Social workers are also demonstrating their effectiveness in home health care agencies, in private corporations, and in medical groups with physicians. The functions performed by social workers in these settings range from direct services to community work, administration, policy planning, and teaching.

Because social workers provide services in such a wide variety of settings, federal and state regulations are influencing the types of services provided and the conditions under which the social worker may practice. Also affecting practice are the standards established by private accreditation bodies and professional organizations. This article explores some of the ways in which the many changes in regulations and standards have affected social work personnel in health services.

The Governmental Role

Social work has been an important part of the health care field since the turn of the century, and legislation and regulations affecting the field have been in place for many years, but only in the last fifteen years has the federal role expanded significantly. Passage of such legislation as the Health Maintenance Organization Act in 1973 and the National Health Planning and Resources Development Act in 1975 extended the scope of government's involvement in health care. The expanded federal role resulted in corresponding increases both in state health activities and in the inclusion of social work services in legislation and regulations.

State health agencies and local health departments administer a variety of programs, which are usually divided into personal health, environmental health, health resources, and laboratory services. About 73 percent of state expenditures in 1981 were for personal health, a proportion that corresponds to the focus of social work in health care.[1] State and local regulations have thus joined federal regulations as a factor in the provision of social work services.

These federal, state, and local legislative and regulatory actions are shaping social work in ways that are not always consistent with the profession's goals and self-definition. Two areas that have been especially affected by federal legislative and administrative actions are social work services in acute-care hospitals and in hospices.

Federal deregulation. The passage of the Social Security Act Amendments of 1965 led to sweeping changes in the health care services of the United States. Medicare (Title XVIII) extended health insurance to millions of elderly, and Medicaid (Title XIX) provided assistance for the medically indigent. Following the enactment of this legislation, the Department of Health, Education and Welfare established regulations that set conditions for the participation of hospitals in these programs. The existing regulations provide standards for hospitals that elect to have social work departments, but they do not mandate social work services in hospitals. According to the American Hospital Association Data Center, however, 70 percent or more of the hospitals they survey have social work departments.[2]

In 1980, the Carter Administration introduced plans to reduce the regulation of hospitals, and the Department of Health and Human Services drafted new Medicare and Medicaid regulations. The new draft deleted many health and safety standards and eliminated references to social work services. Political circumstances intervened to prevent the proposal from going into effect at that time, but in 1982 the Reagan Administration decided on a similar course of action. This initiative met criticism from a number of national organizations, but the proposed revisions were published in the *Federal Register* in January 1983. During the period allowed for public comment, the Health Care Financing Administration, which oversees the programs, received more than 35,000 comments on the proposed changes. Not all the correspondence referred to the deletion of social work standards, but about one-third of the letters did. Letters came from social workers, other professionals, clients, members of Congress, and concerned citizens. Until some decisions are made by the Department of Health and Human Services, however, no action will be taken. Final rules were expected to be published sometime during 1983.

The Department of Health and Human Services asserts that because social work departments were not required by the original regulations, the deletion of social work standards should not have a negative impact on the delivery of services. However, the dramatic growth in the number of hospital social work departments since the Medicare and Medicaid regulations were established suggests that health care providers see these standards as necessary and relevant. This recognition of social work services is also reflected in the standards developed by private, not-for-profit accrediting organizations.

The prospective payment system. Medicare is also undergoing changes in its system of reimbursement that are bound to influence social work practice in hospitals. In an effort to slow rapidly escalating hospital costs, Congress passed legislation in 1983 that created the Medicare prospective payment system. Because it was attached to the popular Social Security Amendments, the legislation moved through Congress quickly.

The prospective payment system is a reimbursement plan designed to encourage cost-effective management of hospitals by paying a fixed rate for services based on patient diagnosis. At present, only inpatient services are covered under the program, and physician services will continue to be reimbursed as usual. The financial incentive for hospitals in this system is that hospitals can keep the difference between the reimbursement rate and their cost if their cost is less, but they must absorb the loss if their costs exceed the allowed rate. Reimbursement levels will be determined by a classification system of diagnosis-related groups (DRGs), which categorizes patients by diagnoses, performance of surgical procedures, age, and discharge status.

The system began in some hospitals in October 1983 and will be gradually adopted by all hospitals over a three-year period. Among the concerns that have been expressed about the system are that it could compromise the quality of patient care and limit access to health care services. Some people feel that the elderly and the poor are likely to be the most negatively affected by the new system because they tend to have more complicated illnesses and multiple diagnoses. The DRGs do not adequately consider the social and environmental factors that often interfere with recovery, especially in the elderly population. It has also been suggested that hospitals might try to manipulate the system. For example, a hospital reluctant to admit patients with more difficult or expensive diagnoses might direct such patients to another facility, a process known as skimming. Cost-conscious administrators might pressure physicians to limit the number of tests they order, to restrict the use of such services as social work or occupational therapy and to try to decrease the length of time a patient remains in the hospital.

The lack of specific references to social work services in the legislation leaves the role of the social worker open to interpretation. The prospective payment system, therefore, offers a challenge for social workers and suggests some new directions for hospital-based workers. It is possible that the focus of services will shift away from counseling and psychotherapy to participation in health education, community liaison work, and outpatient services. Discharge planning will undoubtedly take on greater importance.

Regulation of hospice care. In 1983 legislation was passed that addressed the hospice movement for the first time. With a history going back to Europe in the 1800s, hospice is an alternative to acute care in hospitals for the terminally ill. It is a coordinated program in which an interdisciplinary team provides palliative care and supportive services for dying persons and their families. Care is available twenty-four hours a day, seven days a week. The hospice movement has traditionally been a grass-roots phenomenon. Hospices are frequently affiliated with religious organizations and rely heavily on volunteer support.

As the movement grew and received increased recognition in the United States, it became the subject of regulation. Compliance with the regulations became a condition for hospices to receive Medicare money. The trend is now toward the standardization and professionalization of hospice care. This could threaten the survival of some individual hospices, especially smaller ones.

The first and only organization formed to address issues related to hospice care is the National Hospice Organization (NHO), established in 1977. Members include individuals, care providers, and other organizations. The main goal of NHO is to promote the hospice concept and to maintain standards of care in program planning and patient services. Members monitor health care legislation and regulation relevant to the hospice movement. The National Association of Social Workers (NASW) has participated in NHO's efforts to establish quality standards and has had a representative on its standards committee.

Government involvement in the regulation of hospices is a relatively recent phenomenon. Legislation was first introduced in late 1981 that would make hospice care reimbursable under Medicare. Congress was slow to act until a Congressional Budget Office report, issued in 1982, indicated that hospice services could provide significant financial savings over the traditional system of hospital-based care for the terminally ill. The legislation went into effect November 1, 1983.

The law requires social work as a core service, a reflection of social work's long tradition in the hospice movement. The law also specifies that at least one social worker must be part of the interdisciplinary team. An additional requirement directs that social work services be provided by a social worker with supervision by a physician. In the hospice setting, it may be appropriate to view the physician-medical director as the head of the interdisciplinary team, but it is significant that this legislation attached the supervisory requirement to social work but not any of the other professional service.

Other legislation. A number of other laws and regulations, including several pieces of legislation now under consideration, will affect social work either directly or indirectly. As the previous examples show, the impact of a law or regulation goes beyond simply the inclusion of social work services; many variables need to be considered in evaluating a new piece of legislation or set of regulations. Bills such as one introduced in 1983 designed to protect the disabled from the loss of Social Security Disability Insurance affect clients served by social workers. Other legislation introduced during 1983, such as Senator Inouye's bill allowing reimbursement of clinical social workers under Medicare and Medicaid, deals explicitly with the professional practice of social work.

The Private Role

Government agencies at the state and federal levels are responsible for surveying health care facilities. Aside from governmental regulation, however, health care facilities may seek accreditation by any of a number of not-for-profit standard-setting bodies.

Joint Commission on the Accreditation of Hospitals.

A prominent organization in this category is the Joint Commission on the Accreditation of Hospitals (JCAH). It was formed in 1951 by the American Hospital Association, the American Medical Association, the American College of Physicians, and the American College of Surgeons, and it began to survey and accredit hospitals at that time. The American Dental Association became a corporate member of the JCAH in 1979. Since 1951 the program has been broadened to include health settings other than hospitals, specifically long-term care, psychiatric facilities, and ambulatory health care. In recognition of the extent of the services provided by hospices, JCAH is developing standards for the delivery of care in hospices and is considering establishing a voluntary accreditation program for hospices.

The standards developed by JCAH in each of the foregoing categories all include guidelines for social work services. Both the hospital and the long-term care standards include separate professional sections that specify social work services. The standards for psychiatric facilities also include social work services but are arranged in a format that does not distinguish professional categories. As each of these sets of standards undergoes revision, social workers have been monitoring the way social work services are presented. It has been especially helpful to have social workers as representatives on the JCAH professional and technical advisory committees. Each committee provides expert professional and technical advice regarding the standards and accreditation process.

AC MRDD standards.

Another private standard-setting organization is the Accreditation Council for Services for Mentally Retarded and Other Developmentally Disabled Persons (AC MRDD). The council was established in 1979 to survey and accredit residential facilities and community programs serving the mentally retarded and developmentally disabled. Social work services are included in the AC MRDD standards, but the standards do not address the activities of individual professions. NASW is a member of the accreditation council and has two representatives who serve on the council's board of directors.

Standards for social work in developmental disabilities are especially important as social workers become more involved in the delivery of services to the disabled. Although this area of practice is not new to social workers, the movement to secure the release of people from institutions has given a larger role to social workers in the field. Deinstitutionalization has also exposed social workers in other areas of practice to mentally retarded and to developmentally disabled persons in the community.

The standards developed by JCAH, AC MRDD, and others are important because they recognize social work services. Because approximately one-third of NASW's 92,000 members are employed in health-related settings, it is essential that the quality of services be maintained. These standards help to assure that the patient is receiving appropriate service, that social work is better understood, and that an appropriate level of social work staff is available.

The Professional Role

Professional standards describe the minimum level of functioning generally considered necessary for practice in a given field. Any standard may perform several functions. It can specify a guiding principle, designate educational requirements, describe functions that must be performed, or identify desired outcomes or any other pertinent condition or requirement.[3]

Standards have consistently been a priority of the NASW Delegate Assembly. NASW publishes a Code of Ethics, standards for personnel practices, and other standards that establish the profession's own criteria for high-quality social work practice.

In recognition of the vast number of social workers who are employed in health-related settings, NASW publishes standards for social work services in the health care field. In 1977 a Joint Committee of the American Hospital Association and NASW produced a policy statement on standards for hospital social services. It was replaced in 1981 by standards for social work in health care settings.[4] These standards were prepared by the NASW Health Quality Standards Committee and approved by NASW's Board of Directors. The current standards go beyond the previous effort to a generic definition of social work functions in health settings. They are supplemented by specialized standards for practitioners in the areas of public health, developmental disabilities, and end-stage renal disease.

The professional standards cover core administrative topics in the first section, and specific practice areas are discussed in subsequent sections. The Health Quality Standards Committee describes its work as consisting of

> an initial effort to define core administrative standards meant to be applicable to many health care settings and organizational arrangements and to establish professional expectations for high-quality social work practice.[5]

The core standards include the development of a written plan for providing social work services by a graduate-level social worker; qualifications and responsibilities for the director of social work; and specific requirements for the structure and function of the social work program. Other standards discuss personnel policies, budget, space, facilities, and equipment.

Essential components of the core standards are sections on documentation and confidentiality and on the review, evaluation, and quality assurance of social work services.

Current Issues

The political climate of the United States in recent years has been conducive to deregulating government sponsored programs and industry. These attempts at deregulation all have potential consequences for the health and safety of every citizen. At the same time, the legislative and regulatory actions discussed earlier provide examples of some of the positive and negative effects that might result from government involvement in the delivery of social work services.

The significant number of social workers in the health care field supports the inclusion of social work services in the regulatory standards that affect the health care system. The dramatic response to the proposed elimination of social work standards from the Medicare and Medicaid regulations demonstrates how effective social workers can be in promoting professional standards. Although some critics have said that this is only an effort to obtain professional protection, the key issue is the protection of consumers of services through professional accountability. It is especially important that social workers continue to educate other health professionals, members of Congress, and the community at large about the skills and services the profession has to offer.[6]

MARYANNE P. KEENAN

Notes and References

1. Health Insurance Association of America, *Source Book of Health Insurance Data, 1982–1983* (Washington, D.C.: 1983), p. 31.

2. Telephone conversation, American Hospital Data Center, American Hospital Association, Chicago, Ill., 1983.

3. Maryanne P. Keenan, "Standards for Social Workers in Developmental Disabilities: an

Overview," in Lynn Wikler and Keenan, eds., *Developmental Disabilities, No Longer a Private Tragedy* (Silver Spring, Md.: National Association of Social Workers and American Association on Mental Deficiency, 1983), pp. 41–44.

4. See *Standards for Hospital Social Services,* Policy Statement No. 6; and *NASW Standards for Social Work in Health Care Settings,* Policy Statement No. 6 (Washington, D.C.: National Association of Social Workers, 1977 and 1982, respectively).

5. *NASW Standards for Social Work in Health Care Settings,* p. 1.

6. The author would like to thank NASW intern Beth Linderman for her assistance in the preparation of this article.

INDUSTRIAL SOCIAL WORK (OCCUPATIONAL SOCIAL WORK)

In the United States, industrial (or occupational) social work generally is defined as programs and services, under the auspices of labor or management, that utilize professional social workers to serve members or employees, and the legitimate social welfare needs of the labor or industrial organization. It also includes the use, by a voluntary or proprietary social agency, of trained social workers to provide social welfare services or consultation to a trade union or employing organization under a specific contractual agreement. The employing organizations are not only labor unions and corporations, but often government agencies and not-for-profit organizations.

The Department of Economic and Social Affairs of the United Nations defines industrial social welfare as, "the range of programs, operations and activities carried out at any level or by any group which promotes or preserves the welfare of the worker and protects him and his family from the social costs of the work process and work setting."[1] The three major differences between the international definition provided by the United Nations and the definition commonly accepted in the United States are instructive. First, the United Nations offers a somewhat broader conception of what actually constitutes industrial social welfare activities; second, professional social workers are not emphasized in their guidelines as the principal providers of services; and third, the international definition places little emphasis on the *auspices* of programs and services, which is a central focus of the American definition.[2]

As frequently conceptualized in the United States, industrial social work is a concentration or specialization within the broad conceptual framework of the "world of work." Professional practice in world-of-work settings also includes addressing for example, the need for youth employment training, personnel and guidance services, sheltered workshops for the disabled, and programs of vocational rehabilitation. Although the broader world-of-work rubric is helpful in identifying a conceptually important larger perspective, which includes a general emphasis on the social welfare needs of workers and work organizations, industrial social work per se is narrower and more specific in focus.

The concept of industrial social welfare flows from Titmuss's notion of a third, or occupational, welfare system over and above the social and fiscal welfare systems that have been more commonly understood. Titmuss referred to the occupational system of benefits and services as one in which individuals participate as a result of their employment status.[3] Weiner and colleagues further defined this occupational social welfare system in America as composed of

> benefits and services, above and beyond wages, directed at social and health needs, provision for which is not legislatively mandated. Entitlement to these benefits and services results from affiliation with a job in a particular company, or membership in a particular union, or a dependent relationship to an entitlee.[4]

The conceptualization of an occupational social welfare system and the social work profession's entry into this arena as a site for program development and service delivery are important, given current fiscal trends. Public welfare expenditures, which now total some 400 billion dollars yearly, have been declining for some time. However, the private, occupational welfare system, which also spends about 400 billion dollars annually in the form of employee benefits and services, has been expanding rapidly. In 1980 employers were financing health and welfare benefits to employees and their families at the rate of 32.3 percent of regular pay.[5] The social work profession's willingness to play a role in the development and administration of such benefits and services becomes increasingly important, therefore, as the occupational system takes on an ever greater role in financing services to the more than 100 million Americans in the work force and their families.

Furthermore, industrial social work provides easy access to a population in its natural life space and offers the profession an opportunity to develop a universal service delivery system unencumbered by the usual eligibility and categorical requirements of the public sector. Service here is an earned entitlement, universally available to all participants in the work force without cost and in a familiar environment—the world of work. In Kahn's sense, these are not stigmatized "case services." Rather, these programs and services represent social utilities of the workplace—on tap, as needed, for all work force participants and their families.[6] Like the social worker in the school system or the settlement house worker in the neighborhood, an industrial social worker serves clients from within the functional community of work.

In industrial and other employing organizations, employee assistance or employee-counseling programs are perhaps the best known and most rapidly developing social work services. Usually located in a medical or personnel office, these programs employ the largest number of individual social workers today and represent the fastest growing social work service under the auspices of the major institutional arrangements in the world of work: employers and trade unions. Social workers, however, also serve in company training units, affirmative action offices, corporate social responsibility departments, and human resources divisions. Typical titles might include employee counselor, affirmative action officer, community relations consultant, substance abuse services coordinator, employee resources manager, corporate relocation officer, human resources policy advisor, career planning and development counselor, training consultant, charitable allocations analyst, urban affairs advisor, or coordinator of corporate health and wellness programs.

The majority of social workers employed by organized labor provide services through union counseling and advocacy programs, frequently called personal or membership service units. Such union programs are a major source of employment for industrial social workers, especially in the Northeast. The International Ladies' Garment Workers' Union, for example, employs sixteen master's-level social workers in its Membership Services Unit alone—more social workers than are currently employed in any corporate-sponsored setting in the country.

Professional social workers have assumed responsibility in a variety of individual programs sponsored by union locals and district councils and in the headquarters of international unions and the American Federation of Labor and Congress of Industrial Organizations (AFL–CIO), which oversees and coordinates work of the labor union movement as a whole. Typical titles for social workers employed in these organizations include personal services worker, education program director, occupational safety and health officer, health and security plan manager, membership services coordinator, career training and upgrading advisor, preretirement services worker, day care consultant, legislative analyst, benefit plan administrator, alcoholism program supervisor, community services coordinator, and director of retiree services.

A job description for the prototypical industrial social welfare specialist might list some of the following duties:

• Counseling and carrying out activities with troubled employees, or members in job jeopardy, to assist them with their personal problems and to achieve maintenance of their productive performance

• Advising on the use of community services to meet client needs, and establishing linkage with such programs

• Training front-line personnel (union representatives, foremen, line supervisors) to enable them to determine when changes in job performance warrant referral to a social service unit; and carrying out an appropriate approach to the employee that will result in such referral

• Developing and overseeing the operations of a union or management information system, which will record service information and provide data for analysis of the unit's program

• Conceiving a plan for future programmatic direction, based upon identification of unmet needs and current demographic trends

• Offering consultation to labor or management decision makers concerning human resource policy development

• Helping to initiate community health, welfare, recreational, or educational programs for active and retired employees or members

• Assisting in the administration of the benefit and health care structure and helping plan for new initiatives

• Consulting on the development and administration of an appropriate affirmative action plan for women, minorities, and the disabled

• Advising on corporate giving or labor coalition building, and on organizational positions with relation to pending social welfare legislation.[7]

Historical Background

The relationship between social welfare and industry can be traced to the Middle Ages. In the medieval guilds, funds were set aside to ensure workers' economic security in case of accident, poverty, old age, or death, and loans to young workers were secured by assessments levied on guild members. Laws soon replaced guild levies, but the guild continued to maintain schools and almshouses and was, along with the church, the central social welfare institution for guild workers and their families throughout the Middle Ages and up until the advent of the Poor Laws of 1601. In the early 1800s in Britain and Scotland, leading factory owners began to provide similar benefits, and by the late 1800s many German companies and labor unions began to follow suit.[8]

The historical roots of this field in the United States can be found in what has been termed "welfare capitalism" —those benefits and services provided voluntarily by employers in the late nineteenth and early twentieth centuries in an effort to socialize, retain, and control a raw, unskilled, and badly needed labor force at a time of rapid industrialization.[9] Paternalistic in nature, inconsistent and inadequate in provision, directed at fostering employee dependency and loyalty, these programs were more an instrument of management than a service to workers. Companies hired staff, usually called welfare secretaries, to administer these programs and services, which might include improving sanitation, providing housing, supervising safety, and offering classes.

The welfare secretaries, as the handmaidens of management, increasingly were perceived as policing an immigrant work force to prevent malingering and to discourage workers' identification with a growing trade union movement. Their covert responsibility to investigate employees and to see that labor unions did not gain a foothold in industry ensured the enmity of American Federation of Labor (AFL) President Samuel Gompers and a distrust by workers of employers' motives for providing such programs.

Although initially these welfare secretaries had no formal training, this gradually began to change after World War I. The idea of welfare secretaries received considerable attention from two national organizations whose goals prominently included industrial social welfare services— the National Civic Federation and the American Institute for Social Service. Popple notes that this stimulus was important and that by 1920 more graduates of the New York School for Social Work were taking jobs in industry than in any other setting.[10] Social workers often served in the role of social welfare secretaries, although not always with that title.

Distrust of the emerging social work profession by working Americans was widespread and understandable, given the welfare secretaries' role as messengers of management and the increasingly narrow psychoanalytic approach that had become popular in the profession. This feeling was reinforced by leaders of the growing labor union movement who saw the welfare secretary as inhibiting their organizational drives and confirming their theory that social workers were not only antistrike, but essentially antiunion. During the 1920s, welfare secretaries began dying out, and by 1935 they had largely disappeared, with some of their functions being assumed by personnel officers and some by industrial nurses.

Industrially based social work reemerged during World War II when new groups of employees entered the labor force to respond to a wartime work force shortage. These new workers, many of them women and minorities, needed help in acculturating to the experience of full-time employment in industry and often in balancing the complex roles of employee and single parent. The major employers of industrial social workers were the airplane and munitions industries and the unions representing the shipping industry and merchant seamen. Bertha Reynolds, a prominent social work theoretician and practitioner, was hired to direct the joint labor-management program of the United Seamen's Service, which served members of the National Maritime Union (NMU).

The social workers were accepted in this situation because they were members of the social service union and handled themselves not as therapists, but as advocates for the members. Moreover, the social work profession had established a rapprochement with the trade union movement in the 1930s through active support of CIO organizing drives and through their caring service to unemployed workers during the height of the Great Depression. Reynolds's superb work at the NMU during World War II further strengthened these bonds of trust between organized labor and the social work profession and demonstrated the viability of an alternative model for serving the more than 20 million

Americans who in 1980 were members of organized labor.[11]

Often overlooked as a model for promoting the growth of industrial social work was social workers' participation in the United States armed forces during World War II. With its numbers swelled by a war effort on two fronts, the military became the major national employer. This work force, moreover, had to adapt to new job specifications, in an alien environment, under hostile and anxiety-producing working conditions. Social workers took on major direct service roles in helping to meet the needs of soldiers and their families and thereby established an ongoing role for the profession in the military for the postwar period. In 1946 the Surgeon General's Office established a permanent army commissioned officer corps of social workers, and this corps grew and expanded to the other branches of military service in succeeding years.[12] These professional social workers in the Medical Service Corps of the three branches of the armed forces may be conceptualized as industrial social workers insofar as they work for an employing organization to serve the health and welfare needs of its work force.

Although industry in Europe and South America employed growing numbers of social workers, there was relatively little such activity in the United States during the two decades following World War II. Industry reabsorbed its prewar work force, and the country entered a period of economic and social laissez-faire. The social work profession once again became psychoanalytic in focus, mirroring the inactivity of the nation as a whole with respect to issues of social innovation and organizational change. A few social workers were employed at Kaiser Industries and the J. L. Hudson Department Store in Detroit at this time, but they were the exception.

Wilensky and Lebeaux correctly noted in 1965 that "industrial social work in the European tradition of social workers offering family and other services from outposts in the plant. . . hailed for the past twenty years as a 'new frontier in social work' simply has not materialized in America."[13] The 1965 edition of the *Encyclopedia of Social Work* accurately reflected the times by making no general reference to union or management programs. Skeels's entry in that edition, entitled "Social Welfare Programs of Labor and Industry," provided no mention whatever of industrial social work practice or of the kinds of programs and services under labor and industrial auspices that are so common today.[14]

Modern industrial social welfare practice can be dated from the mid 1960s, when two important events occurred. Management at Polaroid in Boston decided that their innovative employee counseling program was meeting a definite need of this growing corporation and should become a permanent part of the organization. Directed by an experienced social worker, the counseling department had proved its value to the workers and to management both through the direct service function and through its role as human resource consultant to the decision makers of the corporation.[15] At the same time, Weiner and colleagues in New York were establishing a labor-based mental health and rehabilitation program at the Sidney Hillman Health Center of the Amalgamated Clothing Workers of America. With labor and management support and governmental funding, the model brought to workers in the men's clothing industry a service that was sensitive to their cultural style and unmet needs.[16] These two innovations of the late sixties continued into the early seventies and set the stage for the growth and development of the field.

If one were to apply Rostow's paradigm for analyzing the growth of an economy to the growth of a social welfare sector in industry, one might say that the "traditional" period for industrial social welfare was up through the end of World War II. The postwar period, up until the mid 1970s, saw a "development of preconditions" and was followed by a period of "take off" from 1975 to the present. There are signs now that the field may be close to entering the early stages of its "drive to maturity," although it is too early to predict whether Rostow's final phase of "high mass consumption" is realistic in the foreseeable future.[17]

Evolution of Practice

As just noted, there has been a marked growth and expansion of industrial social work practice since the mid-seventies. This growth was not accidental. It reflected a concerted effort and a tremendous concentration of human and fiscal resources; leaders in the educational and practice sectors of social work responded to an idea whose time had come. By the mid-1970s employers were coming to the realization that they had to deal with a changing work force and new social legislation. The Hughes Act, the Vocational Rehabilitation Act, the Occupational Safety and Health Act, the Employee Retirement Income Security Act, the Age Discrimination in Employment Act, and Title VII of the Civil Rights Act were among the new work-related laws to which industry had to become responsive. Women, minorities, and the disabled were entering the work force in great numbers and with new needs. In the movement-oriented spirit of the day, they were voicing their needs for day care, nondiscriminatory assignments, flextime, barrier-free work sites, career-training and upgrading programs, and concessions on some "quality of life" issues.

The permanent attachment of women to the world of work reminded industry of what social workers already knew—that work and family were not separate worlds and that what occurs in one inevitably affects what happens in the other. Therefore, employers needed to understand that linkages to the family, the neighborhood, and the community at large were outcomes not merely of the new mandates of social legislation, but of the changing complexion both of the American work force and of the communities in which they manufactured and marketed their goods and services. Employers needed help from a profession that would offer generalists capable of bringing both clinical and organizational sophistication to bear on industry's new human service agendas.

The trade union movement had to deal with the effects of its own success. As Akabas noted, "When the benefits of labor organization are available to all workers, either through collective bargaining or through employers' unilateral efforts to avoid organization, some new enticement must be offered to achieve union membership growth and loyalty."[18] Responding to this situation, unions began to develop a system of direct services to members; these services were in addition to the occupational social welfare benefits that were essentially fiscal. Organized labor, having won significant financial gains at the bargaining table, now needed to bring in new services to maintain the loyalty of their members to the union and its leaders.

Thus, the human service agenda, in the broadest sense, became markedly greater in size and scope both for labor and industry. Although management's concern for productivity and profit did not disappear, new quality-of-life issues emerged on which managers felt they did not have the requisite expertise. Similarly, although wages and working conditions remained labor's primary agenda, members' concern for "bread and roses" emerged once they had achieved some measure of job security and economic reward. The social work profession's readiness to help labor and management with these issues and its academic and practice preparation to do so created mutually fortuitous conditions for initiating partnership ventures.

Federal agencies in Washington, responding to these conditions and to the various mandates of the new social legislation, began to support social work education and training programs in this arena. Foremost in this effort was the National Institute on Alcohol Abuse and Alcoholism, which began to realize that occupational alcoholism was an issue of growing concern that required federal support for training and for introducing programs at the work site. The National Institute of Mental Health, the Rehabilitation Services Administration, and the Manpower Administration of the U.S. Department of Labor also showed their interest and support for social work initiatives at the workplace. Several philanthropic foundations, especially the Lois and Samuel Silberman Fund and the Johnson Foundation, demonstrated their interest in promoting systematic development of curriculum and practice models for this growing field of practice.

The National Association of Social Workers (NASW) underwrote a two-year joint project with the Council on Social Work Education (CSWE) to promote the preparation of professional social workers for industrial social work practice. The association later provided special program advancement funds to several of its state chapters to further their development of models and standards for industrial practice.

As not-for-profit family service agencies and community mental health centers developed expertise in serving workers and their families, they began offering contractual social service programs to industries in their community. They were joined by Human Affairs, Inc., and other social work–directed proprietary firms that began to market industrial social services to leading corporations.

Several graduate schools of social work provided leadership in conceptualizing industrial practice and in refining models for this field. The first among the landmark events in this area was the establishment of an Industrial Social Welfare Center at the Columbia University School of Social Work in 1970. This was followed by the initiation of industrial social work programs in 1974 at the schools of social work at Boston College, Hunter College, and the University of Utah. Then, in 1978, Columbia University and Hunter College, along with CSWE, sponsored the First National Conference on Social Work Practice in

Labor and Industrial Settings. This conference brought industrial social work practitioners together for the first time so that, from the vantage point of practice, they might begin to define both the generic and the specific. [19] Generous support from NASW and the Lois and Samuel Silberman Fund during the period between 1977 and 1980 permitted the education community to take strides toward (1) refining and then sharing models for teaching and practice, (2) developing sites for student placement and employment, and (3) building a literature to interpret industrial social work both to the profession and to labor and industrial organizations.

The importance of the educational community's undertaking to develop a cohesive conceptual literature for the field cannot be overestimated; it provided a foundation for the steady growth and maturation of industrial social work practice. Models were constructed based on sound social work theory and then tested in the field through graduate practicum arrangements and through pilot labor and industrial programs. Based on historical understanding and on an appreciation of what social work as a profession had to offer, the opportunities, dilemmas, advantages, and risks of industrial practice were explored.

The academic leaders were committed to systematically developing models of policy and practice, rather than merely seizing an opportunity to gain a foothold in a new field of practice. They harnessed resources from government, foundations, universities, and professional organizations to initiate a developmental process. Simultaneously, they obtained sanction from the gatekeeping professional associations, social agencies, and major labor and industrial organizations.

The early leaders recognized the need for a reconceptualization of the area, and this ensured that the emerging literature would be not just descriptive but conceptual as well and would view the emerging field in all its richness and complexity. A relatively sophisticated harnessing of diverse, public and private institutional resources occurred, along with the development of the organizational sanction and support of NASW and CSWE. The resulting proliferation of articles in professional journals;[20] newspapers;[21] and business magazines;[22] monographs;[23] research studies;[24] doctoral dissertations;[25] course outlines and bibliographies;[26] books;[27] and interpretive brochures[28] placed the profession in a good position to enter the competitive labor and industrial arena as a knowledgeable contributor to the needs of workers and work organizations.

Education for Practice

The results of this concentration of attention and resources were remarkable. In 1977 only twenty-six graduate schools of social work had even one industrial social work field placement, and only four had an industrial social work concentration or specialization. Five years later fifty schools had such field placements, seventeen had established formal industrial social work specializations, and twenty-two additional graduate schools were planning to develop an industrial social work concentration in the near future.[29]

In general, most graduate schools have started slowly, first with one or two field placements and then with an elective course offering. This step typically preceded an administrative decision to support a specialization, which would move the school toward hiring a faculty member to provide leadership in conceptualizing and developing the program. A subsequent expansion of required and elective course offerings and the development of a range of practicum opportunities generally marks the advent of a recognized concentration.

With this program firmly in place, a school then typically moves toward conducting occupationally based research, developing new program thrusts, offering human resource consultation to selected labor and industrial organizations, and initiating continuing education courses for experienced practitioners interested in moving into the field. Evidence to date shows that the designation of faculty who will have a primary commitment to developing the new program and building appropriate class and field opportunities is essential to the successful initiation of an industrial social work training program.

Educational preparation for the field has been limited to graduate social work programs almost exclusively. This is appropriate because industrial social work is an area of specialization and CSWE has stipulated that specialization is a graduate-level educational responsibility. Many graduate schools are also assigning a priority to developing continuing education offerings to prepare experienced practitioners to deal with the unique policy and practice issues in the labor and industrial arena.

Current Issues

Like any new venture, industrial social work is not without its issues and controversies. If one accepts the proposition that the existence of such tension is essentially healthy in an open system, then the profession's willingness to acknowledge such disagreement within its ranks can be conceived as a normal and even useful occurrence. Industrial social work teachers and practitioners need not agree on all issues, any more than they would in such established fields as family treatment or child welfare. Especially at this early juncture, industrial social workers recognize that some internal disagreement is a sign of the vigor of the field and is likely to lead to more thoughtful and broadly acceptable resolutions as the field matures.

Focus on alcoholism. An early issue concerned whether direct service programs should focus primarily on substance abuse, particularly occupational alcoholism, or whether the service should be more broadly conceptualized, offering services to workers or members with any personal or emotional problem. Because the early funding for the labor and industrial service programs came largely from the National Institute on Alcohol Abuse and Alco-

holism and the early affiliation of industrial social workers was primarily with the Association of Labor-Management Administrators and Consultants on Alcoholism (ALMACA), the focus on substance abuse prevailed. Leadership was provided by such organizations as ALMACA and the Hazelden Foundation, with little activity from NASW, CSWE, or the schools and agencies of the social work profession.

Today this has changed, partly in response to leadership from within social work, but also in reaction to the needs of the field. Practice experience has taught social workers that alcoholism is not the only, or even the primary, problem of most clients coming for help at the workplace. Most need help with a variety of personal, emotional, family-oriented, and community-centered problems. A "broad-brush" model of service, customarily offered in industry under the auspices of an employee assistance or employee counseling program or, in unions, under a personal services or member assistance program, has become the prevailing model. The focus is direct service, but

> direct service in these settings is an all-encompassing term. It includes counseling, organization of support groups, concrete services, consumer advocacy, linking an individual to community services, training and staff development for union representatives and management personnel, and consultation to union and industrial decision makers.[30]

Confidentiality. Another issue has been whether confidentiality is truly possible in these settings, especially in management-sponsored programs. The placement of such programs generally under the personnel or medical department, both of which have manifest or latent monitoring functions, makes the issue more serious. Because a breach of confidentiality could mean the loss of a worker's job or a stigma that could affect job advancement, the issue of confidentiality takes on special importance in this setting. Because the corporate world is not oriented to human services, the social worker must always be prepared to question managers' understanding of the nature and boundaries of confidentiality and their willingness to respect workers' rights.

Although this issue remains central to all industrial social work practice, instances of actual abuse are extraordinarily rare. Practitioners, however, must acknowledge and respect workers' apprehensions. Under the circumstances, these concerns are appropriate, and the extent to which they are allayed conditions the worker's willingness to use the service. The profession's guidelines for confidentiality, embodied in NASW's Code of Ethics, must be scrupulously observed, and information should be shared only with the voluntary and informed consent of the client.[31]

A question of motives. Some have questioned the motives of the social work profession in embracing the industrial arena as a new setting for practice, especially at a time when corporations dominate the allocation of national resources. They ask whether the profession is motivated to move into the area primarily to demonstrate its capacity for entrepreneurship and to maximize practitioners' income and prestige. Does the trend toward industrial social work mean that social work is or will become less committed to serving the poor, who often are not members of the work force? Given the national trend toward "privatization" of the economy in general and of the human services in particular, is industrial social work another step in this direction by a profession historically committed to the public and voluntary sectors? In view of the recent growth of private entrepreneurship in such service sectors as child care, nursing homes, and home health care and the parallel growth of private clinical practice, will industrial social work become still a further move toward modeling the profession on the profit-making sector?

Although the profession has begun to address some of these ethical issues, the answers to these questions are not yet clear and must await the further evolution and maturation of the industrial field of practice.[32] However, there are several promising signs. First and perhaps foremost is the willingness of leaders in the profession to discuss these issues openly, partly to increase awareness of potential problems and also to ensure that the fundamental issues will be addressed both by individual social workers and by gatekeepers in our professional agencies and organizations. Second, the recent growth of industrial social work in trade union and not-for-profit settings has created a balance in this emerging field of practice that gives promise of a measured and varied perspective within the field. Third, leaders in the development of industrial social work have suggested a broader world-of-work perspective as the arena for specialization, and this has generally been supported by NASW and CSWE. This view of the field casts the net for service more broadly than merely over those with an active and relatively permanent labor force attachment and includes the newly employed, those unemployed and seeking entry, and the disadvantaged and disabled.

Agents of social change. The final current issue is somewhat related to the question of "privatization" and is perhaps the most fundamental of all. Briefly stated, it is whether social work's participation in the world of work will be largely, or even exclusively, as providers of service or also as agents of social change. This issue is an old and honored one in the profession and embraces Richmond's focus on the tension between "retail" and "wholesale," Schwartz's discussion of "private troubles" and "public issues," Wilensky's concern with the "residual" and "institutional," and the Milford Conference's attention to "cause" as well as "function."

Inseparably related to this question is the issue of social control and whether industrial social workers' professional use-of-self will primarily be in service to the individual or to the employing organization. "Concern for the well-being of people, individually and collectively," writes Bakalinsky, "historically has been social work's trademark. Industry, on the other hand, places its primary value on production and profits. Its people are viewed as a commodity having only instrumental value for the industry's central purpose."[33] Walden questions whether industrial social workers will serve only the individual needs of workers or will move organizationally to address collective issues, such as hazardous working conditions, worker dehumanization, and violations of affirmative action.[34]

The willingness of colleagues to raise these questions is helpful: there is a danger that industrial social workers will become more concerned with questions of social service than with issues of social change. The resulting goal displacement, whereby practitioners could become as much agents of social control as providers of social service, is a risk that must be acknowledged and discussed if it is to be avoided.

Ultimately, however, the question cannot be answered easily or absolutely. Social workers have had to deal with these very same dilemmas in such settings as public welfare, corrections, school social work, addiction services, and child welfare. The fundamental social work question is, "Whose agent are we?" Clarity about role and function means that people are the central focus of attention and yet that the social worker develops the organizational sophistication necessary to mediate between individuals and their environment. In industrial social work, no less than in other fields of practice that appear to constrain social work's options, practitioners must hold fast to their dual commitment to being providers of social service and agents of social change. This is a historical mandate of the profession.

Trends and Projections

Growth and development in the emerging field of industrial social work has been rapid and promises to continue at this rate. A marked increase in the number of practitioners in this field is predictable, and with it will come an increase in their iden-

tification of themselves as social workers, informed for their practice by the knowledge, values, skills, and standards of their profession. This change will come in part from the profession's own recognition of the field and thereby of its practitioners. However, it also should emanate from the fact that, in ten years, most industrial social workers will have been trained for the specialization, either during their graduate social work experience or through a social work continuing education program.

Although training for industrial social work is now almost exclusively at the master's level, educational efforts should begin to spread shortly to doctoral education. Tasks for holders of the BSW can also be envisioned, although baccalaureate programs would not train for specialization. The number of accredited schools of social work formally recognizing the world of work and, in turn, industrial social work as a specialization will expand. Factors in this development will include the success of schools with current programs, the profession's interest in pursuing new markets for its graduates, and CSWE's new curriculum standards, which emphasize the need for specialization at the graduate level and suggest the world of work as an appropriate area.

Labor and industry will continue to expand their human service programs, and increasingly they will select social work as a profession of choice for designing and operating these programs. Both in-house and contractual models of service should grow, and there is likely to be a marked increase in the employment of industrial social workers in the public and not-for-profit sectors. Federal agencies, with encouragement and funding from the U.S. Department of Health and Human Services, will be joined by more and more departments of state, county, and municipal governments in sponsoring employee assistance programs for their work forces. In addition, the number of public and voluntary hospitals and universities moving to establish such programs will continue to increase, and they will turn to their social service departments and schools of social work, respectively, to help establish and staff their programs.

With formal recognition of the field and its importance to the social work profession as a whole will come the formation within CSWE, NASW, and other national organizations of permanent constituency structures for industrial social work. The development of regular regional and national conferences, the launching of a professional specialty journal, and the formal establishment of educational and practice standards for industrial social work will be components of maturation over the next ten years. Clearly, the future of industrial social work is secure.

PAUL A. KURZMAN

Notes and References

1. Department of Economic and Social Affairs, *Industrial Social Welfare* (New York: United Nations, 1971), p. 3.

2. Although a discussion of international industrial social welfare programs is beyond the scope of this article, it should be noted that industrial social work practice has existed on a large scale abroad for many years as a permanent and frequently government-supported field of practice. Such countries as France, Germany, Holland, Belgium, Poland, Peru, Brazil, Zambia, and India have well-established industrial social welfare programs and services.

3. See Richard M. Titmuss, *Commitment to Welfare* (New York: Pantheon Books, 1968).

4. Hyman J. Weiner et al., "The World of Work and Social Welfare Policy," (New York: Columbia University School of Social Work, 1971), p. 6. (Mimeographed.)

5. Barry Friedman and Leonard Hausman, "Welfare: Public and Private," *New York Times,* January 5, 1982, p. 15.

6. See Alfred J. Kahn, *Social Policy and Social Services* (New York: Random House, 1973), chapter 3.

7. Sheila H. Akabas and Paul A. Kurzman, "The Industrial Social Welfare Specialist: What's So Special?" in Akabas and Kurzman, eds., *Work, Workers and Work Organizations: A View from Social Work* (Englewood Cliffs, N.J.: Prentice-Hall, 1982), pp. 201–202.

8. See Irl E. Carter, "Industrial Social Welfare: Historical Parallels in Five Western Countries." Unpublished doctoral dissertation, University of Iowa, 1975.

9. Stuart D. Brandes, *American Welfare Capitalism, 1880–1940* (Chicago: University of Chicago Press, 1976).

10. Philip R. Popple, "Social Work Practice in Business and Industry, 1875–1930," *Social Service Review,* 55 (June 1981), pp. 257–269.

11. See Bertha C. Reynolds, *Social Work and Social Living,* "Classics Reprint Series" (Washington, D.C.: National Association of Social Workers, 1975).

12. See Joseph J. Bevilacqua and Paul F. Darnauer, "Military Social Work," in John B. Turner et al., eds., *Encyclopedia of Social Work* (17th ed.; Washington, D.C.: National Association of Social Workers, 1977), pp. 927–931.

13. Harold L. Wilensky and Charles N. Lebeaux, *Industrial Society and Social Welfare* (New York: Free Press, 1965), p. 163.

14. Jack W. Skeels, "Social Welfare Programs of Labor and Industry," in Harry L. Lurie, ed., *Encyclopedia of Social Work* (15th ed.; New York: National Association of Social Workers, 1965), pp. 735–741.

15. See "Counseling and Consultation at Polaroid," *Practice Digest,* 1 (June 1978), pp. 6–7.

16. Hyman J. Weiner, Sheila H. Akabas, and John J. Sommer, *Mental Health Care in the World of Work* (New York: Association Press, 1973).

17. W. W. Rostow, *Stages of Economic Growth* (2d ed.; Cambridge, England: Cambridge University Press, 1971).

18. Sheila H. Akabas, "Labor: Social Policy and Human Services," in *Encyclopedia of Social Work* (17th issue; Washington, D.C.: National Association of Social Workers, 1977), p. 743.

19. See Sheila H. Akabas, Paul A. Kurzman, and Nancy S. Kolben, eds., *Labor and Industrial Settings: Sites for Social Work Practice* (New York: Columbia University, Hunter College, and Council on Social Work Education, 1979).

20. Paul A. Kurzman and Sheila H. Akabas, "Industrial Social Work as an Arena for Practice," *Social Work,* 26 (January 1981), pp. 52–60; Paul R. Brooks, "Industry-Agency Program for Employee Counseling," *Social Casework,* 56 (July 1975), pp. 404–410; Roslyn Yasser and John J. Sommer, "One Union's Social Service Program," in *Social Welfare Forum, 1974 (New York: Columbia University Press, 1975), pp.*

112–120; Martha N. Ozawa, "Development of Social Services in Industry," *Social Work,* 25 (November 1980), pp. 464–470; and "Social Work and the Workplace," *Practice Digest* (entire issue), 5 (September 1982).

21. Barbara Lovenheim, "More Care Given to Employee's Psyches," *New York Times,* April 1, 1979, sec. 3, pp. 3 and 5; Pamela S. Leven, "A New Service from a Seattle Bank: Social Work," *Seattle Post-Intelligencer,* October 5, 1980, pp. 1–2; and David O. Tyson, "Social Workers in Three Trust Departments: Look After Confined Beneficiaries," *American Banker,* October 16, 1980.

22. Sheila H. Akabas and Seth A. Akabas, "Social Services at the Workplace: New Resources for Management," *Management Review,* 71 (May 1982), pp. 15–20; "Hiring Outside Help to Solve People Problems," *Business Week,* January 20, 1975, pp. 30–31; and Daniel D. Cook, "Companies Put Social Workers on the Payroll," *Industry Week,* September 21, 1981, pp. 73–79.

23. Michele Vinet and Constance Jones, *Social Services and Work: Initiation of Social Workers into Labor and Industry Settings* (Seattle: Washington State Chapter of the National Association of Social Workers, 1981); Akabas, Kurzman, and Kolben, *Labor and Industrial Settings;* and *Meeting Human Services Needs in the Workplace: A Role For Social Work* (New York: Columbia University, Hunter College, and Council on Social Work Education, 1980).

24. Melvin A. Glasser et al., "Obstacles of Utilization of Prepaid Mental Health Care," *American Journal of Psychiatry,* 132 (July 1975), pp. 710–715; John Erfurt and Andrea Foote, *Occupational Employee Assistance Programs for Substance Abuse and Mental Health Problems* (Ann Arbor: Joint Institute of Labor and Industrial Relations, University of Michigan and Wayne State University, 1977); and Hans Spiegel, *Not for Work Alone: Services at the Workplace* (New York: Urban Research Center of Hunter College, 1974).

25. Carter, "Industrial Social Welfare"; Lou Ann B. Jorgensen, "Social Work in Business and Industry," unpublished doctoral dissertation, University of Utah, 1979; and Bradley Googins, "The Use and Implementation of Occupational Alcoholism Programs by Supervisors," unpublished doctoral dissertation, Brandeis University, 1979.

26. *Educational Resource Material for Social Work Practice in Labor and Industrial Settings* (New York: Council on Social Work Education, 1979); Sherri R. Torjman, *Mental Health in the Workplace: Annotated Bibliography* (Ottawa: Canadian Mental Health Association, 1978); and Weiner et al., *The World of Work and Social Welfare Policy.*

27. Barbara B. Feinstein and Edwin G. Brown, *The New Partnership: Human Services, Business and Industry* (Cambridge, Mass.: Schenkman Publishers, 1982); Dale A. Masi, *Human Services in Industry* (Lexington, Mass.: D. C. Heath & Co., 1982); and Akabas and Kurzman, eds., *Work, Workers, and Work Organizations.*

28. "We Are Now 'At Work' to Help You Safeguard Your Most Valuable Resource...People" (New York: Columbia University and Hunter College Schools of Social Work, 1981); and "Human Resources Workshops: A Service of Employee Counseling Programs" (New York: Jewish Board of Family and Children's Services, 1983).

29. See "Final Report of the Council on Social Work Education and National Association of Social Workers Project on Social Work in Industrial Settings," Appendix 3 (New York: Council on Social Work Education, March 1980) (mimeographed); and Gary M. Gould, "Industrial Social Work Education Study" (Los Angeles: School of Social Work, University of Southern California, 1982) (mimeographed).

30. Akabas, Kurzman, and Kolben, *Labor and Industrial Settings,* p. 5.

31. For further discussion, see John C. Erfurt and Andrea Foote, *Occupational Employee Assistance Programs for Substance Abuse and Mental Health Programs,* pp. 45–46; Akabas and Kurzman, "The Industrial Social Welfare Specialist," pp. 221–226; and Kurzman and Akabas, "Industrial Social Work as an Arena for Practice," pp. 55–56.

32. See *NASW Code of Ethics,* Policy Statement No. 1 (Washington, D.C.: National Association of Social Workers, 1980); Rosalie Bakalinsky, "People vs. Profits: Social Work in Industry," *Social Work,* 25 (November 1980), pp. 471–475; Paul A. Kurzman, "Ethical Issues in Industrial Social Work Practice," *Social Casework,* 64 (February 1983), pp. 105–111; and Sheila H. Akabas, "Industrial Social Work: Influencing the System at the Workplace," in Miriam Dinerman, ed., *Social Work in a Turbulent World* (Silver Spring, Md.: National Association of Social Workers, 1983), pp. 131–141.

33. Bakalinsky, "People vs. Profits," p. 472.

34. Theodore Walden, "Industrial Social Work: A Conflict in Definitions," *NASW News,* 23 (May 1978), p. 3.

LEGAL ISSUES IN SOCIAL WORK PRACTICE

Law and social work are intimately, if not always affectionately, related. Public social welfare agencies are created, funded, shaped, and even destroyed by the actions and inactions of federal and state legislatures or by executive orders of the president or a governor of a state. The actions of courts and various administrative bodies also affect social welfare agencies.

Law and the Agency

The private, or voluntary, social welfare agencies are also influenced by the law. Most social welfare agencies are chartered under federal or state law as eleemosynary, or charitable, corporations. Incorporation as a charitable organization permits the agency to take advantage of certain benefits the government offers to encourage the development and continuation of organizations that work for the good of the public. The chief benefits that accrue to charitable corporations are exemption from corporate income taxes and often from certain state or local taxes. In addition, charitable corporations benefit from federal and state laws that permit contributors to deduct the amount of their contributions on their corporate or individual income tax returns.

Prior to the emergence of almost universal coverage of charitable corporations by liability insurance, many states protected charitable corporations from liability to civil actions by various means, including the "charitable immunity" rule. This rule insulated charities from the payment of damages for wrongs that they committed; the theory was that potential contributors to charities would be reluctant to support charitable works if they feared that their contributions would be paid out in legal judgments. Although the charitable immunity rule no longer flourishes in the United States—South Carolina, the last state with such a rule, abolished it in 1982—charities still enjoy the favor of various statutes and

legal rules, including limitations on the amounts for which a charity can be sued.

Law provides benefits to charities; it also places certain restraints on their activities. For example, a major restriction prevents charities from lobbying as opposed to merely educating the public for some public good.[1] Other important legal restrictions and issues that have recently changed or threaten to change agency activities need further discussion.

Adoption and surrogate parenting. Law also shapes the services that agencies provide to their clients. In addition to the obvious impact that law has on an agency by virtue of establishing the powers and duties of a public agency and by increasing, decreasing, or withholding funding, substantive law also affects agency services. (Substantive law is that which affects or defines the rights existing between persons or classes.) Adoption, for example, is a matter of state law. State statutes specify the persons eligible to adopt children, the adoption procedures, and a variety of other matters including the nature of home studies and the circumstances in which adoption agencies are to be involved in the process of adoption. Adoption agencies have long argued that competent studies made by specialized agencies should be a part of most or all adoptions. Although state adoption statutes typically provide for agency studies, courts usually have the discretion to waive such studies.[2]

The debate over agencies' authority in adoptions is likely to heat up with the emergence of the so-called surrogate-parenting contracts. Under such contracts, a woman typically contracts with an infertile husband and his wife; the woman is artificially inseminated with the husband's sperm and agrees to deliver the child to the couple for adoption following the child's birth. What makes this an issue, in part, is that the enforceability of surrogate-parenting contracts is legally uncertain at this time.

Bills introduced in various state legislatures seek to clarify the legal issues involved, but surrogate parenting is also an issue because the surrogate mother is typically paid a large sum of money. On the surface, this suggests the contractual selling of babies rather than concern for the best interests of a child. Thus, children's advocates can be expected to push strongly for a greater involvement of social agencies in the process of surrogate adoption.[3]

Abuse and protective services. Substantive law also affects a number of other social work programs. Most notable and widespread are state statutes that assign powers and duties to social agencies to license foster homes and institutions and that define the roles of social agencies with regard to child abuse and neglect and adult protective services. During the late seventies and early eighties, all states revised their statutes dealing with child abuse and neglect, spurred by incentives provided by the Child Abuse Prevention and Treatment Act (P.L. 93-247), which sought to improve each state's ability to uncover child abuse and neglect and to take appropriate action. These statutes establish the major parameters for reporting child abuse and neglect and set out the duties and powers of the courts and involved agencies. In similar but usually less detailed fashion, state statutes also specify the major parameters and components of agency involvement in the protection of developmentally disabled adults from various types of abuse, neglect, or exploitation.

Court interpretations in cases relating to both child and adult protective services have often touched fundamental constitutional issues because protective services statutes granted powers to agencies that traditionally had been reserved for families rather than government.[4]

Employment and information-handling policies. Law also affects many agencies' employment policies and their information-handling and accounting procedures. Government agencies typically function under civil service procedures and state or federal personnel policies.

Perhaps the most difficult and complex problem facing many social agencies is the handling of information. Although social agencies generally function under the professional and often statutorily imposed duty of confidentiality, exceptions exist. In child abuse and neglect, social workers are required to report suspected abuse or neglect. In adoptions, although information must generally be kept confidential, state statutes or courts sometimes require adoption agencies to provide certain information for "good cause," usually medical information for an adopted child.

In recent years the issue of the confidentiality of adoption records has been debated in every state legislature and adoption agency, spurred largely by adult adoptees who wish to know their biological parents or at least to have more information about their preadoptive years. This issue is not easily resolvable because to grant rights to adoptees diminishes the rights of biological parents, and adoption agencies and adoptive parents can be caught somewhere in the middle, having no rights of their own and being unable to satisfy the needs of all parties involved.[5]

Law and the Practitioner

Separate and apart from its effect on social welfare agencies, the law also affects the environment in which individual social work practitioners practice. The salient changes in this area since the mid-seventies involve licensing, issues of privileged information, and malpractice vulnerability.

Licensing. State statutes license social workers for practice, specify which persons can include the words "social worker" as a professional designation, and determine what functions the social worker can perform. The licensing of social workers has been a major issue in most states since the early seventies. Although twenty-eight states have social work licensing or title protection statutes, legislatures have become resistant to licensing "new" professions, sometimes on the rationale that licensing protects the practitioner rather than the client.[6]

Privileged and confidential information. State statutes and case law also regulate the social worker's obligations with regard to information that the social worker receives as part of the professional relationship with a client. Here important distinctions must be noted between privileged information and confidential information.[7] Privileged information is information that a social worker receives as part of a professional relationship with a client or patient and that, according to law, the social worker cannot be ordered by a court to divulge unless the client wishes it. Only a small number of states have statutes that grant the protection of privileged information to social workers, but courts sometimes grant a privilege to social workers depending on the circumstances of the case. The protection of confidential information can have two sources. The first is that provided under the ethics of the social work profession. The other possible source is a state statute that requires information to be kept confidential, that is, revealed to no one without the client's permission, except by order of a court or other competent authority.

Questions of confidentiality and privilege abound in part because of the wide variety of cases and factual situations in which social workers are involved and in part because of the exceptions that statutes contain. Thus, although courts in all states recognize the general ethical duty of a social worker to maintain a confidence, statutory exceptions exist, most commonly in regard to requirements that social workers and other professionals report suspected child abuse or neglect.

Courts have also found exceptions to confidentiality. In California and New Jersey cases involving mental health professionals, courts have held that there is a duty to warn a person who is in danger of

being done bodily harm by a patient.[8] These decisions leave much uncertainty as to the scope of confidentiality, and critics of the California decision have argued that the decision will deter those most in need of professional treatment from seeking it because of the fear that they cannot discuss their problems in confidence.

Malpractice. Courts are sometimes called on to make judgments about the nature of a social worker's practice. Malpractice actions against social workers have increased dramatically since the mid-seventies. Malpractice is commonly defined as the negligent practice of one's profession. *Black's Law Dictionary*, however, gives a much broader definition of malpractice: "Any professional misconduct, unreasonable lack of skill or fidelity in professional or fiduciary duties, evil practice, or illegal or immoral conduct."[9] Malpractice then includes more than the negligent practice of social work; it can mean the violation of an ethic of the profession or of a judicial or statutory duty that is imposed on social workers; and a social worker can potentially be sued for a variety of causes including breach of confidentiality, failure to report suspected child abuse or neglect, trespass, assault, battery, false imprisonment through wrongful confinement in a hospital, and other actions.

At a minimum, the law expects a social worker to practice within the standards and ethics that are established by the profession of social work. Thus, the Code of Ethics of the National Association of Social Workers and the association's standards for practice carry the potential for more than sanctions from a practitioner's professional peers.[10] When malpractice questions develop, courts reasonably look to standards that social workers develop for themselves.

Traditionally, unless the actions or inactions of the worker were extreme, social workers were insulated from liability based on negligence. There are two principal reasons for this. First, to prove a social worker is negligent, it must be shown, in addition to other requisites, that the worker's client or patient was harmed in some manner and also that there was a causal link between the harm and some action or inaction of the worker. These proofs could be difficult to establish if the alleged harm was mental or emotional: (1) there are no sound measures of mental or emotional injury, (2) the client or patient came to the social worker, most likely, because of some mental or emotional difficulty outside the social worker–client relationship, and (3) the sources, causes, and etiology of mental or emotional injury are complex, often obscure, and typically multiple.

A second reason why social workers traditionally had little to fear from negligence actions was that courts were reluctant to find liability for emotional injury unless it was accompanied by some physical injury. The reason for this rule was that courts recognized the difficulties involved in assessing mental or emotional injury and felt that there was great risk of trumped-up suits being brought unless the more easily proved physical injury accompanied the mental or emotional injury. Now, however, many courts no longer require proof of physical injury for a plaintiff to recover damages for alleged mental injury, and juries in recent years have been more willing to side with an injured party than to wrestle with the niceties of law as charged to them by a judge. Whatever the many possible reasons, social workers are no longer "liability proof."[11]

Law and the Client

Law also reaches the clients of social workers, and recent changes in the law have sometimes treated them kindly, sometimes harshly. Persons deeply in debt have been benefited by the Bankruptcy Reform Act of 1978, which broadened the relief available to debtors to such an extent that creditors have cried out against it.[12] Handicapped and aged adults have increasingly been granted rights in education and employment that are long overdue. Women,

minorities, and recipients of Aid to Families with Dependent Children, however, had little to cheer about with regard to changes in the law in the late seventies and early eighties.

Children. Recent changes in the law have greatly affected children, mostly positively. In all states, statutes have improved the reporting of child abuse and neglect; this is a significant advance. Statutes authorizing the payment of subsidies to persons who adopt "special needs" children—minority children, handicapped children, older children, and siblings who need to be together—have passed in all but two states. This encourages the adoption of special needs children and is a significant step forward, although the subsidies seldom are generous and typically are related to the financial situation of the adoptive parents rather than to the needs of the child.[13] Adoption has been further encouraged by a change in the Internal Revenue Code that permits certain expenses of adoption to be deducted from income; some states have similar provisions in their tax codes. Many states have also reviewed their statutes regarding the termination of parental rights with an eye toward removing provisions that might not withstand the challenge to their constitutionality and that would make it easier to terminate the rights of parents who have abused their children or have failed to visit or support them over a specified period of time. These revisions have made it possible for many children to be adopted without the traditional need for a biological parent to give his or her consent to an adoption and have speeded up the process of adoption generally.

Handicapped youngsters have benefited from the passage of the Education for All Handicapped Children Act (P.L. 94-142) and subsequent legislation and court decisions. Although long overdue and facing years of further effort before full compliance can be reached, the act encourages schools to serve handicapped children and to provide them with an education that differs as little as possible from that of their age peers.[14]

Juvenile and family courts have also been changing, especially in regard to child custody. Although not dead, the "tender years" doctrine, which asserts that young children should be with their mother, is rapidly falling into disuse as courts rely increasingly on the "best interest of the child" criterion for determining child custody. Increasingly, too, courts are awarding joint custody of children and are attempting to lessen custody and other disputes by using divorce mediation. California's legislature was the first to enact legislation favoring joint custody and divorce mediation.[15]

Important steps also have been taken by both the Congress and most states to curb the estimated 100,000 cases of parental child snatching that occur in the United States each year. The problem of child snatching exists in part because child custody is a matter of state, not federal, law. Thus an award of custody in one state has often been effectively thwarted by the parent denied custody snatching the child, taking it to another state, and obtaining a court award of custody in that state. Normally one would expect the second state to be bound by the full-faith-and-credit clause of the Constitution, by which the court in the second state would be bound to accept and enforce the decree of the first state, but the U.S. Supreme Court has refused to require full faith and credit in custody matters. However, forty-eight states have enacted, in whole or in part, the Uniform Child Custody Jurisdiction Act. This act provides, at least in theory, that enacting states recognize the validity of court rulings handed down in other states that have enacted it and provides for certain important jurisdictional and procedural uniformity and reciprocity. In addition, many states have made it a crime for anyone to remove a child from a state to avoid a court determination of custody or in defiance of a court award of custody, and Congress enacted the Parental Kidnapping Prevention Act of 1980 (P.L. 96–611), which makes available the Federal Parent Locator Service for the purpose of locating parents who flee with their children.[16]

Domestic violence. Although most domestic violence is technically a violation of criminal law, the police and the courts have long done little to protect members of a household against the violence of one another. In the last decade, however, the legislatures of all states addressed the matter of domestic violence, and all but one state passed legislation designed to deal with the problem. Although the statutes differ from state to state, they all mandate greater involvement by the courts and the police in domestic violence. The central issues involved are (1) whether the state should intrude on the family and, if so, to what extent, (2) whether implementation of the new statutes is possible without additional resources being granted to the courts and police, and (3) whether the police are the proper agents of government to intervene in domestic violence. The question of the enforceability of court orders in domestic situations is also important, as is the question of the extent to which the victimized spouse should have a role in shaping the orders of the court or the punishment that a court might assign to one who commits domestic violence. This area suggests the need for increased involvement of social workers as agents for the court in other ways.[17]

The mentally ill and developmentally disabled. Laws affecting the mentally ill and the developmentally disabled are in a developing state. In *Rouse* v. *Cameron*, an American court first recognized the right of an involuntarily committed mentally ill patient to receive treatment for his illness— above and beyond mere custodial care.[18] In *Wyatt* v. *Stickney* and two connected cases, a federal district court ordered state hospitals serving mentally ill and mentally retarded patients to initiate treatment or release them.[19] The court also approved a list of procedures meant to assure patients of more than mere custodial care.

If mentally ill patients and the developmentally disabled have a right to treatment, what range of treatment modalities are they entitled to? Does a patient have a right to refuse treatment? Under what circumstances? Can the patient sue for damages rather than for mere release from a hospital or the right not to receive certain treatment? These questions are largely unanswered.

Generally an individual has a right to decide whether to submit to medical treatment, a right long recognized in the doctrine of informed consent. Nevertheless, in the case of the involuntarily committed mentally ill, many courts have held that mental patients were ipso facto incompetent to participate in medical treatment decisions, equating civil commitment with a determination of legal incompetency—two different matters.

Recently, the courts have increasingly distinguished commitability from incompetence. Thus, in *Winters* v. *Miller*, the federal court of appeals held that civil commitment did not even raise a presumption of legal incompetence, and other courts since then have expressed the same view.[20] This suggests the need, in many states, for separate determinations regarding commitment and incompetency. Are hospitals that treat the mentally ill likely to become involved in seemingly endless procedural and legal questions, not to mention uncertainty regarding the limits of treatment modalities that professionals can decide?

The case of *Rogers* v. *Okin* does not answer all questions, but it is instructive.[21] It involved a suit in which patients not adjudicated incompetent alleged that they had been forcibly medicated with antipsychotic drugs in violation of their constitutional right of privacy. The trial court held for the patients. The appeals court, however, remanded the case to the trial court, recognizing that although due process rights of patients must be recognized, it also must be recognized that medication frequently is necessary to prevent patients from doing violence to themselves or to others. This case clearly tries to balance patients' rights against the need for protection of patients and others. It also recognizes that professionals need discretion in making difficult judgments regarding individual patients. It does not, however, resolve the many questions that still need to be addressed, and courts will struggle with related cases for years to come before the legal issues involved become reasonably well defined and answered.[22]

Rights of prisoners. Persons confined in America's prisons have a number of important rights, including the right to communicate with an attorney and even a right of access to at least a minimally acceptable law library. Although prisoners enjoy constitutional protections that include protection against cruel and unusual punishment and a guarantee of due process, courts frequently are reluctant to interfere with the administrative discretion of prison officials. The most fertile ground for changes in the law affecting prisoners are (1) a prisoner's right to protection against homosexual or other assaults from other prisoners, (2) the question of whether a prisoner has a right to be protected from certain common conditions in prisons, such as overcrowding of inmates, and (3), perhaps the most likely area for change, the question of whether a state can constitutionally deny a prisoner certain rights enjoyed by other citizens but that are not reasonably related to a prisoner's crime or to any state interest, such as the rights to vote or to drive an automobile.[23]

The weight and mass of law in America change slowly. Still, the somewhat hyperbolic assertion sometimes made by lobbyists and legislators to the effect that no person's life or property are safe so long as the legislature is in session correctly suggests that American law can be changed and often does change in dramatic and sometimes fundamental ways.

Social workers, more than most other professionals, can play a decisive role in changing the law as it affects their clients. Knowledge of social problems and of how such problems affect citizens of a state or community are important attributes of social workers. This knowledge, combined with professional education and experience and a knowledge of community groups and organizations, places social workers in a position to be uniquely effective advocates for reform of the law.

As society continues to become more complex, the need for social workers to devote more of their time, energy, and abilities to being advocates for changes in the law will become even greater than it is at the present. This is the fundamental challenge—and opportunity—that increasingly exists for every social worker.

GEORGE R. SHARWELL

Notes and References

1. "Corporations," 18 *American Jurisprudence 2nd;* and Carol M. Rose, *Some Emerging Issues in Legal Liability of Children's Agencies* (New York: Child Welfare League of America, 1978).

2. "Adoption," 2 *American Jurisprudence 2nd.*

3. Ibid.

4. Roberta Gottesman, *The Child and the Law* (St. Paul, Minn.: West Publishing Co., 1981), chapter 2.

5. Susanna J. Wilson, *Confidentiality in Social Work: Issues and Principles* (New York: Free Press, 1978).

6. Paul and Dorothy Weinberger, "Legal Regulation in Perspective," *Social Work*, 7 (January 1962), pp. 67–75.

7. Wilson, *Confidentiality in Social Work.*

8. Tarasoff v. Regents of the University of California, 551 P.2d 334, 131 Cal. Rpter. 14 (1976); and McIntosh v. Milano, 168 N.J. Supter. 466, 403 A.2d 500 (1979).

9. Henry C. Black, *Black's Law Dictionary*, Joseph R. Nolan and Michael J. Connolly, eds.

(5th ed.; St. Paul, Minn.: West Publishing Co., 1979).

10. *Code of Ethics, NASW Policy Statement No. 1* (Washington, D.C.: National Association of Social Workers, 1980). See reprint in this volume.

11. Louis N. Massery II, and James E. Rooks, Jr., *Handling the Professional Liability Case* (Boston, Mass.: Association of Trial Lawyers of America, 1976), section 4.3.

12. For a lucid discussion of bankruptcy, see Marjorie Girth, *Bankruptcy Options for the Consumer Debtor* (New York: Practising Law Institute, 1981).

13. Gottesman, *The Child and the Law,* chapter 5.

14. Joseph Ballard et al., *Special Education in America: Its Legal and Governmental Foundation* (Reston, Va.: Council for Exceptional Children, 1982).

15. Gottesman, *The Child and the Law,* chapter 8.

16. Sanford N. Katz, "Legal Remedies for Child Snatching," *Family Law Quarterly*, 15 (Summer 1981), pp. 103–248.

17. William L. Prosser, *Cases and Materials on Torts* (Mineola, N.Y.: Foundation Press, 1982), chapter 2.

18. Rouse v. Cameron, 373 F.2d 451 (D.C. Cir. 1966).

19. Wyatt v. Stickney, 325 F. Supp. 781 (M.D. Aia, N.D. 1971).

20. Winters v. Miller, 446 F.2d. 65 (2d Cir. 1971).

21. Rogers v. Okin, 634 F.2d 650 (1st Cir. 1980).

22. Bruce Dennis, *Disabled Persons and the Law: State Legislature Issues* (New York: Plenum Press, 1982); and David B. Wexler, *Mental Health Law: Major Issues* (New York, Plenum Press, 1981).

23. James J. Gobert, *Rights of Prisoners* (Colorado Springs, Colo.: Shepards/McGraw-Hill, 1981); and Alvin J. Bronstein and Philip J. Hirschkop, *Prisoners' Rights* (New York: Practising Law Institute, 1979).

MINORITIES: PEOPLE OF COLOR

The term "minority" is now applied to many more groups than those traditionally encompassed by it. This development has important implications for social policy and for the social work profession and has prompted the introduction of the term "people of color" to identify the populations most affected by racism and the poverty it engendered.[1]

During the 1970s many changes took place in the population of the United States, changes not merely in the composition of the population as a result of the immigration of new minority peoples, but also in the number of groups who, although their oppression was not new, began during that period to define themselves as "minorities." The latter included women, the handicapped, gay men, lesbians, the elderly, and all people with Spanish surnames, not only Puerto Ricans and Mexican Americans. This trend occurred largely because government resources allocation policies entitled groups with minority status to remediation of socioeconomic disadvantages and access to opportunity structures. The new minorities borrowed both ideology and strategy from the traditional racial minorities, notably the black civil rights movement, the Chicano farm workers' struggle, and Indian tribes' insistence on treaty rights.

Defining "Minority"

The growth in the number of groups claiming minority status occurred during a period when political ideology and monetary policy became more liberal, permitting the system to accommodate the thrust for employment opportunities. The number of new minorities grew rapidly and without a concomitant examination of the varying types and levels of oppression. Consequently, the term "minority" lost meaning, and the strategies for resolving minority problems became increasingly numerous and complex. As the political

and economic system shifted from the growth posture of the sixties and early seventies to the tight monetary policies and limited opportunity structure of the late seventies and early eighties, ironically those most affected were, once again, the groups historically entwined in the racism-poverty matrix, those known collectively as people of color. At the same time that new groups justified their claims for services on the basis of minority status, remediation programs for disadvantaged groups were attacked and dismantled, and their funding was curtailed. This contraction of resources forced the social work profession to reexamine the meaning of "minority."

Defining "minority" is difficult in the absence of scientific criteria or formulas. There is no clear meaning of "minority" or "racial minority"; nor is there a consistent pattern of usage for these terms. Race, a highly complex subject, has traditionally been associated with minorities in America and even when approached from abstract or theoretical perspectives, the political, social, and economic implications for the populations involved overpower any neutral conceptualizations.

This dilemma is highlighted in the *Harvard Encyclopedia of American Ethnic Groups*, which involves a comprehensive analysis of 101 ethnic groups but in the end contributes to the blurring of distinctions between race and ethnicity.[2] That encyclopedia has been criticized for overlooking the fundamental distinctions between differences among America's major racial stocks and the differences among various ethnic groups, distinctions that have had and continue to have significant influence on the development and structure of this society.[3] Its effort to develop a "uniform, comprehensive system" of group classification without giving due emphasis to these differences results in a bias of a different order and misrepresents the stratifications of power, differentiation, and stereotyping that are pervasive in this society.

Privilege does exist, and it accumulates from generation to generation. So does institutionalized advantage. Even if a scientific definition of race could be agreed on and race were demonstrated to be insignificant in determining human differences, this would not change the status of those suffering the consequences of generations of discrimination and oppression based on race. The socioeconomic condition of millions of Americans would still be found to be influenced by color, which is race associated. The impact of the Harvard work should not be minimized; it will influence thought and public policy for years. But despite that encyclopedia's valuable information, people of color must be concerned about the uses to which it might be put. Racists have always used color consciousness for discriminatory ends. Now social scientists and social workers must be alert to the possible misuse of "color blindness" as a way to avoid remediation of the effects of past discrimination.

Definitions of "minority" based on proportionate numbers are also misleading. They are neither logical nor functional because, as in South Africa, a numerical minority possessing control of wealth and institutions can negate the legitimate wishes of the majority for freedom and human dignity.

Other possible definitions of "minority" apply such criteria as socioeconomic conditions and cultural acceptance. Both these criteria locate people of color at the lowest end of the spectrum of power and advantage. Regardless of the indicators used, blacks, American Indians and Native Alaskans, Mexican Americans, and Puerto Ricans are clearly identified as minorities.[4] It is precisely this identification that has implications for social policy.

Because of the profession's traditional policy of including all at-risk populations in the category of those deserving remediation, the need to explore definitions and to distinguish among levels and types of oppression still does not come easily to social workers. Ethicist McGuire has posited a helpful set of criteria for determining whether a group is so disadvantaged as to need preference: (1) no alternatives to enforced preferences are available; (2) prejudice against the group has reached the level of depersonalization; (3) bias against the group is not private or narrowly located, but is rather entrenched in the culture and distributive systems of the society; and (4) the members of the victim groups are visible and lack an avenue of escape from the disempowered status.[5]

Groups in America that meet all these criteria include blacks, American Indians, Mexicans, and Puerto Ricans. Women were also cited by McGuire as meeting all of the criteria. In keeping with the focus of this discussion on people of color, women, per se, are excluded. Yet, it should not be inferred that problems do not confront women. As this author has stated elsewhere:

> The situation for women of color is worse and more hopeless than for white women. White women may have been excluded from the financial and power centers, but many have enjoyed derived power and material gains in their roles as daughters, wives, and mothers and thus are reluctant to face change. Although the problem of sexism is still prevalent, changes are occurring that have enabled white women to move well ahead of all people of color. The double income earned by white families widens this gap. Thus, women of color are in multiple jeopardy, facing as they do the combined forces of racism, sexism, and in many cases, poverty.
>
> What this means is that more white women are in a socially advantageous position. Because of their individual and collective relationships to the power structure, they are able to exercise leverage that people of color, regardless of their gender, do not have.[6]

Sociodemographics

People of color account for roughly 20 percent of the U.S. population—a distribution of 12 percent black, 6 percent Hispanic, and 2 percent American Indian, Asian American, and other nonwhites. Not included in these statistics are recent immigrants, such as Southeast Asians, Cubans, and Haitians. People of color increased their numbers faster in the past decade than the general population, a pattern that is expected to continue in view of this group's younger age structure and rate of immigration. The median age of the white population was slightly over 31 years; for blacks it was 24.9; Hispanics 23.2; Asian 28.6; and American Indian, Eskimo, and Aleut 23.0. Blacks and Hispanics are significantly younger than Asians, whose age structure corresponds more closely to that of whites.[7]

Geographically, populations of color are concentrated largely in the South, where roughly 50 percent of the nation's blacks reside, and in the West, where most Mexicans, Asians, and American Indians live. A major shift occurred in the 1970s when, reversing the postwar pattern of blacks moving from the South to the North and West, more blacks moved South, as did other Americans. Puerto Ricans dispersed more during that decade, with less than 50 percent living in New York State in 1980 compared to 64 percent in 1970. The Mexican American population, which nearly doubled between 1970 and 1980, also dispersed and became the second largest minority group in the country. In contrast to the pattern established in the 1960s, these groups moved to metropolitan areas rather than central cities, although over half the blacks and Hispanics still reside in cities.[8] This has a bearing on occupational upgrading. For example, during the seventies, blacks living in suburban areas benefited more from occupational upgrading than did those who resided in cities.[9]

The distribution of people of color has several implications for the states and central cities in which they are concentrated. It could influence election outcomes, service delivery patterns, income maintenance programs, and the utilization of housing and other city services. As the New Federalism of the Reagan Administration shifts fiscal and allocative responsibility for programs from federal to state auspices,

the weight of these distribution patterns will be felt more dramatically by some states than others. The impact on the South and the central cities will be great because a high portion of the poor, especially people of color, live in those areas.

Socioeconomic Conditions

A critical factor affecting people of color in recent years was the election in 1980 of a president who reversed more than fifty years of development in social welfare. Although conservative policies had been initiated earlier, President Reagan was more persuasive and successful in convincing Americans that these programs were unnecessary, even wasteful. In a 1982 editorial entitled "Milking the Poor," the *Wall Street Journal* pointed out that programs benefiting the poor—rather than programs reflecting interests of the middle class, such as social security, Medicare, and certain business subsidies—had been successful targets for the Reagan Administration's budget cuts.[10] Although the Comprehensive Education and Training Act (CETA), Medicaid, food stamps, and other programs that were cut have a larger number of white recipients, the impact of the cuts will be felt more severely by people of color, who have a disproportionate dependence on these programs. Likewise the reduction in the federal work force necessitated by the program cuts had a greater impact on minorities because for them government employment was a major route to the middle class.

Assuming that income is a solid indicator of socioeconomic condition, the status of people of color vis-à-vis the majority white population can be demonstrated statistically. In constant dollars, median family income in the United States remained at about the same level between 1975 and 1980, although income was 53 percent higher ($21,020) in 1980 than in 1975 ($12,710). The median 1980 income for white families was $21,900 whereas for black families it was $12,670 and for Hispanic families, $14,270. Although the decrease was minor in real terms for white and Hispanic families, it reached 6 percent for black families.[11]

The strong emergence of the two-career family during the 1970s increased the gap in income between white families and families of color. This phenomenon, together with the traditional problems of discrimination in employment practices and an increase in the number of families among people of color that were headed by women, put them well behind other families. Traditionally, poor women of color worked to augment the earnings of husbands, fathers, and sons. Consequently, because they were already in the labor force, their income has not produced the same increase in family earnings as has that of white women.[12]

During the period 1964–77, there was a decrease of 15 percent in the number of multiple-earner black families, the result of an increase in the number of single-mother black families and in the entry of non-black women into the labor force. At the same time, there was a 4-percent increase in multiple-earner Hispanic families and a 13-percent increase among white families. An even greater setback took place in the number of black families with no adult earners—a 50-percent increase compared to increases of 29 percent for Hispanics and 34 percent for whites.[13]

The rise in single-parent and no-earner families has had an obvious bearing on the increase in the number of people of color living below the poverty line. The concentration of the poor in families with a female head was clearly demonstrated among blacks, for whom the number increased from 740,000 (59 percent) in 1969 to 1.3 million (71 percent) in 1980.[14] Out-of-wedlock births are increasing among all teenagers and are alarmingly high for blacks—86 percent of the births compared to 36 percent for whites.

During the last decade, there has been a retrenchment in the effort to eradicate poverty. In both 1969 and 1979, roughly 12 percent of the population was below the poverty line. In 1980, 13 percent were in poverty, an increase from 26.1 million to 29.3 million in one year, representing the fastest rise since 1959 when poverty data first became available. The distribution corresponds to prior trends: blacks, 32 percent; Hispanics, 26 percent; and whites, 10 percent.[15]

Unemployment was a major factor in the lower socioeconomic condition of people of color. From 1970 to 1981, the unemployment status of "blacks and other races" increased from 8.2 percent to 14.3 percent; for whites the increase was from 4.5 percent to 6.7 percent.[16] In 1982, unemployment among black youths was over 50 percent, reducing the earning power of families and adding many social costs to communities.[17]

In summary, disturbing socioeconomic trends point out that Americans, and especially people of color, are worse off than they were a decade ago. The increases in female-headed households, out-of-wedlock births, and unemployment among black adult males and teenagers have all taken a toll on families of color. Without major federal intervention, now an unpopular topic, prospects for the future are not good because, historically, the private sector has not viewed communities of people of color as attractive areas for investment.

Education

Any discussion of potential improvement in the economic condition of people of color must examine their opportunity for educational achievement, which has always been viewed as a path "up and out" of poverty. A disturbing fact is the difficulty in securing even basic education for the young of this group, leaving them illiterate and unprepared for participation in the job market. For Hispanic youths, the lack of proficiency in English often further exacerbates their inability to compete for jobs.

In the future the competency of those youths who are fortunate enough to finish school will be increasingly challenged. One example of this is occurring in Massachusetts, where the state board of regents is considering a proposal to tighten admissions standards to state colleges and universities through heavier reliance on Scholastic Aptitude Test scores and class rank and more rigorous high school requirements.[18] Competency measures have traditionally posed problems for people of color because of a variety of factors, including problems with the composition of the test and with the delivery of education and community support systems.

Although the total number of youths in school declined in the United States, black and Hispanic adults increased their participation. The rate of blacks age 25 to 34 completing high school increased faster than for whites of that age group. During the 1970s, the number of blacks enrolled in college more than doubled, an increase that occurred mostly in the early seventies. In 1981, blacks accounted for 10 percent of the college population. Although this upward swing in college enrollment is positive and although the 22-percent rate of blacks completing one to three years compares favorably with the rate among whites, the proportion of young adults who had four years of college was only 12 percent for blacks and 24 percent for whites.[19]

The Reagan Administration's cuts in funds allocated for student loans and financial aid will have an impact on the college enrollment of all students, but particularly people of color. Most students in public institutions who receive aid are from low-income and moderate-income families, with half below the poverty level. These families cannot afford to pick up the slack in federal aid. Prior to establishing final levels of appropriation for student aid for fiscal years 1982 and 1983, Congress was informed that families contributed roughly $180 to black students, $142 to Hispanic students, and $600 to white students in public four-year institutions.[20] In addition, "minorities" are concentrated in two-year colleges rather than in universities where public support of programs is more generous and well established.[21] Consequently, the poorest and most disadvantaged

students are matriculating in the "poorest programs."

Even for those people of color who complete college, the degree has not translated into earnings comparable to those received by whites.[22] Likewise, it is clear that this population group will not be prepared for the high-technology and health professions that will be in demand in the future. Except among Asian Americans, few people of color pursue studies in science and technology.[23] Rather, they have traditionally concentrated in service fields, where pay continues to be less than in industry and where there is now a prediction of turbulence. In education, for example, the lower birth rate has reduced the demand for teachers, and in social work, cuts have reduced job opportunities. Laborers who had finally begun to move into higher positions in the "smoke stack" industries will have difficulty developing new skills necessary for employment as those industries shift to high technology. In the early 1980s, as industry went through a phase of reorganization and technological modernization, not only was there no government impetus for programs to incorporate people of color, but affirmative action also underwent a steady erosion.

Affirmative Action

Affirmative action is basically a moderate form of social redistribution designed to correct continued discrimination. Attempts to dismantle such programs include several legal challenges, of which the *Regents of the University of California* v. *Bakke* is perhaps the most widely known. Although the Supreme Court upheld the constitutional validity of race-conscious *voluntary* programs, the decision represented a moral setback for people of color, who had looked to the court for relief from discrimination and injustice since the 1954 *Brown* v. *Board of Education* decision outlawing the separate-but-equal doctrine.

In a recent decision, *Bob Jones University* v. *United States* (together with *Goldsboro Christian Schools, Inc.* v. *United*

States), which was argued October 12, 1983 and decided May 24, 1983, the Court ruled in an eight-to-one vote against a stance posited by the Reagan Administration, which questioned whether Congress had given the Internal Revenue Service (IRS) authority through the tax codes to help "prevent" racial discrimination by denying tax exempt status to schools that practice racial discrimination.

Bob Jones University and Goldsboro Christian Schools, Inc., practiced racial discrimination on the basis of religious doctrine and sought tax exemption under the Internal Revenue Code of 1954, Section 501 (c) (3). The question became a public policy issue and one of major concern to people of color when the Reagan Administration challenged the position of the IRS. The Court's action, which represents a judicial defeat for the Reagan Administration, upheld the IRS policy, which had been in effect since 1970. In that year,

> a three judge District Court for the District of Columbia, issued a preliminary injunction which prohibited the I.R.S. from granting tax exempt status to private schools in Mississippi that discriminated as to admissions on the basis of race. (Green v. Kennedy, 309 F. Supp. (D.D.C.) app. discussed sub nom. Cannon v. Green, 598, U.S. 956 (1970).[24]

After the ruling, the "I.R.S. concluded that it could no longer legally justify allowing tax exempt status (under Sec. 501 (c) (3) to private schools which practice racial discrimination."[25] The IRS also "announced that it could not 'treat gifts to such schools as charitable deductions for income tax purposes, under Sec. 170.' "[26] All private schools were notified of the policy change by the IRS on November 30, 1970. The policy was "applicable to all private schools in the United States at all levels of education."[27]

In its opinion, the Supreme Court pointed out that the IRS had not exceeded its authority and that its interpretation was "wholly consistent with what Congress, the Executive, and the Courts had previously declared."[28] The Court further declared that

the Government's fundamental, overriding interest in eradicating racial discrimination in education substantially outweighs whatever burden denial of tax benefits places on petitioners' exercise of their religious beliefs. Petitioners' asserted interests cannot be accommodated with that compelling governmental interest, and no less restrictive means are available to achieve the governmental interest."[29]

Affirmative action was also attacked in *Weber* v. *Kaiser Aluminum Co.* (argued March 28, 1979, and decided June 27, 1979), in which race was an issue in training programs, and in *Fullilove* v. *Klutznick* (argued November 27, 1979, and decided July 2, 1980), which involved the awarding of government contracts. In both cases, the Court upheld race as a valid consideration.[30] From a legal frame of reference, these decisions are—over the long term—potential facilitators of affirmative action. In the present milieu, however, they must be implemented by staff of an Administration that has yet to demonstrate support for affirmative action. It would be unwise to underestimate the strength of the executive branch's capacity to thwart judicial and legislative intent, which can be awesome, particularly if there is philosophical disagreement in relation to a program.

A major argument against affirmative action is that this country subscribes to the principle of inclusiveness and that all who prepare well and work hard can participate in its socioeconomic rewards. The enslavement and subsequent caste system for blacks, the exploitation of Chinese, race-conscious immigration laws, the subjugation of Mexican Americans, and centuries of wars with Indians are viewed as historical deviations from an otherwise just system.[31] Tied to the inclusiveness principle is the notion that affirmative acts create reverse discrimination and lead to a backlash against people of color when they are perceived as competing with whites for resources. In the context of a declining economy with a scarcity of employment opportunities and a large supply of labor, tension has risen and has produced an increase in the activities of the Ku Klux Klan and other vigilante groups.

Political Power

The cumulative impact on individuals and families of the conditions so far described in this article has caused people of color to examine, once again, the need for political action. For years, the distribution of people of color in certain states and central cities suggested the potential for increased political power. This was one reason the Voting Rights Act of 1965 was controversial upon initial enactment and subsequent extensions, including 1982. For example, blacks constitute more than 30 percent of the population in Mississippi and South Carolina and from 20 to 30 percent in five other southern states. Similarly, Hispanics constitute 6 percent of the population nationwide but 36 percent in New Mexico, 21 percent in Texas, and more than 15 percent in California and Colorado. Minorities also make up almost half the population in New York City.[32]

Although these groups have yet to realize fully the potential of their numbers and to translate their latent power into effective action, some encouraging signs of change have occurred. In 1982, people of color, notably blacks, helped reverse a twenty-year trend of declining voter participation in midterm elections. They were the decisive factor in the defeat of several conservatives in the South and helped elect more moderate candidates as governors in several states including Massachusetts, New York, and Texas. Their own representation increased in state legislatures and in the House of Representatives. There were also major defeats, including that of Mayor Thomas Bradley of Los Angeles, who narrowly lost the gubernatorial race in California. Still, the Joint Center for Political Studies, a Washington, D.C., firm that monitors and reports on voting behavior, referred to the respect that has been gained recently by these new voters. For example, the gains at the polls were translated into

beginning initiatives for national programs to address employment problems.

The Profession's Response

Social workers have responded to the special problems of people of color and appreciate their need for social justice. The goals of this collective population group—a numerical minority in this country but part of the majority worldwide—are congruent with those of the profession. The alliance social workers have provided through difficult economic and political times during the past decade helped to crystalize the issues facing this country's traditional minorities. Social workers supported many of the forces and candidates for political change. They also spoke out against cuts in social programs. The future of both people of color and social workers is interwoven in the fabric of this society.

Sensitivity to the needs of all deprived, excluded, or discriminated against groups has always been intrinsic to social work ethics and values. The profession must become aware of the differences, both subtle and gross, in the types and levels of discrimination and of the discrete needs that result from these differences, and this awareness requires continued analysis of generalizations about "minorities" and careful attention to the unique situation of people of color. It is a historical anomaly that most American reform movements since the 1840s have begun with this recognition but have quickly expanded to include a variety of worthy causes, invariably leaving people of color back on the bottom rung of the ladder. That this cannot be mere coincidence has implications for every orientation in social work, from psychodynamics to social activism.

JUNE GARY HOPPS

Notes and References

1. For an earlier presentation of similar data and viewpoints, see "Special Issue on People of Color," *Social Work,* 27 (January 1982).

2. Stephan Thernstrom et al., *Harvard Ency-*

clopedia of American Ethnic Groups (Cambridge, Mass.: Harvard University Press, 1981).

3. M. G. Smith, "Ethnicity and Ethnic Groups in America: The View from Harvard," *Journal of Libertarian Studies*, 5 (January 1982), p. 10.

4. Juan Longres, "Minority Groups: An Interest-Group Perspective," *Social Work*, 27 (January 1982), pp. 7–14.

5. Daniel C. McGuire, *A New American Justice* (Garden City, N.Y.: Doubleday & Co., 1980), pp. 129–130.

6. June G. Hopps, "Oppression Based on Color," *Social Work,* 27 (January 1982), p. 4.

7. *Population Profile of the United States* (Washington, D.C.: Bureau of the Census, U.S. Department of Commerce, 1981), p. 15.

8. Ibid., pp. 17–18.

9. Diane Nilsen Westcott, "Blacks in the 1970's: Did They Scale the Job Ladder?" *Monthly Labor Review,* 105 (June 1982), pp. 33–34.

10. *Wall Street Journal,* July 13, 1982, p. 32.

11. *Population Profile of the United States,* p. 47.

12. Harriet McAdoo, "Demographic Trends for People of Color," *Social Work*, 27 (January 1982), p. 17.

13. Ibid., p. 17.

14. *Population Profile of the United States*, p. 42.

15. Ibid., p. 53.

16. Ibid., p. 42.

17. Newly immigrated Cambodians, Laotians, and Vietnamese who had arrived in this country between 1975 and 1977 and were in the labor force were less likely to become unemployed than others in the labor force. See Daniel Montero and Ismael Dieppa, "Resettling Vietnamese Refugees: The Service Agency's Role," *Social Work*, 27 (January 1982), p. 78.

18. Muriel Cohen, "Regents Slow Campaign for Admissions Standards," *Boston Globe*, February 20, 1983, Sec. B, pp. 21–23.

19. *Population Profile of the United States,* pp. 33–34.

20. "U.S. Student Assistance Serves the Truly Needy; Aid Cuts Hurt Low-Income Enrollment, Study Says," *Higher Education and National Affairs,* September 17, 1982, p. 6.

21. McAdoo, "Demographic Trends for People of Color," pp. 19–20.

22. See, for example, "Table 51. Education and Total Money Income in 1980—Persons 25 Years Old and Over by Age, Race and Sex," *U.S. Bureau of the Census, Current Population Reports,* Series P-60, No. 132, *Money Income of Households, Families and Persons in the United States, 1980* (Washington, D.C.: U.S. Government Printing Office, 1982).

23. McAdoo, "Demographic Trends for People of Color," p. 20.

24. Bob Jones University, Petitioner v. United States No. 81-3 and Goldsboro Christian Schools, Inc. No. 81-1, Petitioner v. United States. In writs of certiori to the United States Court of Appeals for the Fourth Circuit, May 24, 1982, p. 2.

25. Ibid. p. 2.

26. Ibid.

27. Ibid.

28. Supreme Court of the United States. Bob Jones University v. United States, No. 81-3, together with Goldsboro Christian Schools, Inc. No. 81-1, May 24, 1983, Syllabus II (slip opinion).

29. Ibid., Syllabi II and III (slip opinion).

30. United Steel Workers v. Weber, 99 S. Ct., *Supreme Court Reporter* (1981), pp. 2721–2753; and Fullilove v. Klutznick, 100 S. Ct., *Supreme Court Reporter* (1981), pp. 2758 and 2814.

31. McGuire, *A New American Justice,* p. 11.

32. *Population Profile of the United States*, pp. 5–6; and Robert D. McFadden, "New York of 70's Portrayed by U.S. Data as a City in Flux," *New York Times*, February 27, 1982, p. 28.

NATIONAL PROFESSIONAL ORGANIZATIONS: COUNCIL ON SOCIAL WORK EDUCATION; NATIONAL ASSOCIATION OF SOCIAL WORKERS

COUNCIL ON SOCIAL WORK EDUCATION

The first national organization concerned exclusively with social work education, the Association of Training Schools for Professional Social Work, was established in 1919 by representatives of seventeen schools of social work in the United States and Canada. The name was shortly changed to the American Association of Schools of Social Work (AASSW). In 1927 AASSW first formulated educational standards for schools that sought admission to the association, and over the years standards were developed and expanded in an effort to ensure that the schools would prepare students to meet the changing requirements of practice. In 1931 AASSW, in cooperation with the American Association of Social Workers, made the landmark decision that professional education for social work would require two academic years of graduate-level study and would culminate in a master's degree in social work (MSW). This policy set the course of professional education in social work for the next forty years.

In 1942 a second national organization of schools of social work, the National Association of Schools of Social Administration (NASSA), was founded by a number of state institutions of higher education, most of which had a strong concern for preparing students for public welfare practice.

NASSA was composed of both graduate and undergraduate social work education programs, as compared to AASSW, which was composed of graduate programs only. The public welfare practice sector was extremely interested in baccalaureate-trained staff because the public assistance agencies utilized this staff level in direct practice in a significant fashion. In addition, NASSA was composed of master's programs that were primarily one year in duration, as opposed to AASSW, in which the two-year program was the primary model.

The appearance of NASSA meant that there were two national organizations claiming to represent social work education, both providing similar membership services, including accreditation and the development of partially conflicting accreditation standards. This situation resulted in sufficient confusion so that in 1946 the National Council on Social Work Education (NCSWE) was established to resolve the difficulties.

NCSWE was established by a voluntary group representing the professional associations in social work as well as major governmental and voluntary agencies. Although governmental agencies such as the National Institute of Mental Health and the Children's Bureau participated in the effort to form NCSWE, there was no specific governmental body that "forced" the two organizations to come together. A national study, the Hollis-Taylor Report, was undertaken by NCSWE funded by a grant from the Carnegie Foundation. This resulted in the creation of the Council on Social Work Education (CSWE) in 1952 as the successor to the two competing groups.

Accreditation for specialization in social work education was initiated by the specialized membership organizations such as those representing medical and psychiatric social work. This continued even after AASSW was organized and began its systematic accreditation of schools. The accreditation process began in 1927 when, as mentioned previously, the schools in the association agreed to formulate and maintain educational standards and to apply these to all new schools seeking admission to membership.

When CSWE was established in 1952, the professional associations clearly conceded that this new organization should assume the national responsibility for accrediting graduate social work education. The overall responsibility for professional social work education thus was assigned to CSWE.

According to its bylaws, the purpose of CSWE is to provide the leadership and service required

> to assure an adequate supply of appropriately educated professional, paraprofessional and technical social work personnel needed to plan, administer, provide, and improve social services and other related human services. The Council shall be concerned with the quantity and quality of social work education at all levels . . . . [CSWE shall] carry out its purpose through accreditation as well as through other standard-setting activities, consultation, conferences and workshops, research, publications, special projects, and through other means.[1]

Governance

Governance of CSWE is vested in a national Board of Directors composed of three officers and twenty-one members who serve three-year terms. This group is elected by members of the House of Delegates and is structured to represent the various constituencies such as graduate school deans and directors, baccalaureate program directors, undergraduate and graduate faculties, and practice agency representatives. The Board of Directors formulates specific policy necessary to manage the affairs of the council as a corporate body. A House of Delegates composed of 235 elected representatives of constituency groups meets annually and establishes the general goals, reviews program activities, recommends program priorities, determines the dues schedule, elects the Board of Directors, and approves changes to the bylaws. The Commission on Accreditation is responsible for the ongoing activity of the council's accreditation responsibilities. All commission and committee members are appointed by the council president. Other standing bodies are the commissions on educational planning, minority groups, and the role and

status of women. Other committees may be established and terminated by the Board of Directors, as needed. The House of Delegates establishes the classes and requirements of membership in the council. Members may be either individuals or organizations.

Membership

Full members. As of July 1982 CSWE had 2,465 full members and 1,404 affiliate members for a total of 3,869. On July 1, 1983, there were 88 accredited graduate programs plus 5 in candidacy and 343 accredited undergraduate programs plus 6 in candidacy. Other organizational members include public and private social welfare agencies, practitioner organizations, and related voluntary and public organizations concerned with educational preparation for the human services.

Affiliate members. Any interested person or organization can be an affiliate member. Such members include educational institutions that are interested in social work education but that do not meet accreditation requirements: agencies, organizations, and institutions not otherwise eligible for full membership; professional libraries and associations; and international organizations.

Accreditation

The function of accreditation is officially assigned to CSWE by the national, nongovernmental Council on Post-secondary Accreditation and by the accreditation and institutional eligibility staff of the U.S. Department of Education. The CSWE Commission on Accreditation is a permanent, semiautonomous body. Its members are appointed for a three-year term by the president of CSWE according to the bylaws, which provide that of the twenty-five members, sixteen must be full-time faculty in accredited schools and programs of social work. Seven members are appointed as members-at-large representing other constituencies. Two members are appointed as citizen representatives.

Prior to July 1, 1974, CSWE accredited only graduate schools of social work. Since then undergraduate programs have been eligible to apply for accreditation; if accredited, they become full members of CSWE. A well-developed set of standards establishes the criteria for accreditation and guides the accreditation process at both educational levels. Each institution's accreditation is reviewed every seven years.

Accreditation offers schools and programs a number of advantages. The most important of these is an assurance of having met minimum standards for the quality of the educational process. The quality assurance functions as a consumer protection device for prospective students. Accreditation also affords eligibility to apply for certain publicly funded grants. The school or program is eligible to apply for governmental grants only if accredited. This means, in fact, that only those students enrolled in accredited schools or programs are eligible for such financial assistance as these grants provide.

Graduation from an accredited MSW or BSW program is a criterion for acceptance into the National Association of Social Workers (NASW), the professional association for social work. A similar requirement determines eligibility for taking the state examination in all the states that have licensing and certification laws for social work. In addition, graduates of accredited undergraduate programs can apply for advanced standing in MSW programs, which in some cases enables the BSW graduate to receive the MSW degree in less than two years.

The effect of accreditation on the quality of education among the many and diverse institutions that sponsor programs is being studied. This is a difficult and time-consuming task, but it appears certain that accreditation can improve and strengthen many schools and programs and also help eliminate the inadequate ones.

Accreditation has been well accepted by the social work profession. It prevents the development of inadequate educational programs, ensures quality, and stimulates improvement. Although accreditation imposes certain limitations on schools and faculties, it assures better programs than might otherwise have been developed. The limitations include the requirement that educational programs adhere to a national curriculum policy statement and that certain aspects of the educational program structure such as off-campus and part-time programs also are subject to restrictions for the purpose of assuring minimum quality. The fear that accreditation would stifle initiative and experimentation or promote uniformity has proved unfounded. Any responsible accrediting body must compromise between the two values of complete academic freedom and the guarantee of minimum quality.

In 1981, the Board of Directors of CSWE adopted a plan to strengthen and expand the council's program in areas beyond accreditation. In the process of development, with implementation planned for 1985, is a series of program activities that will come under the rubric of The National Center for Social Work Education. Specifically, these programs include:

1. A national faculty academy to further develop and expand educational skill and knowledge of current faculty members as well as to provide an opportunity for preparation of new teachers.

2. A national institute for administrators in social work education. This will provide seminars for newly appointed deans and baccalaureate program directors, directors of field practicum, and admissions program directors.

3. A national center for social work research. This unit will attempt to increase the capability of social work research production in colleges and universities throughout the nation.

Issues

A revision of the national Curriculum Policy Statement (CPS) took place in 1983. CPS provides guidelines for the development of curricula on both the MSW and BSW levels of professional education. The accreditation standards were revised simultaneously. Both new documents were scheduled for implementation on July 1, 1984. A clearly defined continuum between the various levels of social work education still remains an elusive and controversial goal, and this is implicit in both documents. Although both CPS and the accreditation standards aim at maintaining and strengthening the quality of the educational programs, they also provide opportunities for schools and programs to experiment with different structures for organizing social work education. In the late 1970s and early 1980s, substantial changes in the social and economic ethos of the American society gave rise to increasing criticism of the social service system and attacks on the social work personnel who administer these programs. Inevitably, questions arose regarding the content and adequacy of social work education and its relevance to effective practice. This has had a negative impact on the funding of domestic social programs and has resulted in the curtailment of many social services and of many educational programs for social work. More students on both the BSW and MSW levels are seeking part-time programs, and the traditional full-time student is becoming rarer, giving way to students involved in a variety of time structures. Schools and programs are also experiencing a high demand for off-campus and extension activities.

The severe cutbacks in funding and the Reagan Administration's "new federalism" approach of block grants may radically change social service delivery systems and greatly alter social work practice both in form and in content. Social work education, with the leadership of CSWE, needs to keep abreast of these changes and to respond accordingly.

ARTHUR J. KATZ

Notes and References

1. "By-laws of the Council on Social Work Education" (New York: Council on Social Work Education, March 1974), p. 1. (Mimeographed.)

NATIONAL ASSOCIATION OF SOCIAL WORKERS

The National Association of Social Workers (NASW) is the organizational representative of the profession of social work in the United States. Its 92,000 professional members constitute the critical mass of trained social workers who, through democratic participation in NASW's policy-making activities, define the qualifications for the profession, establish practice standards, and advance the expert views of the profession.

Since its formation, NASW has organized practitioners with baccalaureate and graduate degrees in social work and raised them from a semiprofessional status to full professional recognition. Thus, according to the model provided by Greenwood, social work has met the criteria for a learned profession in the following ways. [1]

1. As demonstrated in the curricula of 88 graduate and 326 undergraduate schools of social work, in the extensive publications programs of NASW and commercial firms regarding theory and practice, and in the curricula standards of the Council on Social Work Education (CSWE), social workers have developed a transmittable body of knowledge that they utilize to make professional and technical judgments.

2. Social workers have developed a personal, interactive authority with individuals, groups, and communities, and this authority is recognized by millions of clients.

3. Social work has received community sanction, as reflected in citizen support of 52,000 voluntary and public social agencies and in legislative sanctioning of social work licensing in more than one-half of the fifty states.

4. To regulate the activities of practitioners, social workers have implemented national and international codes of ethics and established professional and practice standards.

5. Through NASW's organizational structures and programs, social workers maintain a professional culture.

Professional Amalgamation

Five broad periods are discernible in the general development of the social work profession since World War II. The periods overlapped, but each had a distinctive emphasis. During the period of professional amalgamation (1950–1962), members of the local and national units of six specialty associations and one general membership association—the Association for the Study of Community Organization (founded 1946), the American Association of Group Workers (1936), the American Association of Medical Social Workers (1918), the American Association of Psychiatric Social Workers (1926), the American Association of Social Workers (1921), the National Association of School Social Workers (1919), and the Social Work Research Group (1949)—intensively examined and debated the basic role and responsibility of social workers in society, the fundamentals of their education, and the duplication of activities by the various organizations.

Throughout this period the demand for a unified profession gradually escalated among the members of the seven separate organizations, and after several years of discussion and negotiation in a Temporary Inter-Association Council, the National Association of Social Workers was formed by merger in July 1955. It became operative on October 1, 1955, with a combined membership of 22,027.

The heritage of the seven organizations is evident in NASW's early structure. Although NASW assumed responsibility for general governance, policy formation, legal regulation, publications, personnel practices, public relations, and other broad functions that had previously belonged to the largest amalgamating organization, the American Association of Social Workers (AASW), the educational authority and technical practice interests of the specialty associations were maintained through the section executive committees and through representation on the Board of Directors. Thus, the primary activities of the previous organizations continued even as NASW's national board and staff and its local chapters struggled to reach administrative and program integration.

During this period, "NASW was built by attracting and holding members through an appeal to their need for status and improved salaries."[2] Starting in 1957, NASW annually published minimum salary standards, and in a joint effort with the Council on Social Work Education that lasted fourteen years, NASW provided financial support for a National Commission for Social Work Careers.

After five years, in accordance with the original merger agreement, NASW initiated an extensive review of its functions, organization, and structure. This review culminated in 1962 in major changes. The new NASW structure followed a balance-of-powers concept, although it delegated increased authority to the national Board of Directors. It also reserved ultimate policy-making authority for the general membership; continued representative governance in elected bodies—the Delegate Assembly, the national and chapter boards of directors, and the various councils and commissions—each of which had separately delegated powers; and provided autonomy to elected nominating committees at national and chapter levels. These organizational changes marked the culmination of the period of amalgamation and the achievement of a rational structure for executing the responsibilities of the association.

Professional Consensus

A quest for professional consensus was the hallmark of the second phase of the profession's postwar development, and it lasted from 1956–1967. This was a period of debate and parliamentary struggle to reach an agreement on vital practice issues and major public policies. After 1962, the search for professional consensus involved the twenty-two councils and commissions of NASW's three divisions—the Division of Practice and Knowledge, the Division of Social Policy and Action, and the Division of Professional Standards—in what became a costly attempt to define their respective roles and to formulate program activities. These deliberations were executed through a process of national committee study, usually involving local chapters and their committees, and the reports issued by these committees were next reviewed by the association's Board of Directors. The committee reports and the recommendations of the Board of Directors were then discussed, often heatedly, at meetings of the local chapters. The whole process culminated in decisions at the biennial meetings of the Delegate Assembly.

At the beginning of this period, eighteen policy statements of the predecessor organizations were adopted as tentative working documents and, "after review and study, were approved with amendments at the association's first Delegate Assembly in 1956."[3] The social policies covered the following subjects: social insurance, public welfare, juvenile delinquency, health, rehabilitation, education, housing and urban development, public recreation and leisure-time services, economic and labor conditions, military service, corrections, immigration, civil rights and liberties, social aspects of foreign policy, peace and disarmament, income maintenance, family planning, and social policy goals for voluntary social agencies. Consensus was also obtained on practice standards with the adoption of a Code of Ethics (1960), procedures for the adjudication of grievances (1967), and standards for social work personnel practices (1968).

It was also during this period that the Commission on Social Work Practice made fundamental contributions toward the clarification and definition of social work practice.[4] The concern for professional standards and public recognition led to NASW's formation of a separate corporation to initiate a quality assurance mechanism for the profession, the Academy of Certified Social Workers (ACSW). NASW members in good standing were given the opportunity of receiving blanket approval for ACSW standing. Subsequently, certification was administered as a quantitative standard and was awarded upon successful completion of a master's degree program, two years of supervision by an ACSW member, and annual renewal of NASW membership. In 1970, the corporation was dissolved and integrated into the NASW structure, and objective testing converted the ACSW recognition into a qualitative standard.

The redesigned organization, with its policy and recognition activities, attracted social workers until, in 1967, its membership reached approximately 50,000. At that point, membership gains leveled off for several years as the next phase in the association's life began.

Professional Ambivalence

The third overlapping period in the history of the professional association's development can be characterized as a phase of professional ambivalence (1965-1971). A knowledge explosion in the social sciences, the student revolts, and the militant civil rights and Black Liberation movements precipitated widespread challenges to social institutions and mores. Social agencies, schools of social work, and NASW were caught in ambiguous positions as they tried to contribute to the improvement of society and, simultaneously, to respond to charges that their practices and ideology were establishment oriented.

New and liberalizing organizational and cultural concepts and action strategies were introduced into the profession. Ambivalence regarding the ends and means of social work practice produced a costly conflict over the emphasis on casework rather than social policy, heightened criticism of educational criteria for practice, encouraged organizational fragmentation, and stirred professional sadomasochism about the state of the art.

NASW attempted to meet these challenges by expanding its continuing education program, holding its first national symposium in 1965, increasing its career thrust through work force studies, and strengthening legislative action. Nevertheless, bitter dissension among the membership, program limitations, and financial disaster resulted when NASW's national leadership focused the association's resources on "the urban crisis and related public welfare problems."[5]

Membership dissatisfaction brought action at the 1969 Delegate Assembly, creating new policy directions for NASW and the profession. Student and black caucuses besieged the assembly with demands that NASW programs emphasize social action. The assembly ended by giving an overriding priority to eliminating racism and poverty; this action was tempered by the adoption of a balanced program emanating from the Western States Chapter Coalition, again a reflection of the professional ambivalence of the time.

Professional Unity

Although first viewed as a period of organizational rehabilitation and reorganization, the years between 1969 and 1975 were essentially focused on developing professional unity. After much internal controversy over the implementation of the priorities set by the 1969 and 1971 assemblies, NASW obtained organizational unity by a combination of (1) vigorous execution of the Delegate Assembly priorities; (2) improved administrative and membership services, (3) adherence to the principle of maintaining balanced programs, and (4) increased professional visibility. For example, all activities were reviewed regularly for their significance relative to eliminating racism and poverty. The staffing of the national office was changed from 14 percent minority to 43 percent. To demonstrate the practicality of equal opportunity and affirmative action goals, NASW achieved 30 percent minority leadership in national elected and appointed offices even though minority membership was only 15 percent.

During this entire period, it was necessary to reduce the budget radically to repay prior deficits; it was also necessary to streamline the volunteer structure. However, the membership's confidence returned as modern management techniques were

introduced into the association—stringent fiscal controls, accountability, accrual accounting, functional staffing and personnel administration, and computer technology. The establishment of definitive policies, standardized operating procedures, improved information, increased interaction between the national office and chapters, and the development of chapter guides resulted in an increasing sense of organizational integration. As a result, the membership of the 178 chapters in 1972 approved a dues standardization program and thus provided valuable financial underpinning for both national and the local chapters.

This was a critical period during which NASW and all social service supporters were engaged in a defensive struggle against radical attacks by the federal administration of President Richard Nixon. NASW gave special attention to "social action," which was subsequently recognized as a means of providing community service—of translating social work expertise into public services and policies. This emphasis helped support moving the national office from New York to Washington, D.C., in 1972.

To expand NASW's legislative lobbying, the Educational Legislative Action Network (ELAN) was devised. This organization increased the political participation of NASW's membership by assigning local social workers to work with their national and state legislators for social work legislative and policy goals. The national ELAN office collaborated with local social workers in this and provided information via a newsletter, *The Advocate for Human Services*, which was first issued in 1971. NASW also intensified its legislative activities during this period by participating in many coalitions with other special interest groups, a practice that became routine after the success of the NASW-led Social Services Coalition in 1974, which defeated retrogressive regulations and helped create Title XX of the Social Security Act.

As the 1970s wore on, the gradual advancement of the balanced program concept—equitable attention to the basic organizational functions of practice advancement, standards development and promotion, community service, and membership service—began reducing the rivalry among special interests. It also helped the membership maintain a focus on goals specific to the profession.

NASW supported practice advancement mostly through continuing education activities, including seed money grants to initiate chapter workshops and national projects related to school social work, mental health training, and vendorship recognition for clinical social workers. The biennial national symposium was made a permanent feature, and the publications program was broadened from serving only national organizational units to the policy of serving the needs of the profession.

Prior to 1970 NASW exercised its responsibility to social work education through an annual subvention to CSWE and through service on CSWE's Board of Directors and committees. In 1970, however, recognizing education as an integral component of the profession, NASW took greater responsibility for making independent recommendations to CSWE, and it eliminated overlapping representation in favor of direct negotiations through the NASW-CSWE Joint Board Committee. NASW also initiated direct collaboration with the schools of social work, built a national faculty and student liaison system, and began a national fieldwork training program. In 1970, by a national membership referendum, NASW accepted the baccalaureate social work degree as a sufficient criterion for regular membership in the association. The Delegate Assembly had debated this possibility in 1965, 1967, and 1969, and the 1970 referendum constituted a formal recognition of the expansion of social work education.

Stimulated by the recognition of the BSW, the association increased its efforts to analyze the labor force of the social service industry. This resulted in the delineation of a six-level classification system, with two preprofessional and four professional levels. In 1974 NASW's *Standards*

for Social Service Manpower, which used education as the basis for differentiation, introduced a rational personnel classification scheme for use by social agencies and became an important tool for more efficient utilization of social service personnel. This classification system, in turn, became a foundation for the creation of a model licensing statute that identified three levels—preprofessional, entry, and advanced. This model licensing bill became the basis for a major thrust by the association for state licensing.

These advances were paralleled by the creation of a social work test of competence, instituted in January 1971, as a qualitative requirement for ACSW status. At the same time, NASW mounted intensive efforts to obtain acceptance of the ACSW as the criterion for vendorship recognition, to insert social worker standards in federal legislation (Health Maintenance Organizations, Professional Standards Review Organizations, and so forth), and to define social work specialties.

During this period between 1969 and 1975, then, NASW provided a structured arena for resolving ambivalence and conflicts and took specific steps to deal with its internal and external organizational problems. The association also established a sound financial, organizational, programmatic, and ideological base for the profession, and this produced a new spirit in the association's leadership and members.

Professional Assertiveness

The period from 1974 until 1983 can best be characterized as one of professional assertiveness. A unique professional identity grew as NASW shifted from defensive tactics to an offensive strategy. Despite the more sophisticated struggle required to support social programs and professional services during the national administrations of Ford, Carter, and Reagan, the association became more aggressive in advancing its policies and programs.

A qualitative leap was taken in social work's community service function as the membership-supported legislative activities led to the organization of the Political Action for Candidate Election (PACE) subsidiary under the new Federal Elections Campaign Act. Formed during the 1975 presidential election, PACE, with some forty chapter duplicates, now raises funds and supports social service–oriented candidates at all levels of government. Political action has become a standard activity and is now defined as an inherent professional function.[6]

This same assertiveness developed in all the community service activities. Successive task forces originated social service proposals. Delegate Assemblies adopted additional public policies. Campaigns to support and improve social services and to provide legislative analysis and testimony became standard for national and chapter units. The profession has provided consistent leadership in coalitions on children and youths, health care, social security, mental health, human rights, public employees, and other issues.

The NASW structure also benefited from the drive for unity. Strengthened by the single corporate structure of NASW, the 1975 consolidation of chapters eliminated the election of bodies representing the standing fields of practice, leaving only three elected national bodies—the Delegate Assembly, the Board of Directors, and the Nominating Committee. A national structure was instituted for addressing issues on an ad hoc basis, and it rapidly expanded to include units devoted to special interests, but the activities of these units remained under the control of a central program planning and budgeting system and the Board of Directors.

This system was rapidly adopted by the chapters, along with an accrual accounting program, which reduced unaccounted chapter funds from 39 percent in 1974 to 2 percent in 1981. A three-year planning cycle, which included a shift to a triennial Delegate Assembly in 1981, was constructed from Delegate Assembly actions and is now in place for the entire association.

The most important effects of the shift toward unity and assertiveness were the membership's support for a 50 percent dues increase and the adoption in 1977 of the Program Advancement Fund, which takes the first 5.5 percent of each member's dues to fund grant projects of significance to the profession as a whole.

The professional association's growing confidence and assertive outlook was demonstrated in two additional actions by the Board of Directors. NASW extended its internal affirmative action program to the entire association and successfully implemented this expanded program. In 1978 the association adopted a policy statement on the organization of professional social workers.[7]

The profession's increased assertiveness also sparked drives for legal recognition of social workers in state licensing. Strengthened by increased recognition of the differential classification concept, these drives achieved more legal regulation in ten years than had been obtained in the prior fifty years; more than half the states now regulate social workers. At the same time, the association fought a national trend toward declassifying social work positions. This effort emphasized the importance of developing detailed standards for the classification of social work practice in 1981 and classification validation processes for social services positions in 1982.

The publication of a *Register of Clinical Social Workers* in 1976 set a new standard for practice in the field, as did standards for hospital social services (1977), social work services in schools (1978), social work practice in child protection (1981), continuing education (1981), and social work in health care settings (1981).[9] (The last standards superseded those published in 1977 for hospital social services.)

NASW mounted special campaigns to obtain recognition of the profession and its standards in voluntary and governmental regulatory bodies, such as the Joint Commission on Accreditation of Hospitals and Professional Standards Review Organizations. The association's Code of Ethics was revised in a format similar to that of the

International Code; the revised code was also designed for specific application and enforcement.

At the same time, NASW's volunteer leadership increasingly recognized the necessity for an independent practice representation in educational policy. Cooperating with CSWE and the Undergraduate Social Work Curriculum Development Project, NASW in 1976 approved and advocated a standard baccalaureate curriculum. The association also developed an objective examination for BSW licensing and achieved its goal of including practice representatives on the site-visit teams CSWE's Commission on Accreditation sent to graduate and undergraduate programs applying for accreditation. Through CSWE, NASW also financed a project to develop an industrial social work curriculum and to stimulate its use in schools of social work.

In other education-related actions, the increasingly unified and assertive association in 1980 adopted policy positions on the accreditation standards, which CSWE was then in the process of revising. These position statements were influential in strengthening the final standards. NASW also instituted a practice of releasing the results of the ACSW examinations to individual schools of social work to show them how their graduates' results compared to national averages. The most significant achievement for both education and practice was the completion in 1979 of a policy document by a joint NASW–CSWE task force defining specialization in the profession.[10]

The enterprising outlook of the period was also reflected in the profession's development and utilization of knowledge. Two landmark conferences were held to define the conceptual frameworks of social work, and a variety of national and special symposia demonstrated greater integration of theory and practice. Aided by NASW's national Practice Improvement Program, the number of continuing education offerings vastly increased in the association's fifty-five chapters. The expansion of knowledge

and new technologies, particularly in the health field, gave added impetus to the assertiveness of social workers, causing them to seek increased opportunities to exchange knowledge and to foster recognition of practice specializations. Groups of practitioners began organizing around practice interests such as renal dialysis, genetics counseling, and perinatal services. NASW volunteer leaders, trying to avoid fragmentation of the profession, sought to develop organizational forms through studies and demonstration units to meet practitioners' specialty interests. Formal recognition of these specialty concerns was established in 1980 by delineating criteria for the formation of Practice Advancement Councils.

NASW's publication programs also expanded during this period of professional assertiveness. New periodicals focused on research, health, education, and general practice, and the association also sponsored such special offerings as the "Social Work Classics" and subject reprint series. (NASW publishes the *Encyclopedia of Social Work* and many other books and journals; listings are available from NASW's national office in Silver Spring, Md., or its editorial office in New York City; for a list of NASW's periodicals, see Table 1.) This growth in the association's publishing efforts was paralleled by a geometrical proliferation of social work journals and books offered by commercial houses. Complementing this expansion of the publishing activities in social work was an increased emphasis on the fundamental requirement for a profession—research. NASW sponsored a national conference on the future of social work research and initiated a program of research into practice effectiveness.

The increasing unity and assertiveness felt by NASW's leadership and members also expanded their horizons. Recognizing the integral interrelationship among foreign and domestic social and economic problems and the needs to advance social workers' expertise and policies in international matters, NASW took the leader-

TABLE 1. PERIODICALS PUBLISHED BY THE
NATIONAL ASSOCIATION OF SOCIAL WORKERS

Title of Periodical	Year Established	Circulation
NASW News	1955	98,000
Social Work	1956	100,000
Health and Social Work	1976	5,000
Social Work Research and Abstracts	1977	4,100
Social Work in Education	1978	1,500
Practice Digest	1978	3,200

ship in reconstructing the International Federation of Social Workers. A practitioner exchange program was conducted with Kenya, Mexico, and Jamaica, and an international travel program, new services for overseas members, and an international development program were also started during this period. In cooperation with such organizations as the American Association for the Advancement of Science, the Council on Hemispheric Affairs, and the

TABLE 2. PRESIDENTS AND EXECUTIVE DIRECTORS OF THE NATIONAL ASSOCIATION OF SOCIAL WORKERS

Name	Term of Office
Presidents	
Nathan E. Cohen	1955–1957
John McDowell	1957–1959
John C. Kidneigh	1959–1961
Norman V. Lourie	1961–1963
Kurt Reichert	1963–1965
Howard Gustafson	1965–1966
Helen E. Cassidy	1966–1967
Charles I. Schottland	1967–1969
Whitney M. Young, Jr.	1969–1971
Alan D. Wade	1971
Mitchell I. Ginsberg	1971–1973
Lorenzo H. Traylor	1973–1975
Maryann Mahaffey	1975–1977
Arthur J. Katz	1977–1979
Nancy A. Humphreys	1979–1981
Mary Ann Quaranta	1981–1983
Robert P. Stewart	1983–
Executive Directors	
Joseph P. Anderson	1955–1969
Chauncey A. Alexander	1969–1982
C. Annette Maxey	1982–1983
John E. Hansan	1983–

National Education Association, NASW undertook to provide active leadership on human rights.

Summary

With 92,000 members in fifty-five chapters in the fifty states, New York City, and Washington, D.C., and the Virgin Islands, Puerto Rico, and Europe, NASW is the largest organization of professional social workers in the world. It is a single nonprofit corporation, operating under Section 501–c–6 of the Internal Revenue Code. Its policies and program are established by a triennial Delegate Assembly of representatives elected through chapters and by a twenty-five member Board of Directors elected in a national election among the members. (For a list of NASW's presidents and executive directors, see Table 2.)

NASW operates five subsidiaries: (1) the Research and Education Fund, which is devoted to the support of scientific, educational, and philanthropic activities under Section 501–c–3 of the Internal Revenue Code, (2) the Insurance Trust, which administers group life, disability, and health insurance programs for the membership, (3) PACE (Political Action for Candidate Election), which raises funds to assist social service–oriented legislators, (4) the Professional Liability Program, which provides low-cost liability insurance, and (5) the Legal Defense service, which provides assistance to members engaged in legal action as a result of actions taken as a professional social worker.

NASW's primary functions include practice advancement, community services, collective membership services, and the implementation of service and practice standards. The association operates on an annual budget of approximately $11 million, of which nearly $4 million is spent from chapter budgets.

CHAUNCEY A. ALEXANDER

Notes and References

1. Ernest Greenwood, "Attributes of a Profession," *Social Work,* 2 (July 1957), p. 45.

2. Bertram M. Beck, "Professional Associations: National Association of Social Workers," in *Encyclopedia of Social Work* (17th ed.; Washington, D.C.: National Association of Social Workers, 1977), p. 1090.

3. Mitchell I. Ginsberg, "Preface," in *Goals of Public Social Policy* (New York: National Association of Social Workers, 1963), p. 4.

4. See NASW Commission on Social Work Practice, Subcommittee on Fields of Practice, "Identifying Fields of Practice in Social Work," *Social Work,* 7 (April 1962), pp. 7–14.

5. *From Crisis to Challenge to Change,* Report (New York: National Association of Social Workers, 1969), pp. 9–10.

6. Chauncey A. Alexander, "Professional Social Workers and Political Responsibility," in Maryann Mahaffey and John W. Hanks, eds.,

Practical Politics: Social Work and Political Responsibility (Silver Spring, Md.: National Association of Social Workers, 1982), pp. 15–31.

7. "Policy Statement on Organization of Professional Social Workers," (Washington, D.C.: National Association of Social Workers, 1978). (Photocopied.)

8. *NASW Standards for the Classification of Social Work Practice,* Policy Statement No. 4 (Washington, D.C.: National Association of Social Workers, 1981); and Robert J. Teare, Catherine Higgs, Thomas P. Gauthier, and Hubert S. Feild, *Classification Validation Processes for Social Services Positions* (6 vols.; Silver Spring, Md.: National Association of Social Workers, in press).

9. See *NASW Register of Clinical Social Workers; NASW Standards for Hospital Social Services,* policy statement No. 6; *NASW Standards for Social Work Services in Schools,* Policy Statement No. 7; *NASW Standards for Social Work Practice in Child Protection,* Policy Statement No. 8; *NASW Standards for Continuing Professional Education,* Policy Statement No. 10; and *Standards for Social Work in Health Care Settings,* Policy Statement No. 6 (all Washington, D.C.: National Association of Social Workers, 1977, 1978, 1981, 1981, and 1981 respectively).

10. National Association of Social Workers–Council on Social Work Education Task Force on Specialization, "Specialization in the Social Work Profession," *NASW News,* 24 (April 1979), p. 20.

POLITICAL ACTION

In this article, political action is defined as the deliberate efforts of individuals and groups to influence public policy decisions by participating in electoral politics, identifying problems that require governmental attention, informing policymakers about alternative courses of action and their likely consequences, influencing their choices in this regard, and advocating change. Put more abstractly, political action consists of activities intended to advance information and preferences so that they are reflected in how, when, and to whom resources are allocated.

This article examines the roles social workers play in political action—as individual professional practitioners, as agency employees, and as members of the professional associations. It first surveys the history of political action in the profession, gives a brief description of the extent and variety of political activities in social work, and reviews the ideological stances that inform these activities. It then discusses current and emerging roles taken by social workers as they attempt to influence policy development.

The methods and techniques of political action are not unique to social work. They derive, instead, from a variety of disciplines and professions, such as law and political science, and from the experience of those inside and outside the social work profession who have been intimately involved in the political process. Social work both draws from and contributes to this fund of knowledge and experience, as do other groups in society. What makes skilled political action important to the profession is that social work, like other professions, is an interest group that seeks to promote certain attitudes and social objectives through government institutions.[1] These attitudes and objectives are not narrowly self-serving, but constitute a commitment to equity and distributive justice, to a social and economic environment that facilitates healthy growth and development, and to a system of social services that prevents social problems and cares for those in need.[2]

In a political system characterized by an increasing number of well-organized interest groups, the profession and its members can hope to press its interests effectively only if it can mobilize for sophisticated political action.[3] Lack of involvement or competence in political action would effectively deprive social work of a vehicle for advocating its interests in the policy arena and would leave the field to others who may or may not pursue similar objectives.

History

Since social work began to emerge as a self-conscious occupational group at the turn of the century, the profession has generally embraced the idea that individual and collective action to reform social and economic institutions or to change harmful environmental conditions is a part of its domain. To be sure, there have been internal divisions on ideology and substantive policy issues and sharp differences about the relative emphasis social work education and practice should give to political action as opposed to the provision of direct services. Nevertheless, a persistent, normative theme in the professional subculture has continued to define political action as a core responsibility.

The persistence of this credo in social work is in large part a result of the legacy of political action by social work pioneers in the decades just before and just after the turn of the century. The list of accomplishments from that era remains one of the dramatic chapters in the profession's history. Social workers and those closely identified with the profession played significant parts in such varied developments as the First White House Conference on Children (1909), the establishment of the Children's Bureau, the enactment of child labor legislation, the development of juvenile courts, the passage of legislation establishing Mothers' Pension programs, and the modernization of local public welfare. At the municipal level, social workers, most prominently those connected with the settlement houses in large cities, became intimately involved in a variety of reform efforts aimed at improving housing and educational, recreational, and health services for the inner-city poor. The most visible political influence exercised by social workers of that era came during the 1912 presidential election, when Jane Addams, Paul Kellogg, and others helped to fashion the platform of the Progressive party and campaigned extensively for its candidate, Theodore Roosevelt.[4] The list of that era's politically influential social workers is too long to include here, but among them are persons credited with shaping the social conscience of the profession, including Jane Addams, Edward Devine, Lillian Wald, Julia Lathrop, Robert Woods, Florence Kelley, and Homer Folks.

The course of the profession's involvement with political and social action since those early times has been extensively described and analyzed and will not be detailed here.[5] Suffice it to say that between 1915 and 1960 social work grew increasingly preoccupied with developing direct-practice functions and techniques and gave relatively less attention to effecting broad social change.[6] There were exceptions to this trend. During the Great Depression, for example, social workers were prominent advocates for social insurance, federal aid for relief, and related New Deal programs.[7] In the 1950s and early 1960s, social workers were often vocal critics of restrictive and punitive public assistance policies and argued for humane and rehabilitative programs.[8] On the whole, however, the bulk of the profession's members and institutional resources—its schools, associations, research efforts, and literature—were invested in extending and refining social work practice with individuals.

The profession was never entirely comfortable in giving disproportionate attention to individual dysfunction and adjustment. Throughout this period, a dissenting cadre lamented social work's retreat from social responsibility, and when a unified professional association was created in 1955, those committed to this role for social work managed to establish a division through which the association was to pursue this broader purpose.[9]

The 1960s and 1970s witnessed a gradual but significant resurgence of professional interest in political action. In the sixties, two related developments served to rekindle this interest. First, a number of broad-based social movements sought to empower segments of society that had previously had little influence on policy development or resource allocation. Minorities, students, poor people, women, the aged, and opponents of war, each in turn and sometimes in concert, organized to call attention to social and economic inequities and to press their claims on governmental institutions. Many social workers who participated in or supported these movements came away from the experience with a heightened sense of the need for institutional change and an awareness of the complexities of the political process.

At the same time and continuing into the early seventies, legislation created a large number of new programs that were directed at changing the social conditions that gave rise to such problems as poverty, racism, and delinquency. The theoretical orientation behind many of these programs focused on environmental deficits rather than individual pathology as the critical variable in social change. This orientation required the social workers involved in these programs to develop such technologies as grassroots organizing, advocacy, planning, citizen participation, and lobbying—forms of practice that relied heavily on the understanding and skilled use of political processes.[10]

These developments were reflected in an expanded commitment to social action by the National Association of Social Workers (NASW) and by social work education, where there was a substantial increase in the number of students who matriculated in community organization concentrations

—from 1.5 percent of all graduate students in 1960 to 9 percent in 1969.[11] Although there continued to be internal criticism that social workers were not sufficiently involved in political action, the profession in the late sixties and early seventies was more oriented to the need for political involvement than at any time since the Great Depression.

The period from the early seventies to this writing has witnessed a continued interest in political action, although the social and political contexts have changed markedly. A sustained period of high inflation and slowed economic growth, growing public concern over the "uncontrolled" rate of expenditures for social programs, and a tide of political conservatism have brought the policy gains of the sixties and early seventies under severe scrutiny. Several policy trends that emerged in the seventies and accelerated during the Reagan administration threaten to erode government's commitment to social welfare. The severe budget cuts in entitlement programs during the last several years are the most visible indication of this trend, but perhaps equally important is the devolution of policy authority for social programs to the states and localities.[12] The moves toward block grants, deregulation, local discretion, and local financing and the concomitant shift of responsibility to states are placing many policy decisions closer to home. Among other things, these developments make it increasingly important that social workers become involved in political action at state and local levels to protect existing programs and to advocate for groups like the unemployed, women heads of households, and minorities, whose situations grow steadily worse.[13]

Involvement in Political Activity

To what extent are social workers involved in political action? Because no national data are available, it is impossible to give a definitive answer to this question, but it is possible to suggest something of the profession's general posture in this regard.

Since the late 1960s, in response to the social unrest of that era and to the heightened political awareness in the profession, NASW has directed increased attention and resources to political action. Reorganized in 1969, in part to augment activity in the political arena, NASW has maintained a staff of paid lobbyists to advocate selected social policy goals. NASW lobbyists played an important role in, among other activities, developing and maintaining the coalition that was instrumental in gaining passage of the social services legislation that ultimately became Title XX of the Social Security Act.[14]

In 1971, as part of a strategy to expand the involvement of its members in political action, NASW established the Educational Legislative Action Network (ELAN). A national network connecting state chapter members with one another and with the national office, ELAN facilitates information exchange and coordinates action on state and federal legislation. The network thus serves as both a catalyst and a conduit for political action among social workers.[15] In 1975 NASW established Political Action for Candidate Election (PACE) to raise funds for contributions to political candidates whose records indicate support of human services programs. Legally separate from NASW and its state chapters, PACE established a base for influencing voters directly. In the 1982 national election, for example, PACE raised $130,000, which was distributed among two hundred candidates for congressional office. In addition to these monetary contributions, five thousand social workers are estimated to have devoted some fifty thousand hours of work to various congressional campaigns in 1981. In a special NASW-sponsored project in 1982, social workers were also responsible for registering an estimated ten thousand new voters in six congressional districts involving PACE-endorsed candidates.[16]

None of this is to suggest that these political action mechanisms are as strong or effective as many in the profession would like them to be. Nevertheless, it is fair to say that the political action capability of the profession has increased significantly in the last decade and, with it, the opportunities for social workers to become involved in influencing social policy.

The political activities of social workers are, of course, not restricted to the professional associations. Social workers also work to influence policy development in their roles as agency employees, as members of political parties, as elected political officials, and as organizers and participants in broad-based social action groups.[17] Evidence regarding the extent of these involvements is reflected in Wolk's survey of social workers in Michigan.[18] In this study of 289 social workers, Wolk found that approximately two-thirds had participated in three or more of the following political activities: engaging in political discussions, financial contributions to political pressure groups, attendance at political meetings, membership in political organizations, participation in political campaigns, communicating with legislators, and testifying before legislative committees. It is impossible to generalize these findings to all social workers, but Wolk's findings suggest that, as a group, social workers may be more politically involved than is often assumed.

Ideological Orientations

Political action in social work has two major ideological orientations. The first, which may be characterized as the social reform orientation, is probably the dominant one in the profession. Adherents of this orientation reconcile themselves more or less comfortably to the major political and economic institutions in this country, but do not accept the inevitability of the social problems and hardships that have been associated with this system. In their view, such problems as structural unemployment, racism, sexism, inadequate social and health services, and the myriad other problems that plague society, although deeply rooted, can be significantly ameliorated or contained through governmental intervention, enlightened social responsibility on the part of corporations, and an informed, politically active citizenry. Social workers with this social reform orientation see political decision making in the social policy arena as resulting from the interplay of multiple, diverse interests, rather than from the dictates of a few economic and political elites. To enhance its political power in this pluralistic system, the profession seeks to increase access to and influence with decision makers by using traditional political methods, such as coalition, education, persuasion, and compromise.

A second ideological stance found in the profession is often referred to as radical social work. The radical orientation starts with the proposition that existing social and economic institutions are inherently exploitive and oppressive for the mass of people in this society. It sees social work's liberal, reformist tradition, its efforts to mitigate the excesses of capitalism notwithstanding, as having incorporated the values and perspectives of this system. The profession is thought to reinforce the status quo by treating its victims rather than addressing the underlying defects of a system that is inexorably exploitive and inequitable.[19] Proponents of this radical orientation contend that, even as social work seeks to reform aspects of the society, the profession and the organizations through which it functions benefit from existing arrangements.[20] Thus, it is not surprising, in this view, that social workers do not pursue political action aimed at fundamentally changing the existing order because to do so would jeopardize their occupational interests as currently defined.

Although radical social workers differ regarding the strategies and tactics of political action, they generally reject as inadequate the traditional methods and processes of political influence. Rather, the ideology of radical social work suggests a broad approach to political action, with the objective of transforming societal institutions through mass collective action. Social workers are seen as potentially instrumental in this struggle, but only as they join with other movements involving workers, clients, and social activitists. Although there is no single strategic posture in radical social work, some of the forms of political action proposed are as follows: the building of local collectives to model, in microcosm, alternative institutional forms; altering the political consciousness of social workers to make them more aware of their conserving role in the system and of the personal changes they must make to contribute to social change; the unionization of social workers in a radicalized labor movement to challenge the legitimacy of social welfare agencies; and the democratization of social agency practices.[21]

The profession includes adherents to both of these ideological perspectives and to an infinite number of political positions to the left, right, and between these poles. An ideological stance does not necessarily dictate the particular role one chooses to play in political action, but it does much to condition the goals, expectations, and strategic parameters one brings to a role. In the next section, six political roles are discussed. Social workers of both the reformist and radical ideologies participate in this array of roles, but the reformers are more often engaged in traditional, institutional capacities, such as policy analyst or lobbyist, whereas those with a radical orientation more often choose to influence policy through less traditional roles, such as community organizer and agency advocate.

Political Action Roles

Social workers engage in a variety of political activities as individuals and as members of organized groups. This section briefly discusses six political roles, some of which social workers have long been involved in and some of which are emerging and are likely to receive more attention in the years ahead. In each case, the text briefly describes the context within which the role is carried out, the resources that social workers in this capacity call on to influence decision makers, and the strategies or tactics they are likely to use in the various contexts.

Internal policy analyst. Internal analysts are employed by governmental agencies and legislative bodies to assist decision makers in understanding the nature and magnitude of social problems that may require policy attention, assessing the comparative strengths and limitations of alternative policy options, monitoring policy implementation to check for compliance and detect problems, and evaluating the effects of policy. These functions may be performed by management or supervisory personnel, but the concern here is primarily with persons whose duties are substantially directed at providing information and analytic support to high-level policymakers. The best examples of the positions in which this role is dominant are the professional staffs of legislative committees; personnel in offices of planning, policy analysis, and evaluation in local, state, and federal health and welfare agencies; and the staffs of individual legislators.

The internal analyst's influence on policy formulation can be considerable. Proximity and regular interaction with decision makers are important assets, but to the extent that the policymaker comes to rely on the analyst as a major source of information and ideas, the analyst is, of course, in a critical position to condition the decision maker's perceptions of problems and ways of dealing with them. The analyst selects and synthesizes technical information regarding policy options and outcomes but may also provide the decision maker with perspectives on the political constraints, costs, and consequences under which such choices are inevitably made.[22] Some policy analysts also assist decision makers in negotiating the compromises and forging the coalitions that are necessary to achieve support for important policy decisions.

External policy analyst. Employed in universities, profit and nonprofit research corporations, and social agencies, external analysts are retained through grants and contracts to perform research and analysis on policy issues of concern to government policymakers. Such persons may study emerging social problems to assess their incidence, prevalence, and correlates; assess existing policy arrangements and suggest modifications; evaluate pilot or demonstration programs to determine if they are suitable models for policy adoption; and assess the impact that has been produced by extant policy.[23]

Although the work of external analysts often influences the policy process, there are significant barriers to its utilization for decision making. Lack of timeliness, the perceived irrelevance of the research or analysis once it is completed, and the economic or political infeasibility of acting on the findings and recommendations of analysts are among the problems often encountered.[24] External analysts often have the potential to influence by virtue of their recognized expertise, but they must deal with the liability of being removed from the political environment of the decision maker. In most instances, they lack the opportunity for ongoing interaction with policymakers and often find it difficult to understand the policymakers' questions or to discern what information they need. In some instances, external analysts prefer to pursue areas of inquiry that are viewed as critical in the academic community even though these questions are removed from the concerns of decision makers.

There is increasing awareness of this dysfunction between external analysis and decision making and a growing appreciation that, if researchers and academics are to have a greater impact on policymaking, they need to devote as much attention to promoting decision makers' utilization of their work as they now do to the conduct of the research itself. Despite these problems, opportunities for external analysts continue to arise because government agencies often do not have the time or expertise to meet all their own information needs. In addition, because the external analysts' position outside government allows them some freedom to explore unconventional or unpopular ideas, such persons are in a position to offer fresh perspectives on policy issues.

Professional lobbyist. Professional lobbyists are retained by interest groups to advocate or oppose legislative proposals. The word "professional" is not meant to imply that such persons have particular educational credentials, but simply that they are substantially engaged in the practice of lobbying, often for pay. Although there is no count of how many social workers are employed as lobbyists, observation suggests that there is a significant number. This article has already spoken of the lobbyists employed by NASW's national office. Some NASW state chapters also employ lobbyists to work on state legislative matters. Social workers also serve in this capacity for groups and associations in such areas as mental health, poverty, and child welfare.

Professional lobbyists in social welfare may be employed by nongovernmental agencies or associations or by agencies of government. State departments of social welfare, for example, often deploy staff members to liaise with the legislature to promote or oppose bills that bear on departmental jurisdictions.

Lobbyists play an important part in the policymaking process. Those who represent social welfare interests are not likely to have large expense accounts, extensive support and research capabilities, or a powerful constituency, resources that have come to be associated with major business and professional lobbies. Rather, the social worker-lobbyist is more likely to derive influence from personal credibility with legislators, expertise or the ability to call on expertise, personal persuasiveness with legislators and their staffs, and skill in the processes of negotiation and compromise.[25]

Given limited resources, social work lobbyists must work with their constituencies to forge clear legislative agendas before a legislature goes into session and to build a solid group of supporters who can be pressed into action—for personal contacts, letters, testimony, and the like—at critical points in the policy process. Keeping constituents informed of the need for modifications in strategy or in the substance of their proposals is also important to maintaining the active support and involvement of the sponsoring organization. Because of limited resources, social work lobbyists often find it necessary to ally with lobbyists representing other human service organizations to create a united front and enhance the influence that can be brought to bear. Building and maintaining these coalitions is a complex task requiring considerable political and interpersonal skill.[26]

The social work advocate. In addition to the social workers whose principal professional activity is lobbying, there are those, far greater in number—especially among community organizers, planners, administrators, and academics—who occasionally become involved in advocating policy issues.[27] With the exception of the academics, these practitioners often become involved in advocacy as part of their jobs. Administrators of social agencies, for example, are likely to represent their agency's interests in legislative hearings or through personal contacts with legislators.

Direct service practitioners are less likely to be active in the policy process. This is unfortunate because it is those in day-to-day contact with clients who see firsthand the adverse effects of environmental problems and policy limitations. For some decades now, there has been considerable interest in the role that frontline workers might play in policy formulation. Hamilton, Beck, Specht, Briar and Briar, and others have pointed out the contributions that can be made by direct service practitioners, particularly in the aggregation and analysis of the client problems that result from harmful social conditions, inadequate social provision, or deficits in the operation of delivery systems.[28] Such a worker is often in a position to detect the emergence of new social problems before they come to the attention of planners and administrators—an early warning system, in effect. Workers can also help catalyze the interest of policymakers by providing palpable evidence of social problems, which are often treated as abstractions in legislative deliberations. Frontline workers are also likely to be among the first to know whether a new policy is being implemented as intended and whether it is working.

Although it is not unusual for direct service practitioners to become engaged in political action, far wider involvement is possible. Lack of training in political action, real or imagined constraints that agencies place on advocacy by workers, and a tendency to see clients' problems as individual dysfunctions rather than as a result of the person-environment interaction are obstacles to the wider involvement of workers in the policy process.[29] Agencies, schools of social work, the professional associations, and unions all have responsibilities for facilitating and supporting the advocacy efforts of direct service practitioners.

A major issue for agency employees acting as advocates is the extent to which it is necessary to have the concurrence of employers before publicly airing client problems or policy recommendations. NASW, through a grievance procedure and a legal defense service, has sought to provide some protection to workers whose jobs are threatened because they have spoken out on matters requiring the attention of policymakers. Still, those who independently advocate on public policy issues may risk dismissal, disciplinary action, and other sanctions. This risk must be weighed against the social workers' ethical responsibility to take action to improve the social conditions of the individuals and groups served.[30] When the employing agency fails to recognize or take a stand on a policy issue that adversely affects the welfare of its clientele, the social worker should take responsibility for seeing that this issue is brought to the attention of policymakers.

Political partisan. As individual citizens and as members of professional associations, social workers also play a role in the policy process through partisan political activity. This may take several forms. As already mentioned, NASW's PACE provides financial and campaign support to political candidates whose platforms are consistent with the association's policy positions. In addition, social workers become actively involved as campaign workers for candidates who are supportive of human services.[31] Writing statements on policy issues, soliciting contributions, advising the candidate on strategy matters, and helping with the myriad small details of campaigns are among the activities in which partisans become involved.

Those who make significant contributions of time and expertise are, at the very least, likely to gain the ear of the candidate and perhaps influence the candidate's views on social welfare issues. After the election, campaign workers usually have ready access to the official. In some cases, supporters who have been central actors in the campaign are offered positions on the legislator's staff. In any case, involvement in partisan campaigns, especially if it is early and continuous, creates an obligation that the social worker can later use as a conduit for influence.

Organizer. Social workers also become involved in political action as organizers of community groups that have been adversely affected by social and economic conditions, that have been discriminated against or systematically denied entitlements, or that have been ineffective in pressing for policies and programs to meet their needs. Such social work organizers act in a variety of contexts, including community action agencies, public interest groups, minority group associations, feminist organizations, and unions.

In some instances, they join in ad hoc movements that have emerged to address the problems of hunger and unemployment, inadequate housing or the exploitation of tenants, unfair law enforcement practices, and so on. In any case, the social work organizer is more likely than the social worker involved as an advocate or in another political role to work collaboratively with persons who are directly affected or victimized by the social conditions that are to be changed.

The organizer's role involves efforts to mobilize affected populations; to assist them in crystallizing issues and identifying their common interests; to study the problems and develop an analysis of causes and a factual basis for arguments and proposals; and to develop an organizational infrastructure that will make it possible to acquire resources, plan, recruit members, and carry out strategies.[32]

Organizers and the groups with which they work tend to call on a wider range of strategies and techniques than do social workers in other political action roles. Strategies used to influence decision makers vary from collaborative (education, joint problem solving, rational persuasion) to conflict (public protests, marches, strikes, media exposés), with the choice based on calculated self-interest rather than stylistic constraints.[33] At the same time, organizers often attempt to affect policy at several points rather than focusing their attention primarily on top-level policymakers. They may, for example, protest an agency's practices to dramatize an inequitable law, join in a class-action suit to prevent the implementation of a social policy, or conduct a large demonstration to call public attention to legislative inaction. Although these tactics may be used by social workers in other political roles, the contexts in which they operate and the conventions that surround their roles are more likely to limit their flexibility than in the case of the social work organizer.

Conclusion

Each political role in which social workers engage has a distinct contribution to make to the development of humane, progressive social policies. Over the past twenty years, these roles have become increasingly well defined, and the repository of experience and institutional support from which social workers draw as they participate in political action has grown. The current challenges to social justice and social provision demand, as never before, that social workers take up these roles.

RINO J. PATTI

Notes and References

1. David B. Truman, *The Governmental Process* (2d ed.; New York: Alfred A. Knopf, 1971), pp. 33–36.

2. Chauncey A. Alexander, "Professional Social Workers and Political Responsibility," in Maryann Mahaffey and John W. Hanks, eds., *Practical Politics: Social Work and Political Responsibility* (Silver Spring, Md.: National Association of Social Workers, 1982), pp. 22–25.

3. Willard C. Richan, *Social Service Politics in the United States and Britain* (Philadelphia: Temple University Press, 1981), pp. 38–43.

4. Allen F. Davis, "Settlement Workers in Politics, 1890–1914," in Mahaffey and Hanks, *Practical Politics,* pp. 41–42. For other accounts of social workers' political activities during this period, see Robert H. Bremmer, *From the Depths: The Discovery of Poverty in the United States* (New York: New York University Press, 1956), pp. 201–259; and Frank J. Bruno, *Trends in Social Work, 1874–1946* (New York: Columbia University Press, 1948), pp. 133–240.

5. Bruno, *Trends in Social Work, 1874–1946,* pp. 342–352; Nathan E. Cohen, *Social Work in the American Tradition* (New York: Dryden Press, 1958); Bertram M. Beck, "Shaping America's Social Welfare Policy," in Alfred J. Kahn, *Issues in American Social Work* (New York: Columbia University Press, 1959), pp. 193–201; and Daniel Thursz, "Social Action," in *Encyclopedia of Social Work,* Vol. 2 (Washington, D.C.: National Association of Social Workers, 1977), pp. 1274–1275.

6. Roy Lubove, *The Professional Altruist: The Emergence of Social Work as a Career, 1880–1930* (Cambridge, Mass.: Harvard University Press, 1965).

7. June Axinn and Herman Levin, *Social Welfare: A History of the American Response to Need* (New York: Dodd, Mead & Co., 1975), pp. 161–196.

8. Winifred Bell, *Aid to Dependent Children* (New York: Columbia University Press, 1965); and Gilbert Steiner, *Social Insecurity: The Politics of Welfare* (New York: Rand McNally & Co., 1966), pp. 141–179.

9. Beck, "Shaping America's Social Welfare Policy"; Herbert Bisno, "How Social Will Social Work Be?" *Social Work,* 1 (April 1956), pp. 12–18; and Alexander, "Professional Social Workers and Political Responsibility," p. 20.

10. Fred M. Cox and Charles Garvin, "Community Organization Practice, 1865–1973," in Fred M. Cox et al., eds., *Strategies of Community Organization* (Itasca, Ill.: F. E. Peacock Publishers, 1974), pp. 53–57.

11. Ibid., p. 69.

12. John L. Palmer and Isabel V. Sawhill, "Perspectives on the Reagan Experiment," in John L. Palmer and Isabel V. Sawhill, eds., *The Reagan Experiment* (Washington, D.C.: Urban Institute, 1982), pp. 1–28; and Diana M. DiNitto and Thomas R. Dye, *Social Welfare Politics and Public Policy* (Englewood Cliffs, N.J.: Prentice-Hall, 1983), pp. 32–43.

13. Michael F. Gutkowski and Jeffrey J. Koshel, "Social Services," in Palmer and Sawhill, *The Reagan Experiment,* pp. 307–328.

14. Richan, *Social Service Politics in the United States and Britain,* pp. 151–179; and Paul E. Mott, *Meeting Human Needs: The Social and Political History of Title XX* (Columbus, Ohio: National Conference on Social Welfare, 1976), pp. 38–45.

15. David J. Dempsey, "Establishing ELAN in a State Chapter," in Mahaffey and Hanks, *Practical Politics,* pp. 227–240.

16. "10,000 New Voters Registered," *NASW News,* January 1983, p. 8.

17. Maryann Mahaffey, "Lobbying and Social Work," and William H. Whitaker, "Organizing Social Action Coalitions: WIC Comes to Wyoming," in Mahaffey and Hanks, *Practical Politics,* pp. 69–84 and 136–158, respectively.

18. James L. Wolk, "Are Social Workers Politically Active?" *Social Work,* 26 (July 1981), pp. 284–285.

19. Jeffry H. Galper, *The Politics of Social Services* (Englewood Cliffs, N.J.: Prentice-Hall, 1975), pp. 88–110.

20. Frances F. Piven and Richard Cloward, *Poor People's Movements* (New York: Pantheon Books, 1977), pp. 7–27.

21. Galper, *The Politics of Social Services,* pp. 175–186; and Paul Adams, "Politics and Social Work Practice: A Radical Dilemma," in Mahaffey and Hanks, *Practical Politics,* p. 21.

22. Walter Williams, *Social Policy Research and Analysis* (New York: Elsevier Publishing Co., 1971), pp. 169–172.

23. David G. Gil, *Violence Against Children: Physical Child Abuse in the United States* (Cambridge, Mass.: Harvard University Press, 1970); and Robert Moroney, *The Family and the State: Considerations for Social Policy* (London, England: Longman, 1976).

24. Carol Weiss and Michael Bucuvalas, *Social Science Research and Decision Making* (New York: Columbia University Press, 1980),

pp. 16–26; and Ilene Bernstein and Howard Freeman, *Academic and Entreprenurial Research* (New York: Russell Sage Foundation, 1975), pp. 137–140.

25. Mahaffey, "Lobbying and Social Work," pp. 70–72; and Rino J. Patti and Ronald B. Dear, "Legislative Advocacy: One Path to Social Change," *Social Work,* 20 (March 1975), pp. 108–114.

26. Richan, *Social Service Politics in the United States and Britain,* pp. 233–236; and Whitaker, "Organizing Social Action Coalitions," pp. 146–155.

27. Wolk, "Are Social Workers Politically Active?" p. 286.

28. Gordon Hamilton, "The Role of Social Casework in Social Policy," *Social Casework,* 33 (October 1952), pp. 315–324; Beck, "Shaping America's Social Welfare Policy"; Harry Specht, "Casework Practice and Social Policy Formulation," *Social Work,* 13 (January 1978), pp. 42–52; and Katharine Hooper Briar and

Scott Briar, "Clinical Social Work and Public Policies," in Mahaffey and Hanks, *Practical Politics,* pp. 45–54.

29. Alexander, "Professional Social Workers and Political Responsibility," pp. 26–27.

30. "Profession of Social Work: Code of Ethics," in *Encyclopedia of Social Work,* p. 1067. See also p. 262 of the present volume.

31. William H. Whitaker and Jan Flory-Baker, "Ragtag Social Workers Take on the Good Old Boys and Elect a State Senator," in Mahaffey and Hanks, *Practical Politics,* pp. 161–180.

32. Jack Rothman, "Three Models of Community Organization Practice," in Fred M. Cox et al., eds., *Strategies of Community Organization* (Itasca, Ill.: F. E. Peacock Publishers, 1974), pp. 22–39; and Douglas Biklen, *Community Organizing: Theory and Practice* (Englewood Cliffs, N.J.: Prentice-Hall, 1983), pp. 100–110.

33. Biklen, *Community Organizing,* p. 89.

PRACTICE TRENDS

It has been suggested that what is most distinctive about social work is its diversity. If that is true, social work is more distinctive now than ever before. An expanding diversity is evident in many aspects of social work practice, including the variety of fields of practice, the wide array of theoretical orientations and interventive approaches, and the increasing range of research tools to advance the knowledge base for practice. Such changes constitute the central focus of the following overview of current trends in the practice of social work.

Before describing these trends, some clarification of the nature of social work practice is in order. Because this is not the place for a lengthy discussion of this important but complex subject, it is sufficient to note that social workers seek to improve the quality of life for all persons by providing rehabilitative and preventive services and social supports to individuals, families, groups, organizations, and communities and by working to bring about needed changes in the society. This definition, although less than perfect, is sufficiently broad to encompass the variety of the social work profession, and yet it places some boundaries on a profession that quite often seems diffuse to observers who do not have a detailed knowledge of it.

The practice of most social workers consists of providing services directly to individuals, families, and groups, and the prevalence of this form of practice, which is often called direct practice, is reflected in this review. However, many social workers perform other practice roles, including community organization, consultation, social action, policy practice, administration and management, research, and professional education. In addition, it should be noted that these latter professional roles are often performed by social workers engaged primarily in the area of direct practice.

Clinical Social Work

A relatively visible recent trend among practitioners primarily identified with direct practice is the clinical social work movement. Actually, this movement is neither new nor recent; its origins can be traced at least to the 1960s and the emergence of the clinical social work societies. In recent years the movement has been associated, although neither formally nor exclusively, with the expansion of private practice among social workers. The importance of this movement was recognized by the National Association of Social Workers (NASW) in its establishment of a Task Force on Clinical Social Work. This led to the convening, by NASW, of a National Invitational Forum on Clinical Social Work in Denver in June 1979 and to the sponsorship of a national NASW symposium on clinical social work in 1982. A purpose of the 1979 invitational conference was "to further the definition of clinical social work as a contribution to the profession as a whole."[1] The search for definition permeates the sizable body of literature that has accompanied the clinical social work movement.

Because the leadership of this movement emphasizes that the definition of clinical social work is still in the process of being formulated, it is not easy to state confidently what clinical social work is. Even the characterization of clinical social work as a movement may not be widely shared among those identified with clinical social work, even though one leader in the field suggests that clinical social work arose, in part at least, as a "backlash" against the criticisms in the 1960s of direct practice—then called social casework—as being irrelevant and failing to be committed to social change.[2]

Many of the definitions of clinical social work that have been generated at conferences bear striking similarities to earlier definitions of social casework, if allowances are made for terms such as "ecology" that were not widely used by social workers ten to twenty years ago. In fact, the "remarkable degree of consensus" that is reported to have emerged at the national forum in Denver focused on the *process* of clinical social work, the components of which, again, resembled the definitions of the casework process two or three decades earlier.[3] What is new, then, in the clinical social work movement?

The continuity with the past is not surprising in view of the purposes of NASW's organized efforts to address the interests and needs of clinical social workers. As the clinical social work movement developed, it included a number of social workers who were critical of the rest of the profession, especially of NASW, and some of these disaffected social workers advocated that clinical social work should become a separate profession, or at least should create an organization independent of NASW. In an attempt to heal this division within the profession, NASW is encouraging a consensus that would recognize the identity of clinical social workers and, at the same time, clearly identify clinical social work as an integral component of social work. NASW thus appeals to concepts that are rather general and based on traditions familiar to all the various constituencies involved. Whether NASW's objective will be achieved is a political question that can only be answered in the future. Thus far, it appears that many clinical social workers have responded positively to NASW's initiatives.

A close look at the specifics of clinical social work suggests that the "remarkable degree of consensus" Ewalt reported at the Denver forum in 1979 will need to be sturdy to overcome the equally remarkable diversity described in the *Handbook of Clinical Social Work* that appeared in 1983.[4] The *Handbook* presents a wide variety of perspectives, practice models, theoretical orientations to practice, and points of view about a number of key issues in clinical social work. The *Handbook*, of course, was written with no

specific political objective, and it did not seek to achieve a consensus.

It is difficult to see how the diversity of perspectives in the *Handbook* could be encompassed in one practice model, unless the model is so general as to be of limited practical utility or unless it is a different kind of consensus than the one reached in Denver, namely a new consensus that, among other things, would celebrate diversity and make a commitment to using an empirical approach to resolve controversy. Historically, the social work profession has not always tolerated difference and division easily and comfortably. Perhaps clinical social work will become an arena in which social workers find a way not only to tolerate, but to welcome the excitement and clarity that can be generated by controversy.

Theoretical Perspectives

From the 1920s until relatively recently, the theory and practice of social work with individuals and families was informed predominantly by psychodynamic perspectives derived primarily from Freudian and neo-Freudian theories of human behavior. Even the theoretical controversies in this area of social work practice—such as the diagnostic-functional debate that was a lively issue for several decades—were disputes over issues within a single overall perspective, not over fundamentally different theoretical perspectives. Thus, although relatively few social workers were doctrinaire followers of classical Freudian theory, most social workers, over many decades, were influenced heavily in their training by derivatives of Freudian theory, such as the developmental theories of Erik Erikson.

The theoretical perspectives informing social work practice have been expanding in recent years. The behavioral perspective, introduced into social work in the 1960s, is now in widespread use in the profession, and its applications have been extended to work with groups,[5] administration,[6] and social change.[7] The behavioral approach has been supplanted, to some extent, by the cognitive-behavioral perspective, which gives increased emphasis to cognitive variables in intervention.[8] The behavioral perspective has also been incorporated, along with certain other perspectives, into yet another perspective, called the empirical model of practice. In this model, methods and techniques for empirically assessing effectiveness are integrated into the practice process so that feedback about effectiveness can guide the practitioner's decision regarding intervention.[9]

The ecological perspective is another orientation that has been introduced into social work in recent years.[10] This perspective draws heavily on the language of the environmental movement and is focused primarily on relations between persons and environments. This perspective bears a striking similarity to the psychosocial perspective, which also focuses on person-environment interactions and which has been an integral part of most models of social work practice since the early beginnings of the profession. What the ecological perspective claims to bring to the traditional focus on person-environment interactions is an increased capacity to conceptualize the environmental components of these interactions. To accomplish that, social work theorists developing the ecological perspective tend to rely on concepts of general systems theory.

One of the limitations of the ecological perspective, thus far at least, is that the concepts and principles used tend to be general and even vague, making it difficult to derive from them specific guides that can be applied by practitioners. This weakness, which is recognized by a number of the advocates of the ecological perspective, results in part from the reliance on general systems theory, which is essentially an orientation and a framework, not a theory; it generally has not been capable of generating testable hypotheses or practice prescriptions. A few ecological theorists in social work have made use of the behavioral perspective, which is focused on person-environment interactions, is compatible with a systems orientation, and is

capable of precise specification of interventions and hypotheses.[11]

Thus, the search for more effective ways of implementing social work's focus on person-environment interactions continues. It is a search worthy of the profession's best efforts because this perspective focuses on a significant dimension of human problems, a focus that no other profession has taken as one of its central contributions.

Practice Research

In 1973 Fischer published his conclusion, based on a review of the accumulated research at that time, that casework, or the direct practice of social work, was not effective.[12] That summary statement has cast a pall on the field and provided support to the critics of the profession.

Almost a decade later, in 1982, Reid and Hanrahan published a review of the research on practice conducted subsequent to Fischer's review. They found that social workers were effective in more than 80 percent of the studies reviewed.[13]

Why such a striking difference in slightly more than ten years? Whereas most of the studies reviewed by Fischer compared the interventions by social workers—using whatever interventions they ordinarily would use—to nonintervention or intervention by untrained workers, most of the studies reviewed by Reid compared a specific interventive strategy to a different, usually less specific intervention approach. In other words, the research reviewed by Reid indicated that *how* social workers intervened made a difference; that is, some interventions are more effective than others. This conclusion differs from an assumption implicit in many of the earlier studies reviewed by Fischer, namely that all that social workers do is essentially similar and comparable.

The research reviewed by Reid indicates that if social workers use effective intervention methods, their practice is effective; they are less effective if they use ineffective methods. Further, the more effective methods tended to be structured, focused, and specific. Thus, it is important for the practitioner to know which methods are most effective and how to use them in practice.

The research reviewed by Reid reflects the growth of practice research during the past decade. The methodology of clinical research is receiving increased attention in schools of social work, in practice as well as research courses, and among practitioners themselves there is growing interest in clinical research. These developments may well be the most important current trend in the field in view of the important influence that research and advances in practice knowledge can be expected to have on the future development of the profession. (See also RESEARCH DEVELOPMENTS.)

Specialization

The trend toward specialization currently is strong in social work, even though efforts to formulate a coherent framework for specialization within the profession have been less than successful. Specializations continue to be defined according to (1) the population served, as in the case of child welfare and aging, (2) the focal problem, as in the field of substance abuse, (3) the practice setting, as in corrections or health, or (4) some combination of one or all of the above. Conceptual confusion about the most appropriate basis for specialization may not be a real problem, but lack of clarity about how much difference justifies establishing a specialization remains an issue.

A prominent specialization that has emerged in recent years is industrial social work, sometimes called occupational social work or occupational social welfare. To a considerable extent, this specialization consists of introducing social work services and social services into a new setting—new, at least, in the recent history of social work—the workplace. However, some social workers in this specialization are arguing for a broader perspective that would take the workplace itself as the object of intervention. Recent developments in this specialization are discussed elsewhere in this volume. (See INDUSTRIAL SOCIAL WORK.)

Health care continues to be a fertile source of subspecialties, probably because of the extent of specialization in other health professions. The movement of social workers into subspecialty areas in health care—such as renal dialysis, oncology, pediatric pulmonary care, and pain control, to name a few—has often led to the formation of an informal association of social workers practicing in that area and, to that extent at least, to the formation of a subspecialty in the profession of social work. (See also HEALTH CARE REGULATIONS AND STANDARDS.)

How to avoid the problems that can follow from overspecialization remains an issue for social work. This question is receiving increased attention from social work educators and the professional associations.

Prevention

Prevention is hardly new to social work. The need for prevention has been asserted, periodically, throughout much of the profession's history. For the most part, however, the call for prevention has been rhetorical because the knowledge base was lacking to support primary and secondary prevention and because of obviously strained attempts to interpret as prevention the treatment of problems after they have appeared.

What is different about the current emphasis on prevention in social work, and in related disciplines, is that research-generated knowledge on prevention is being developed. The expanding base of empirical knowledge about the relative effectiveness of alternative preventive approaches will make it possible to design preventive interventions with greater confidence than was possible when the only guidelines available were theoretical speculations.[14] This is an important step forward because one of the objections to funding prevention programs is the uncertainty about their effectiveness. If these research efforts continue to expand and if they continue to generate positive results, they can be expected to provide a powerful impetus for practitioners to increase their prevention activities and for agencies to give greater emphasis to prevention in their programs. (See also PREVENTION.)

Political and Social Action

There are indications that political and social action among social workers, including practitioners, have increased in recent years. These activities are discussed at length in a chapter on the subject elsewhere in this volume. (See POLITICAL ACTION.) The topic is mentioned here only to call attention to it as an important trend in social work practice.

Many clinical practitioners have been drawn into political and social action out of their interest in obtaining or protecting licensing legislation and in securing third-party vendor status for reimbursement of social work services, especially in private practice. These efforts often entail participation in coalitions with other groups and therefore broader involvement in and support for other social issues and concerns.

Increased participation in social and political action by practitioners, as part of their practice, is supported increasingly by perspectives that link direct practice to policy development and that view individual cases as belonging to classes of cases with similar problems that can often be best addressed through advocacy and systemic change rather than through individual treatment.[15]

Prospects

This brief review of current trends in social work practice omits several important trends that are discussed elsewhere in this volume, such as practice developments related to ethnic minorities; to women; and to the use of computers for management and accountability and as aids to decision making in practice. (See MINORITIES;

PEOPLE OF COLOR; WOMEN'S ISSUES; and COMPUTERS.)

Taken together, the trends described here indicate that social work practice is in a period of active and significant change. Many of these changes appear to be directed internally, to the profession and its practices, which is hardly surprising during a period when the political climate is not supportive of social programs and has even been somewhat hostile to social work. Most promising perhaps, many of the trends are not defensive but are affirmative efforts to strengthen the foundations and methodology of practice—through conceptual clarification and especially through research. If these efforts produce demonstrably successful results—and Reid's review of recent practice research indicates that successful results are feasible (see RESEARCH DEVELOPMENTS)—the strength, vitality, and social utility of social work services may very well increase markedly over the next decade.

SCOTT BRIAR

Notes and References

1. Patricia L. Ewalt, "Preface," in Patricia L. Ewalt, ed., *Toward a Definition of Clinical Social Work: Papers from the NASW Invitational Forum on Clinical Social Work* (Washington, D.C.: National Association of Social Workers, 1980), p. iii.

2. Carol H. Meyer, "Selecting Appropriate Practice Models," in Aaron Rosenblatt and Diana Waldfogel, eds., *Handbook of Clinical Social Work* (San Francisco: Jossey-Bass, 1983), pp. 736–737.

3. Patricia L. Ewalt, "Social Work Process as an Organizing Concept," in *Toward a Definition of Clinical Social Work*, p. 88.

4. Rosenblatt and Waldfogel, *Handbook of Clinical Social Work*.

5. Sheldon D. Rose, *A Casebook in Group Therapy: A Behavioral-Cognitive Approach* (Englewood Cliffs, N.J.: Prentice-Hall, 1980).

6. Lawrence M. Miller, *Behavior Management: The New Science of Managing People at Work* (New York: Wiley Interscience, 1978).

7. Robert L. Burgess and Don Bushell, Jr., *Behavioral Sociology: The Experimental Analy-*

sis of Social Process (New York: Columbia University Press, 1969).

8. Sharon Berlin, "Cognitive-Behavioral Approaches," in Rosenblatt and Waldfogel, *Handbook of Clinical Social Work*, pp. 1095–1119.

9. Steven P. Schinke, "Data-Based Practice," in Rosenblatt and Waldfogel, *Handbook of Clinical Social Work,* pp. 1077–1094.

10. Carol B. Germain and Alex Gitterman, *The Life Model of Social Work Practice* (New York: Columbia University Press, 1980).

11. James K. Whittaker, *Social Treatment: An Approach to Interpersonal Helping* (Chicago: Aldine Publishing Co., 1974).

12. Joel Fischer, "Is Casework Effective? A Review," *Social Work,* 18 (January 1973).

13. William J. Reid and Patricia Hanrahan, "Recent Evaluations of Social Work: Grounds for Optimism," *Social Work,* 27 (July 1982), pp. 328–340.

14. See, for example, Lewayne Gilchrist, Steven Schinke, and Betty Blythe, "Primary Prevention Services for Children and Youth," *Children and Youth Services Review*, 1 (1979), pp. 379–391.

15. Katharine Hooper Briar and Scott Briar, "Clinical Social Work and Public Policies," in Maryann Mahaffey and John W. Hanks, eds., *Practical Politics: Social Work and Political Responsibility* (Silver Spring, Md.: National Association of Social Workers, 1982), pp. 45–65.

PREVENTION

"Primary prevention" generally refers to those scientific practices aimed at *preventing* predictable physical, psychological, or social problems for individuals or populations at risk; maintaining or *protecting* current strengths or levels of health; and *promoting* the desired goals and potentials of people.[1] Primary prevention is an interdisciplinary endeavor. Wittman described the contribution social work had made to this endeavor up to 1977.[2]

Since that time, powerful social forces have been at work indirectly and directly helping to realize some of the long-unfulfilled promises of primary prevention, including those described by major contributors to social work, from Mary Richmond and Homer Folks to Lydia Rapoport and Ludwig Geismar.[3]

Among the indirect forces creating a receptive climate for primary prevention are recognition of the magnitude of the psychological and special problems for which existing manpower and techniques are inadequate;[4] the spiraling costs of treatment and rehabilitation, without corresponding gains in health or mental health;[5] the uninspiring and contradictory outcome studies involving traditional interventive theories and methods;[6] the documentation of the inequality in the availability and quality of treatment for people of different social classes, cultures, and races;[7] the attitudinal shift toward an emphasis on holistic health, exercise, and nutrition and on controlling one's lifestyle;[8] the agonizing changes that followed the recognition of scarcity both in the physical environment, with its limited natural resources, and in the social context, with its limited funds that must be allocated between 'guns and butter;'[9] and the moral objections to allowing large numbers of persons to undergo pain and suffering that could have been avoided if those persons had been given access to the wide variety of tools and procedures that are currently known and available within the profession of social work.

The Approach

In 1977 the Task Panel on Prevention (part of the President's Commission on Mental Health) stated that primary prevention is a cluster of strategies differing qualitatively from the approaches that dominated the mental health field in the past.[10] These strategies are proactive rather than reactive; they seek to identify and to build adaptive strengths and skills in people so as to avoid predictable problems or to attain desired objectives and reduce weaknesses or limitations that hamper individuals' attainment of such objectives. The preventive strategies are systems oriented; they are concerned with simultaneously reducing the many sources of stress in the social and physical environments inhabited by people and with building up the supports available in these environments.

Primary prevention is often concerned with total populations, especially groups at high risk, such as infants and children, the aged, minority people, persons with alternative lifestyles, and other groups social work has traditionally been concerned with. Primary prevention approaches these people with a fundamentally different orientation, however, seeking to engage and optimize their strengths, rather than to be preoccupied with their weaknesses. This reflects a paradigmatic shift away from the disease-medical model, which focuses on a sick individual and seeks specific causes, such as a particular bacterium or an inferred psychological trauma, that have specific pathologic effects, such as tuberculosis or the Oedipal reaction.[11] Primary prevention generally applies a public health/social learning model, which takes the person in the environment as its unit of consideration, precisely the focus traditionally sought by the mainstream of social work theory.[12] Rather than look for a specific cause of a specific symptom, the preventive model looks at the entire configuration of forces and structures that are related to states of health or disorder in people. Many sources of stress and limitation, in interaction with available strengths and skills, result in a given set of events. For example, there is considerable evidence that it is the overall accumulation of stresses, regardless of their specific origin, that is correlated with the emergence of one or another type of illness or disorder.[13]

Thus, the main tools and strategies of preventive/promotive helping involve the education of individuals and this modification of environments, both taken together and in the broadest context. The statement is, in effect, an exact restatement of traditional social work values, which other disciplines are rediscovering and refashioning in their own image. One of the reasons for the reemergence of the preventive/promotive goals in other disciplines, such as social psychiatry, community psychology, public health nursing, and the emerging paraprofessions, is that social work has not provided sufficient leadership.

For example, there has been a veritable explosion of empirical studies in primary prevention in the last half dozen years, but few social workers have been involved in this research. Nance sampled seven principal journals of social work and found that fewer than 3 percent of the articles published between 1976 and 1980 specifically related to preventive social work and that, of these, most were reports of programs rather than theoretical or empirical papers.[14] Among the reasons for this neglect are the magnitude of the pool of current victims needing aid and the crisis-and-pathology orientation of the helping professions generally. Funding sources and apparent public demand favor the remediation of current victims. Almost all sectors of society pay lip service to the desirability of prevention, but it is doubtful that any has yet found effective ways of realizing this goal. Among the recent substantive contributions made by social workers to primary prevention research are those by teams under the direction of Schinke, who uses the cognitive-behavioral approach to prevent unwanted teenage pregnancy;[15] Reinherz, who uses screening tools

with preschoolers to identify children at risk;[16] and Feldman and Caplinger, who use group work with predelinquents.[17]

In contrast, social workers have made numerous contributions to the programmatic or conceptual literature in primary prevention. Examples of these include the work of Porter and his colleagues, who have used community development techniques in achieving preventive/promotive goals in small communities in Appalachia;[18] Silverman's summaries of the activities of many self-help groups, including her own work in widow-to-widow programs;[19] Carlson and Davis's discussions of programs for the prevention of domestic violence;[20] Libassi and Turner's presentations of strategies for promoting competence among older persons; and Brown's work addressing the same concern among women;[21] Germain's analyses of how modifying the physical environment can contribute to primary prevention;[22] Middleman and Swenson's descriptions of the social environment's contribution, with special reference to natural helping networks;[23] and Patterson and Irvin's work illustrating social work perspectives in day care and in early mother-infant bonding.[24] The workplace is also becoming a center of preventive/promotive thinking and action: Employee assistance programs once focused narrowly on alcohol-related problems, but in recent years, companies have begun projects encompassing family and community orientations.[25] This, moreover, is only a small sampling of current writings by social workers.

Developments

The 1980s began with an Administration dedicated to reversing the general trend of federally supported health and welfare programs. In some cases the Reagan Administration eliminated programs entirely; in others it provided limited block grants to states for local choice in programming and funding. Despite these cutbacks, major policymakers have placed primary prevention among the leading goals on the national agenda. For example, Schweiker stated that "disease prevention and health promotion are at the very top of my agenda as Secretary of Health and Human Services."[26] The Surgeon General's report regarding the health status and goals of the American people identified fifteen major areas for preventive/promotive action, from accident prevention and the promotion of proper nutrition, to the prevention of substance abuse and the promotion of healthful lifestyles.[27] However, the conventional programs and skills of social work are not directly suited to the majority of these areas, and this suggests that there is still room to advance national priorities dealing more directly with mental health and social competence.

Legislation passed during this period, such as the 1980 Mental Health Systems Act, mandated funds specifically for primary prevention. Even in these years of austerity, the Office of Human Development Services in the Department of Health and Human Services requested applications for preventive programs in the belief that the role of the federal government is "to adopt and implement national policies or programs aimed at promoting economic growth and prosperity and thereby reducing the need for social services."[28] Conservatives view primary prevention as an economical solution to the endless expenditures for health and welfare programs, a solution that, rather than depending on the federal government, calls into play the strength and initiative of individuals. Liberal politicians view primary prevention as a means to achieve social goals through collective action; that this approach also promises to be cost-effective is an added attraction for them. These favorable, albeit contradictory, views of primary prevention frequently generate conflict over specific pieces of federal legislation, but they suggest that by providing evidence of the effectiveness and efficiency of preventive/promotive efforts, social workers and other helping professionals can ensure their inclusion on the national agenda, regardless of which party is in power.

Also assuring that prevention continues to receive attention on the national level are the activities of major mental health organizations, such as the National Mental Health Association, and specialized organizations, such as the National Committee against Child Abuse and Neglect. These organizations provide forums for examining a broad spectrum of topics and for launching action on specific concerns.

Regional confederations also play a role in preventive/promotive planning. For example, the Southern Regional Educational Board has long been interested in sponsoring conferences that clarify the meaning of prevention in that region, developing standards for preventive/promotive activities, and reporting evaluations of projects.[29] Social workers and other helping professionals have made contributions through these regional organizations.

At the state level, primary prevention has increased dramatically in the past few years. Johnston reviewed policies of the fifty states in mental health, including the nine states that had formed separate prevention units or appointed prevention directors in their mental health systems since 1974.[30] She noted that the general trend of the state's role in mental health had changed from caregiver, in the form of large state mental hospitals, to coordinator and facilitator of community mental health services, some of which are preventive in nature. Although only in operation for a decade at the most, these state-level prevention units have helped to "provide a climate conducive to preventive activities, increase the occurrence and co-ordination of preventive efforts, develop guidelines on acceptable prevention programs, and increase the quality and quantity of evaluations of preventive services. States without an organized preventive focus have generally not made these accomplishments."[31]

At the local level, progressive cities and counties are reorganizing their limited resources to include preventive/promotive efforts along with traditional treatment and rehabilitation programs. For example, to bring the best current thinking to bear on local problems and potentials, Westchester County, New York, hosted a conference on primary prevention.[32] Paster's report of her work with disadvantaged community groups on police-community relations, deteriorating housing, and single room occupancy hotels illustrates how community mental health centers have attempted to reorient their handling of preventable problems.[33] Ambrosino described how a family service agency adapted to changing needs in a rapidly growing suburban area by integrating its traditional counseling function with preventive/promotive efforts in family life education and family advocacy.[34] His agency has also been responsible for many innovative programs in prevention, such as Levenstein's doll demonstrator project, in which social workers showed disadvantaged parents how to communicate with their children by means of age-related toys.[35]

Local communities bear the major responsibility for providing mental health services through such organizations as schools, voluntary organizations, self-help groups, health maintenance organizations, and community mental health centers. Usually, primary prevention constitutes only a small proportion of these services. For example, only about 5 percent of staff time in community mental health centers funded by the federal government goes to the mandated activity of "consultation and education," which is the most likely form that prevention would take in these settings.[36]

Increasingly, in the absense of other sources of these services, prevention/promotion activities are passing to the hands of businesses, churches, and other citizen groups and individuals. Programs in stress management, employment assistance, and preretirement education are coming to be recognized as good business as well as good sense. An important element in these developments is the cost-effectiveness of primary prevention. For example, a statement by the National Institute on Alcohol Abuse and Alcoholism indicated that "for every dollar a company spends on an alcoholism program, it recoups eight dollars in increased productivity, decreased absenteeism and accidents."[37] Today there is em-

pirical confirmation of the folk saying about an ounce of prevention being worth a pound of cure.

Knowledge Base

The knowledge base for primary prevention has increased enormously since the mid 1970s. The past few years have seen the founding of several journals devoted entirely to primary prevention: the *Journal of Primary Prevention*, *Prevention in Human Services*, and the *Journal of Preventive Psychiatry*. In addition, the *American Journal of Community Psychology*, *Hospital and Community Psychiatry*, the *Journal of Community Health*, and the *Community Mental Health Journal* all offer considerable content coverage in this area. However, until recently, it was rare to find articles on primary prevention in any social work literature, except for materials on crisis intervention, which is more appropriately viewed as early treatment of an existing problem than preventive action taken before a problem has occurred.

The Vermont Conferences on the Primary Prevention of Psychopathology provided a continuing forum for preventive/promotive thinking, research, and practice. The volumes emerging from these proceedings are among the best materials on prevention to date.[38] In addition, a number of other books have appeared, some written by social workers, that offer an extensive range of materials for teaching.[39] The Council on Social Work Education's projects on integrating primary prevention in the social work curriculum have made public a wide array of teaching approaches.[40] The proportion of the papers presented at national professional conferences that concern prevention has also increased in recent years.

Overall, the availability of materials on primary prevention directly accessible to social workers and social work educators is far greater than it was in the mid 1970s. Efforts by professional bodies to put this information to active use have not, as yet, borne fruit, but they continue.

Criticism and Response

Some social workers note that identifying populations at risk may itself risk labeling such populations and creating unanticipated social problems.[41] Any such negative labeling, including the kind that is so pervasive among practitioners in treatment and rehabilitation settings, represents a risk to be condemned. However, such criticism fails to recognize the essence of primary prevention in promoting the strengths and potentialities of people, a form of labeling that is likely to have positively reinforcing and synergistic effects. Other critics caution helping professionals against rushing into unfounded claims about what primary prevention can accomplish, but this point is equally worth applying to claims for treatment and rehabilitation success as well. Thus, these are important and necessary criticisms, but they are not unique to primary prevention as a helping modality, and they tend to ignore the positive emphasis of primary prevention.

Other critics find a lack of clarity in the conceptual premises of primary prevention and point to a shortage of substantial empirical linkages on which to develop practice. For example, some critics demand that a specific cause be known before true preventive efforts can be implemented; because few causes of social problems are ever known specifically, this implies that there can be no primary prevention. This line of reasoning fails to recognize prevention's paradigmatic stance that causation is not limited to one factor as in the classical medical model, but rather that every social event has multiple causes in systematic relationships, so that it is sufficient to break the pattern at any significant point in the system to accomplish some preventive/promotive objective.

Other critics, pointing to the limited rigorous empirical base for the "benevolent gamble" of pursuing primary prevention in the mental health area, note that support of prevention will take funds and resources away from needed areas of treatment and rehabilitation. Because at present less than 5 percent of all federally funded projects are directed toward primary prevention, this is not the central issue. Rather, the question should be what balance among prevention/promotion, treatment, and rehabilitation is optimal for this society, given present and foreseeable conditions? Underlying this issue is the *malevolent certainty* that critics fail to consider—that each day will bring a new crop of victims to treatment, many of whom could have been prevented from appearing had the society but used the knowledge and skills currently at its disposal.[42]

The Future of Prevention

Half a century ago, a great preventive social worker, Homer Folks, in a paper entitled "Preparing a President for 1980," noted that a child had then recently been born who would be elected to the presidency in 1980, and he asked if it would not be wonderful if society could find that child and "guard his health, his surroundings, his education, his associates, his travel, his ambitions. . . ." But Folks was wise enough to recognize that the then contemporary sciences simply did not know enough to guarantee a perfect philosopher-king for the 1980s. Rather, he suggested telling the parents of that presidential child that "we will provide for you all those things which are needful, which are beyond your reach" and thereby help the parents to raise this child to a wise and secure maturity. Folks concluded his paper with a fundamental axiom for all preventive/promotive social work: since we cannot predict which particular parents were raising the president for the 1980s, then "we must decide what are the major needs for all children who are to become useful, competent, public-spirited citizens."[43]

Perhaps, the nation's president for the year 2030 has recently been born. Whether preventive social work fulfills its enormous potential for contributing to the prevention of predictable problems and the promotion of desired ends remains to be seen.

MARTIN BLOOM

Notes and References

1. Public Health Service, U.S. Department of Health, Education, and Welfare, *Healthy People: The Surgeon General's Report on Health Promotion and Disease Prevention*, Publication No. PHS 79-55071 (Washington, D.C.: U.S. Government Printing Office, 1979).

2. Milton Wittman, "Preventive Social Work," *Encyclopedia of Social Work* (17th ed.; Washington, D.C.: National Association of Social Workers, 1977).

3. Murray Levine and Adeline Levine, *A Social History of Helping Services: Clinic, Court, School, and Community* (New York: Appleton-Century-Crofts, 1970).

4. George Albee, *Mental Health Manpower Trends* (New York: Basic Books, 1950); and "The Fourth Mental Health Revolution," *Journal of Prevention*, 1 (1980), pp. 67–70.

5. Morton Hilbert, "Prevention," *American Journal of Public Health*, 67 (1977), pp. 353–356.

6. See, for example, Joel Fischer, "Does Anything Work?" *Journal of Social Service Research*, 1 (1978), pp. 215–244; Sol Garfield, "Effectiveness of Psychotherapy: The Perennial Controversy," *Professional Psychology: Research and Practice*, 14 (1983), pp. 35–43; and William Reid and Patricia Hanrahan, "Recent Evaluations of Social Work: Grounds for Optimism," *Social Work*, 27 (1982), pp. 328–340.

7. Julian Rappaport, *Community Psychology: Values, Research, and Action* (New York: Holt, Rinehart & Winston, 1977).

8. See, for example, Russell Whaley, *Health* (Englewood Cliffs, N.J.: Prentice-Hall, 1982); and Carolyn Swift, "Encouraging New Lifestyles: PLUS Puts It All Together," *Journal of Prevention*, 1 (1980), pp. 44–46.

9. See, for instance, Thomas P. Gullotta, "An Unorthodox Proposal for Funding Primary Prevention," *Journal of Primary Prevention*, 2 (1981), pp. 14–24; and William G. Hollister, "Fiscal Myopia or Constituency Building," *Journal of Primary Prevention*, 3 (1982), pp. 3–5.

10. President's Commission on Mental Health, *Task Panel on Prevention*, (Washington, D.C.: U.S. Government Printing Office, 1978).

11. Ibid.

12. See, for example, Carel B. Germain and Alex Gitterman, *The Life Model of Social Work Practice* (New York: Columbia University Press, 1980).

13. President's Commission on Mental Health, *Task Panel on Prevention*.

14. Kathy Nance, "Understanding and Overcoming Resistance to Primary Prevention," *Social Work Research and Abstracts*, 18 (1982), pp. 32–40.

15. Steven Paul Schinke, Lewayne D. Gilchrist, and Richard W. Small, "Preventing Unwanted Adolescent Pregnancy: A Cognitive-Behavioral Approach," *American Journal of Orthopsychiatry*, 49 (1979), pp. 81–88; and Lewayne D. Gilchrist, Steven Paul Schinke, and Betty Jean Blythe, "Primary Prevention Services for Children and Youth," *Children and Youth Services Review*, 1 (1979), pp. 379–391.

16. Helen Reinherz and Carol L. Griffin, "Identifying Children at Risk: A First Step to Prevention," *Health Education*, 8 (1977), pp. 14–16.

17. Ronald Feldman and Timothy E. Caplinger, *The St. Louis Conundrum: The Effective Treatment of Anti-Social Youth* (Englewood Cliffs, N.J.: Prentice-Hall, 1983).

18. Robert Porter, John Peters, and Hilda Heady, "Using Community Development for Prevention in Appalachia," *Social Work*, 27 (1982), pp. 302–307.

19. Phyllis Silverman, *Mutual Help Groups: A Guide for Mental Health Workers*, Publication No. ADM 78-646 (Washington, D.C.: Department of Health, Education, and Welfare, 1978).

20. Bonnie E. Carlson and Llane V. Davis, "Prevention of Domestic Violence," in Richard H. Price et al., eds., *Prevention in Mental Health: Research, Policy, and Practice* (Beverly Hills, Calif.: Sage Publications, 1980).

21. Mary Frances Libassi and Nathalie S. Turner, "The Aging Process: Old and New Coping Tricks," and Prudence Brown, "Women and Competence," both in Anthony N. Maluccio, ed., *Promoting Competence in Clients: A New/Old Approach to Social Work Practice* (New York: Free Press, 1981).

22. Carel B. Germain, "The Physical Environment and Social Work Practice," in Maluccio, *Promoting Competence in Clients*.

23. Ruth R. Middleman, "The Pursuit of Competence through Involvement in Structured Groups," and Carol R. Swenson, "Using Natural Helping Networks to Promote Competence," both in Maluccio, *Promoting Competence in Clients*.

24. Glendora Patterson, "Consultation in High School–Based Day Care Settings: Interfacing of Developmental and Sociocultural Needs," and Nancy A. Irvin, "Early Maternal-Infant Bonding: Institutional Practices and Research,"

both in Robert C. Jackson, Jean Morton, and Miriam Sierra-Franco, eds., *Social Factors in Prevention* (Berkeley, Calif.: School of Public Health, University of California, 1979).

25. Sheila Akabas and Paul Kurzman, eds., *Work, Workers, and Work Organizations: A View from Social Work* (Englewood Cliffs, N.J.: Prentice-Hall, 1982).

26. Richard S. Schweiker, "Promotion/Prevention: Programs, Policies, and Prospects," in *Proceedings of the Conference on Alcohol, Drug Abuse, and Mental Health Promotion/Prevention at the Worksite* (Washington, D.C.: Alcohol, Drug Abuse, and Mental Health Administration, Public Health Service, and U.S. Department of Health and Human Services, 1981), p. V. 1.

27. Public Health Service, U.S. Department of Health, Education, and Welfare, *Healthy People*.

28. *Federal Register*, December 7, 1982, p. 55112.

29. See, for example, *Guideline Standards for Preventive/Promotive Services in Mental Health* and *Definitions for Preventive/Promotive Services in Mental Health* (Atlanta, Ga.: Southern Regional Education Board, both 1980).

30. Judith E. Johnston, *The Role of the State Mental Health Authority in Prevention* (Nashville, Tenn.: Center for the Study of Families and Children, Vanderbilt Institute for Public Policy Studies, Vanderbilt University, 1980).

31. Ibid., p. 74.

32. Eugene Aronowitz, ed., *Prevention Strategies for Mental Health* (New York: Prodist, 1982).

33. Vera Paster, "Organizing Primary Prevention Programs with Disadvantaged Community Groups," in Donald C. Klein and Stephen E. Goldston, eds., *Primary Prevention: An Idea Whose Time Has Come,* Publication No. ADM 77–447 (Washington, D.C.: Alcohol, Drug Abuse, and Mental Health Administration, 1977).

34. Salvatore Ambrosino, "Integrating Counseling, Family Life Education, and Family Advocacy," *Social Casework,* 60 (1979), pp. 579–585.

35. See John Madden, Phyllis Levenstein, and Sidney Levenstein, "Longitudinal IQ Outcomes of the Mother-Child Program," *Child Development*, 47 (1976), pp. 1015–1025; and the original paper, Phyllis Levenstein, "Cognitive Growth in Preschoolers through Verbal Interaction with Mothers," *American Journal of Orthopsychiatry*, 40 (1970), pp. 426–432.

36. Stephen E. Goldston, "Primary Prevention: A View from the Federal Level," in George W. Albee and Justin M. Joffe, eds., *The Issues*, "Primary Prevention of Psychopathology," Vol. 1 (Hanover, N.H.: University Press of New England, 1977), pp. 297–315.

37. Schweiker, *Promotion/Prevention*, p. V-3. See also Morton Hilbert, "Prevention"; and R. B. Albritton, "Cost-Benefits of Measles Eradication: Effects of a Federal Intervention," *Policy Analysis*, 4 (1978), pp. 1–21; and Martha Ozawa, "Development of Social Services in Industry: Why and How?" *Social Work*, 25 (1980), pp. 464–470. In "How Much Is a Life Worth?" *Social Policy*, 9 (1979), pp. 4–8, Amitai Etzioni points out that, although a favorable cost-benefit ratio is possible, it represents a value choice between how much prevention a society desires and how much it is willing to pay for it.

38. These volumes include: George Albee and Justin Joffe, eds., *Primary Prevention of Psychopathology: The Issues* (Vol. 1, 1977); Donald Forgays, ed., *Environmental Influences* (Vol. 2, 1978); Martha Whalen Kent and Jon E. Rolf, eds., *Social Competence in Children* (Vol. 3, 1979); Lynne A. Bond and James C. Rosen, eds., *Competence and Coping During Adolescence* (Vol. 4, 1980); Justin M. Joffe and George W. Albee, eds., *Prevention Through Political Action and Social Change* (Vol. 5, 1981); and Lynne A. Bond and Justin M. Joffe, eds., *Facilitating Infant and Early Childhood Development* (Vol. 6, 1982) (all Hanover, N. H.: University Press of New England).

39. Klein and Goldston, *Primary Prevention*; Jackson, Morton, and Sierra-Franco, *Social Factors in Prevention*; Carel B. Germain, ed., *Social Work Practice: People and Environments: An Ecological Perspective* (New York: Columbia University Press, 1979); Price et al., *Prevention in Mental Health*; Martin Bloom, ed., *Life Span Development: Bases for Preventive and Interventive Helping* (New York: Macmillan, 1980), and *Primary Prevention: The Possible Science* (Englewood Cliffs, N. J.: Prentice Hall, 1981); David Biegel and Arthur Naparstek, eds., *Community Support Systems and Mental Health: Research, Practice and Policy* (New York: Springer Publishing Company, 1981); and Maluccio, *Promoting Competence in Clients*. See also such governmental publications in primary prevention as Silverman, *Mutual Help Groups*; Louisa Messolonghites, *Primary Prevention in Drug Abuse: An Annotated Guide to the Literature*, and Thomas C. Harford,

Douglas A. Parker, and Lillian Light, eds., *Normative Approaches to the Prevention of Alcohol Abuse and Alcoholism,* Publication Nos. M 76-350 and ADM 79-847 (Washington, D.C.: U.S. Department of Health, Education, and Welfare, 1977 and 1980, respectively); and Public Health Service, U.S. Department of Health, Education, and Welfare, *Healthy People.*

40. See Milton Noble, ed., *Primary Prevention in Mental Health and Social Work: A Sourcebook of Curriculum and Teaching Materials* and *Manual of Course Outlines in Primary Prevention in Mental Health and Social Work* (New York: Council on Social Work Education, both 1981).

41. For recent criticisms of primary prevention, see Neil Gilbert, "Policy Issues in Primary Prevention," *Social Work,* 27 (1982), pp. 293–297; Jack Zusman and H. Richard Lamb, "In Defense of Community Mental Health," *American Journal of Psychiatry,* 134 (1977), pp. 887–890; H. Richard Lamb and Jack Zusman, "Primary Prevention in Perspective," *American Journal of Psychiatry,* 136 (1979), pp. 12–17; and Allen S. Mariner, "Benevolent Gambling: A Critique of Primary Prevention Programs in Mental Health," *Psychiatry,* 43 (1980), pp. 95–105. Although the various critics tend to make the same general points, each paper has a distinctive emphasis. For example, Gilbert emphasizes labeling and unanticipated consequences in prevention. Lamb and Zusman, like some earlier critics, take prevention to task for claiming more than it could deliver and for its weak empirical base. Mariner emphasizes, as do others, the would-be diversion of funds from treatment to prevention.

42. See, for example, Michael J. Begab, "The Major Dilemma of Mental Retardation: Shall We Prevent It?" *American Journal of Mental Deficiency,* 78 (1974), pp. 519–529. Begab noted that with the knowledge about mental retardation in hand in 1974, helping professionals could prevent half of all new cases; recent developments likely would raise this estimate even higher.

43. Homer Folks, *Public Health and Welfare: The Citizens' Responsibility. Selected Papers of Homer Folks* (New York: Macmillan Publishing Co., 1958), pp. 378–379.

RECLASSIFICATION AND LICENSING

Since the early 1960s, there has been tremendous growth in the number and type of social welfare programs in the United States. Federal expenditures for social insurance, social services, and public assistance increased tenfold between 1961 and 1980.[1] The social service labor force kept pace with this expansion. In 1960, the number of "social workers" estimated to be working in the United States was 105,000. Twenty years later, that figure was reported to be approximately 385,000, and more and more people were taking specialized training in social work in preparation for entering this labor force.[2] The number of people enrolled in MSW programs grew from 4,972 in 1960 to 22,313 in 1981, and in 1981 the number of students in BSW programs reached 26,602.[3]

By the early 1980s, times had changed. The United States was beset by economic difficulties that rivaled the Great Depression. There was grave concern about the economy and its ability to sustain continuous growth in expenditures, particularly for social and health insurance. Beginning in the 1970s, three successive presidential administrations sought ways to control and curtail expenditures.

But economics was not the only reason for scrutiny and concern. During the sixties and seventies, the realization grew that, as a broad-based cure for the nation's ills, social programs had severe limitations. This caution was leavened periodically by reports of program ineffectiveness, waste, or fraud. This gradual loss of innocence has been characterized succinctly by Briar as the emergence of the "age of accountability."[4]

Because the delivery of social services is a labor-intensive undertaking, it is not surprising that concerns with cost containment and accountability attached themselves to matters relating to labor force utilization. Social work has paid considerable attention in recent years to the formulation of standards for practice. The National Association of Social Workers (NASW),

through periodic position statements on the classification and regulation of practice, has endeavored to provide leadership in this area.[5]

Reclassification

At the heart of a number of labor force issues is the fact that available data for the public sector indicate that many, if not most, individuals who provide social services do not have specialized training in social work at either the graduate or undergraduate level.[6] Furthermore, the connection between specialized social work preparation and access to social services jobs has appeared to weaken in recent years. This phenomenon has been called declassification.[7] Data on this process of erosion, permitting comparisons of employment patterns at different times, are not available. In the past decade, however, several surveys have been carried out that, despite methodological problems, shed light on the situation.

Between 1977 and 1979, the American Public Welfare Association (APWA) conducted a national survey of state human services personnel.[8] Thirty-seven states and the District of Columbia responded to the survey.[9] From the perspective of the profession, the findings were mixed. Despite its newness at the time of the survey, the BSW degree already had some visibility; seventeen states made a distinction between the BSW and other bachelor's degrees in hiring requirements for direct services. Twenty-four jurisdictions indicated that a distinction was also made between the MSW and other master's degrees at the direct service level. Nevertheless, workers without specialized social work training clearly predominated in direct service positions. Approximately 28 percent of the workers held either BSW or MSW degrees; 64 percent possessed degrees in other fields.

Fifteen states recognized the BSW and

twenty-three recognized the MSW in hiring for supervisory positions. At this level, social work training was more prevalent. Half of the supervisors had either BSW or MSW degrees; only 47 percent of the incumbents held degrees in other areas. In twenty-eight reporting jurisdictions, it was possible, although not necessarily frequent, for direct services workers to become supervisors without graduate training of any kind.

Other data about personnel requirements came from studies carried out by NASW. An NASW project entitled "Classification Validation Processes for Social Service Positions" was funded by the Children's Bureau from 1979 to 1981. The first phase of the study was designed to collect information about job requirements for child welfare and social service positions. In 1980, a request for training and education requirements was sent to the state merit agencies in the fifty states and the District of Columbia. Despite NASW's attempts to standardize the terminology in the request, the twenty-nine responding states used different terms and an assortment of job descriptions. These responses, moreover, were based on documents that articulated policies that might not be carried out in practice. That different states responded to different surveys further complicated the task of comparing the data sets obtained in this and other studies. Although comparisons with the APWA data or with survey data collected by NASW in 1975 must be made cautiously, some conclusions can be drawn.

First, it is clear that social work does not have a proprietary hold on social service positions in the public sector; nor did it have one in the recent past. In the most recent job descriptions, the terms "social work" and "social worker" appear less frequently. This is apparently the result of an increasing tendency to define and label jobs in functional rather than disciplinary terms. The BSW still has visibility. In the 1980 survey, ten states mentioned the BSW as fulfilling an entry requirement, but it was cited as a sufficient rather than as a necessary credential. Fifteen states specified the BSW as sufficient for attaining more advanced positions in direct service. However, none of the states providing data stipulated the BSW as the sole requirement for employment in direct service. Many states consider "related" education to be a substitute for social work education; in addition, work experience can often substitute for formal education. Twenty-two states permitted experience to be substituted for the bachelor's degree. At the supervisory level, social work education (BSW or MSW) plus varying amounts of experience were required in sixteen states, but experience could often be substituted for education on a year-for-year basis. Twelve states required some level of graduate training for supervisory positions, but the nature of the training varied from one state to another.

Second, social service classification systems are undergoing change. At the time of the 1980 NASW survey, over a third of the responding jurisdictions reported activities associated with the revision of job classes or personnel requirements. A number also indicated that efforts were under way to carry out validation studies of selection procedures or training and education requirements. Documents describing these activities were requested as part of the survey.[10]

Third, great variability was apparent among the states in the way staffing patterns and requirements for personnel were specified. The one consistency was inconsistency. Social work was mentioned frequently, but no combination of training or experience predominated. Many states accepted "related" education in lieu of social work, but there was no uniform interpretation of this term. When it was defined, and often it was not, the disciplines referred to were psychology, sociology, guidance and counseling, education, and child development. Work experience was often used as a substitute for education, but, again, there was considerable variability. In some instances "life" experience was a substitute; in others, the experience component had to be in the general field or in the specific career ladder.

Rationale for Job Requirements

There is little evidence to support the contention that changes in the requirements for social services jobs flow only out of a widespread animosity toward the profession of social work. Although such a motive is probably a factor in some instances, the reasons for altering job requirements seem as varied as the requirements themselves. A number of these reasons are given in the following section.

Fiscal austerity. As stated earlier, social service delivery is a labor intensive activity. Applicants with less training and education are generally perceived as cheaper to hire and employ. Thus, minimizing credential requirements is seen as one way of containing or curtailing costs.

Competition. In times of austerity, there are usually cutbacks in social service and social welfare appropriations. This results in increased competition among related disciplines for decreasing numbers of jobs.

Service integration. Trends toward functional integration and away from disciplinary specialization have already been noted. These trends, combined with the lack of a commonly accepted definition of social services and social work at the agency level, have made the approach of allowing a variety of backgrounds to satisfy job requirements seem like a logical strategy to many employers. This approach probably contributed to the advent of non–social workers as managers in public sector social service organizations. Although social workers have never been in the majority in such agencies, they have traditionally been in influential management positions. With the rise of functional management specialists, this influence is waning.

Shortages. There have been and still are genuine shortages of trained social work personnel in many localities. Although often a result of uneven distribution, such shortages have prompted employers to broaden the pool of applicants from which they can draw.

Perceived ineffectiveness. Social services do not usually result in quick or dramatic outcomes. By attempting to identify itself with the social service industry, social work sometimes bears the stigma for its perceived lack of results. Also, this perception of ineffectiveness does not reinforce the notion that high standards of performance are necessary.

Mistaken notions about risk. Social interventions are often perceived as benign, that is, as involving few risks to clients or society if things go wrong. To those holding this view, experimentation with job requirements would not seem to be inappropriate or dangerous.

Job mobility. As has been noted, most social service systems contain many workers without specialized social work education. The career aspirations of these workers are enhanced by the mobility that results from the broadening of job requirements. Any bargaining agents representing such employees would routinely reinforce this position through their characteristic emphasis on experience and seniority.[11]

Perceptions about clients. The public generally has a negative image of the welfare recipient. The notion of requiring highly trained professionals to deliver services to these "undeserving" individuals can thus seem paradoxical, and this attitude contributes to a reduction in employment standards.

Patronage. Jobs perceived as low-risk activities providing nebulous services to largely undeserving clients can become prime targets for patronage. To facilitate this type of political appointment, credential requirements are sometimes modified or dropped.

Affirmative action. The requirement of educational credentials can usually be shown to have an adverse impact on minorities whose access to higher education and professional training has traditionally been limited. This fact, coupled with current requirements that recruitment and selection procedures not discriminate against protected groups, have raised the specter of lawsuits. Rather than run such risks, employers sometimes choose to drop the requirements.

It is clear that the determination of social service job requirements is based on much more than a presumption that certain forms of technical preparation impart the necessary competence. Available data suggest strongly that job specifications and work requirements are formulated in an atmosphere that is an exotic mixture of technology, economics, and politics.

Legal Regulation of Practice

This less-than-ideal link between social work training and incumbency in social services jobs has made the legal regulation of social work practice an important professional concern. Legal regulation has two basic objectives: protection of a title and protection of a practice. Considerable confusion surrounds legal regulation because the terminology associated with it differs from state to state and because the same process of regulation may accomplish different ends in different places. Three terms appear with regularity. "Registration" generally refers to the simplest form of regulation and provides little control. It involves a listing of those who wish to be associated with an activity and is most often used for title protection without an examination requirement. A second term, "certification," is used at times to refer to both title protection and practice regulation. Most often it is simply title protection with an accompanying examination requirement. The third term is "licensing." In principle, this is the highest level of regulation because it restricts both the title and activity to those who have met certain requirements.[12] In practice, however, licensing is an ambiguous mechanism with many variations.

Despite its flaws, licensing is the form of regulation preferred by NASW.

Puerto Rico was the first jurisdiction to regulate social work practice; a certification and licensing law was enacted there in 1934. In 1945, California passed a voluntary registration act for the master's-level social worker. Little activity took place until New York and Oklahoma enacted legislation in 1965.

Until 1969, NASW took the position that social work, as an agency-based profession, would be adequately protected by title protection (registration). In 1969, recognizing the proliferation of "social work" titles applied to jobs not restricted to social workers and the need to develop standards for practice not based in agencies, NASW's Delegate Assembly adopted a position favoring licensure to control practice. By 1972, the Professional Standards Cabinet had revised the existing guidelines and developed a model statute, which was promulgated among the chapters.[13] The effort paid off. Between 1972 and 1977, legislation was enacted in fifteen states. In eleven of these, the legislation involved licensure.

In 1976, NASW issued a more comprehensive statement on legal regulation.[14] This document set forth eight "essential elements" for the adequate regulation of practice: (1) an emphasis on licensure, (2) a recognition of all levels of practice based on professional knowledge and skill, (3) the establishment of criteria for autonomous practice, (4) valid means of assessing competence, (5) coverage of all settings in which practice occurs, (6) periodic license renewal and a continuing education requirement, (7) privileged communications, and (8) sanctions and accountability. Language relating to eight elements is included in the NASW model statute.

Statutes. The most recent state law regulating social work practice was enacted in 1983. At present twenty-nine states or jurisdictions have some form of legal regulation. To facilitate description and comparison, the salient characteristics of the various statues are summarized in Table 1.

TABLE 1. SUMMARY OF CHARACTERISTICS OF STATE REGULATIONS

State	Type[1]	Year Passed/ Amended	Exams	Levels	Education	Excluded Groups[4]	Privileged Communication	Penalties[5]	Cont. Education Required
Alabama	L	1977	Yes	4	BSW/MSW	a, c	No		Yes
Arkansas	L	1975/1981	Yes	3	BSW/MSW	c	Yes	d	Yes
California	R	1945/1981	Yes	1	BA/BSW/MSW	a, b	Yes		No
	L	1968/1973	Yes	1	MSW				
Colorado	R/L	1975/1981	Yes[2]	3	BA/MSW		Yes	e	Yes
Delaware	L	1976	Yes	1	MSW	a, b	Yes	e	Yes
Florida	R	1981	Yes	1	MSW	a, c	No	e	Yes
Idaho	L	1976	Yes[3]	3	BSW/MSW	c	Yes	e	No
Illinois	R	1967	Yes	2	BA/MSW	c	Yes	d, f	No
Kansas	L	1974/1980	Yes	3	BSW/MSW		No	e	Yes
Kentucky	L	1974/1976	Yes	3	BSW/MSW	a	Yes	e	Yes
Louisiana	L	1972	Yes	1	MSW	a, b, c	Yes	d, f	No
Maine	R/L	1969/1978	Yes	4	BA/BSW/MSW	a	Yes	d	Yes
Maryland	R	1975/1981	Yes	4	BSW/MSW	a, c	No	d, f	Yes
Massachusetts	L	1977	Yes	4	BA/BSW/MSW	a, c	Yes	d, f	Yes
Michigan	R	1972/1975	No	3	BA/MSW		Yes		No
Montana	R	1983	Yes	1	MSW	a, b, c	Yes	e	Yes
New York	R	1965	Yes	1	MSW		Yes	e	No
North Carolina	R	1983	Yes	3	BSW/MSW		Yes	e	Yes
North Dakota	L	1983	Yes	3	BSW/MSW	c	No	e	Yes
Oklahoma	R	1965/1980	Yes	2	BSW/MSW		Yes	d	No
Oregon	R	1977/1979	No	1	MSW	a, b, c	No	e	No
Puerto Rico	L	1934/1940	No	1	BA/BSW/MSW	c	No		No
Rhode Island	R	1961	No	1	MSW		No	d	No
South Carolina	R	1968	No	1	MSW		No	d, f	No
South Dakota	L	1975	Yes	4	BA/BSW/MSW	c	Yes	d, f	Yes
Tennessee	R	1980	No	2	MSW		No	d, e	No
Texas	R	1981	Yes[3]	4	BA/BSW/MSW		No		Yes
Utah	L	1972/1977	Yes	4	BSW/MSW		No		Yes
Virginia	L	1966/1975	Yes	2	MSW	a, b, c	Yes	d	Yes

[1] L = licensing, R = registration.
[2] Not required for private or independent practice.
[3] Not required for private agency employees.
[4] (a) public employees; (b) private agency employees; (c) student.
[5] (d) fine; (e) misdemeanor; (f) imprisonment.
Source: *State Comparison of Laws Regulating Social Work* (Silver Spring, Md.: National Association of Social Workers, July 1983).

Twelve of the statutes provide only for registration or certification. Fourteen states establish licensing. Three states provide for both mechanisms. Most states require some form of an assessment, usually an examination, as a prerequisite for licensing. Since 1972, most of the statutes have been multilevel, specifically recognizing the BSW graduate and providing some type of coverage for this degree. In specifying background requirements, the states use a mixture of formal education and experience. A number of states specify "related" education and experience but leave definitions up to various regulatory bodies, such as licensing boards, that are charged with administering the statutes at the state level. Although the training and education requirements the various statutes establish for applicants who wish to be certified and licensed to practice social work are generally more consistent than the requirements set for hiring, there still is little uniformity from state to state.

In the past ten years, considerable progress has been made in the regulation of social work practice. As of September 1982, NASW estimated that approximately 77,400 social workers were covered by various state statutes. This is far from full coverage of the labor force described earlier, but many statutes specifically exclude agency-based workers, especially in the public sector. Once enacted, regulations such as these are far from permanent. As of March 1982, nineteen states had sunset laws or some form of scheduled regulatory review.[15] Given the present climate of antiregulatory sentiment, passage of additional laws has come more slowly. Also, "sunset" provisions in most states suggest the need for continuous monitoring of existing statutes.

Social workers differ in their attitudes toward practice regulation. Some are of the opinion that existing regulations do not go far enough in extending coverage and providing control.[16] Others, particularly practitioners who are members of minority groups, often argue against any control at the state level, perceiving licensing as a means of restricting access to jobs by requiring qualifications, such as degrees and exams, that are likely to be discriminatory. Future policies on licensing must take these disparate points of view into account. NASW, which still strongly supports licensing, is revising its model statute.

Examinations. NASW's *Standards for the Regulation of Social Work Practice* requires "a valid means of objectively assessing the qualifications, knowledge, and competencies of applicants for licensure...."[17] This is typically done by means of a paper-and-pencil examination, although California and Virginia also have an oral component to their examinations. Various private corporations and a number of individual states have attempted to develop examinations. Like other features of state regulation, the exams vary widely, as do the mechanisms for administering them. In 1977 NASW developed the *Social Work Examination for Licensing* (SWEL) to assess performance at several practice levels corresponding to those designated in NASW's standards for classifying practice. The states were slow to adopt SWEL, and NASW discontinued the program in 1980.

During the early 1980s, the American Association of State Social Work Boards (AASWB) attempted to set up a national licensure testing procedure. The multilevel examinations developed for AASWB by an independent testing firm attempt to assess qualifications at both the BSW and MSW levels, a range of coverage somewhat broader than that of the ACSW exam.[18] Although the first administration of the AASWB exams was scheduled for 1983 in several states, these tests are likely to face the same problems encountered by the SWEL program and the examination procedures developed by private groups. Any examination program, if it is to be used on a widespread basis for licensing, must first surmount the differences in statutory provisions. There is no doubt that a need exists for a consistent mechanism of applicant assessment from state to state, but smoothing out differences requires legislative action and considerable negotiation.

The Importance of Validation

The data on manpower utilization in social work clearly show that social agencies throughout the country, although they deal with similar problems, clients, and programs, employ labor forces that differ remarkably in the extent of their specialized training and work experience. Social workers who are dismayed by this state of affairs are propelled by a belief that specialized competencies are imparted by programs of study in social work and that these competencies are essential for practice. this belief lies at the heart of the desire for practice classifications based on levels of education and for social work credentials as requirements for licensure and jobs. In short, this position avers the job relatedness of social work training.

As stated earlier, this position is increasingly challenged, and applicants with degrees in other fields are competing for jobs traditionally held by social workers. Employers without social work backgrounds often lack information on which to evaluate claims of unique qualifications. In addition, because both the processes leading to credentials and the traditional methods of assessing competence can often be shown to penalize minorities, the profession has the burden of demonstrating the jobrelatedness or validity of its credentialing procedures if it wishes to adhere to its educational standards. Federal regulations based on civil rights legislation mandate that any qualifications set up as minimal requirements for jobs, if they can be shown to have an adverse impact on minorities, must be demonstrated to be "business necessities."[19]

Establishing the validity of credentials and licensing procedures for a profession as diverse as social work is difficult. Although the technology of validation has a long history, there are formidable obstacles to the use of traditional validation strategies with social work jobs. Social workers function in a wide range of settings and engage in highly abstract activities; cases, moreover, vary tremendously in difficulty and complexity. Measures of job performance are few and unreliable, giving little support to validity claims.

Efforts to remedy this situation are under way. The NASW study funded by the Children's Bureau was described earlier in this article. One product of this three-year project was a model that agencies or schools of social work can use to validate the content of social work curricula as minimum requirements for jobs.[20] This model was subjected to limited pilot testing during its development; its usefulness awaits demonstration on a broader scale. Further, in 1983 NASW undertook to validate the content of the ACSW examination. The first step was job analysis of NASW members nationwide; the findings are expected to guide a revision of ACSW assessment procedures to reflect more closely the content of the jobs social workers perform. The AASWB exams described earlier have also incorporated the findings of a job analysis of licensed social workers in a number of states. These and other investigations should demonstrate the validity of social work's personnel standards and provide support for the political efforts necessary to maintain those standards.

ROBERT J. TEARE

Notes and References

1. See U.S. Bureau of the Budget, *The Federal Budget in Brief: Fiscal Year 1960,* and U.S. Office of Management and Budget, *Special Analysis, Budget of the United States Government: Fiscal Year 1982* (Washington, D.C.: U.S. Government Printing Office, 1959 and 1982, respectively).

2. These estimates are based on definitions of the term "social worker" contained in U.S. Department of Labor, Manpower Administration, *The Dictionary of Occupational Titles* (3rd and 4th eds.; Washington, D.C.: U.S. Government Printing Office, 1965 and 1977); and U.S. Bureau of Labor Statistics, *Occupational Outlook Handbook* (1961 and 1980-81 eds.; Washington, D.C.: U.S. Government Printing Office, 1961 and 1980), pp. 269 and 452, respectively.

3. Miriam Dinerman, *Present Social Work Curricular Patterns: Baccalaureate and Masters*

(New York: Silberman Foundation, 1981); and Allen Rubin, *Statistics on Social Work Education in the United States, 1981* (New York: Council on Social Work Education, 1981).

4. Scott Briar, "The Age of Accountability," *Social Work,* 18 (January 1973).

5. For an excellent discussion of the activities of professional associations, see Bertram Beck, "Professional Associations: National Association of Social Workers," and Ernest Witte, "Professional Associations: Council on Social Work Education," *Encyclopedia of Social Work* (17th ed.; Washington, D.C.: National Association of Social Workers, 1977), pp. 1084–1093 and 1081–1084, respectively.

6. See "An Analysis of Hiring Requirements for Social Service Classifications in State Merit Systems" (Washington, D.C.: National Association of Social Workers, 1975) (mimeographed); Robert J. Teare et al., *Classification Validation Processes for Social Service Positions —Volume 1: Overview* (Silver Spring, Md.: National Association of Social Workers, in press); Ann Shyne and Anita Schroeder, "National Study of Social Services to Children and Their Families," Publication No. OHDS 78-30150 (Washington, D.C.: U.S. Children's Bureau, U.S. Department of Health, Education, and Welfare, 1978); "Survey of State Human Services Personnel" (Washington, D.C.: American Public Welfare Association, 1979) (mimeographed); and Robert Teare, *Social Work Practice in a Public Welfare Setting* (New York: Praeger, 1981).

7. The term "declassification" is a misnomer because it implies the complete removal of requirements for training or experience. In practice, alteration rather than removal of requirements is usually the case. Consequently, the term "reclassification" is more appropriate and has been used in its stead in this article.

8. "Survey of State Human Services Personnel."

9. There were some problems with the data. Definitions were not provided for terms such as "direct service" or "supervisory positons." Also, some jurisdictions did not reply to all the questions, and numbers of incumbents were not always provided and were often based on estimates.

10. For a summary of the activities in eighteen states, see Hubert S. Feild, Robert J. Teare, and Thomas P. Gauthier, *Classification Validation Processes for Social Service Positions— Volume 4: An Analysis of States' Classification*

Validation/Job Analysis Studies of Social Service Positions (Silver Spring, Md.: National Association of Social Workers, in press).

11. In the APWA survey, twenty-three states reported having at least one collective bargaining unit representing their employees.

12. For elaborations, see David A. Hardcastle, "Public Regulation of Social Work," *Social Work,* 20 (January 1977), pp. 14–20; and Benjamin Shimberg, *Occupational Licensing: A Public Perspective* (Princeton, N.J.: Educational Testing Service, 1980).

13. *Legal Regulation of Social Work Practice* (Washington D.C.: National Association of Social Workers, 1973).

14. *Standards for the Regulation of Social Work Practice,* Policy Statement No. 5 (Washington D.C.: National Association of Social Workers, 1976).

15. *The Status of Sunset in the States: A Common Cause Report* (Washington, D.C.: Common Cause, March 1982).

16. See Hardcastle, "Public Regulation of Social Work"; and Myles Johnson, "Missing the Point of Licensure," *Social Work,* 22 (March 1977), p. 87.

17. For the latest version of these standards, see *NASW Standards for the Classification of Practice,* Policy Statement No. 4 (Silver Spring, Md.: National Association of Social Workers, 1981), p. 6.

18. The Academy of Certified Social Workers (ACSW) is an NASW program that provides for the evaluation of social workers through the use of a nationwide examination procedure. In use since 1971, the examination aims its content at the "independent professional level," which is defined as requiring an accredited MSW degree plus two years of experience.

19. Equal Employment Opportunity Commission, Civil Service Commission, Department of Labor, and Department of Justice, "Adoption of Four Agencies of Uniform Guidelines on Employee Selection Procedures," *Federal Register,* March 2, 1979, pp. 11996–12009. For a discussion of case law relating to these guidelines as they apply to social work, see Teare et al., *Classification Validation Processes for Social Service Positions—Volume 1: Overview.*

20. *Job Analysis Procedures and Instruments,* Vol. 2, and *Curriculum Analysis Procedures and Instruments*, Vol. 3, (Silver Spring, Md.: National Association of Social Workers, 1982).

RESEARCH DEVELOPMENTS

As a highly diversified profession, social work makes use of research from many sources. Most of the scientific work generated by the social sciences and human services is relevant to the profession's broad range of interests. Only a fraction of this empirical base is social work research in the strict sense of studies that both deal with social work concerns and are produced by social workers or under the auspices of social work schools or organizations. This relatively small body of research is of critical importance to social workers, however, because it addresses questions of direct relevance to their activities and provides substance for the claim that social work is an autonomous profession with its own scientific underpinnings. This article focuses on selected developments in social work research since approximately the middle of the 1970s. It considers four aspects of social work research: its infrastructure, content, results, and methodology.

Infrastructure

The social work research enterprise depends on a complex infrastructure consisting of such elements as skilled personnel, organizational supports, professional climate, financial resources, and channels of dissemination. This infrastructure has experienced gains, losses, and other changes during the period under review.

On the positive side, continuing emphasis in the profession on the need for an accountable, scientifically based practice has elevated the importance of research. Concrete expressions of this development have included national and regional conferences on research utilization sponsored by the Council on Social Work Education, the 1978 National Conference on the Future of Social Work Research sponsored by the National Association of Social Workers, and the appearance of two professional journals devoted to research, *Social Work*

Research and Abstracts and the *Journal of Social Service Research.* Also, the production of doctorates continued to increase, adding to the growing body of dissertation research and to the pool of professionals with advanced training in research methods.[1] On the negative side, funding for research has become increasingly difficult to acquire in the wake of reduced federal support for domestic programs. Competition for available government and private funds has become more intense, and social agencies, which have been hard pressed to maintain their basic service programs, have been less willing to devote time and money to research.

One of these developments, the increased output of doctorates, is a long-term and important change in the infrastructure, a change that has begun to have an overriding effect on the social work research enterprise. The major impact, thus far, has been in schools of social work, where the majority of doctoral graduates have found employment. According to the most recent statistics available (1980–1981), almost half the faculty in graduate schools of social work possess doctorates, although not always in social work, and the proportion has been steadily increasing.[2] Having a doctorate is by no means equivalent to having research interests or competence, but faculty with doctorates are likely to be more involved in research, to be more skilled at it, and to make more use of it in teaching than faculty without the degree.[3] Moreover, university administrations, which are becoming increasingly selective and demanding, are motivating faculty to engage in research and scholarly activities as well as to obtain doctorates.

These developments are contributing to a growing dominance of social work research by its academic cadres. For example, in a content analysis of all articles in major social work journals, Grinnell found that the proportion of research articles authored by academics has been increasing.

Over three-fourths of the articles published in the recently established research journals had academic authorship.[4] In a survey of social work research articles abstracted in *Social Work Research and Abstracts* from 1980 through 1982, the present writer found that the authors of almost 80 percent of the articles were located in academic institutions. In his review of the deliberations of the National Conference on the Future of Social Work Research, Fanshel cited repeated references at the conference to the "decline in the importance of agency-based research" and the shift to "university and government sponsorship."[5]

The emergence of the academic setting as the center of gravity in social work research is one consequence of the upgrading of the profession's educational arm, and it offers opportunities for new partnerships between schools, which can provide research expertise, and agencies, which can provide clients, practitioners, and good research questions. Still, it would be unfortunate if agencies were to assume an entirely subordinate role in this partnership. At the least, if research findings or empirically based service models are to have an impact on practice, they need to be tested, evaluated, and reworked by the agencies in which they are to be used. For this task, there is no substitute for agency staff with research know-how.

Content

What do social work researchers study? The question is of considerable importance considering the range of possible topics in a field as diverse as social work. It is also difficult to answer, even if one limits attention to published or abstracted studies. Although a good deal of the profession's research literature can be accessed through such sources as *Social Work Research and Abstracts*, major social work journals, and periodic reviews of social work research, much of it is not so readily identified.[6] For example, many studies are published in books or in non-social work journals. Moreover, the interdisciplinary nature of much relevant research complicates efforts to distinguish between social work research and other kinds, and the classification of the subject matter of any study is no simple task.

Nevertheless, some observations can be made. The great bulk of social work research can be classified into the following categories: (1) studies concerned with the behavior, personality, and problems of individuals, families, and small groups, both client and nonclient, (2) investigations of the characteristics, utilization, and outcome of service, (3) research on the social work profession, interdisciplinary concerns, and the attitudes, orientations, and training of social workers, and (4) studies of organizations, communities, and social policy. Approximations of these categories emerged in two independent content analyses of abstracts of research studies, thus providing a measure of cross-validation for this kind of classification.[7]

The social work research literature, including dissertations, published or abstracted since 1975 can be roughly mapped in terms of these categories. Different content analyses have indicated that about a quarter of the studies fall into the first category, understanding people.[8] An additional quarter fall into the second category, service characteristics and outcome. Studies of social workers, the profession, training, and the like account for another quarter, and from 15 percent to a quarter are accounted for by the fourth category, organizations, communities, and social policy. The variation in the last category appears to depend on whether the content analysis relates to published articles or dissertations —the latter tend to show higher proportions of studies in the last category; another source of variation appears to relate to differences in how studies are sampled and coded.

Although no short-term trends are apparent, one long-term trend emerges in both published articles and dissertations: studies concerned with social work education have increased markedly since the sixties. This trend may be related to the shift noted earlier to university-based research.

The broad range of social work research —which some feel amounts to a scattered focus—becomes apparent when its content areas are further subdivided, for example, by type of client or nonclient population, problem, service, and so on. Few content areas have attracted concentrations of studies. Although this is perhaps inevitable in a field as broad as social work, it highlights the profession's dependence on research from the social sciences and other disciplines. Moreover, the relative emphases in content raise questions about priorities. For example, should studies of social workers and their training occupy as much as a quarter of the profession's research output, a proportion that may well be increasing? Should not the study of the nature and outcomes of social work services occupy a more prominent place in social work research than is currently the case?

Results

The chief purpose of social work research is to enhance the knowledge base and technology of social work practice. This requires that the research yield significant and relevant results. It is beyond the scope of this article to attempt even a cursory review of the entire body of results produced by contemporary social work research. Instead, the article examines one important cluster of findings to demonstrate that noteworthy progress has been achieved in recent years.

In the early seventies, social work was presented with an accumulation of research evidence suggesting that its individualized services had been unable to demonstrate their effectiveness.[9] The evidence took the form of reviews of a series of field experiments, conducted largely in the sixties, that evaluated professional casework and other services against controls involving no treatment or lesser treatment. In most experiments, the professional services were not able to demonstrate superiority over no service or inferior service. Although the studies were roundly criticized for method-

ological shortcomings and sampling limitations, their results could hardly be taken as an endorsement of the types of intervention tested. The findings put the profession in the uncomfortable position of having to apologize for either its flawed research or its inadequate services.

Fortunately, this picture began to change in the early seventies. An exhaustive review of the controlled studies published between 1972 and 1981 revealed that when social work intervention was pitted against a lesser or no-treatment condition (approximately twenty-five experiments), the intervention proved to be clearly superior in all but a few of the studies.[10] This welcome turnaround in the results of controlled outcome evaluations appeared to be a consequence of several factors. Compared to the interventions examined in the experiments of the 1960s, the interventions were better structured, and their goals were more limited and specific, reflecting the influence of behavioral and other structured treatment approaches that were little in evidence in the earlier experiments. Moreover, the recent experiments were generally better designed than their predecessors. The recent experimental programs showed more evidence that they had been preceded by pilot testing, they were more likely to have been conducted under the direction of the experimenters, and they tended to have made greater use of observational and other objective measures.

More effective interventions and better means of evaluating them may thus have accounted for the more optimistic results of the post-1972 experiments. In part, the gains were achieved through a pulling back from the ambitious experiments of the earlier period. The later experiments tended to use smaller samples and shorter follow-up periods. The effects of service they examined were more readily achieved and were often limited in scope, for example, an improvement in specific social skills. However, this approach of accomplishing more by doing less does not account for the positive outcomes of several recent experiments that used large samples and achieved significant impact in the lives of the clients served.[11] Clearly, a milestone has been achieved.

Methodology

Recent developments in the methodology of social work research have included the emergence of developmental research paradigms; applications and extensions of single-system methodologies; and the growing impact of computer technology, which has made possible the growth of agency information systems and the use of complex models of data processing and analysis. This section discusses the first two of these developments and related issues.

Developmental Research. A new strategy for the construction, testing, and modification of social work programs and models has emerged in recent years. Usually referred to as developmental research, this strategy has as its objective the creation of empirically based service approaches.[12] The primary goal is not the generation of knowledge, which is the conventional application of research, but rather the building of intervention technology. The developer, who combines expertise in both research and practice, resembles an engineer who uses scientific understanding and techniques to construct rather than to investigate. The primary end product is not a research report but rather a service model delineated in such forms as practice manuals and program designs. In creating this product, the developer makes use of research in different ways: in designing an initial version of the model, the developer draws on existing research findings about target populations and intervention methods; data are collected on how practitioners apply the model and on the apparent outcomes of its application; and this information is then used to improve the model's strategies and methods. More rigorous tests of the model's effectiveness may later be conducted by means of controlled experiments.

As a means of improving programs, a developmental research strategy overcomes,

at least in theory, a number of the inadequacies of conventional research. It provides a direct route between research activity and the improvement of service. The self-corrective powers of research can be used in a systematic and efficient way in constructing programs and the means to evaluate them. Inherent conflicts between "program people" and researchers are obviated. Some instransigent obstacles to research utilization are also bypassed. To utilize the fruits of developmental research, it is not necessary for practitioners or decision makers to digest and apply research reports; rather, they can apply the service technology produced by the research. This still-evolving strategy of research is a major advance. Thomas puts it more strongly:

> Developmental research may be the single most appropriate model of research for social work because it consists of methods directed explicitly toward the analysis, development, and evaluation of the very technical means by which social work objectives are achieved.[13]

Limitations in this strategy need also to be taken into account. Developmental research is in an inchoate stage of development. Little is known about the best project designs to use at different stages of program development or about how study results can best be used to inform this development. Bias in evaluation is difficult to avoid if the model developers are also the evaluators. Problems of utilization—not of research findings, but of the service models themselves—need to be solved. Although it is fashionable to use the vocabulary of engineers and to refer to the service models produced by developmental research as "products," these products are usually not apparatuses that can be made to work everywhere, given proper instructions. They consist rather of complicated guidelines for practitioners and are often incomplete and too general. Proper use may require substantial training changes in accustomed work habits and practice beliefs, all of which may encounter agency and staff resistance. Unlike an apparatus, a practice model can be readily picked apart by users, who may incorporate some elements into their own practice, usually after refashioning them somewhat, and junk the rest. As a result of such obstacles, the "dissemination" of service models of proved effectivenes into an ongoing program provides no assurance whatsoever about the effectiveness of the model or the parts of it that may be used in the program. Dissemination does not even provide assurance that the model will be used at all.

Much of the recent research in social work appears to fit, at least in part, the developmental research paradigm. In most of the recent service experiments referred to in the preceding section, for example, developers devised and evaluated models they helped perfect, usually making use of previous research and often conducting preliminary tests of their approaches. In a sense, the developmental research paradigm is an effort to systematize this kind of experimental work and to provide guidance for it.

The best articulated example of developmental research is seen in Rothman's efforts to develop and test ways of introducing innovations into community agencies.[14] Rothman's work is distinctive in its deliberate use of principles for developing service models. Although Rothman's approach, referred to as social R&D, is modeled after research and development operations in industry, it is a type of developmental research. It is of additional interest in showing how developmental research, which has been used largely in clinical settings, can be applied to practice at the community organizational levels.

Single-system design and the practitioner-researcher. In the late sixties, the single-system design, which had become the major research design in behavior modification, began to be introduced in social work, usually in the context of behavioral intervention. In the seventies, applications of these designs—also referred to as single-case and single-subject designs—increased considerably. Advances have been made in

adapting them to the diversities of social work practice, and they have been used as a basis for what might be termed the practitioner-researcher movement in social work.[15]

Single-system designs were introduced as a means of assessing the effects of interventions with individual clients. Observational data on target behavior or problems are collected prior to, during, and after the intervention and are used to form a profile of change over time. This time series gives an indication of whether a change in the behavior or problem is associated with the intervention tested. Through various manipulations of the intervention—for example, by withdrawing it or starting it at different times with different problems or clients—it is possible to achieve a high degree of control over extraneous factors that might explain change, a degree of control comparable to what might be achieved in a controlled group experiment.

Applications of this design are increasing, although the number of published social work studies that have used it is still small.[16] In adapting the design to social work contexts, researchers have attempted to broaden its scope to include families, small groups, organizations, and communities.[17] Retrospective baseline data obtained in the initial session and followed immediately by an intervention have been used in place of extensive preintervention baselines to avoid delays in treatment. Although observational data are still the norm, a variety of client self-reports and other types of measuring instruments have been introduced.

The design has proved extremely useful as a means of assessing the effectiveness of behavioral or quasi-behavioral forms of intervention and has provided an excellent way for students to engage in research on their own cases. At the same time, applications have pointed up certain limitations that have yet to be overcome. The use of single cases severely restricts the generalizability of any findings. In theory, generalization can be achieved through replication, but few replication series have yet appeared. Moreover, the design has been little used apart from behavioral forms of treatment. Requirements for the specification of change targets and for quantitative measurement have been obstacles to the design's broader application. However, ways of resolving these obstacles have been suggested.[18] Also, examples of the use of single-subject designs with nonbehavioral interventions have appeared.[19]

Single-system designs have been given a central role in what might be termed the practitioner-researcher movement. According to the proponents of this movement, agency practitioners should take an active role in evaluating the effectiveness of their own practice and in applying developmental research to improve their interventive techniques.[20] Case-by-case evaluative and developmental efforts, it is argued, would promote accountability and result in a more empirically based, effective practice with only modest allocations of resources. Moreover, the results of this integration between practice and research would be likely to be utilized because this research would be produced by practitioners themselves.

How much of an impact this movement has had thus far is hard to ascertain. It has been an important influence in student training in a number of schools, and students have successfully tested it in various fieldwork settings and in doctoral dissertations. It has not yet had a noticeable impact on the ranks of agency practitioners, but this impact may grow as students trained in the use of single-case methods begin to exert a wider influence in agencies. If so, as Briar suggests, agencies will need to "create the organizational and institutional supports practitioners need to perform as practitioner-scientists."[21] This is a goal that hard-pressed agencies would find difficult to realize at present. Also, the conflicts between service and research objectives that Thomas has detailed need to be reconciled.[22]

More apparent than any increase in the numbers of practitioner scientists has been the adoption of empirical models of practice and of orientations that cast interven-

tion targets in specific measurable terms and use systematic observation, goal attainment scaling, standardized instruments, consumer questionnaires, and structured recording for treatment planning or evaluative purposes. Agency and government accountability systems that require the reporting of case events and outcomes have augmented and reinforced this trend. Although these developments do not add up to an implementation of the practitioner-research concept, they may reflect a growing incorporation of research viewpoints and methods into the fabric of agency programs.

WILLIAM J. REID

Notes and References

1. Allen Rubin, *Statistics on Social Work Education in the United States, 1981* (New York: Council on Social Work Education, 1982).

2. Ibid. p. 10.

3. See, for example, Stuart A. Kirk and Aaron Rosenblatt, "The Contribution of Women Faculty to Social Work Journals: A Research Note." To be published in a forthcoming issue of *Social Work*.

4. Richard M. Grinnell, Jr. "Qualitative and Quantitative Articles in Social Work Journals," unpublished manuscript, LaTrobe University, Bundoora, Victoria, Australia, 1983; and Richard M. Grinnell and Martha L. Royer, "Authors of Articles in Social Work Journals: A Research Note," to be published in a forthcoming issue of the *Journal of Social Service Research.*

5. David Fanshel, "The Future of Social Work Research: Strategies for the Coming Years," in David Fanshel, ed., *The Future of Social Work Research* (Washington, D.C.: National Association of Social Workers, 1980), pp. 3–18.

6. For major reviews appearing since 1975, see Fanshel, *The Future of Social Work Research;* and Henry S. Maas, ed., *Social Service Research: Review of Studies* (Washington, D.C.: National Association of Social Workers, 1978).

7. Ann A. Abbot, "Social Work Doctoral Dissertations, 1960-1974: Content, Method, Quality, and Relevance for Future Research Productivity." Unpublished doctoral dissertation, Graduate School of Social Work and Social Research, Bryn Mawr College, May 1977.

8. For the content analyses that were the basis for this and subsequent observations in this section, see William J. Reid, "The Subject Matter of Social Work Research," Editorial, *Social Work Research and Abstracts*, 14 (Fall 1978), p.2; Patricia Hanrahan, "Trends in the Subject Matter of Social Work Research," unpublished manuscript, School of Social Service Administration, University of Chicago, 1978; Abbot, "Social Work Doctoral Dissertations, 1960–1974"; and Shirley Jenkins et al., "Abstracts as Data: Dissertation Trends, 1975–79," *Social Work Research and Abstracts*, 18 (Spring 1982), pp. 29–34. The analysis of all the social work studies abstracted in *Social Work Research and Abstracts* from 1980 through 1982 was conducted by the author.

9. Joel Fischer, "Is Casework Effective? A Review," *Social Work*, 18 (January 1973), pp. 5–20.

10. William J. Reid and Patricia Hanrahan, "Recent Evaluations of Social Work: Grounds for Optimism," *Social Work*, 27 (July 1982), pp. 328–340. The twenty-five experiments include studies in both the main review and the update.

11. See, for example, Mary Ann Jones, Renee Neuman, and Ann W. Shyne, *A Second Chance for Families: Evaluation of a Program to Reduce Foster Care* (New York: Child Welfare League of America, 1976); William J. Reid, *The Task-Centered System* (New York: Columbia University Press, 1978); Richard B. Stuart, Srinika Jayaratne, and Tony Tripodi, "Changing Adolescent Deviant Behavior Through Reprogramming the Behavior of Parents and Teachers: An Experimental Evaluation," *Canadian Journal of Behavioural Science*, 8 (March 1976), pp. 133–143; and Myrna M. Weissman et al. "Treatment Effects on the Social Adjustment of Depressed Patients," *Archives of General Psychiatry*, 30 (June 1974), pp. 771–778.

12. See, for example, Edwin J. Thomas, "Generating Innovation in Social Work: The Paradigm of Developmental Research," *Journal of Social Service Research*, 2 (Fall 1978), pp. 95–116; and William J. Reid, "The Model Development Dissertation," *Journal of Social Service Research,* 3 (Winter 1979), pp. 15–25.

13. Edwin J. Thomas, "Mousetraps, Developmental Research, and Social Work Education," *Social Service Review*, 52 (September 1978), p. 470.

14. Jack Rothman, *Research and Development in the Human Services* (Englewood Cliffs, N.J.: Prentice-Hall, 1980).

15. See, for example, Scott Briar, "Incorporating Research into Education for Clinical Practice in Social Work: Toward a Clinical Science in Social Work," in Allen Rubin and Aaron Rosenblatt, eds., *Sourcebook on Research Utilization* (New York: Council on Social Work Education, 1979), pp. 132–140; Srinika Jayaratne and Rona Levy, *Empirical Clinical Practice* (New York: Columbia University Press, 1979); and Martin Bloom and Joel Fischer, *Evaluating Practice: Guidelines for the Accountable Professional* (Englewood Cliffs, N.J.: Prentice-Hall, 1982).

16. See, for example, Elsie Pinkston et al., *Effective Social Work Practice: Advanced Techniques for Behavioral Intervention with Individuals, Families and Institutional Staff* (San Francisco: Jossey-Bass, 1982).

17. Tony Tripodi and Janice Harrington, "Use of Time-Series Designs for Formative Program Evaluation," *Journal of Social Service Research*, 3 (Fall 1979), pp. 67–78.

18. Judith C. Nelsen, "Issues in Single-Subject Research for Nonbehaviorists," *Social Work Research and Abstracts,* 17 (Summer 1981), pp. 31–37.

19. See, for example, Neal Broxmeyer, "Practitioner-Research in Treating a Borderline Child" *Social Work Research and Abstracts*, 14 (Winter 1978), pp. 5–11; and Jeanne Haynes, "Application of Single-Subject Design to Psychosocial Casework," paper presented at Annual Program Meeting, Council on Social Work Education, Phoenix, Ariz., 1977.

20. Scott Briar, "Toward the Integration of Practice and Research," in Fanshel, *Future of Social Work Research*, pp. 31–37.

21. Ibid., p. 36.

22. Edwin J. Thomas, "Research and Service in Single-Case Experimentation: Conflicts and Choices," *Social Work Research and Abstracts*, 14 (Winter 1978), pp. 20–31.

RESIDENTIAL TREATMENT FOR CHILDREN

The Child Welfare League of America recognizes only a few types of group care settings for children who are dependent or have behavioral or emotional difficulties.[1] In actual practice, however, these institutional services take many forms, including residential treatment centers, group homes, crisis and shelter care facilities, children's psychiatric facilities, and respite care facilities. In many states and jurisdictions, important child welfare institutional services are provided under mental health, juvenile correction, and developmental disabilities auspices.

Estimates of the numbers of children in residential institutions suffer from many of the same flaws that plague child welfare census figures generally. Despite the inadequacy of census data, however, a number of individuals and organizations have made helpful estimates. Kadushin, for example, reported that in 1976 there were some 152,000 children in noncorrectional institutions, including institutions for dependent neglected, physically handicapped, mentally handicapped, and emotionally and psychiatrically impaired.[2] Taking a somewhat broader view, the Children's Defense Fund estimated that there were nearly 500,000 children in out-of-home care who were the responsibility of public child welfare agencies. This figure reflected foster family placements as well as group care placements and was extrapolated from a 1975 survey of 140 randomly selected counties.[3] In 1977 another national study of social services to children and their families estimated that approximately 28 percent of the 1.8 million children receiving public child welfare services were in foster family and residential care placements and that, of these, nearly 79 percent were in foster family placements.[4] This study thus yielded a lower figure for residents of child care institutions than the previous two. This inconclusiveness in the census figures for public wards in substitute child care was a major reason recent federal child welfare legislation stipulated that a comprehensive inventory be conducted of the children in such care.[5]

Pappenfort and his colleagues at the University of Chicago are in the process of carrying out a follow-up to their comprehensive 1966 census of child care institutions.[6] No population figures are yet available from the new study, but preliminary data indicate the following:

• While the number of residential group care facilities has increased markedly since 1966, there has been a decline in the number of children and youth in care.
• The rate of growth in numbers of facilities has been concentrated in the category of juvenile justice facilities for children and youth considered delinquent or status offenders and in mental health facilities.
• Facilities in all categories have declined in size over the past sixteen years. In 1966, less than 50 percent of the facilities surveyed had fewer than 26 children and youth in residence. The majority of all facilities surveyed in 1982 were of that size.
• Among the facilities surveyed in 1982, the number of children were almost evenly divided among public and private facilities. Slightly more than one-third of all children were in juvenile justice facilities, one-fourth were in mental health facilities and about one-fifth were in child welfare facilities. The remainder of children were in short-term care facilities.[7]

There is considerable overlap among the various types of group care for children, and the terms used to define their characteristics lack precision. These problems are evident in the way the Child Welfare League of America describes the respective aims of residential treatment and group home service. First, residential treatment:

To provide treatment in a group care therapeutic environment that integrates daily group living, remedial education and treatment services on the basis of an individualized plan for each child, exclusively for children with severe emotional disturbances, whose parents cannot cope with them and who cannot be effectively treated in their own homes, in another family, or in other less intensive treatment-oriented child care facilities. Service elements include: (1) study and diagnosis to determine appropriate service and to develop a treatment plan for each child; (2) work in behalf of or directly with children and youth in a therapeutic milieu during placement (including provision of group living facilities and essentials of daily living such as dental care, and child care supervision); (3) provision of treatment services as needed by each child (social work, psychiatry, psychology, remedial education); (4) work with parents while child is in placement; (5) postplacement activities during readjustment period.

The purpose of group home service is described in the same professional directory as follows:

To provide care and treatment in an agency-owned or operated facility that assures continuity of care and opportunity for community experiences, in combination with a planned group living program and specialized services, for small groups of children and youth whose parents cannot care for them adequately and who, because of their age, problems, or stage of treatment, can benefit by such a program. Service elements include: (1) exploration to determine appropriate service, development of a plan for services, and preparation for placement; (2) work in behalf of or directly with children and youth during placement (including provision of facilities and the essentials of daily living, such as meals, clothing, arrangements for education, recreation, religion, medical-dental care; child care supervision; social work, psychiatry, psychology, special education, vocational and employment counseling; (3) work with parents while child is in placement; (4) postplacement activities during readjustment period.[8]

Although these statements are correct in their implication that the most severely disturbed child can benefit from placement in restrictive residential treatment centers, they fail to suggest the reality of present practice. Today it is common to treat even severely disturbed children in less restrictive, family-oriented settings.[9] Moreover, the statements fail to acknowledge the extent to which the considerations involved in any decision to place a child in institutional care still lack adequate definition:

The decision to place a child in residential treatment is presently a highly individualized matter based on a complex set of idiosyncratic factors defying categorization. The literature does not indicate agreement on consistent criteria or universal guidelines and it is not certain whether institutions diverse in origin, philosophy, policy, and clientele can agree on a basic set of premises.[10]

In short, group and institutional care cannot be described as a single entity. Rather, this segment of the child welfare service continuum contains a range of residential placements that are different from each other but that overlap considerably in definition, purpose, and population served.

Outcome Research

The research on residential child care suffers from the same problems found in most studies in the area of child welfare:

Absence of Controls. For ethical and practical reasons, many studies omit the use of control groups required in the classic experimental design. Although this omission leaves the interpretation of results open to question—particularly with respect to "success"—one cannot, for the sake of establishing a control group, deprive troubled children of needed care and treatment. Hence, many outcome studies have tended toward a comparison group design—testing differential approaches to residential and nonresidential treatment on a similar populations of referrals.

Poorly Defined Service Units. In such an all-encompassing service strategy as milieu treatment, it is often difficult to specify exactly what a service unit consists of and also to identify which interventions are most potent in changing behavior. While such questions are not of paramount interest to the clinician concerned primarily with positive movement in an individual case, they are of concern to executives and planners charged with the responsibility for program expansion.

Improper Selection of Outcome Criteria. All too often residential programs have allowed themselves to be evaluated on a narrow range of criteria—grades in school, recidivism, absence of police contact—which either are not directly related to services offered or which occur in community environments where the residential program has little involvement, much less control.

Sample Selection. Troubled children and youth are seldom randomly assigned to different residential programs; instead, placement depends on such factors as severity of problem, prognosis for positive change, and available bed space. These factors may definitely bias sample selection in a number of ways. For example, some programs may engage in a "creaming-off" operation— accepting only the best-risk children in order to positively dispose toward program successes. This problem of nonrandom assignment, particularly when coupled with the absence of a control group, can confound the interpretation of results from a program —particularly a demonstration project seeking funds for expansion on the basis of a high degree of success in the pilot phase.

Lack of Utility. Because many of the studies of residential child care are outcome studies—often conducted by outside researchers—many child care practitioners doubt the value of the research enterprise and feel that its findings are of little use in shaping day-to-day practice. Almost by definition, outcome research cannot be directly useful, since it does not focus on the treatment process as it is occurring but on a "payoff" that occurs, if at all, long after children have left care.[11]

Several developments hold promise as means of reducing these problems and broadening the types of research carried out in residential treatment. For example, such group care programs as the teaching family model have incorporated evaluation directly into their training procedures and operational policies so that program staff and supervisors receive continuous feedback on treatment effectiveness.[12] Other promising developments include the use of single-case evaluation procedures[13] and goal attainment procedures.[14] In addition, many residential programs are now actively soliciting consumer feedback on treatment effectiveness from the children, their families,

referring agencies, and collateral helpers. The Who Cares project of the British National Children's Bureau regularly brings together children and youth in substitute care settings to elicit their views on a wide range of questions, including which staff are most helpful to them and the children's degree of "connectedness" to the broader community.[15]

Certain related and recurrent findings are apparent in the research on residential treatment. The absence of a clear relationship between residential and postresidential performance has turned up in a number of studies, including the follow-up study by Allerhand, Weber, and Haug:

> Perhaps the most striking finding of the study is that none of the measurements of within-Bellefaire performance at discharge, either in casework or in cottage and school roles, were useful in themselves in predicting postdischarge adaptability and adaptation. Only when the situation to which the child returned was taken into account were performances at Bellefaire related to postdischarge adequacies. In a stressful community situation, strengths nurtured within the institution tended to break down, whereas in a supportive situation, these strengths tended to be reinforced.[16]

Taylor and Alpert reached a similar conclusion regarding the importance of postdischarge continuity and support:

> Social and behavioral adaptation is in large part a function of environmental situation and is *not* transferred from one dissimilar situation to another (i.e., from institution to community).[17]

Such findings underscore the power of the postdischarge environment as a predictor of a child's adjustment regardless of adjustment and progress while in the program. Other studies suggest that if social supports are available in the community to which the child returns, the maintenance of the treatment gains made in the residential setting is significantly greater.[18]

These and similar findings argue for a much more prominent role for family work and community liaison before, during, and after residential placement. A number of practice models representative of what might be termed ecological approaches to child treatment are emerging to address this concern.[19]

Future Trends and Issues

Virtually all the issues for residential treatment that were identified in the 1977 *Encyclopedia of Social Work* are still prominent considerations. These include continuing concerns about the spiraling costs of care; issues of effectiveness, efficiency, and accountability; changes in treatment philosophy; concern with the development of closer community linkages; and continuing confusion over goals and purposes.[20] The issues that stand out as of paramount importance in shaping future directions in this sector of child welfare services are these:

Residential treatment as part of the service continuum. Although residential treatment is not a panacea for the problems of troubled and troublesome children, it is clear that there is, and will continue to be, a need for services away from the child's family of origin. Residential institutions need not be thought of as an end-of-the-line alternative, but as a viable part of the overall service continuum in child welfare. As in the past, group care remains isolated from the rest of child welfare services, but it is increasingly apparent that this should not continue to be the case. Foster family care, home-based intervention, adoption, and other child services or service strategies have their limitations as well.

The task is to work towards a time when group care services are part of an integrated continuum of care that begins with preclusive prevention, extends through a whole range of family-centered, home-based options, and ends with secure treatment institutions for those few children who need them. As has been suggested elsewhere, what is needed in child welfare is a continuum of care that softens the distinction between residential and nonresidential options.[21] Such a continuum would include foster care, respite care, shelter care,

day treatment, and crisis services, along with a variety of community-integrated residential options. The key issue in developing a service plan for a child would not be whether the child remained at home or was placed out, but would focus instead on how the elements in the total environment could be mobilized into a powerful force for change.

Ecological factors and residential treatment. As the outcome research so clearly indicates, success in residential care, however defined, is largely a function of the supports available in the posttreatment environment and has much less to do with either the presenting problem or the type of treatment offered. Consequently, what has come to be known as the ecological perspective has profound implications for residential children's services.[22] This perspective views the residential environment as a complex interplay of many different elements, both within and outside the formal service context. Notable here are the quality of the linkages between the residential program and such important community systems as the family, the neighborhood, the peer group, the world of work, and other potential sources of support in the community. A Massachusetts experiment that focused on deinstitutionalization in juvenile corrections highlighted the importance of these community linkages as they interact with the formal service program.[23]

One implication of the move toward an ecological approach is that social workers in residential care will be spending less time in direct treatment of children and more time working with and through the environment, particularly in creating or maintaining social support networks for the children and their families.[24] At the same time, funding agencies will favor models of care and treatment that are able to document and track the progress of children, that are oriented to teaching basic life skills, and that place increased responsibility on direct care staff for major therapeutic work with children and families.

Increasing numbers of voluntary child welfare agencies will seek to combine residential and in-home services as a means of diversifying their programmatic funding bases.

Parents as partners in residential treatment. If the residential center is to be seen as a temporary support for families in crises rather than as a substitute for families that have failed, the center must engage families as full and equal partners in the helping process. Traditionally, and for a variety of reasons, parents have been kept at arm's length from the process of treatment in institutional settings. In *The Challenge of Partnership*, Maluccio and Sinanoglu document a variety of ways in which the parents of children in foster and residential care can assume meaningful roles in helping, including parenting education, family support groups, family participation in the life-space of the residential institution, and family therapy.[25] As in adoption and foster family care, the enormous potential of the helping power of parents has only barely been tapped. Permanent-planning efforts for children in residential treatment will generate a variety of guardianship and shared care options to augment the traditional outcomes of a return home, adoption, and long-term foster care.

JAMES K. WHITTAKER

Notes and References

1. *Directory of Member Agencies* (New York: Child Welfare League of America, 1983).

2. Alfred Kadushin, *Child Welfare Services* (3d ed.; New York: Macmillan Publishing Co., 1980), p. 554.

3. *Children without Homes* (Washington, D.C.: Children's Defense Fund, 1978), p. 2.

4. A. W. Shyne and A. G. Shroeder, *National Study of Social Services to Children and Their Families* (Washington, D.C.: National Center for Child Advocacy, 1978).

5. United States Code, P.L. 96-272.

6. Donnell M. Pappenfort, Dee M. Kilpatrick, and Robert W. Roberts, eds., *Child Car-*

ing: Social Policy and the Institution (Chicago: Aldine Publishing Co., 1973).

7. Donnell M. Pappenfort and Thomas M. Young, "National Survey of Children's Residential Institutions and Alternative Programs: A Status Report" (Chicago: School of Social Service Administration, University of Chicago, 1983), p. 5. (Photocopied.)

8. *Directory of Member Agencies,* pp. xx-xxi.

9. Thomas Cherry, "The Oregon Child Study and Treatment Centers," *Child Care Quarterly*, 5 (Summer 1976), pp. 146–155; Edmund T. Dimock, "Youth Crises Services: Short-Term Community-Based Residential Treatment," *Child Welfare*, 56 (March 1977), pp. 187–196; and Julian S. Rubenstein et al., "The Parent Therapist Program: Alternative Care for Emotionally Disturbed Children," *American Journal of Orthopsychiatry,* 48 (October 1978), pp. 654–662.

10. Anthony N. Maluccio and Wilma D. Marlow, "Residential Treatment of Emotionally Disturbed Children: A Review of the Literature," *Social Service Review*, 42 (June 1972), p. 239.

11. James K. Whittaker, *Caring for Troubled Children: Residential Treatment in a Community Context* (San Francisco: Jossey-Bass, 1979), pp. 187–188.

12. Dean L. Fixsen, Elery L. Phillips, and Montrose M. Wolf, "The Teaching Family Model: An Example of Mission-Oriented Research," in Charles A. Catania and T. A. Brigham, eds., *Handbook of Behavior Analysis* (New York: Halsted Press, 1978).

13. Srinika Jayaratne and Rona Levy, *The Clinical-Research Model of Intervention* (New York: Columbia University Press, 1979).

14. Harvey L. Johnson et al., "Program Evaluation in Residential Treatment," *Child Welfare*, 55 (April 1976), pp. 279–291.

15. R. Page and G. A. Clark, eds., *Who Cares?* (London, England: National Children's Bureau, 1977).

16. M. E. Allerhand, R. Weber, and M. Haug, *Adaptation and Adaptability: The Bellefaire Follow-up Study* (New York: Child Welfare League of America, 1966), p. 140.

17. Delores A. Taylor and Stuart W. Alpert, *Continuity and Support Following Residential Treatment* (New York: Child Welfare League of America, 1973), pp. 45–46.

18. R. H. Nelson, M. J. Singer, and L. O. Johnson, "The Application of a Residential Treatment Evaluation Model," *Child Care Quarterly,* 7 (1978), pp. 164–175; and W. W.

Lewis, "Ecological Factors in Successful Residential Treatment," *Behavioral Disorders*, 7 (1982), pp. 149–157.

19. P. Dokecki, "The Liaison Perspective on the Enhancement of Human Development," *Journal of Community Psychology*, 5 (1977), pp. 13–17; N. Hobbs, *Troubled and Troubling Children* (San Francisco: Jossey-Bass, 1982); A. N. Maluccio and P. A. Sinanoglu, *The Challenge of Partnership: Working with Children of Parents in Foster Care* (New York: Child Welfare League of America, 1981); and R. W. Small and James K. Whittaker, "Residential Group Care and Home-Based Care: Toward a Continuity of Family Service," in Shiela Maybanks and Marvin Bryce, eds., *Home-Based Services for Children and Their Families* (Springfield , Ill.: Charles C Thomas, publisher, 1979).

20. James K. Whittaker, "Child Welfare: Residential Treatment," in *Encyclopedia of Social Work* (17th ed.; Washington, D.C.: National Association of Social Workers, 1977), pp. 169–175.

21. Small and Whittaker, "Residential Group Care and Home-Based Care"; and James K. Whittaker, "The Changing Character of Residential Child Care: An Ecological Perspective," *Social Service Review*, 22 (March 1978), pp. 21–36.

22. Whittaker, *Caring for Troubled Children*.

23. Robert B. Coates, Alden D. Miller, and L. E. Ohlin, *Diversity in a Youth Correctional System* (Cambridge, Mass.: Ballinger Publishing Co., 1978).

24. James K. Whittaker and J. Garbarino and associates, *Social Support Networks: Informal Helping in the Human Services* (New York: Aldine Publishing Co., 1983).

25. Maluccio and Sinanoglu, *The Challenge of Partnership*.

SEXUAL ORIENTATION

In recent years, important changes have occurred in the cultural and social norms that influence the sexual behavior of Americans, and many people have become more open-minded in this area. However, a great deal of confusion still exists, particularly on the subjects of homosexuality and sexual orientation. This confusion is found not only among the clients of social workers but among the professionals themselves. This article examines the meaning of homosexuality, reviews current knowledge on the antecedents of sexual orientation, and briefly considers appropriate areas for social work intervention.

Definitions

Homosexuality must be understood in the context of human sexual identity. According to Moses and Hawkins, sexual identity is composed of three factors that are often confused: gender identity, gender role behavior, and sexual orientation.[1] "Gender identity" refers to the individual's perception of himself or herself as male or female; it is fixed by the time a child is 3 or 4 years old and is remarkably resistant to change after this critical period.[2] "Gender role behavior" refers to behavioral responses that a culture associates with appropriate male or female behavior. In American culture, for example, men are supposed to be strong, self-reliant, and unemotional, and women are expected to embody the opposite set of characteristics. There is currently much controversy about such gender role differences.

The term "sexual orientation" refers to a preference for members of one's own or the opposite gender as the objects of sexual and affectional needs. It is important to include an affectional aspect in this definition because uninformed observers have interpreted sexual orientation as a purely sexual phenomenon. It is not. The satisfaction of affectional needs is identical for heterosexuals and homosexuals. This definition correctly classifies both forms of behavior as variations of human sexual expression.

Although for the majority the three components of sexual identity are consistent—for example, female identity, female role behavior, and heterosexual orientation—they may operate independently. For the majority of homosexuals, gender identity and gender role behavior are consistent with gender; most male homosexuals, for example, are comfortable with themselves as men and act in a typically masculine manner and are thus indistinguishable from heterosexual men. A small minority of homosexuals adopt opposite-gender role behavior, sometimes deliberately to assert their homosexuality.

Social workers are often confused about what terms to use in describing their homosexual clients. There are different views about this even among homosexuals. Gays generally avoid the word "homosexual" in describing themselves because this label implies a clinical diagnosis and focuses on the sexual rather than the affectional aspect. Many gays feel that this label is imposed by "straight" professionals on their unwilling and often abused minority. Whereas the term "homosexual" came into use only recently, "gay" has been used for centuries and is a label that gays choose for themselves.[3] Until recently it was a code word familiar only to gays. Today it is widely used and is preferred by most gay men and women. Some women object to both "homosexual" and "gay" because these terms are commonly understood to refer only to men. These women prefer to be called lesbians.

"Sexual preference" is another term that has caused confusion. Some people have taken this term to mean that homosexual *choose* to be homosexual. It would be more accurate to say that gays and lesbians do not choose how they feel but rather how to act in response to their feelings. To avoid this confusion, it is better to use the term "sexual orientation."

Becoming Homosexual

Why are there homosexuals? That this society has arbitrarily chosen to select sexual behavior as a relevant criterion for categorizing individuals says more about its attitude toward sex than it does about the individuals labeled heterosexual or homosexual. Categorization by a sexual criterion reflects society's negative view of sexual expression and its concern with regulating sexual behavior.[4] This becomes apparent when studying other societies in which homosexual behavior is nearly universal or in which individuals who pursue same-sex relationships are not set apart from others by labels.[5] This is essentially the perspective of a branch of sociology that has contributed greatly to an understanding of homosexuality—societal reaction theory.[6]

Despite American society's definition of homosexuality as an arbitrary social expression, the phenomenon is real and complex. Moses and Hawkins, for instance, believe that sexual orientation is composed of four independent factors—sexual attraction, sexual activity, affectional attraction, and fantasy—each of which can change over time.[7]

Berger has proposed a multidimensional model for the formation of a homosexual identity.[8] This model discards the traditional binary notion that individuals are either heterosexual or homosexual in favor of a holistic model that views sexual orientation as existing on a continuum from exclusive heterosexuality to exclusive homosexuality. Overwhelming research evidence supports such a model. For instance, large-scale surveys conducted by Kinsey and his colleagues in the late 1940s and early 1950s showed that most men and women have a mix of heterosexual and homosexual experiences and feelings.[9] Statistically, exclusive homosexuality or heterosexuality is atypical.

In Berger's model, homosexual identity formation is a developmental process characterized by three independent tasks: sexual encounter, social reaction, and identity. The term "sexual encounter" refers to such overt sexual activity as kissing, fondling, or intercourse. "Social reaction" refers to the labeling of the individual by others as homosexual or heterosexual. Being labeled as homosexual often exerts a formative effect on the development of a homosexual orientation, but it is neither necessary nor sufficient for the development of such an orientation. The importance to the individual of those doing the labeling, the period of time over which the labeling occurs, and, most important, the individual's perception of how others regard him or her (which may be different from their actual views), are other important factors.

Homosexual identity formation also depends on a number of identity tasks. All homosexuals have experienced a period of identity confusion in which discrepancies in perception lead to psychological discomfort. The discrepancy may arise between any of the components of the homosexual identity process: sexual encounter, social reaction, and identity. For instance, the individual's view of himself as heterosexual (identity) may be discrepant with a recent sexual experience with a person of the same sex (sexual encounter). Other discrepancies may arise between two aspects of the individual, as when a self-labeled heterosexual experiences homosexual fantasies.

For individuals who come to view themselves as homosexual, the identity confusion is resolved by self-labeling as homosexual. This gives rise to the need for identity management, or ways to conceal or share this "new" information with others. At this point, peer association is an important part of solidifying a homosexual identity. The individual finds validation of the self-label by associating with others who have similarly labeled themselves. In addition, the homosexual peer culture enhances self-esteem and reinforces the new identity by serving as a legitimating reference group with a homosexual world view, as opposed to the heterosexual world view of the culture at large.

At this stage, some homosexuals adopt a militant posture vis-a-vis the heterosexual community. Although this may give rise to such temporary behaviors as revealing one's homosexuality in all social situations, it, too, serves to solidify a homosexual identity. Eventually, the great majority of homosexuals reach a stage of self-acceptance as a result of mastering the preceding identity tasks. Although issues of identity management, self-labeling, and militancy usually continue to occur as the environment presents new challenges (for example, the arrival of a a new co-worker who is gay or a change in existing relationships), the individual is comfortable being himself or herself, and this is reflected in interpersonal relations.

This model can help the social worker understand phenomena that have been sources of confusion to professionals who deal with homosexuals. It illustrates that sexual experience and a homosexual identity are independent phenomena. Some individuals who are firmly committed to a homosexual identity have had no same-sex experience. This commitment is likely to be an accurate indicator of subsequent identity and must not be dismissed as irrational. It is also true that some individuals with extensive homosexual histories are still able to view themselves as completely heterosexual.

The model also suggests that the phenomenon of "latent homosexuality" is meaningless. Because it is the client's view of his or her behavior and perceptions that is crucial to identity formation, it is wrong to assume that a client is a "latent" homosexual on the basis of experiences that the worker, but not the client, labels as homosexual.

Causes

What causes homosexuality? This question has been heatedly debated since the nineteenth century. It may be the wrong question. Homosexual advocates believe that heterosexual investigators, who have done most of the research in this area, have been obsessed with establishing an "etiology." This would reinforce the now out-dated notion that homosexuality is an illness (or a case of arrested development, as Freud theorized) and the majority view that homosexuals are different. Although early approaches emphasized the distinctness of homosexuals, the modern view is that the antecedents that determine homosexuality are no different from those that determine heterosexuality. In other words, the correct question is, "What determines sexual orientation—both homosexual and heterosexual?"[10]

Despite years of research an answer still is not available. However, a great deal more is known about what does *not* determine sexual orientation. Individuals are not likely to become homosexual or heterosexual as a result of parental or sibling relations or of peer relationships in childhood or adolescence. Even preadult sexual behaviors, heterosexual or homosexual, have no influence on subsequent sexual orientation. Research on hormonal and other physical differences has not convincingly identified any causal factors. The only two variables that correlate with adult sexual orientation may simply be other ways of measuring sexual orientation itself: gender nonconformity (homosexuals were less likely to conform during their youth) and preadult homosexual feelings.[11]

Some early researchers claimed to have shown that homosexuality resulted from pathological family relations.[12] These studies, however, have been largely discredited for their poor methodology.[13] The most widely accepted view is that environmental factors are the primary influence in determining sexual orientation. However, a group of Kinsey Institute researchers has suggested a strong biological base, particularly hormonal events in utero, modified by early childhood experiences.[14] The case is far from closed.

Areas for Intervention

Can social workers be helpful to gay men and lesbians? The recent involvement of social workers in gay and lesbian social service settings suggests that they can. Social work values and objectives suggest many types of intervention that can be initiated by individual social workers and by the profession as a whole. Such activities include working for changes in specific laws, educating staff members in social service institutions to the needs of gays and lesbians, linking gays and lesbians to special resources, and engaging in problem-solving and counseling activities with such clients and their families. The following are the principal areas in which intervention can take place.

Legal matters. The current legal system was established to regulate heterosexual relations. Although homosexuals are only sometimes singled out for punishment, their rights and needs are often in jeopardy as a result of the legal system.[15] This is particularly true for gay and lesbian couples. For instance, it is not uncommon for one partner of a same-sex couple to lose all of his or her lifelong investment in an estate that was in the other partner's name. Legal precautions often are not undertaken by a gay couple because of a lack of information, an unavailability of sympathetic legal help, or a desire for anonymity that precludes joint ownership. In such cases, at the partner's death, members of the blood family, who may not have seen the deceased for decades, can take legal title to the estate.

There are a number of such inequities in the legal system. Other examples are the gay spouse's inability to sue a third party for wrongful death and the absence of survivor's benefits. This situation is beginning to improve as more and more lawyers gain expertise in using the legal system to help their homosexual clients through wills, relationship contracts, and other methods.

Another legal area of concern is the absence of federal protection against discrimination in housing, employment, and public accommodations. The small amount of research available shows that employment discrimination is a serious problem.[16] Although forty-two localities and states have some form of protection against discrimination, gays and lesbians in most localities have no legal recourse when they find themselves victims of unfair discrimination.

Lesbian and gay parents. It is commonly recognized that a fifth of the gay men and an even higher proportion of the lesbians in the United States have at some time been heterosexually married.[17] Many of these have children. Many gay men and women long to have children of their own, just as heterosexuals do. The stereotype of homosexuals as child haters is untrue.

Lesbians often have children as the result of a heterosexual marriage that occurred prior to the realization of their attraction to other women. When the heterosexual relationship is abandoned in favor of a relationship with another woman, the children usually remain with the mother. Some gay men and women marry primarily for the opportunity to have children. A recent development in the lesbian community is the use of Artificial Insemination by Donor (AID) in which a single lesbian or a lesbian couple acquires a natural child without a heterosexual relationship.[18]

A great tragedy in the gay and lesbian communities is that the legal system often deprives a parent, usually the mother, of her child solely because that parent is homosexual. If a custody battle comes to court, the lesbian mother has only a 15 percent chance of keeping her child.[19] The generally unfavorable attitude of judges seems to have been unaffected by research showing that children of homosexual parents are no more likely than other children to be disturbed and that the chances are that they will be heterosexual.[20]

Parents of lesbians and gays. Most gays and lesbians "come out" (reveal their homosexuality) by their teens or early twenties. It is common for children to come out to their parents some months or years later. At times parents may accidentally discover their child's homosexuality at a much earlier age; for instance, by reading a letter or overhearing a conversation.

Families react to the discovery of a child's homosexuality in ways that are as diverse as families' reactions to any crisis. The family's reaction is a function of its pattern of conflict resolution, openness of communication, and attitudes toward human sexuality.

This event often leads to a period of tension or estrangement between the child and the rest of the family. The child who chooses to "tell" has usually had several months or years to handle this information and may be impatient with parents or siblings who seem to need too much time to adapt. Parents may be bewildered. They may believe they have erred in their child rearing or worry that their child will be immoral or lonely or ostracized. They may be ashamed for others to learn of their family "secret."[21]

Despite occasional extreme reactions, most families come to terms with a child's homosexuality. As the public becomes more familiar with gay and lesbian lifestyles, families are accepting their gay and lesbian children more readily. Self-help groups of Parents of Gays are now active in many cities across the country. Acceptance by the individual's family is central to his or her emotional well-being. As one gay man expressed it "We have a right to belong to the families of the world."

Racial and ethnic minorities. Much of the last decade's social activism in favor of gays and lesbians occurred in a white and middle-class context, but homosexuality is as common among racial and ethnic minorities. The situation of such persons is often especially troublesome because they are subject to double discrimination—as gays or lesbians and as minorities. Ethnic and racial minorities are at times prevented from full participation even in the homosexual community, as when they are discouraged from entering gay bars or clubs.

Some minority homosexuals have responded by identifying with their racial or ethnic group and denying their connection to the gay and lesbian community. This step may be a difficult one because some minority cultures are particularly punitive toward homosexuals. In general, cultures that place a premium on machismo and have rigid notions of appropriate male and female behavior are least accepting of homosexuality, particularly among males. A male who loves other males is seen as having capitulated to the white oppressor because machismo is believed to be necessary for the struggle against oppression. Only recently have minority gays formed their own self-help groups.[22]

Disabled gays. Physical and emotional disabilities isolate individuals from the mainstream of society. Disabled gays and lesbians are doubly isolated. Because homosexuals are a minority and because displays of same-sex interest are severely sanctioned, access to other gays is a central concern for all gays and lesbians. A gay or lesbian who is blind, deaf, or wheelchair-bound faces almost insurmountable barriers to reaching other gay people and resources. Many bars and organizations are not accessible by wheelchair. Only a handful of large cities have organizations or social networks for disabled gays and lesbians. In some gay male communities that place an emphasis on goods looks, physical disabilities are not well accepted.

Mainstream organizations for the disabled often hold conservative attitudes toward sexuality and are also not accepting of gays and lesbians. Helping professionals often find it difficult to accept that their disabled clients have *any* sexual needs; they would certainly be at a loss to help a disabled gay man or lesbian. Mainstream agencies need to learn that gays are born with or acquire disabilities just like everyone else, and the gay and lesbian community needs to open its doors to this minority within a minority.

Adolescents. Many social workers believe that an adolescent cannot possibly be homosexual, but research shows clearly that the majority of gay men realize they are gay between the ages of 9 and 15 and that the majority of lesbians are aware of their sexual preference before the age of 20.[23] Many children are openly gay in their early teens. This is particularly difficult to accept in a society that does not recognize that children have sexual needs.

Adolescents are often in a difficult position. Just when they need to reconcile their emerging sexual feelings with their self-view, they find no role models of well-adjusted homosexual adults or teens. Their access to other gays is severely limited. For instance, they are too young to enter a bar legally and may not have the transportation to get to a meeting. Their emotional and financial dependence on potentially rejecting parents often makes it dangerous to pursue a gay or lesbian lifestyle or even to look for support and guidance from the adults to whom they are the closest. Many adolescents are forced to submerge their needs until they turn 18 or 21. In some cities Gay Youth Support groups are available.

The elderly. American society is afflicted with catastrophic stereotypes about gay and lesbian aging. Gay men are said to become increasingly effeminate, isolated, and lonely as they age and to prey on young boys for their sexual outlet. The older lesbian purportedly turns into an unhappy "witch" who spends her days alone. Several studies show these stereotypes to be largely untrue. Most older homosexuals are emotionally well adjusted, only a minority live alone, and most have a lover or a network of close, supportive friends. Although the level of sexual activity may decrease with age, most continue to have sex, are satisfied with it, and relate sexually with age peers. Several researchers have suggested that in some ways, being gay or lesbian actually facilitates adaptation to aging. For instance, in their early lives, homosexuals tend to acquire greater self-reliance and role flexibility, which serve them well in adjusting to the changes that accompany old age.[24]

Substance abusers. Many observers believe that substance abuse is greater among gays and lesbians than among het-

erosexuals. There are reasons to believe this is true. In many communities, the "bar" is the only place where homosexuals can socialize openly. The result is long hours spent in an atmosphere of drinking. This, combined with the stress of being homosexual in a homophobic society, can lead to problem drinking. Other drugs have become associated with a gay male lifestyle, in particular, "poppers" (amyl and butyl nitrite), which are used publicly in discos and, privately, to enhance sexual pleasure.

Most treatment programs are not responsive to the needs of gay and lesbian clients. Treatment personnel may not understand the stresses experienced by a gay person, may create an atmosphere in which the gay client is afraid to "open up," or may fail to involve a lover who is maintaining the problem. Some programs pressure the client to convert to heterosexuality as part of an explicit or implicit treatment plan.[25] A promising development in this area is the formation of Gay Alcoholics Anonymous groups across the country.

The gay and lesbian network. The last decade has seen a proliferation of social services run by and for the homosexual community. Most social workers are unaware of this. Every major city and many smaller ones offer social services to gays and lesbians. Larger cities offer a range of specialized services for subpopulations such as gay parents, parents of gays, deaf gays, interracial gay couples, aging gays, and gays with cancer.

There are two characteristics of this gay and lesbian network of which social workers should be aware. First, these services are organized on a separatist model. This is, in part, a response to the unwillingness of mainstream agencies to be more responsive, or to provide any services at all, to the gay and lesbian community. Second, many of these services have had a bias against professional involvement. This reflects the gay and lesbian community's historical antipathy to professionals who have oppressed homosexuals by defining them as ill and subjecting them to "treatment."

In recent years, as more social workers and other professionals have "come out" and involved themselves in gay and lesbian services, this attitude has been changing.

Homosexuality is a complex phenomenon. It may never be fully understood, but the information gathered over the past thirty-five years is more than enough to promote informed practice on the part of social workers.

RAYMOND M. BERGER

Notes and References

1. A. Elfin Moses and Robert O. Hawkins, *Counseling Lesbian Women and Gay Men* (St. Louis, Mo.: C. V. Mosby Co., 1982), pp. 28–40.

2. John Money and Anke A. Ehrhardt, *Man and Woman, Boy and Girl* (Baltimore, Md.: Johns Hopkins University Press, 1972), pp. 176–179.

3. John Boswell, *Christianity, Social Tolerance, and Homosexuality* (Chicago: University of Chicago Press, 1980), pp. 41–44.

4. Richard W. Smith, "Why Are Many Societies Sex-Negative? A Social-Functionalist Theory," *Counseling Psychologist, 5* (1975), pp. 84–89.

5. See, for example, Boswell, *Christianity, Social Tolerance, and Homosexuality,* pp. 49–51.

6. See Howard S. Becker, *Outsiders: Studies in the Sociology of Deviance* (New York: Free Press, 1963); and Martin S. Weinberg and Colin J. Williams, *Male Homosexuals: Their Problems and Adaptations* (New York: Penguin Books, 1975).

7. Moses and Hawkins, *Counseling Lesbian Women and Gay Men,* p. 43.

8. Raymond M. Berger, "What Is a Homosexual? A Model for Practice," *Social Work, 28* (March 1983), pp. 132–135.

9. Alfred C. Kinsey, Wardell B. Pomeroy, and Clyde E. Martin, *Sexual Behavior in the Human Male* and Kinsey et al., *Sexual Behavior in the Human Female* (Philadelphia: W. B. Saunders Co., 1948 and 1943, respectively), pp. 650 and 473, respectively.

10. See Alan P. Bell, Martin S. Weinberg, and Sue K. Hammersmith, *Sexual Preference: Its Development in Men and Women* (Bloom-ington, Ind.: Indiana University Press, 1981).

11. Ibid., pp. 186 and 188.

12. See, for example, Irving Bieber et al., *Homosexuality: A Psychoanalytic Study* (New York: Basic Books, 1962).

13. Moses and Hawkins, *Counseling Lesbian Women and Gay Men,* p. 9.

14. Alan P. Bell, "Sexual Preference: A Postscript," *SIECUS Report, 11* (November 1982), pp. 1–3.

15. "Homosexuality and the Law," *Journal of Homosexuality* (entire issue), 5 (Fall–Winter 1980).

16. Pat Califia, "Documenting Discrimination," *Advocate,* November 25, 1982, pp. 17–18; and *Employment Discrimination in New York City: A Survey of Gay Men and Women* (New York: National Gay Task Force, 1981).

17. Alan P. Bell and Martin S. Weinberg, *Homosexualities: A Study of Diversity among Men and Women* (New York: Simon & Schuster, 1978), pp. 162 and 166.

18. Gillian E. Hanscombe and Jackie Forster, *Rocking the Cradle: Lesbian Mothers, A Challenge in Family Living* (Boston: Alyson Publications 1982).

19. Brenda Maddox, "Homosexual Parents," *Psychology Today, 16* (February 1982), pp. 62–69.

20. Ibid.

21. Charles Silverstein, *A Family Matter: A Parent's Guide to Homosexuality* (New York: McGraw-Hill Book Co., 1977).

22. Thom Beame, "On the Issue of Race and Black and White Men Together," *Advocate,* December 23, 1982, pp. 21–23.

23. Karla Jay and Alan Young, *The Gay Report* (New York: Summit Books, 1979), p. 105.

24. Raymond M. Berger, *Gay and Gray: The Older Homosexual Man* (Urbana Ill.: University of Illinois Press, 1982); James J. Kelly, "The Aging Male Homosexual: Myth and Reality," *Gerontologist, 17* (August 1977), pp. 328–332; and Deborah G. Wolf, "Close Friendship Patterns of Older Lesbians," paper presented at the convention of the Gerontological Society, Dallas, Tex., November 1978.

25. Gary Schoener, "The Heterosexual Norm in Chemical Dependency Treatment Programs: Some Personal Observations," *Stash Capsules, 8* (1976), pp. 1–4.

SOCIAL ISSUES: EMERGING TRENDS

For present purposes, the author will discuss social issues exclusive of economic issues. However, social and economic issues and related family and personal needs and problems are intimately intertwined and share complex causal dynamics. In the following discussion, therefore, the reader should not ignore the transition in the United States from a "production" economy to a "service" economy, the latter accounting in 1980 for 70 percent of the labor force.[1] Also pertinent is the high unemployment of the early 1980s and the related anxiety as to whether some of the unemployed will ever again find satisfactory and sufficiently remunerative work. The larger backdrop involves as well the obvious need to renew the nation's industrial plant and to redirect it wisely in the context of the international economy.[2] On an ideological level, the disillusionment with big government on the political right and left, together with the fascination with the marketplace and market devices as alternative loci and means of service delivery have created a shortage of funds for the social services and have disrupted traditional patterns of operation.[3]

A given course of individual and interpersonal behavior is not defined as an issue or social problem except in a societal context. That is, before any course of conduct is widely conceptualized as seriously deviant and costly and as an appropriate object of policy, it must threaten established institutions, beliefs, or people; waste resources; or must intrude into the lives of significant numbers of influential people. Therefore, when any specific social issues or problems are highlighted and dealt with, as a matter of policy, it is not easy to know precisely whether the phenomena themselves are changing and increasing or whether there are elements in the societal context that lead to more frequent recognition. Perhaps people are being made more aware that the behavior in question is present, which leads to more regular reporting and counting of the behavior and more visible and specific labeling of it—all as prelude to the intended increase in societal intervention.

These observations are pertinent to the national preoccupations during the last decade and a half with a series of social issues that are widely perceived as serious social problems. Among such problems are child neglect and abuse, spouse abuse, adolescent runaways, out-of-wedlock births, teenage pregnancy and child bearing, sexually transmitted disease, and the homelessness of adults as reflected in the prevalence of "bag ladies" and "bag men" and in the large numbers of the deinstitutionalized and rootless people who have become visible in our large cities.

To achieve intellectual coherence in the present article, the author will posit that once the political and economic context is specified, the "issues" or "social problems" (depending on one's perspective) are best reviewed and interpreted against a background of certain demographic and structural changes in the family. Such changes perhaps do yield hypotheses about interrelationships. Whereas (1) there is absolutely no way to distinguish adequately between increases in a phenomenon and increases in reporting and taking notice of it and (2) there is no way to obtain absolute frequencies of occurrence for certain societal problems (because one is dependent upon identification, reporting, assessment, standardization, compilation, validity and reliability, and publication), the central demographic and structural tendencies in American families in recent years do provide a milieu in which "problems" or "issues" of this sort could very well increase.

One might therefore hypothesize that what these issues represent is a combination of greater visibility and also greater real frequencies but that it is not possible to attach precise percentages to these components. The numbers that appear in official reports and research publications in several of these fields clearly represent a combination of "best guesses" and institutional advocacy.

Specifically, the widely published and publicized data on child and spouse abuse, runaways, and homelessness are probably highly inaccurate. Trend data on these phenomena are therefore also highly unreliable.[4] Pregnancy and childbirth information as well as information about disease are all more precise because of the nature of the health and public health reporting systems and the availability of time series.

However, skepticism about the numbers does not at all signify that the phenomena in question are not significant indicators of need, concern, maladjustment, distress, deprivation, deviance, and so forth. Whatever the words chosen, these issues merit public attention and action. Nor are they small matters. They affect significant elements of the population.

Note that this discussion has moved somewhat away from a stress on problems and issues alone to the identification of a "need." In effect, there is a not-too-sharp boundary between the demographic and social trends that are said to generate problems (child abuse, for example) and those that highlight emerging "needs" (family support or child care services, for example). In a sense, this distinction involves a strong element of social evaluation and preference. Thus, in the 1950s most day care was entered through a diagnostic doorway; a caseworker decided whether it was a "solution" to a family's problems. Today, most day care is seen as a public social utility and is used by parents for the socialization and development of their children and to cope with child care needs when parents work. Day care is no longer seen as a problem but as a normal state of things.[5]

A Context of Change

It is not the purpose of this article to unravel the chain of causal interrelations among economy, polity, culture, mobility, technology, and demography that explain present structural and functional tendencies in families and other primary groups in the United States. For present purposes, the identification of such tendencies is sufficient. The family and community are seen as the context for the social problems that are the focus of this article, whatever the theory about where the causal chain begins. In all likelihood, in our complex system, causality may be conceptualized beginning at several points, depending upon one's purpose.

American families are changing in significant ways, but there is no serious belief anywhere that the family is declining as the primary institution of development, socialization, and expressiveness. Moreover, all evidence confirms that Americans retain a general identification and satisfaction with family above all other institutions.[6] None of this is to ignore important changes in the family, such as the following.[7]

•There are fewer husband-wife-children families of the traditional mold—an at-home mother, a working father, their two, three, or four children, with no history of divorce or separation—than ever before.

•Because families are significantly smaller than ever before, many children grow up without the social support of other siblings or with only one sibling, this at a time when a high percentage of parents are separating or divorcing. In addition, large numbers of children are leaving home in adolescence.

•High rates of marriage, divorce, separation, out-of-wedlock birth, and remarriage ensure that close to half of all children will experience some period of life in a one-parent family, usually a female-headed family. Parental divorce or separation inevitably worsens the economic situation of children and mothers. Well over half of all children will grow into maturity after an experience of living with stepparents, stepsiblings, or stepgrandparents. Many will have had traumatic experiences related to divorce, separation, or child support.

•Well over half of all children—indeed over 40 percent of those age 1—have working mothers. Many are reared under unstable, shifting, and constantly repackaged child care arrangements. A significant number of school-age children are on their own from the time they are dismissed from school until 6:00 or 7:00 P.M.

•Working parents in two-earner families have begun to redefine roles, and men are helping more at home. However, the inequities are still major, and working women have "two jobs." Family life is often pressured and breathless. Marketplace services and social supports have not yet produced affordable and accessible alternatives for large numbers of people.

•About a fifth of all families with children are now single parent, and more than half of these families live in poverty.

•After declining in the 1960s, poverty in families with children has risen again to the point that over one-fifth of all children are affected. More than half of all children in poverty are in female-headed families; 56 percent of all children and over two-thirds of black children who live in female-headed families are poor. These families in particular lack marketplace or social support services.

•Immediate family members, relatives, and neighbors help many people, but high rates of mobility, estrangement, and practical problems of daily life leave many other families under pressure and without access to buttressing from their immediate residential and kin communities.

•Neighborhood, family, and role transitions inevitably create tension and conflict, particularly for those who are also under economic pressures. The primary groups and social environments of modern Americans are full of such tensions and conflicts, and those affected by them are often people who have themselves been deprived and are handicapped or disturbed.

Problems at the Forefront

In this context, therefore, the high rates of child abuse, homelessness, and so forth become understandable. For many, families have lost much of their stabilizing role. They are often not anchored in a local context that reinforces traditional norms. The exceptions to this trend may include the majority, yet at all social levels there are parents, often young parents, coping alone with parenthood, household management, and interpersonal relationships without access to role models or immediate supports. Many of them, moreover, are economically deprived and poorly educated; they lack the skills essential to the job market and are concentrated in inner-city areas that offer neither opportunity nor minimal comfort. Many are members of underprivileged minority groups, particularly blacks and Hispanics.

This, at least, is one aspect of the picture. Another is more positive. Family and community changes have made internal family events more visible and more accessible to community assistance. Abuse and neglect may have afflicted earlier generations, but community norms and family codes kept it all hidden in the primary group. Nor were there, in earlier times, generally recognized rights that justified community intervention or organizations dedicated to converting private problems into public issues. The remainder of this section identifies some of the issues that have occupied the nation's attention in recent years.

Child and spouse abuse. If there are explosions of these phenomena, they are readily understood, no matter how much deplored, in the context of the foregoing changes in the family. Regardless of whether the perpetrators are emotionally disturbed and deviant—studies reporting such conclusions contain impressive evidence—personality clearly is the intervening variable between the societal context and the proscribed behavior. Personality is also a product of the developmental context, however, and disturbance and deviance may be increasing because of the structural and functional changes in the family and because of the absence of a supportive societal context, or they may merely have become more visible because now there is no intimate social environment to absorb them and the shock waves they create for primary groups. In either case, they are important social problems requiring societal response.

In the late nineteenth century, another time of great social change, with immigration and the juxtaposition of culturally diverse groups living in economically extreme statuses, the child protection issue was highlighted for the first time, and a national movement and state legislation were created to cope with it.[8] The 1970s and 1980s have seen the process repeated: the old intervention systems, particularly the child welfare and family service agencies, were no longer deemed adequate, and new organizations, networks, and services, came to stage center under the banner of child abuse and spouse abuse or "family violence" and received funds, attention, and legislative sanction.[9]

The statistical estimates, which often represent "reported cases" as though they were validated, may be blown up by true believers or by those who would build the "industry." In the children's field, the numbers often combine physical abuse of a severe sort with what is usually described as neglect or even dependency. Nevertheless, experts agree that no fewer than a million cases require the attention of the network every year; the cases requiring ongoing attention and surveillance or justifying the use of authoritative measures are far fewer. The child abuse response system, a component of child welfare, includes state mandatory reporting laws, case registers, emergency response arrangements to protect children under police or social work auspices, case evaluation systems, arrangements for case integration so that endangered children remain in view, intensive services to families and children, child removal arrangements, prosecution provisions, and self-help groups.[10] For about a decade federal research and demonstration funds have encouraged the development of this response system, and other federal funds have sponsored advertising, public education, and reporting programs. By 1983 direct federal involvement in these delivery systems was clearly winding down.

The data on spouse abuse are even less reliable. This problem has long been invisible and even now is only partially able to "come out." It has inspired the same types of response strategies applied to child abuse, but on a far smaller scale, and, in addition, includes the need to provide family shelters for "battered spouses." Because cases often become visible in the midst of family crises, physical protection is a valid concern. There has even been a tendency to focus too much on the emergency shelter. As in child abuse, these cases often lead to prosecution or social intervention, or both. The development of other responses has been slow and subject to local emphases despite advocates' efforts to ensure expansion through federal funding. States and localities have been cooperative, however, making portions of their social service funds available for this purpose.[11]

Adolescent runaways. This is another manifestation of the same phenomenon—changes in primary groups. Adolescents have always run away, and until modern times the nonfarm adolescent or the adolescent not needed on the family farm was expected to move away and into apprenticeship and boarding arrangements. Today, large portions of our youth move away to college, often permanently, at age 18 or thereabouts. However, what now occurs with disturbing frequency is that high school youths disappear or run away; this is not part of a planned departure for work, training, or apprenticeship. It is often precipitated by an incident relating to drugs, school problems, pregnancy, clashes about peer or boy-girl relationships, delinquency, or several such incidents at once. The claim of a million such "cases" each year is, like the claims relating to child and wife abuse, impossible to evaluate.[12]

Many American families have few "shock absorbers"—relatives or community members close by who might offer a youth an alternative living arrangement during the height of a family crisis. Since the 1960s, many young people have been on the road. Of these, many never return home or contact their families again.

The federal response has been limited to legislation supporting local efforts to create "hot lines," "crash pads," and multipurpose centers for runaway youths. Some of the programs focus on drug-related problems. Much of the innovative work has been of the volunteer or self-help variety. Some programs have been funded by foundations and local philanthropies or United Ways. Most center in those cities to which many young people flock, although the cities seem to change from time to time in their attractiveness to runaway youths.

Adolescent pregnancy and childbearing. These phenomena are more accurately documented as social issues because they are easier to identify and count and because public health statistics and related biostatistical and epidemiological research have strong traditions and sanctions. More than one million teenagers become pregnant in the United States each year; in 1980 there were over half a million births to this age group, accounting for 16 percent of all births. There was an equal number of abortions. About half the teenagers who carried their babies to term gave birth outside marriage; most had conceived outside marriage. Available data suggest that many divorce before 20.

Most teenage families with children are single-parent families. An extremely high proportion are headed by poor, poorly educated, and occupationally unskilled young women who prove to be unable to break out of the situation, thus creating disadvantaged circumstances for their own children. There is evidence as well of long-term, negative health effects. Although many teenage mothers are supported by their own families, others turn to public assistance. More than half of the recipients of Aid to Families with Dependent Children (AFDC) were teenagers when they bore their first child. It is estimated, as well, that about 60 percent of the children born to teenage mothers outside of marriage subsequently become AFDC recipi-

ents.[13] Despite large increases during the 1970s in white adolescent sexual activity, pregnancy, and out-of-marriage childbearing, all these phenomena and abortion are still more prevalent among blacks.

Whatever one's views about the traditional family and teenage sexuality, the data summarized here indicate serious social problems: poverty, poor education, inadequate occupational preparation, and health difficulties. For example, early childbearing is associated with high rates of risk for low-birthweight infants and low Apgar scores and perhaps cognitive deficits as well.

The controversy surrounding abortion and Congress's closing off Medicaid and other public funds for this purpose has perhaps increased teenage childbirths in recent years. The prevalent intervention strategies seek to decrease teenage sexual activity, to increase the use of contraception, to make the contraception more effective, to enable teenagers who become pregnant to be more deliberate in their decisions about how to resolve the pregnancy, and to guarantee that those who do bear and rear children will do so under conditions that maximize their own and the child's likelihood of decent life chances. The goal of assuring access to abortion is a controversial intervention.

This range of goals has generated a diversity of intervention models, ranging from family planning, abortion, and well-baby services in the public and nonprofit health systems, to special programs in the schools and to various direct counseling, treatment, educational, and job strategies in the social service system. The Federal Office of Adolescent Family Life has distributed its limited funds for innovative experimentation and demonstration projects, state-of-the-art reports, and research. State and local governments and nonprofit organizations have also taken part. The pattern has yielded a diverse, diffuse "nonsystem" with limited coverage. Abortion services are often lacking because of state and city policies in response to the cutoff of federal funds by Congress. In some places, abortion services are simply not available. The services available to pregnant teenagers are sometimes single purpose and narrowly specialized, but many programs, recognizing the complexity of the problem, strive for comprehensiveness, attempting no less than to socialize the teenage parents and to ensure their education, employment, family stability, and economic self-sufficiency. Health services may be provided for the children as well. Some comprehensive and effective services often cannot meet identified local needs; others report underutilization.

Homelessness. This phenomenon may be seen either as another problem category or as a symptom of several different types of problems. During the early 1980s, for the first time in almost half a century, homelessness came to the forefront as a public issue. Lacking a systematic federal or state response, localities improvised. Public agencies and voluntary nonprofit groups offered modest facilities, usually emergency shelters for individuals or families. A small amount of federal aid became available in 1983. Advocates have offered numbers at local and national public hearings, but there has been no systematic accounting of the homeless.

The emergency of homelessness as a public issue illustrates the manner in which major issues at any one time tend to absorb, take over, or redefine related phenomena. The new thing in the early 1980s was the appearance in cities of relatively young people with no place to stay. They were unemployed, had come to communities to look for jobs, or had been ousted from residences for nonpayment of rent. They either were not eligible for assistance, given the unevenness and inadequacy of general assistance in most jurisdictions, or were eligible for grants too low to pay for housing. They began to crowd the public and private shelters or the "flop houses," joining the alcoholics and drug addicts and mentally ill already there.

The crowding created new visibility. In the public perception all this was related to the big city, single-room occupancy (SRO) housing problem. These former hotels were always difficult places, and now they were housing single adults, some employed but many on welfare; deinstitutionalized aged; alcoholics; drug addicts; mental hospital dischargees; developmental center dischargees; and prison parolees. By virtue of this diversity and pathology, SROs were poor places to live: they endangered many of their occupants and were constantly deteriorating physically. Nor was the situation helped by landlords. As some cities began to experience general housing shortages in the 1980s because of the lack of new construction during the stagflation, many landlords tried to upgrade their properties, closing down some SROs and adding to the homeless totals.

Unemployment also began to affect low-income families with children: some could not meet rental or mortgage payments and were on the streets under emergency circumstances. Others were the victims of fires, unsafe buildings, or buildings poorly maintained or heated in cold weather. By 1982–83 all these phenomena had been combined in a "homelessness" category that provided anecdotal copy for the daily press and TV broadcasts, generated public legislative hearings, and justified emergency measures.

As of late 1983 no comprehensive initiatives to address the problem were visible despite the many local efforts and programs. New York City, for example, expended considerable public funds to expand and upgrade public shelters, and churches and other voluntary facilities added spaces. The courts mandated improvement in the quality of such arrangements following class-action litigation.

Like many of the other problems discussed here, "homelessness" is on the public agenda in part because the family and kin systems and intimate neighborliness, long the shock absorbers for primary group crises, do not function as efficiently as they once did for many Americans, even if they do for others. Nor are they ever likely to again. Solutions depend on separate responses to the different components of the problem, not on one magic program: there need to be more realistic community care resources if mentally ill or aged are to be deinstitutionalized successfully; unemployment benefits and related income supplementation must be expanded for those affected by the job market; a network of emergency family shelters is needed for use in crises following fires, building collapses, eviction, or incidents of family violence; and society must respond seriously to the problem of marginal singles who for lack of education and because of personality disorders and predilections cannot make it in today's economy and do not even have permanent addresses from which to seek jobs, training, financial aid, or rehabilitation. Basic attention also needs to be addressed to the problems of a housing market that prices decent dwelling units beyond the reach of many single-earner and two-earner families. It is perhaps this problem on which all the others rest.

Foster care and adoption. Child welfare and foster care and adoption statistics are part and parcel of the same societywide circumstances of family disruption discussed here. One obviously cannot discuss child abuse and neglect, family violence, homelessness, runaways, and adolescent pregnancy and childrearing without attention to developments in the foster care and adoption systems. These problems have received serious and more systematic public attention, however.

The Child Welfare and Child Adoption Assistance legislation of 1980 has been protected by Congress against Reagan Administration cutbacks and is being implemented in many states. This legislation gives priority to protecting children in their own families, returning them to their families, insuring adoption for those who cannot return to their families, and assisting those who would adopt children but cannot afford to do so. The legislation authorizes federal funding for these purposes, provides policy guidance, and requires states to develop plans to implement public goals. It focuses in particular on the allegedly excessive use of foster care and creates financial incentives for protecting the children's own families and for returning displaced children home as soon as possible.

The Response

Before entering the usual prevention/treatment debate these troublesome phenomena immediately generate, it may be useful to the social work professional, whose interventions span a broad range, to think of the society's response in yet another, overdue way—as a response to normality or normalcy rather than to pathology. The family changes described yield pathological phenomena that society cannot but deal with because they are so troublesome and demand outreach, authority, intervention, and attention. However, the concerned society should also note that family changes generate not only problems but also needs. If two-earner families, single-parent families, and families away from relations are all trying to rear children, it is clear that many families need institutional buttressing. There are children who need care while their parents work; there are families that need resources to permit them to shop, live comfortably, get home on time, support their children's learning and recreation, obtain health services, participate as citizens, interact with neighbors and friends, and have fun and satisfaction.

A focus on normalcy requires attention to income, housing, health care, child care, shopping facilities, recreation, leisure time resources, libraries, cultural programs, and social centers. In short, society needs to recognize that the families described here are what we have. They are not to be seen only as problems; they represent the new normative phenomena of our age. A responsive society that recognizes this should experience less pathology.

In their efforts at early intervention with families that tend to place their children in foster care, child welfare agencies feature family life education, mutual aid, referral for financial assistance, visiting homemakers, and so forth. Each of these has its unique value and place, but basic prevention obviously requires more potent initiatives—attention to what are described here as the normal circumstances of everyday families, not just families that are entering the child welfare network.

If the economic and social are intimately intertwined and if family change is to be interpreted in broader cultural, political, and material context, prevention must mean social policy, and the factors that create preconditions for the social problems highlighted here must have a policy address. Wise societies, and certainly pluralistic, democratic societies, do not attempt to engineer their family structures. Such efforts in police states are not attractive to Americans. However, humane, democratic, pluralistic Western industrial societies have learned to identify *the policy preconditions for stable primary group living.* Absent such preconditions, and there is no reason to expect that services or therapeutic interventions will make an impressive impact on family violence, runaways, teenage parenting, homelessness, or the channeling of the resulting cases into the child welfare, protective services, mental health, and correctional systems. Although each deserves elaboration, the policy ingredients are merely listed here:

•A job and income policy responsive to the changing realities of the economy and labor force and comprehensive in the populations it includes.

•A training and education policy that prepares all adults for useful and successful roles in a changing economy.

•An income transfer system that offers income supplementation, substitution, and replacement for people in different risk categories, so as to sustain consumption while maintaining the primacy of work as the route to income claims.

•A health policy that ensures equitable access to needed medical and hospital services by other than marketplace criteria, that creates for both consumers and providers incentives for prevention and comprehensive service delivery, and that insures all people against economic catastrophe in times of illness.

•A housing policy that faces the gap between marketplace housing costs and the maximum expenditures possible for all but high-income earners.

•A personal social services policy that features education, socialization, and practical supportive services attuned to the two-earner family, the single-parent family, the isolated family, and the frail aged, providing information, help, social experiences, mutual aid, and counseling.

Such a policy context would create hope that family and group living could evolve in a way that would gradually decrease the incidence of the social problems highlighted in the earlier section. Given the complexity of the phenomena and the limited knowledge involved, it cannot be expected that all the problems would disappear. Those that remained could be addressed by a general or personal social service system that would be used for helping and treatment, as appropriate. Because this system would not attempt to substitute services for social policy, it could hope for an increased impact.

Such a social service system would also need to depart significantly from the ad hoc fragmentation and the inadequacy that characterize present efforts. It is difficult to conceive of any rationale for not improving the system as rapidly as possible, even in the absence of general policy formulation. Millions of people clearly are affected by a pattern of services and responses that are neither sufficient in their levels nor adequate in their delivery arrangements. The following related problems require both immediate and long-range attention:

Categorical "selling" versus balanced, integrative systems. Special labels, an aura of new crises, and reports about desperate people attract the media and win legislative sponsors. They even appear to generate new funds. This is the history of initiatives responding to child abuse, spouse abuse, and deinstitutionalization. The experience of a decade and a half suggests that this is an almost irresistible trap.

The child abuse initiatives of the 1970s shook up the child welfare field, which, obviously, had not been attending to some of its domains. Publicity about family violence highlighted the failings or limited coverage of family service systems. In both instances and others, there was a price: an emphasis on problems outside their necessary context, a tendency to dramatize and to "sell," even to be careless about the numbers and the boundaries. Thus, allegedly abusive families and neglectful families sometimes are not distinguished from one another or from the other categories that feed into the child welfare system— families whose adult members may need to relinquish childrearing; families with children out of control; or families in marital conflict, accompanied in some cases by the violence of one parent against the other.

If the dedication is truly to early intervention—to intervention even before it is clear if the basis for response is delinquency, abuse, neglect, marital violence, a child runaway, or some other problem—there is something to be said for a more inclusive "family service" umbrella. Nothing precludes giving such a unit or service the capacity to turn to the legal system to protect children or a spouse. This broader view of families and their crises generates a capacity for more diverse interventions. It also solves another problem—the tendency for public funding to follow fashion, favoring a newly dramatized category and ignoring the old seemingly intractable problem. Experience does not argue for turning down initiatives of well-meaning political figures or public administrators who want to provide for specific "favored" categories. However, integrated systems that cover diverse groups of troubled families and permit broad coverage are likely to be better at nonstigmatizing and diverse interventions and to take a more balanced view of all family members and their needs. The families that come in under different labels are often just one family at different moments in the course of its problems. A working philosophy might be to abandon categorical labeling for holistic perspectives at every opportunity.

Demonstration projects versus an ongoing system of services. The appeal of the new categories does not ensure large or permanent investments. Even when there is a positive response to a disclosure of urgent need, Congress usually votes modest funding authorizations that specify research and demonstration strategies. Sometimes, as in the case of child abuse, there is also money for public education, for state-of-the-art compilations, and for clearinghouses. There may also be funding on three-year or five-year cycles for regional resource centers. Conferences and newsletters are financed. All of it depends on annual appropriations, responses to competitive requests for proposals (RFPs), or grant applications. Then, with careful attention to political balance and claims, the money is distributed.

The initial activity may be impressive: new energies are generated, new ideas stimulated, new channels opened. Attention flows away from other less adequately funded domains. Professional associations and educational institutions respond. The problem gets visibility. Then, an inevitable countertrend occurs: *There is no coverage.* Three-year and five-year cycles end, projects die, and money shifts from place to place.

The past two decades have seen the rise and fall of large numbers of these demonstration initiatives in social welfare. Now the lessons have emerged: A research and demonstration strategy can be justified as a partial response, a first stage, but not as a total social strategy. If research and development is planned without provision as to what will come next, programs are truncated. Some projects are refunded, but most are not. The local contribution occasionally becomes a coverage budget, but most initiatives do not continue after the federal presence disappears. In recent years, given the philosophy of the Reagan Administration, even demonstration budgets have been cut, and the casualties are particularly numerous. In any case, the sum total of all research and demonstration initiatives cover only a small part of the national need. In most localities, nothing significant occurs.

The lesson of these enterprises is that the demonstration route may have validity if it includes provision for systematically assessing results and translating them into coverage programs. This has not yet been the case with the problems mentioned here. Child welfare is no exception because it was part of the initial social security initiative in 1935 and was never adequately implemented. The 1980 legislation was an improvement.

Observers of this pattern of demonstration projects that do not lead to coverage programs tend to note alternative strategies of reform: (1) to advocate broader legislation that, from the beginning, describes exactly how a demonstration project will automatically be translated into a coverage service, or (2) to seek legislative backing for general social service systems that are standardized, offer national coverage, and are so organized as to respond to a multiplicity of needs.

Developmental provision and socialization services. As was suggested earlier, a family-oriented personal social service system supporting normal families to meet normal needs may prevent some of the problems described here. Moreover, because families find it difficult to go to units that are only problem-oriented, particularly units that are known to specialize in the most stigmatized and demeaning of all problems, violence and abuse, a personal social services network that includes developmental provision and socialization activities in a unit also responsible for case services could well offer many families easy access to a stigma-free program in which they can both receive counseling and have access to help if problems arise.

This proposal is offered not as a definitive answer but as an alternative hypothe-sis. The research literature does not reveal whether everyday agencies that help normal families with normal needs can also cope with severe problems without a major change in image and therefore in accessibility.

If this type of strategy works, it would suggest the formation of personal service centers that take a holistic view of the family and combine developmental and socialization services with case services. Umbrella organizations of this kind would have specialized units for dealing with specific needs, difficulties, and problems. Such units could successfully carry out the prevention mission specified by the Adoption Assistance and Child Welfare Act of 1980 and also be a meeting ground for mutual aid and self-help activities, give special attention to the needs of single-parent families, and serve as community centers.[14] One would assume a diversity of public and private auspices and funding mechanisms, at least in an experimental period.

Sorting out strategies. The programs described in this article are funded in a diversity of ways and on many conflicting principles—federal leadership, extreme devolution, mixed policies, and so forth. They were, after all, enacted under different administrations with different, even opposing philosophies and in response to special needs as they captured public attention. The programs include a social service block grant, developed from what was once Title XX; the child welfare and adoption assistance legislation, which carries a strong policy of federal carrots and sticks; various categorical grant programs from which the Reagan Administration now seeks to withdraw the federal government as a policy and operational influence; and new legislation by which Congress is attempting to mandate additional categorical programs. This type of hodgepodge does not permit sensible programming at either state or local levels and certainly provides no grounds either for decent coordination or for the coverage services described. Those concerned with emerging social problems cannot ignore the debates about federalism, about the meshing of the public and private auspices, and about future patterns of funding and accountability.

The experience of the past several decades suggests that, in a society constantly redefining the roles of various levels of government and various public and private sectors, the sorting out process is also continuous. The major social policy initiatives listed earlier—income, housing, jobs, and the like—deal with national needs only the national government has the capacity to fund. Similarly, comprehensive, reliable local social services require national financial participation. This does not mean, however, that the diversity both of the society's family patterns, lifestyles, and needs and of the potential responses to emerging problems could not be reflected in a pluralistic delivery system. A nationally supported policy, with federal fiscal participation and certain policy and delivery minima specified by the national government, could nonetheless allow substantial state and local variations both in substance and in delivery structures. This is not on the immediate horizon, however.

ALFRED J. KAHN

Notes and References

1. Eli Ginsberg and George J. Vojta, "The Service Sector of the U.S. Economy," *Scientific American,* 244 (March 1981), pp. 48–55.

2. See, for example, Barry Bluestone and Bennett Harrison, *The Deindustrialization of America* (New York: Basic Books, 1982); Robert Reich, *The Next American Frontier* (New York: Time Books, 1983).

3. John L. Palmer and Isabel V. Sawhill, eds., *The Reagan Experiment* (Washington, D.C.: Urban Institute Press, 1982); George Gilder, *Wealth and Poverty* (New York: Bantam Books, 1981); Eugene J. McAllister, ed., *Agenda for Progress* (Washington, D.C.: The Heritage Foundation, 1981); and Williard Gaylin et al., *Doing Good: The Limits of Benevolence* (New York: Pantheon Books, 1978).

4. George Gerbner et al., *Child Abuse: An Agenda for Action* (New York: Oxford University Press, 1980); Richard J. Gelles, "Violence Towards Children in the United States," *American Journal of Orthopsychiatry,* 48 (October, 1978), pp. 580–592; Sheila B. Kamerman and Alfred J. Kahn, *Social Services in the United States* (Philadelphia: Temple University Press, 1976), pp. 141–181; Barbara Shore, "Social Services for Selected Oppressed Groups," in Neil Gilbert and Harry Specht, eds., *Handbook of the Social Services* (Englewood Cliffs, N.J.: Prentice Hall, 1981), pp. 215–233; and Philip Hovda, "Child Welfare: Child Abuse," *Encyclopedia of Social Work* (17th ed.; Washington, D.C.: National Association of Social Workers, 1977), pp. 125–129.

5. Kamerman and Kahn, *Social Services in the United States,* chapter 2.

6. Angus Campbell and Phillip E. Converse, eds., *The Human Meaning of Social Change* (New York: Russell Sage Foundation, 1972); Angus Campbell, Phillip E. Converse, and Willard L. Rogers, *The Quality of American Life* (New York: Russell Sage Foundation, 1976); Frank M. Andrews and Stephen B. Withey, *Social Indicators of Well-Being: Americans' Perceptions of Life Quality* (New York: Plenum Press, 1976).

7. "Births, Marriages, Divorces, and Deaths for 1982," *Monthly Vital Statistics Report,* 31 (March 14, 1983), pp. 1–3 and 10; George Masnick and Mary Jo Bane, *The Nation's Families: 1960–1990* (Cambridge, Mass.: Joint Center for Urban Studies, 1980); U.S. Bureau of the Census, *Current Population Reports,* Series P-20, P-23, and P-60 (Washington, D.C.: U.S. Department of Commerce, 1980, 1981, 1982, and 1983; *National Journal,* August 13, 1983, p. 1706; and *New York Times,* August 3, 1983, pp. A-1 and B-4.

8. Robert M. Mulford, "Protective Services for Children," in *Encyclopedia of Social Work,* pp. 1115–1121; Hovda, "Child Welfare: Child Abuse"; Alfred J. Kahn, *Planning Community Services for Children in Trouble* (New York: Columbia University Press, 1963), pp. 312–349.

9. Gerbner et al., *Child Abuse;* Shore, "Social Services for Selected Oppressed Groups."

10. Ibid. See also Kamerman and Kahn, *Social Services in the United States.*

11. Murray A. Straus et al., *Behind Closed Doors* (Garden City, N.Y.: Doubleday & Co., 1980).

12. "Shelters and Streets Drawing More 'Throwaway Kids,' " *New York Times,* June 3, 1983, p. D-15.

13. Kristin A. Moore and Martha R. Burt,

Private Crisis, Public Cost: Policy Perspectives on Teenage Childbearing (Washington, D.C.: Urban Institute, 1982); Frank Furstenberg, *Unplanned Parenthood: The Social Consequences of Teenage Childbearing* (New York: Macmillan Publishing Co., 1976); U.S. Bureau of the Census, *Current Population Reports*, Series P-20, No. 371, "Household and Family Characteristics" (Washington, D.C.: U.S. Department of Commerce, 1982).

14. Alfred J. Kahn and Sheila B. Kamerman, "Personal Social Services and the Future of Social Work," in Kay Dea, ed., *Perspectives for the Future: Social Work Practice in the '80s* (Washington, D.C.: National Association of Social Workers, 1980), pp. 3–17; Alfred J. Kahn and Sheila B. Kamerman, *Helping America's Families* (Philadelphia: Temple University Press, 1982), pp. 229–241.

UNEMPLOYMENT

Unemployment, a persistent social problem in American history, affected more than 10 percent of the labor force in the first quarter of 1983. Because of the growth of the labor force, the jobless in the early 1980s outnumbered those of the depression in the 1930s. Although the actual rates of unemployment are less than half those estimated for the 1930s, the recurring escalations in the unemployment rate raise serious questions about the acceptability of such widespread joblessness and its social costs.

In the 1930s social workers helped to bring the needs of the jobless to the forefront, and in the early 1980s the recognition grew that unemployment and its consequences are social work issues.[1] This article develops a profile of the unemployed, describing their social, psychological, and economic problems. It then explores ways in which social workers can systematically focus services on the needs of jobless clients and promote improved employment opportunities and policies.

Profiles of the Unemployed

Official rates of joblessness are increasingly seen as indicators not just of an available labor pool or the functioning of the economy, but also of individual, family, and community needs. The Bureau of Labor Statistics calculates national unemployment statistics from the monthly household surveys it conducts in sample communities.[2] Interviews determine whether a member of the household has been out of work in the last week and has looked for work during the past four weeks. Excluded from the unemployment count are "discouraged workers" who have not searched for work in the past four weeks. Such workers numbered well over a million in 1982.

Rates of joblessness are presented in monthly or yearly averages. Jobless rates tend to obscure the incidence of the problem by reporting counts at fixed times rather than the number of persons who have been affected at some time during the year. The incidence or prevalence of unemployment generally runs at least twice that of the annualized rate. Thus, for 1982 at least 20 percent of the work force was affected by joblessness at some time during the year.[3] Data on incidence thus present a more accurate indication of the numbers of persons at risk because of joblessness.

The terms "cyclical," "seasonal," "frictional," and "structural" help to differentiate among various types of joblessness. Structural unemployment reflects the persistence of disproportionately high rates of joblessness among ethnic minorities, youths, women, older workers, and such other groups as the disabled, offenders, and Vietnam veterans. Even during an expanding economy, higher rates of joblessness afflict these groups because of structural barriers. Their participation in the labor market is impeded by labor market discrimination that affects job acquisition and retention and by skill deficits or skill obsolescence among the workers. For example, in January 1983, rates of unemployment were 20.8 percent among blacks, 22.7 percent for youths, and 45.7 percent for black youths.[4]

Those whose joblessness results from downturns in the business cycle are referred to as cyclically unemployed; it is usually expected that most such workers will be reabsorbed into their jobs when the economy improves. Others whose jobs fluctuate with the seasons are called seasonally unemployed workers. "Frictional unemployment" refers to workers who are "in between" jobs and is taken to be a fixed attribute of any labor market, including one promoting full employment. Underemployment is another type of unemployment and has compelled increased attention in recent years. The term refers to workers laboring in jobs not commensurate with their skills, training, or expectations, given the type or amount of work they are prepared to perform. Underemployment becomes an increasingly significant issue during recessionary periods, when jobless workers, to tide themselves over, will often take jobs rendering them underemployed.

Economic Impact

It is often assumed that the jobless can weather their unemployment because now, unlike during the depression of the 1930s, access to social welfare programs mitigates the financial impact of wage loss. In addition, the Reagan Administration has argued that the high percentage of unemployed workers in families with other wage earners leaves a relatively small proportion with financial hardships.

Unemployment insurance benefits cushion the potentially devastating loss of wages. Yet, because such benefits generally do not exceed 50 percent of one's wages, the income losses often reduce personal and family standards of living; cause the relinquishment of lifelong possessions, such as homes, cars, and other property; and scale down expectations about the future, such as financing college for children, caring for aging relatives, or preparing for one's own retirement.

The average weekly unemployment benefit for 1982 was $123.22, which places a family of four with no other income below the poverty line.[5] Because benefits do not replace wages, many jobless skid into the ranks of the poor. A study of the jobless in 1980 found that the median income of their families was 21 percent lower than for comparable families free of joblessness. Moreover, the incidence of poverty among families of single-parent jobless women increased to 39 percent.[6] Of the 11.446 million out of work in January 1983, over half did not have access to unemployment insurance benefits. Some were not covered because they were newly entering or reentering the labor market; others were denied benefits because of restrictions in eligibility mandated by the Reagan Administration.

Aggravating the economic insecurity of unemployment is the loss of health benefits for workers and their families. As of January 1983, an estimated 11 million jobless workers and their families were without health coverage because of layoffs.[7] Economic insecurity among the jobless may be less immediately devastating than during the thirties, but it nonetheless causes hardships and irrevocable losses. Unemployment compensation, food stamps, and public assistance may camouflage and slow the inevitable economic skid downward that is necessitated by reduced income. Even so, sharp increases in mortgage foreclosures, utility shutoffs, and bankruptcies indicate the financial crisis engulfing some of the jobless. Indeed, the growing numbers of homeless and the emergence of "tent cities," soup lines, and food lines attest not just to increasing economic hardships, but also to the deficits in social welfare policies and services.

Many communities have been increasingly afflicted by temporary or permanent plant closures resulting from declining demand, bankruptcy, or capital flight to nonunion, low-wage sections of the country. The ripple effects of such closures, especially in single-industry towns, often cripple the viability of shopkeepers and public services. Attempts to curb the profound effects of plant closure have culminated in proposals to regulate the closures process so that states can mobilize resources to address the redevelopment, retraining, and service needs of the community and its residents. However, even if such legislation were enacted on a wide basis, the declining tax revenues that accompany increased joblessness would limit the financing of services and perhaps prevent them from keeping pace with the intensified needs of the jobless and their families. For example, during the recession of the early 1980s some of the state employment services sharply reduced the number of job search classes they offered. Despite such cutbacks in state and federal services, however, the costs of income transfer programs escalate during recessions. This means that unemployment compensation costs increase. It was estimated, as one example, that unemployment insurance costs in 1975 were four to six times greater because the economy was operating at rates of 7 percent rather than 5 percent unemployment.[8]

Social Costs

In recent years, intensified interest in the social costs of joblessness has prompted a number of attempts to study such consequences. It is generally recognized that not all jobless workers experience hardships and that some already living with marginal incomes even prefer the benefits of unemployment compensation and nonwork. Also, workers spared prolonged unemployment often remain relatively free of the negative consequences that can result from long-term joblessness.

For a number of years, research on joblessness has been dominated by the studies of Brenner, who found statistically significant correlations between unemployment rates and admissions to mental hospitals, suicides, homicides, incarceration, and stress-related health disorders.[9] Such correlational studies examining the link between unemployment and crime or unemployment and mental health have generated controversy because they lack sufficient causal evidence. Moreover, a longitudinal study generated findings that call into question Brenner's research and the premise that job loss produces psychiatric symptoms.[10]

Some argue that unemployment does not cause mental illness or other problems but merely "stimulates" such predispositions.[11] Thus, the correlational link found between unemployment and spouse[12] and child abuse[13] may also be disputed, not because there is no relationship, but because the nature of the relationship— whether the unemployment is a cause or a stimulus—awaits further inquiry.

Interviews with the jobless reveal a range of stresses, including problems of morale, family conflict, and health. A longitudinal study has shown that blood pressure rises

with the news of a layoff and remains high until reemployment has occurred.[14]

Differences in the way researchers evaluate single-outcome studies, such as the link between joblessness and mental health, often obscure the need to examine the varied ways in which the stress of joblessness is expressed. Researchers need to examine the range of human costs associated with joblessness. Age, gender, and ethnic differences in coping with the consequences of unemployment remain relatively unaddressed in research, but these and other factors need to be included to obtain a more accurate reflection of the coping problems faced by various groups of workers.

Longitudinal, single-interview, and correlational studies depict social, psychological, health, interpersonal, and financial correlates of unemployment. Such findings underscore the way unemployment may be personalized in the sense that it impairs psychological and social functioning. Rather than politicizing their joblessness, workers become victims not just of their condition, but also of their inability to speak out about their plight or to advocate policies ensuring job entitlements or income security.

It has been argued that such personalized symptomatology stems from the self-blame that the long-term jobless experience. Self-recrimination may help the worker endure job rejections and an aversive job search, but its corrosive effects may underlie some of the social and psychological symptomatology uncovered in research on the effects of joblessness.[15]

Unemployed or Unemployable

Some of the presumed human costs of joblessness, such as institutionalization, addictions, and terminal illness, may temporarily or permanently disable workers so that reemployment may not be appropriate or feasible. For some, surviving the consequences of unemployment, whether these consequences are financial, social, or psychological, may be as important as acquiring a new job. A few studies have shown work to be a therapeutic antidote to the effects of unemployment for men and women, youths, and aged workers, but little is known about the "survival thresholds" for various groups of workers.[16] Even if they are available, social interventions, including social services, income supports, and job and training programs, may not come in time to curb the temporary or irreversible economic or human costs of unemployment. For example, workers and their families who lose their homes as a result of mortgage foreclosures are often unable to retrieve such losses.

For some, unemployment may be permanent not solely because of its side effects, such as illness and institutionalization, but because of the nature of the job market. The steady elimination of jobs in the 1980s resulted from plant closures, automation, and international competition and may leave a substantial number of workers permanently without jobs in their regular line of work. Despite modest retraining programs to increase the employability of permanently dislocated workers, many jobless will be forced to solve their problems in a climate that generally reflects laissez-faire approaches to the labor market.

Reentry

Few longitudinal studies provide a comprehensive analysis of how the jobless attempt to reenter the labor market. Some jobless seek retraining; others start their own business even though the risks of small business failure are high. Still others tide themselves over with part-time temporary jobs; underemployment of this kind is often a substitute for unemployment. Little is known about the human costs of underemployment for workers and their families. One research effort discovered that morale problems persisted among half the jobless workers who had taken part-time temporary jobs.[17] Such jobs were reminders of workers' inability to find work in their regular occupations, and job discontent heightened the possibility of their being fired, a threatening assault against what in many cases was an already damaged self-image.

Leads to jobs are often hard to come by. Studies show that job leads are most frequently acquired through word of mouth. Yet unemployment tends to isolate workers from work-based helping networks, thus cutting them off from valuable sources of leads. Much job seeking is consequently random, inefficient, and counterproductive. During recessionary times, prolonged searches often increase the frequency of rejections, thus potentially damaging the worker's self-esteem and motivation to seek work. Other unemployed workers find the requirement that they search for a job as a condition for drawing unemployment benefits to be a harassment, given the limited jobs available.

Policymakers and the public tend to believe that it is possible to obtain a job even during a recession if the worker is sufficiently motivated to pursue the job search. They often remark that there are plenty of good jobs if the jobless just "look harder." Although perhaps not held culpable for losing their jobs, many jobless find themselves blamed for their prolonged unemployment and inability to become reemployed.

With the exception of a few "jobs bills" and modest retraining programs, the general policy response to the jobless has been relatively laissez-faire. In contrast, intervention in the economy has been direct and deliberate. It is assumed that aggregate policy measures that stimulate the demand for goods and services will produce trickle-down effects that will reabsorb jobless workers more efficiently than programs aimed specifically at producing or retraining workers. Thus, in lieu of targeted approaches to their reemployment, many workers must await such expanding job opportunities. Despite aggregate economic as well as targeted retraining approaches to the jobless, each wave of joblessness permanently expels a substantial number of workers from the labor force.[18] Although more research is needed to explain such attrition, it is assumed that some workers become discouraged, involuntarily retired, or unemployable.

Unemployment and Inflation

It has been increasingly recognized in recent years that the provision of employment opportunities is a governmental responsibility. Despite the 1930s efforts to relieve the hardships of the jobless through job creation and unemployment insurance, official policy initiatives to promote full employment did not begin until after World War II. These initiatives culminated in the Employment Act of 1946. This act and its sequel, the Full Employment and Balanced Growth Act of 1978, were framed, in part, by the dictum that some unemployment is an inevitable by-product of attempts to curb inflation. This belief derives from the Phillips curve, which postulates an inverse correlation between levels of unemployment and inflation. Recent fluctuations in the business cycle have produced a condition called stagflation in which high rates of unemployment and inflation persist simultaneously, and this has led some economists to question the existence of such a simple relationship between unemployment and inflation.

To curb the inflationary consequences of the expansion phase of the business cycle, restrictions are imposed, in part by the Federal Reserve Board, on the availability of money. Strict monetary policies hike interest rates and decrease government spending. This, in turn, puts a damper on investment, production, and the demand for goods and services. In response, many employers attempt to curb an erosion of their profits by cutting costs through reduced production and through layoffs.

As the anti-inflationary benefits of recession become dwarfed by rising worries over unemployment, political pressures mount to loosen the grip on the flow and supply of money. The scales then begin to tip, creating a political mandate for the re-stimulation of the demand for goods and services. Such aggregate stimulation may

be produced by lowering interest rates, by increasing governmental spending, and possibly even by tax cuts. Unfortunately, the basic rate of unemployment has increased with each recent business cycle. In the 1950s and 1960s, an optimum balance between inflation and unemployment was thought to occur when unemployment was 4 or 4.5 percent, but in the 1970s and early 1980s, unemployment rates between 6 and 8 percent came to be seen as producing that balance.

Federal Programs

Government programs for the jobless have pursued the dual strategies of income maintenance and job creation. Increasingly liberalized eligibility for unemployment insurance benefits now makes it theoretically possible for over 90 percent of the current work force to be aided in the event of a layoff. Benefits, financed by employers' payroll taxes, run for twenty-six weeks except during deep recessions when eligibility may be extended for up to sixty-five weeks. Because coverage still is not extended to those entering or reentering the labor market, a substantial number of jobless may be unaided. Policies such as those used during the Reagan Administration to restrict eligibility and access to extensions also limit the amount and duration of benefits. Trade adjustment assistance is available for a small number of workers who lose jobs because of increased imports. Readjustment allowances provide income support and allowances for workers to relocate and search for jobs. Since this program was enacted in 1975, over a million persons have drawn these benefits.

Federal job creation strategies to assist the jobless were initiated in the 1930s but did not resume again until the 1960s. In the sixties a number of programs addressed the needs primarily of the disadvantaged jobless and their communities. Programs such as the Area Redevelopment Act provided funds to impoverished communities, and the Manpower Development and Training Act addressed the training needs of those whose joblessness was caused by technological change. The largest of the job creation programs of the 1960s was the Neighborhood Youth Corps.

Programs to employ welfare recipients also were pursued in the 1960s. These included the Community Work and Training Projects of 1962 and the Equal Opportunity Act of 1964, which expanded the eligibility for employment programs. The Work Incentive Program of 1967, the best known of these programs, broadened further the focus on work as a contingency for receiving welfare.

The Emergency Employment Act (EEA) of 1971 and the Comprehensive Employment and Training Act (CETA) of 1974 emphasized public service employment; both measures were enacted in response to recessions. EEA was intended to create public employment that was to cushion recessionary cycles; CETA increasingly addressed "special needs" workers, such as veterans, women, aged, and offenders, and communities with high rates of joblessness.

In the 1970s, by usually absorbing over one million workers annually, CETA brought down annual unemployment rates by at least 1 percent. With the demise of this legislation in 1982, a modest retraining bill entitled the Job Training Partnership Act was enacted to provide a limited amount of training and retraining for workers, including those displaced from jobs. In 1983 recession relief through the "jobs bill" was anticipated from the creation of public jobs for an estimated 450,000 jobless workers.

Clearly, a continuum of income, employment, and job placement and training services to aid the jobless remains an elusive policy agenda. Even so, initiatives pursued by European countries, several of which sponsor programs that begin to approximate such a continuum, provide models for future U.S. policy initiatives.

Toward Full Employment

Some argue that there are few social problems as pervasive yet as preventable as unemployment.[19] The lack of relevant human services for the jobless and of comprehensive job creation, wage replacement, and training programs for them, suggests not only that preventive approaches to the problem are missing, but also that the policy and service responses to its victims have largely been ad hoc. Pressures to promote full-employment policies evolve from the recognition that work is central to the economic, social, and psychological well-being of the 100 million or more members of the labor force. Yet, for the most part, jobs have remained a rationed privilege that, except during a few periods in American history, have not been made available to all Americans who wished to work.

Proponents of full employment, whose work culminated in 1978 in the passage of HR 50, the Full Employment and Balanced National Growth Act, argue that the job entitlements for all who wish to work should be a basic human right and that employment guarantees are essential to ensure that the achievements in civil rights can be more fully realized. Lacking access to a job, wages, and benefits blunts a person's opportunities for exercising skills and developing one's potential. Despite its sponsors' attempts to ensure job guarantees, HR 50, when finally passed, subscribed to the goals of reducing joblessness in 1983 by 4 percent overall and by 3 percent among adults. These goals were lined up side by side with the goal of reducing inflation by 3 percent in 1983.

Whatever the shortcomings of HR 50, full employment provides a useful framework for examining the benefits of current and proposed employment and training initiatives. Legislation that creates work for only a small portion of the 11 million or more jobless pales in the face of full-employment goals. Some full-employment advocates are calling for the full implementation of HR 50, others are designing legislation to accomplish the goals originally intended for HR 50.[20] As unemployment continues to take its toll, pressures for full employment will increase.

Some might claim that demographic changes, especially the decline in available workers because of lowered birth rates, will produce a glut of unfilled jobs by the 1990s. Such predictions, however, fail to account for the possible elimination of mandatory retirement for older workers, which will increase the available labor pool. In addition, jobs will continue to be lost to robotics and other forms of automation. Thus, full employment may not so easily result from the projected demographic changes, but may require economic and employment planning to distribute work more evenly, such as through shortening the work week, and to promote the creation of jobs in both the public and the private sectors.

Social Work and the Unemployed

Many workers and their families seek help from social workers in coping with the stress of joblessness. Some define their needs in psychological or interpersonal terms and, in doing so, tap the counseling resources many social workers are well equipped to provide. In other cases, the presenting problem is the need for a job, and this need may somewhat elude the service repertoire of many social service agencies. In either case, the social work assessment must discern the degree to which unemployment is the precipitant of the client's problems and to what extent the restoration of improved functioning depends on the acquisition of a job. An assessment that explicitly examines the client's perceived need for work must sort out the extent to which the disabling consequences of joblessness, such as depression or health problems, need to be addressed before job seeking can be aided.[21]

That jobs may be a therapeutic antidote for such symptoms of unemployment as depression or psychosomatic disorders suggests that the ability to marshal employment resources is important to social work practice. To promote more effective social work practice, some agencies have developed job banks and thus function as an employment exchange for their clients. Others have developed services that explicitly address the personal coping problems the jobless and their families face as a result of prolonged unemployment.

The efficacy of psychodynamic or behavioral counseling often depends on first freeing clients from physical deprivation and hardships. During recessions, service effectiveness may require a clinical repertoire that includes assistance with vocational assessment, retraining, and job placement. It has been argued that social workers should expand their job-related services, not just because they fortify other interventions, but because such services are absent from other service sectors. It is estimated that only 5 to 10 percent of those seeking help from the Employment Service acquire the services they need[22] and that job placement rates run about 10 to 15 percent among those seeking work.[23]

One social service program that integrated employment and counseling services for the jobless found heightened service effectiveness (placement rates of 30 percent) and increased client satisfaction with the services.[24] Some CETA programs also integrated employment and social services. Obviously such services should not be limited to targeted training and employment approaches. It may be, however, that the experiences of social workers in implementing CETA programs will enable others in the profession to bring more integrated service models into traditional social service agencies.

With the resurgence of attention to unemployment as a major social problem, social workers are in key positions to empower the jobless. Instead of reinforcing the tendency among the unemployed to blame themselves for their plight, social workers can help these workers organize for self-help mutual aid and for collective advocacy. This kind of intervention should be an essential component of the social work contribution.

The growth of occupational social work has helped to strengthen an awareness of the meaning of work and joblessness as a human service issue. Several occupational social workers have successfully negotiated social service contacts with employers that extend human services to unemployed as well as employed workers.

Because of the profound toll joblessness takes not just on workers but also on their families, services need to be mobilized for family members as well. Some families, unable to interpret the behavior of their discouraged, jobless member, interpret listless behavior as reflecting a lack of interest in their well-being and of motivation to find a job. Effective coping depends on the support jobless workers receive from their families and other helping networks.[25] Thus, mobilizing members of such networks before the unemployed become too damaged and unintentionally punitive is an essential component of social work practice with the jobless.

Church and union support networks are emerging in various parts of the country as useful support systems for jobless members. Social workers may seek to deliver certain services through these networks rather than wait for the unemployed to overcome concerns about the stigma of seeking counseling and come directly to the agencies. Coalitions of social service providers, unions, and church groups may redress other needs of the jobless, such as promoting plant closure regulations, alternatives to layoffs, and moratoriums on evictions, mortgage foreclosures, utility cutoffs, and property repossessions.

Education and Research

Although many agree that unemployment is a major social problem, it has not received significant attention in the curricula of social work education. Social work students are often trained in fieldwork placements that serve jobless clients, but the explicit planning, design, and testing of services to meet the needs of this underserved population has, for the most part, not occurred. Perhaps growing interest in the world of work will elevate the pheno-

menon of joblessness to a more central place in the social work curriculum. Increased sensitivity to the problems graduates of social work programs themselves endure during periods of joblessness may also foster increased attention to the issue.

The problem of unemployment compels a human service response. The social work profession can play a pivotal role in designing and testing strategies to reduce the trauma of long-term joblessness. Even during periods of economic recovery and growth, high rates of joblessness persist among the structurally unemployed, such as women, ethnic minorities, youths, older workers, and those whose jobs are lost to technological changes or the transnational flight of capital. Those left behind are reminders that, for the social work profession, unemployment is not an issue solely of service development.

The profession needs to embrace the position that work, as a major foundation of social and economic well-being, is a human right that no longer can be neglected. As the profession presses for such entitlements as a minimum income, health care, and housing, it must also advocate for job guarantees. Each recession poignantly demonstrates that many workers and their families are just a layoff away from welfare, mortgage foreclosures, and impaired functioning. Preventive intervention necessitates the promotion of full employment policies that guarantee jobs for all who wish to work, thus making work a basic human right.

KATHARINE HOOPER BRIAR

Notes and References

1. Clarke A. Chambers, *Seedtime of Reform* (Minneapolis: University of Minnesota Press, 1963). See also National Association of Social Workers news release, Silver Spring, Md., November 22, 1982.

2. Jobless rates expressed as percentages constitute the ratio of the number of unemployed to the total in the labor force (the sum of those unemployed and employed). See John H. Per-

cavel, "The Nature of the Contemporary Unemployment Problem," in Michael J. Boskin, ed., *The Economy in the 1980's: A Program for Growth and Stability* (New Brunswick, N.J.: Transaction Books, 1980), pp. 83–115.

3. Katharine Hooper Briar, "Unemployment: Toward a Social Work Agenda," *Social Work*, 28 (May–June 1983), pp. 211–216.

4. Committee of Economic Advisors, *Economic Indicators* (Washington, D.C.: U.S. Department of Labor, April 1983), p. 12.

5. *Critical Choices for the '80's* (Washington, D.C.: National Advisory Council on Economic Opportunity, August 1980), pp. 50–51.

6. Sylvia Lazos Terry, "Unemployment and Its Effect on Family Income in 1980," *Monthly Labor Review* (April 1982), pp. 35–43.

7. "Millions of Jobless Lose Health Insurance Coverage," *Jobs Impact*, February 4, 1983. *Jobs Impact* is a biweekly published in Washington, D.C., by the National Committee for Full Employment.

8. See *The Cyclical Behavior of Income Transfer Programs: A Case Study of the Current Recession*, Technical Analysis Paper No. 7, Office of Income Security Policy (Washington, D.C.: Department of Health, Education and Welfare, October 1975), pp. i–ii.

9. M. Harvey Brenner, *Estimating the Social Costs of National Economic Policy* (Washington, D.C.: Joint Economic Committee, U.S. Congress, 1976).

10. S. Kasl and S. Cobb, "Some Mental Health Consequences of Plant Closings and Jobloss," in Louis Ferman and Jeanne Gordus, eds., *Mental Health and the Economy* (Kalamazoo, Mich.: Upjohn Institute, 1979).

11. Kathleen Fisher and Susan Cunningham, "The Dilemma: Problem Grows, Support Shrinks," *Monitor*, 14 (January 1983), p. 2.

12. Susanne K. Steinmetz and Murray Strauss, "General Introduction: Social Myth and Social System in the Study of Intra-familial Violence," in Susanne Steinmetz and Murray Strauss, eds., *Violence in the Family* (New York: Harper & Row, 1974), p. 9.

13. Robert L. Light, "Abused and Neglected Children in America: A Study of Alternative Policies," *Harvard Educational Review*, 43 (November 1973).

14. S. C. Cobb and S. Kasl, "Blood Pressure Changes in Men Undergoing Jobloss: A Preliminary Report," *Psychosomatic Medicine* (January–February 1970).

15. Katharine H. Briar, *The Effect of Long-Term Unemployment on Workers and Their Families* (San Francisco: R & E Research Press, 1978).

16. Katharine Briar et al., "The Impact of Unemployment on Young, Middle-Aged, and Aged Workers," *Journal of Sociology and Social Welfare*, 7 (November 1980), pp. 907–915.

17. Briar, *The Effect of Long-Term Unemployment on Workers and Their Families*.

18. G. A. Akerloff and B. G. Main, "Unemployment Spells and Unemployment Experience," *The American Economic Review* (December 1980).

19. P. R. Cain-Kaudle, *Comparative Social Policy and Social Security* (New York: Dunellen, 1973), p. 202.

20. Bertram Gross, "Grass-Roots National Planning in a Global Perspective," statement presented at the Conference on the Role of the Public Sector in Restoring the Economic and Social Health of the Nation, sponsored by the House of Representatives, Washington, D.C., February 1983.

21. Katharine Hooper Briar, "Helping the Unemployed Client," *Journal of Sociology and Social Welfare*, 7 (November 1980), pp. 895–906.

22. Miriam Johnson, *Counterpoint, the Changing Public Service* (Salt Lake City, Utah: Olympia Publishing Company, 1973).

23. Stanley H. Ruttenberg and J. Gutchess, *The Federal State Employment Service: A Critique* (Baltimore, Md.: Johns Hopkins University Press, 1970), p. 78.

24. *Start-Up* (Seattle, Wash.: United Way of King County, 1974).

25. Susan Gore, "The Effect of Social Support in Moderating the Health Consequences of Unemployment," *Journal of Health and Social Behavior*, 19 (1978), pp. 157–165.

VOLUNTEERS

Volunteers perform a diversity of tasks, respond to an uncharted array of motivations, derive a wide range of satisfactions, and labor in an uncounted number of agencies, both public and voluntary, and in informal settings. The volunteer community is complex, extensive, and not yet fully mapped, although research and survey techniques have improved in the past two decades or so. It is safe to say that at one time or another almost everyone has been a volunteer.

Since the early 1970s, growth and change in the volunteer community have reflected the demographic, economic, and social changes that have affected society as a whole, including sharp increases in the proportion of older persons, greater empowerment of minorities and the poor, important changes in the nature of the workplace and the work force, rapid expansion of the concept of corporate social responsibility, the women's movement, the gradual shift from the 1970s' emphasis on privatism to an emphasis in the 1980s on the Judeo-Christian ethos of caring, and ongoing financial constraints resulting, in part, from inflation, the energy crisis, and high levels of unemployment. Moreover, the newer forms of volunteering—self-help, human support groups; informal block and neighborhood organizations; consumer, public interest, and advocacy volunteering; and a markedly increased use of the initiative as a form of political action—also reflect emerging social and political realities. Among them are widespread alienation from or mistrust of major political and economic institutions, the inability of many so-called traditional volunteer organizations to revise their programs to respond to the needs and expectations of today's volunteers, a serious disillusionment with the professional helping establishment, and a resolution on the part of many people to get some measure of control over events and forces affecting their lives.

Numbers

Studies have shown a remarkable increase in the number of volunteers during the last two decades. In 1965 the Department of Labor reported a total of 22 million volunteers.[1] In 1974 the Census Bureau found 37 million volunteers, an increase of 68 percent over the 1965 study.[2] In 1981 a Gallup poll reported a total of 84 million volunteers, an increase of 127 percent over the figures for 1974 and 280 percent over the 1965 study.[3] Methodologies and definitions differed among these studies, however. For example, volunteers who did religious volunteering only were not counted in the 1965 study; the Gallup survey included for the first time the so-called informal volunteers, those who work alone rather than with an organization.

None of these surveys attempted to determine the number of volunteers working in public agencies as compared with voluntary organizations. One responsible source estimated that 20 to 30 percent of all organized volunteer groups are government operated.[4]

Using the Gallup survey as a base, the organization known as Volunteer: The National Center for Citizen Involvement estimated the total value of volunteer time for the year 1981 to be $64.5 billion.[5]

In 1974 the typical American volunteer was a married, white woman between 25 and 44 who held a college degree and was in the upper-income bracket. This profile had changed little by 1980. However, the growing number of persons 65 and over, now numbering over 25 million, is increasingly regarded as a national resource. Not only are more and more older persons volunteering, but substantial numbers are currently not involved but would like to be. The 1965 report identified 1.5 million volunteers 65 and over. Louis Harris surveys found that this number had increased to 4.5 million in 1974 and to 5.9 million in 1981.[6] By virtue of including informal volunteering, the 1981 Gallup survey produced a figure of 9.1 million volunteers from this age group.

Older persons are now healthier, more economically independent, and better educated than were earlier generations of the elderly, and these characteristics correlate with higher volunteer rates at all ages. The potential for volunteers among the 65 and older age group is thus higher than ever.

Where Volunteers Work

Although the total number of volunteers has been increasing dramatically, the number active in social welfare has either declined or remained constant. However, further definitional problems arise. For example, during the week ending November 13, 1965, 21.6 percent of all volunteers engaged in some kind of educational activity, and 19.8 percent (4.4 million persons) were found in "social and welfare service" such as, according to the report, "homes for the aged or orphans, legal aid, travelers aid." Volunteers in health service settings came to 17.3 percent; civic or community action, 12.7 percent.[7]

During the week ending April 13, 1974, 50 percent of all volunteers devoted themselves to religious-oriented activities. Education and health each commanded 15 percent of all volunteers, and 14 percent worked in civic and community action settings. Citizenship activities claimed 12 percent and recreation groups 11 percent. Seven percent, or 2.6 million persons, participated in "social and welfare," which this time was defined as persons who "worked with the aged and in orphanages."[8]

During the last three months of the 1981 Gallup survey, religious volunteering accounted for 11 percent of all volunteers; education, 10 percent; work-related and community action volunteering, 5 percent each; political activities, 4 percent; "social/welfare," recreation, and general fundraising each accounted for 3 percent. For social/welfare this works out to a total of 2.5 million persons. In the Gallup survey social/welfare was defined as such areas as "the Salvation Army, the National Association for the Advancement of Colored People, homes for the aged, family planning, orphanages, drug rehabilitation, hot lines, etc."[9]

What Volunteers Do

Because formal surveys and other reports indicate that volunteers participate in a wide range of helping activities, it is difficult to achieve a simple classification of what volunteers do. This is evident in the following sample of volunteer positions reported in the Gallup survey: office holder, poll watcher, fund raiser, rescue squad member, nursing home worker, school board member, room mother, coach, usher, choir member. The author has developed the following categories to help classify such diverse activities:

Service. This is the traditional activity of an individual helping another individual. It includes personal support (home-delivered meals, help with marketing, friendly visiting, and the like), shared expertise, and technical assistance.

Issue/change/advocacy. This includes a wide range of activities generally directed toward change—change in the way systems operate, institutions function, and rights and entitlements are protected or extended.

Citizen participation. Although there are different perceptions of this category, a widely accepted formulation emphasizes volunteer activities that relate to the functioning of government, including participation in planning and policy development through boards and committees, in channeling communication and information, and in monitoring and evaluating public programs.

Governance. This activity refers to volunteers who serve on boards of directors and similar bodies in the voluntary sector that have policymaking responsibilities.

Self-help. At least two perceptions of self-help activities are common. One refers to volunteer activities that improve a block or neighborhood or that empower people. Another common application of this category is to self-help groups, such as Alcoholics Anonymous, which deal with the problems of individuals.

Fundraising. The fundraising may be general—part of a United Way campaign, for example—or for a particular organization, such as participation in an alumni funding campaign for one's college or university.

Why People Volunteer

As demand for volunteers increases and as traditional pools of volunteers change, the question of why people volunteer becomes increasingly important. Motivation is personal, reflecting each individual's interests and needs and ranging across a continuum from altruism to enlightened self-interest and frequently becoming a mixture of the two. Enlightened self-interest may include a desire to make a significant impact on a neighborhood or community problem and to have an experience that is meaningful in terms of one's personal career goals. Most people volunteer for one of the following reasons:

Self-help, mutual aid. This category of motivation involves the historically developed principles of mutual help in times of need and the concept that those who have experienced and coped with a problem are best able to help others beset with the same problem.

Religious. Throughout recorded history, voluntary acts of caring, serving, compassion, and sacrifice have been founded on the timeless religious principles, including justice and mercy. Whether the help is rendered in the form of neighbor helping neighbor or through organizations, the impulse to turn outwards from the self to the needs of others without thought of mone-

tary reward reflects one of humanity's noblest impulses and civilization's greatest promise.

Economic. Motivations vary from the desire to acquire new skills or prepare for a new career to attempts to save money by working in a food co-op or other cooperative enterprise.

Justice and other causes. The desire to make societal institutions—governmental, for profit, and voluntary organizations—work more effectively prompts many to direct their efforts toward assuring that they or others receive their rights and entitlements under law. Others choose to support such causes as environmental conservation and the control of nuclear weapons.

Personal. This category covers a wide range of concerns, from the belief that one owes something to society, which was Andrew Carnegie's motive, to pure enjoyment in what one does. Some volunteers want public or social recognition. Others need to be active, wish to socialize, or want to make some use of their talents and attain a degree of self-fulfillment in so doing.

This understanding of why people volunteer suggests that organizations interested in retaining volunteers must give serious thought to creating opportunities for the volunteer to engage in useful and fulfilling activities, something in which they definitely feel needed and that is related to their interests. The heightened expectations of volunteers place new responsibilities on the managers of volunteer programs. A volunteer program can no longer be an add-on operation to which management gives casual attention.

If there is a central truth about successful volunteer programs, it is that today an agency should see its volunteer program as an extension of its staff. This is not to say that volunteers are considered to be staff or that personnel policies should be the same. Rather, to have an exemplary volunteer program, the organization must develop a comprehensive management system for the volunteer program that is parallel to and compatible with its staff system. Volunteers deserve and require, precisely as paid staff do, job descriptions, supervision, training, recognition, and opportunities for growth and promotion.

This kind of a program reflects the accelerating professionalism of volunteer services and emphasizes a collegial relationship among volunteers and staff. That relationship is based on mutual trust and on a mutual respect for the skills each brings to the job and for what each accomplishes.

The Self-Help Phenomenon

The self-help movement is a fast-growing segment of volunteer activity. Self-help activities generally fall into three groups. The first are the human support self-help groups that are directed toward meeting special needs. Modeled on Alcoholics Anonymous, such groups deal with a variety of problems, such as drug addiction, gambling, smoking, and obesity and go by such names as Addicts Anonymous, Checks Anonymous, Nar-Anon, Mended Hearts, Weight Watchers, and Gamblers Anonymous. There are now an estimated 500,000 of these groups, reaching perhaps 15 million persons.[10]

A second group of self-help activities falls in the category of neighborhood improvement—block improvement associations, clean-up programs to convert abandoned lots into playgrounds, neighborhood crime watch groups, block fairs to raise money for local purposes, and so on. No one knows how many of these self-help groups exist, in part because such organizations are often transitory.

A third array of self-help activities defies simple classification. It includes such things as bartering services or goods, networking, monitoring consumer prices, energy conservation, food co-ops, and community gardens. Some observers have called these activities "self-reliant volunteering." Again, no one knows how many persons engage in these activities.

Each of these forms of self-help activity have common elements. They emerge from self-interest, whether stimulated by inflation, the energy crisis, or a desire to improve the quality of life. They often attract participants because self-help groups seem to have a high rate of success in achieving collective goals or in motivating individual participants to achieve personal objectives. They are informal, that is, they are unconnected with established organizations, public or private. They are probably undercounted in all surveys.

The Volunteer Network

Over a relatively short period an impressive infrastructure aimed at serving and facilitating the use of volunteers has developed. In 1981 a tabulation of state and local organizations disclosed the following numbers: local volunteer bureaus, voluntary action centers, or other community-wide volunteer centers—300 to 350; statewide offices of volunteer citizen participation—25; local colleges and universities offering courses in volunteerism to volunteers or volunteer directors—50 to 75; local high schools offering courses in volunteerism to their students—50 to 75; volunteer clearinghouses in colleges and universities—400 to 450; local volunteer community placement programs in churches and synagogues—300 to 400.[11]

Several national organizations focus exclusively on the promotion and improvement of volunteer activities:

• Volunteer, the National Center for Citizen Involvement, was created on July 2, 1979, by the merger of the National Center for Voluntary Action and the National Information Center on Volunteerism. It is dedicated to stimulating and strengthening voluntary action and volunteer involvement; its membership includes local voluntary action centers and volunteer bureaus.

• Founded in 1980 to replace the earlier Association for Administrators of Volunteer Services, the Association of Volunteer Administrators is the professional association for those working in the field of volunteer management.

• The Association of Volunteer Bureaus coordinates the interests of some 190 volunteer bureaus in the United States and Canada. In 1979 this organization published an important manual, *Standards and Guidelines for the Field of Volunteerism*.

• The Association of Voluntary Action Scholars is a professional, scholarly organization concerned with better understanding citizen involvement and volunteer participation. Among its publications is the *Journal of Voluntary Action Research*.

Other national organizations are concerned with volunteering as it relates to particular constituencies or memberships. These include the Association of Junior Leagues, the National Council of Jewish Women, Independent Sector, the National Association of Volunteers in Criminal Justice, and Church Women United. The largest national voluntary organizations are those that achieve their program objectives through the utilization of volunteers. These include the American Red Cross, United Way of America, Young Men's and Young Women's Christian Associations, and Big Brothers and Sisters.

Barriers to Full Utilization

Negative relationships between volunteers and professionals are regarded by many as the greatest single barrier to the effective use of volunteers. According to a report by the National Forum on Volunteering,

> the resistance of helping professionals to volunteer involvement is . . . pervasive. . . . In field after field—education, social services, museums and libraries, health care— the major barrier to effective volunteer involvement lies in the inability or unwillingness of paid helping professionals to accept volunteers as legitimate partners in the helping process. . . .
> These attitudes include the ill-defined professionalism that dictates that only those who are specially trained can provide human services, an insecurity about their jobs

or their own capabilities, fear that volunteers will act as monitors and evaluators of their efforts, fear that in times of budget reduction they may be replaced by volunteers, and ignorance about the capabilities and commitment of volunteers.[12]

In the 1980s reductions in public funding of human service programs focus attention on volunteers as potential replacements for staff or as substitutes for additional staff and threaten to intensify the resistance of paid staff to volunteers.

Social work has begun serious efforts to attack this problem. The National Association of Social Workers and the Council on Social Work Education are cooperating with the Association of Junior Leagues, Volunteer, the Family Service Association of America, and other voluntary organizations in a project to find ways to enhance the effectiveness of volunteers and to improve the means of preparing social work students to work with volunteers.

Among the themes to emerge from this long-term project to address the problems in volunteer-professional relationships was an endorsement of the importance of an atmosphere and attitude of collaborative effort between professional staff and volunteers. A report the project issued in 1981 suggested that "all people in positions of leadership, both academic and operational, should take seriously the responsibility of emphasizing the team approach both didactically and in their own attitudes and actions."[13] The report observed that volunteerism

> must be integrated into schools and agencies at various levels and functions. It is necessary for boards to state policies regarding the importance of volunteerism, for staff to realize that it is an integral part of their responsibilities, for budget directors to fund, for volunteers to commit, for students to study and for the community to respect.[14]

The report also called for materials—case studies, teaching modules, handbooks, bibliographies—that would help schools of social work educate and train people in the use of volunteers.

President's Call for Volunteers

The widely publicized call of President Reagan for more volunteers provided important support for volunteerism nationwide. Not since President Nixon's call for additional volunteers in the early 1970s has the White House given such direct leadership in the recruitment and utilization of volunteers. Volunteering benefits from visible and compelling White House interest and attention.

President Reagan's position on the subject has two sides, however. His call for increased volunteering coincided with substantial reductions in the federal budgets for human service programs. Some of these reductions directly affect voluntary agencies. For example, for the period 1982 to 1985, direct reductions in outlays to voluntary agencies total $33 billion, the largest part in the form of reduced grants, contracts, and the like, with a potential loss to social welfare and community agencies of one-quarter to one-third of their total revenues.[15] Other reductions affect the voluntary sector indirectly. The president's proposals call for a reduction of $115 billion in government-administered programs, about $40 billion of which is in social welfare and income maintenance.[16] Many of those denied government benefits turn to the voluntary sector for help.

When these presidential initiatives are taken together, neither increased private giving from individuals, foundations, and corporations nor any realistic expectations of increases in the number of volunteers can make up the deficit. Observers cite three resulting problems:

1. There is a hazard and a tragedy in the possibility that, at some future time, it will be asserted that the failure to solve local problems came about because people simply did not volunteer.

2. Local volunteers are increasingly being drawn into problems brought about, not by local decision, but by federal default. An example is the local soup kitchen: in responding to this rapidly expanding, urgent need across the country, volunteers are often denied the opportunity of meeting some locally determined priority or need.

3. Reductions in agency staff have strained volunteers' commitment to the principle that they not fill the positions of paid employees. Volunteers have always embraced this principle as a moral issue, but there is evidence that they are increasingly setting this principle aside to maintain some essential services.

The public often fails to understand that it costs money to put volunteers in the field, and this has resulted in policy contradictions. In one midwestern state, a call for more volunteers to serve in a financially stricken program coincided with the elimination, in the name of economy, of the position of volunteer director. It will be remembered that in California in the seventies, as an initial aftermath of Proposition 13, the budgets of twenty-two voluntary action centers were promptly reduced as a means of saving money.

Another important initiative by President Reagan was the creation late in 1981 of the Task Force on Private Sector Initiative. The task force's final report, issued in December 1982, contains several recommendations of significance to volunteers and volunteering.[17] The heart of the report was the recommendation that a goal be adopted of doubling individual cash contributions and the number of volunteers within the next four years.

Volunteering and Public Policy

These developments all point to the importance of having a clear and consistent public policy toward volunteers and volunteering. Although many federal departments may by law encourage volunteering and citizen participation—the Department of the Interior, via Volunteers in the Parks; the Department of the Agriculture, via 4-H clubs and extension programs; the Small Business Administration, via the Service Corps of Retired Executives (SCORE); the Department of Health and Human Services; the Justice Department; and the

Department of Housing and Urban Development. The federal agency with primary responsibility to encourage, support, and strengthen volunteer involvement is ACTION. Despite the importance of its volunteer programs—Foster Grandparents, the Retired Senior Volunteer Program, and Volunteers in Service to America (VISTA) are among the better known—ACTION has suffered in the past from lack of a clear, coherent mission. Successive presidential administrations have viewed it variously as a clearinghouse, a technical assistance program, an umbrella for federal programs, and an antipoverty program.

The impact that various federal actions and policies have on volunteering suggests the need for an overarching federal policy. The general principles that should underlie such a policy are the following:

1. Government, especially at the federal and state levels, should encourage, facilitate, and stimulate volunteering under both public and voluntary auspices.

2. Government should recognize independence, freedom, diversity and heterodoxy as inherent values of volunteering, of voluntary organizations and of society as a whole.

3. Government should recognize the historical value of voluntary organizations as seed beds of innovation, experimentation, and, if in accord with their own priorities, as instruments of public policy through purchase of services and other contractual arrangements.

4. Government should see public and voluntary efforts as complementary, and take appropriate initiatives to bring about collaborative efforts.

5. Government should recognize the supreme importance of the voluntary sector being strong and independent, thereby creating a delicate balance between the governmental, for-profit, and nonprofit sectors.[18]

The critical attribute of any federal policy toward volunteerism is that it be specific, clearly articulated, consistent, and encouraging of citizen participation.

Corporate and Labor Volunteering

A recent survey issued by Volunteer, the National Center for Citizen Involvement, disclosed that 333 companies have some form of employee volunteer program. A total of 239 companies sponsor released time programs under which an employee is afforded an opportunity to pursue community interests on company time. Forty companies reported social service leave programs, an extended leave under which an employee may be away from the job for up to three years.[19] The rationale for these programs is corporate self-interest, recognition of the corporation as a powerful community institution and citizen, the need for corporate talent and resources for problem solving, and a desire to maintain the pluralistic nature of American society.

In the past decade, organized labor has moved from its traditional collaboration with United Ways to the formation of independent community service councils, United Labor Agencies (ULAs). Union members who volunteer through these organizations work in all community agencies and provide various services for the whole community, but they give priority to providing services for union members. Sixteen of these ULAs have been formed since 1971. The principal motivations underlying this development are the same as for corporate involvement—to offer a broader opportunity for members to engage in volunteer community service.

For the Future

Among the items near the top of volunteerism's agenda for the future are new and innovative methods of recruiting volunteers. Just as business segments potential markets to pinpoint its advertising dollars, so organizations using volunteers need to think about potential volunteer markets. For example, data and experience suggest that older persons will be a rich source of recruitment for the next several decades. Despite widespread concern that the large numbers of women entering the labor market would reduce the numbers of volunteers, more working women are now volunteering than ever before. But agencies have had to adapt their schedules to accommodate this valuable source of volunteers.

Similarly, organizations must seize the initiative in developing sources of released-time volunteers from corporations and from organized labor. It is also important that recognition be accorded to new motivations for volunteers; for example, recognition of the enlightened self-interest that leads a person to see volunteer experience as a means of entrance into the labor market.

It is also important to support organizations, such as local voluntary action centers and state offices of volunteering, that work to improve methods of recruitment, placement, and training and to strengthen networking and collaboration among organizations. Destructive competition is evident in all too many communities today as funds are reduced and the demand for volunteers increases.

The most important item on the agenda is that steps be taken to eliminate existing barriers to constructive volunteer and professional collaboration in education, health, social welfare, and other professional fields. Until this problem is tackled constructively and comprehensively, as the profession of social work has done, volunteer programs will fail.

GORDON MANSER

Notes and References

1. Manpower Administration, U.S. Department of Labor, *Americans Volunteer,* Monograph No. 10 (Washington, D.C.: U.S. Government Printing Office, April 1969).

2. *Americans Volunteer, 1974: A Statistical Study of Volunteers in the United States* (Washington, D.C.: ACTION, 1975).

3. *Americans Volunteer, 1981* (Princeton, N.J.: Gallup Organization, 1981).

4. Wayne D. Rydberg and Linda J. Peter-son, eds., *A Look at the Eighties: Crucial Environmental Factors Affecting Volunteerism.* (Appleton, Wisc.: Aid Association for Lutherans), p. 19.

5. "Dollar Value of Volunteer Time," *Voluntary Action Leadership* (Spring 1982), p. 33.

6. *Myth and Reality of Aging in America* and *Aging in the Eighties* (New York: Louis Harris & Associates, 1974 and 1981, respectively).

7. Manpower Administration, U.S. Department of Labor, *Americans Volunteer,* p. 34.

8. *Americans Volunteer, 1974,* p. 8.

9. *Americans Volunteer, 1981,* p. 22.

10. *The Voluntary Sector in Brief* (New York: Academy for Educational Development, 1979), p. 2.

11. Ivan H. Scheier, " 'Other-than-National' Organizations and Volunteering," in *Shaping the Future, Report of the National Forum on Volunteerism* (Appleton, Wisc.: Aid Association for Lutherans, 1982), p. 33.

12. Rydberg and Peterson, *A Look at the Eighties,* p. 54.

13. Florence S. Schwartz, ed., *Voluntarism and Social Work Practice.* (New York: Association of Junior Leagues, 1981).

14. Ibid.

15. Lester M. Salamon and Alan J. Abramson, *The Federal Government and the Nonprofit Sector: Implications of the Reagan Budget Proposals* (Washington, D.C.: The Urban Institute, 1981).

16. Ibid.

17. See "President's Task Force Completes Mission," *Building Partnerships News,* undated, ca. December 1982. (this publication is a semi-monthly periodical issued by the President's Task Force on Private Sector Initiative.)

18. Gordon Manser, "Should America Have a National Public Policy on Volunteerism?" Paper presented at the Annual Meeting of the Voluntary Action Center, Kansas City, Missouri, April 16, 1982.

19. Kerry Kenn Allen et al., eds., *Volunteers from the Workplace* (Washington, D.C.: National Center for Voluntary Action, 1979).

WOMEN'S ISSUES

Since the early 1970s, the women's movement has significantly affected the practice of social work with women. Linked as it was with other human liberation efforts, the movement's emphasis on social, economic, and political rights for women stimulated social workers to reassess the state of their practice with women. In a profession in which women are in a majority both as workers and clients, this analysis was both fitting and timely.

In reflecting on the recent two decades, it is easy to lose sight of the rich history from which this analysis arose. From its earliest days, social work was enlivened by the leadership of outstanding women who shaped future directions for practice. Mary Richmond, Jane Addams, Florence Kelley, and Bertha Reynolds helped anchor the profession to its values regarding social equality. They and others vigorously advocated social policies that would allow women, children, and people of color to have dignified lives.[1] Like the reassessment that occurred a half century later, their efforts were linked with other social reform movements, including the first women's movement.

A renewed recognition of systematic sexism as a factor affecting social work practice was an important feature of the analysis that began in the late 1960s. Central to this concern was an assessment of the extent to which social work had been influenced by destructive, constricting views regarding the capacity of women to determine their own lives. Even though social work has had a historic commitment to end social divisions based on gender, class, ethnicity, race, and physical-emotional conditions, the profession has also been shaped by the cultural forces of the society. Because societal values have supported a view of women as deficient beings with limited rights and status, it is not surprising that this view was absorbed by social workers socialized in that dominant value system.

The feminist perspective, which fueled much of the momentum of the women's movement, was instrumental in helping the profession analyze the nature of its practice with women. Although feminism is not a singular ideology, proponents characteristically emphasize the societal customs and beliefs that maintain women in subordinate roles and produce negative consequences for women's social, physical, and emotional well-being. This perspective was a reminder that social forces in the environment were important variables to take into account.

Some of the renewed awareness of sexism in the profession centered around the differential treatment accorded women and men in the mental health system. Enlightened by the Broverman study, social workers became aware that stereotypical views of women as passive, dependent, and emotionally fragile had seeped into professional clinical judgments.[2] Whereas stereotypical masculine traits of independence, assertiveness, and decisiveness corresponded to views of a mentally healthy adult, stereotypical feminine traits did not. In effect, conventional female attributes did not stack up against the general norms of mental health.

As this double standard of mental health became more clearly understood, increased attention was paid to the treatment of women in the mental health system. Chesler made the case that psychiatric facilities view women as impaired because professionals work from a masculine concept of mental health.[3] Because women can be judged mentally ill for exhibiting traditional feminine traits and equally so for exhibiting aggressive, confronting, masculine traits, they are locked in a double-bind situation.

In the attempt to account for sex-related differences, accepted psychological theories reinforced these social and professional stereotypes. Weisstein pointed out that theories of human behavior reinforced existing stereotypes by asserting that women were destined, by their nature, to be receptive, nurturing, pliable, and emotionally responsive.[4] Because social work draws heavily on theories from the behavioral sciences, scores of students in social work and related disciplines were exposed to theories that assumed women to be inherently deficient.

In a comprehensive analysis of research on clinical treatment, Seidan discussed ways stereotypical expectations of women infiltrated theories used to explain women's behavior. As one example, she pointed to the "blame-the-mother" tradition apparent in theories of psychopathology.[5] This view cited the child's central, early relationship with his or her mother as the cause of the child's later personality problems. Women were thus blamed for their performance in a role about which society gave them little choice.

Sexism in Practice

The wave of awareness quickly gained momentum during the 1970s. The needs of special client populations began to receive attention. Women as victims of battering and rape, elderly women, minority women, lesbians, and poor women were among those whose needs social workers began to address. In its first special issue devoted to women's concerns, *Social Work* published an important collection of articles on the impact of sexism on practice.[6] This edition was a major recognition by the profession that such issues deserved concerted attention and action.

Throughout this period recognition grew of the common denominators in women's lives. Each identifiable group, whatever the experiences unique to its circumstances, shared with all other women the emotional and physical costs of tyranny. In demonstrable ways, social institutions, norms, and customs set up impermeable barriers to keep women "in their place." The exhortation to "behave like a lady" epitomized the kind of constraint to which all women were subject. The collective recognition of this constraint was the seedbed for a common purpose and for a vision that challenged the way things were.

As needs of client groups began to be assessed from a social rather than an exclusively psychological perspective, social workers began to take into account the larger social forces that created the problem and to emphasize service delivery and the development of innovative service models. Attempts to alter old patterns of service to women have typically taken two separate but complementary forms. One pattern has been the development of grassroots programs by women suffering from a common condition. The most widely recognized crisis service has been shelter homes for battered women. Shelters developed in England but quickly spread to the United States.[7] They were recognized as a needed resource for women making a transition from a violent domestic situation to an independent life for themselves and their children. Self-help efforts also sprang up to help victims of rape, incest, and many other conditions in which women shared a common bond.[8] Programs such as these gained from the phenomenon of women's consciousness-raising groups, which were common in the early 1970s. Women came to understand that a key factor in achieving personal and social change was the support of like-minded peers who could help challenge oppressive social norms.

That many services to women in crisis have been developed without the aid of professionals indicates the power of grassroots efforts but must also be seen, in part, as a failure by social agencies to respond to the needs of women clients. Professional intervention that maintains the status quo and fails to include an analysis of the larger social context cannot be considered a responsible approach. For example, professionals who told battered women that their husbands' abusive behavior could be controlled by the women's compliance left the women with no viable alternative but to return home and try harder. That many women felt disenfranchised from the services offered through social agencies must be taken as an indictment of the quality of social work practice.

Nonsexist Practice

In the past few years, awareness of this anomaly has led to an increasing number of books and articles on the subject of improving social work practice with women. The first social work book on the subject was appropriately entitled *Alternative Services for Women*.[9] This and succeeding books attempted to demonstrate the subtle and overt expressions of sexism in practice and to offer practice alternatives for the delivery of social services.[10] Such services are based on the assumption that social workers can practice from a point of view that, in contrast to prevailing social myths, serves to empower women.

The notion of empowerment comes directly from social workers' belief in the capacity of people to determine the course of their lives. In seeking to empower women, social work attempts to help women see their lives in a broader social context and to help them construct an environment in which they have the best chance to develop their strengths. Social workers have special insights about the interaction of societal forces and individual development that enable them to help women clients develop a richer understanding of their capacities to grow and change.

Finding creative ways to unlock the positive potential people possess is a central goal of social work practice. Whether in direct service, supervision, administration, or planning, social workers continually search to find ways to help women move beyond society's narrow definitions of their capacities. Although social workers' own power is limited by agency goals and resources, they can work collectively to find ways in which their viewpoint can be transmitted in social work's spheres of influence.

The principles that guide social work services to women come from an understanding of three interrelated phenomena:

the nature of authority, the nature of change, and the role of the social environment in human development. These phenomena help pinpoint the differences between sexist and nonsexist models of practice. Sexist practice typically assumes that persons with professional certification have the right to assume a dominant role in the professional relationship. Based largely on what is thought to be superior specialized knowledge, the professional person retains control of the interaction through explicit means, such as making formal diagnoses and treatment plans, and implicit means, such as the use of professional jargon and setting the length of appointments. Although the client is generally recognized as a participant in the change process, the professional is often seen as the one who acts to bring about a desired change. Moreover, this viewpoint is often locked within a narrow understanding of behavioral causes. Depending on the preferred theory, a sexist practitioner is likely to ascribe behavior to a single cause and prescribe treatment within one modality. Given the psychological bias of many theories, the cause of the problem is thought to reside in the individual or in the individual's interaction with intimate others.

Nonsexist practice significantly alters the assumptions related to authority, change, and causality. Professional knowledge is acknowledged and given credit, but a conscious attempt is made to share knowledge with clients and thus to involve the client and elicit the client's own power and resourcefulness. Therefore, professional jargon, esoteric diagnoses, and complex treatment approaches are used sparingly, if at all. Nonsexist practice also tends to assign greater value to knowledge based on life experience. This speaks to a belief in women's ability to know what is best for themselves and to draw on that knowledge to make changes they desire. The source of change is more clearly seen to be the client. The practitioner does not cause change to happen but facilitates and strengthens natural growth impulses already present.

The practitioner's understanding of how personal experience is shaped by social and institutional forces creates a broad context in which professional helping takes place. Rather than focusing on factors exclusively within the client's own personality and life experience, the practitioner recognizes that there are universal dynamics that affect all women. That a woman may exhibit deep dependency needs is seen to have both societal and personal causes. Because society has created a role for women that has made them economically and socially dependent on others, nonsexist practitioners recognize that it does women a major disservice to attribute this solely to factors in their individual development.

Professional Values

The principles on which nonsexist practice is based are clearly compatible with the values underlying social work. The focus on women's capacity to determine the course of their lives, to develop the resources they need for growth, and to see their lives in a larger social context all reinforce the ethos of social work. Thus, the knowledge gained from an analysis of social work practice with women can strengthen practice with all clients.

No treatment of women's issues in social work could be complete without addressing the status of women in the profession. Social work has always been identified as a "woman's profession" because the majority of social workers are women. In an early article entitled "The Compassion Trap," Adams, a social worker, zeroed in on the care-taking role of the profession.[11] She argued that social work has served as an extension of a role women perform in society—providing the social glue to hold together the victims of a competitive social system. She also pointed out that the low social status of the profession corresponds exactly to the low social status of women and women's domestic work.

One can disagree with her suggestions for resolving this dilemma, but Adams did pinpoint a double-edged issue that needs further consideration: the larger social dynamics that lead to society's ambivalent acceptance of social work as a profession, and the effect of social attitudes and customs on the status of women in the profession. In 1971, Scotch called attention to discriminatory practices that resulted in salary differences for men and women in social work.[12] These differences were partly related to males' disproportionate advancement in administrative positions, but salary differences also favored men even when the positions were the same.

Once signaled as an issue, the social and economic consequences of sexism in the profession received increasing attention. Research in social work and other fields made it clear that women were less likely to enter into the high administrative echelons in social agencies and in academia.[13] Instead, they typically clustered in the direct service and supervisory ranks. Documentation and analysis in other fields showed that this pattern is virtually universal. Although the pattern is changing in noticeable ways, aided both by increased awareness and by programs such as affirmative action, the women who do make it to the top are still the exception rather than the rule.

Social work has acknowledged the disparities in economic and social rewards in its ranks and has taken steps to institute changes. In 1975, the National Association of Social Workers created a National Committee on Women's Issues, which took as its responsibility the development of programs to eliminate sexism in the professional association, the profession, and society. In Washington in 1980, the committee sponsored the First National Conference on Social Work Practice with Women. Motivated by similar concerns, the Council on Social Work Education instituted a parallel group called the Commission on the Role and Status of Women and, through this and other commissions, added accreditation standards that required schools of social work to include material on women's issues in their curricula. Thus, the groundwork has been laid for increased understanding of and sensitivity to the needs of women both as social work professionals and as social work clients.

The heightened awareness of the various forms of sexism in social work practice has underscored some important lessons for the profession. Social workers have been reminded of the energy-sapping impact of negative images and beliefs. The corrosive effect of oppressive social messages lies in their power to obscure and distort an individual's sense of personal worth whenever society's definition of self supplants a person's own deep knowledge about self. Given the tremendous force of social definitions, it is no wonder that women are often unaware of the power they have to assert more honorable definitions of who they are. That many women are locked into stereotypical behavior reveals more about the powerful social dynamics that shape behavior than about presumed attitudes of women.

Social workers have also developed a deeper awareness of how institutional structures of society contribute to and maintain the status quo. In close tandem with the ideological processes of social definitions, formal and informal policies at all levels reinforce a limited view of women's abilities. Affirmative action and other programs have been initiated to counter and reduce the impact of sexism, but they have not significantly touched the underlying belief system that supports discriminatory practices.

Changing social work practice to take these lessons into account continues to be challenging, particularly in light of the current political climate. The conservative ideology of the times is antithetical to the values that support the professional orientation of social work. Examples are numerous: the Equal Rights Amendment failed to be ratified; in these times of high unemployment, the numbers of poor women and their children are growing at alarming rates; the president has called for a private sector response to social troubles, implicitly encouraging women to return to the role of charity givers. These and all related developments demonstrate the strength and direction of the current process of social definition.

The power of the profession must ultimately come from the same source as client power—from the ability to construct and maintain a point of view in the midst of energy-defying obstacles. It would be fortunate if the political climate were more supportive of this effort, but the challenge cannot be put aside because it is not. Social workers must learn to establish a view of practice that, within environmental constraints, defines the profession. This definition should come from a profound understanding of social work values and of the way in which those values must inform practice. The lessons derived from an analysis of work with women can guide the process of improving professional practice with all who use social work services.

ANN WEICK

Notes and References

1. For further discussion, see Susan T. Vandiver, "A Herstory of Women in Social Work," in Elaine Norman and Arlene Mancuso, eds., *Women's Issues in Social Work Practice* (Itasca, Ill.: F.E. Peacock, 1980), pp. 21–38.

2. Inge Broverman, et al., "Sex-Role Stereotypes and Clinical Judgments of Mental Health," *Journal of Consulting Psychology*, 34 (February 1970), pp. 1–7.

3. Phyllis Chesler, *Women and Madness* (New York: Doubleday & Co., 1972).

4. Naomi Weisstein, "Psychology Constructs the Female," in Vivian Gornick and Barbara K. Moran, eds., *Woman in Sexist Society* (New York: Basic Books, 1971), pp. 207–224.

5. Anne M. Seidan, "Overview: Research on the Psychology of Women. II. Women in Families, Work and Psychotherapy," *American Journal of Psychiatry*, 133 (October 1976), pp. 1111–1123.

6. "Special Issue on Women," *Social Work* (entire issue), 21 (November 1976).

7. Del Martin, *Battered Wives* (San Francisco: Glide Publications, 1976).

8. Doris A. Stevens, "Rape Victims," in Naomi Gottlieb, ed., *Alternative Social Services for Women* (New York: Columbia University Press, 1980), pp. 235–251; Blair Justice and Rita Justice, *The Broken Taboo* (New York: Human

Sciences Press, 1979); and *Child Sexual Abuse: Incest, Assault, and Sexual Exploitation*, U.S. Department of Health and Human Services Publication No. (OHDS) 81–30166 (Washington, D.C.: U.S. Government Printing Office, 1981).

9. Gottlieb, *Alternative Social Services for Women.*

10. Norman and Mancuso, *Women's Issues and Social Work Practice*; and Ann Weick and Susan T. Vandiver, eds., *Women, Power and Change* (Washington, D.C.: National Association of Social Workers, 1981).

11. Margaret Adams, "The Compassion Trap," in Gornick and Moran, *Woman in Sexist Society,* pp. 555–575.

12. C. Bernard Scotch, "Sex Status in Social Work: Grist for Women's Liberation," *Social Work*, 16 (July 1971), pp. 5–11.

13. See, for example, Cynthia Epstein, *Woman's Place* (Berkeley, Calif.: University of California Press, 1970); and Roslyn H. Chernesky, "Women Administrators in Social Work," in Norman and Mancuso, *Women's Issues and Social Work Practice,* pp. 241–262.

Part 2

STATISTICAL AND DEMOGRAPHIC TRENDS

The statistical material that follows is intended to provide readers with updated information about developments since the 1977 edition of the Encyclopedia. In this respect it is like the previous statistical supplement, which was published in 1980. However, the material presented here does not simply meet the need for more recent data but also attempts to portray many important social and economic changes that have occurred in recent years and that present social workers and others with situations that are qualitatively new.

The wide range of materials covered here addresses the diversity of interests that users bring to this publication. It also reflects the rich stores of data that are available not only from the Bureau of the Census, the Bureau of Labor Statistics, the National Center for Health Statistics, and other governmental agencies, but also from the Organization for Economic Cooperation and Development, the European Community, the International Labor Organization, the World Health Organization, and other international bodies. The comparative data presented in Section 9 helps to put U.S. experience and policy into international perspective.

The purpose, then, has been to provide users with ready reference to demographic developments; trends in employment and underemployment; social and economic patterns in the experience of women, immigrants, Hispanics, and blacks; changes in health and mental health programs; and other areas not previously covered in comparable scope and depth. In most cases, these tables avoid excessive detail in order to present as clear and understandable a picture as possible, leaving the interested user to consult original sources for greater depth or detail. The brief captions that accompany the tables permit the reader to understand at a glance the significance of the statistical material contained in the tables and indicate the authors' judgment of the key inferences to be drawn. The aim has been to achieve a balance, presenting neither an overly rosy nor a morbidly pessimistic view of the American economic and social scene in the early 1980s.

SUMNER M. ROSEN
DAVID FANSHEL

GUIDE TO STATISTICAL SECTIONS

SECTION 1

Demographic Characteristics of the Population of the United States

TABLE 1.1. POPULATION OF THE UNITED STATES, 1790–1980, WITH PROJECTIONS TO 2050
(IN THOUSANDS)

The total U.S. population will increase from 230 million in 1981 to 268 million in 2000, reaching an all-time high of 309 million in 2050 before beginning to decline. The nonwhite proportion has risen since 1940.

Year	Total Population Residing in U.S.	Number White	Number Nonwhite[a]	Percentage White
1790	3,929	3,172	757	80.7
1800	5,308	4,306	1,002	81.1
1810	7,240	5,862	1,378	81.0
1820	9,638	7,867	1,771	81.6
1830	12,866	10,537	2,329	81.9
1840	17,069	14,196	2,874	83.2
1850	23,192	19,553	3,639	84.3
1860	31,443	26,923	4,521	85.6
1870[b]	39,818	34,337	5,481	86.2
1880	50,156	43,403	6,753	86.5
1890	62,948	55,101	7,846	87.5
1900	75,995	66,809	9,185	87.9
1910	91,972	81,732	10,240	88.9
1920	105,711	94,821	10,890	89.7
1930	122,775	110,287	12,488	89.8
1940	131,669	118,215	13,454	89.8
1950	150,697	134,942	15,755	89.5
1960[c]	179,323	158,832	20,491	88.6
1970	203,236	178,098	25,138	87.6
1980	226,505	194,779	31,726	86.0
2000[d]	267,990	220,801	45,189	83.1
2050[d]	308,857	238,100	70,756	77.09

[a]1790–1850, black only.
[b]Revised to include adjustments for undernumeration in southern states.
[c]Beginning in 1960, figures include Alaska and Hawaii.
[d]Projections for 1980 and 2000 assume that women reaching the childbearing age will have an average of 1.9 births, net immigration will be 450,000 per year, and the mortality rate will improve slightly.
Source: For the 1790–1970 data, see *Historical Statistics of the United States, Colonial Times to 1970* (Washington, D.C.: U.S. Bureau of the Census, 1976); for the projections, see *Current Population Reports, Population Estimates and Projections,* Series P-25, No. 922 (Washington, D.C.: U.S. Bureau of the Census, 1982).

TABLE 1.2. MINORITY POPULATION AS PERCENTAGE OF TOTAL IN CITIES OF 500,000 OR MORE, 1970 AND 1980[a]

The black population increased in all but four of these cities. The Hispanic population is large in several cities and is a majority in one city. Blacks and Hispanics combined constitute a majority in six cities.

| | 1970 | 1980 | |
City	Black	Black	Hispanic
Baltimore	46.4	54.8	1.0
Boston	16.3	22.4	6.4
Chicago	32.7	39.8	14.0
Cleveland	38.3	43.8	3.1
Columbus (Ohio)	18.5	22.1	0.8
Dallas	24.9	29.4	12.3
Detroit	43.7	63.1	2.4
Houston	25.7	27.6	17.6
Indianapolis	18.0	21.8	0.9
Jacksonville	22.3	25.4	1.8
Los Angeles	17.9	17.0	27.5
Memphis	38.9	47.6	0.8
Milwaukee	14.7	23.1	4.1
New Orleans	45.0	55.3	3.4
New York	21.1	25.2	19.9
Philadelphia	33.6	37.8	3.8
San Antonio	7.6	7.3	53.7
San Diego	7.6	8.9	14.9
San Francisco	13.4	12.7	12.3
San Jose	2.5	4.6	22.3
Washington	71.1	70.3	2.8

[a]Based on 1980 populations.
Source: *Statistical Abstract of the United States, 1982–83* (103d ed.; Washington, D.C.: U.S. Bureau of the Census, 1982), pp. 22–24.

TABLE 1.3. LIFE EXPECTANCY AT BIRTH, 1950–1980

Life expectancy increased for all groups; significant differences remain between men and women and between whites and nonwhites.

| | All | | White | | Nonwhite | |
Year	Male	Female	Male	Female	Male	Female
1950	65.6	71.1	66.5	72.2	59.1	62.9
1960	66.6	73.1	67.4	74.1	61.1	66.3
1970	67.1	74.7	68.0	75.6	61.3	69.4
1979	69.9	77.6	70.6	78.2	65.5	74.2
1980[a]	—	—	70.5	78.1	65.3	74.0

[a]Provisional data.
Source: Public Health Service, *Health—United States, 1982,* DHHS Publication No. (PHS) 83-1232 (Hyattsville, Md.: U.S. Department of Health & Human Services, National Center for Health Statistics, 1982), p. 53.

TABLE 1.4. PERCENTAGE OF THE POPULATION MARRIED AND DIVORCED, 18 YEARS AND OVER, 1960–1981

In the two decades after 1960, the percentage of married persons in the population declined steadily, with an accompanying increase in the percentage divorced; these trends hold for whites and nonwhites.

Sex and Race	1960	1965	1970	1974	1975	1976	1977	1978	1979	1980	1981
Percentage married:											
Male	76.4	76.2	75.3	73.7	72.8	72.2	70.9	70.1	69.2	68.4	67.8
White	77.3	76.9	76.1	74.9	73.9	73.4	72.3	71.7	70.7	70.0	69.6
Black and other	68.4	70.2	65.4	63.1	63.5	62.0	60.6	58.4	57.5	56.3	55.2
Female	71.6	70.5	68.5	67.6	66.7	66.2	65.3	64.2	63.5	63.0	62.4
White	72.2	70.9	69.3	68.8	68.0	67.6	66.7	65.9	65.2	64.7	64.1
Black and other	66.3	67.6	62.6	58.9	57.3	56.2	55.4	52.6	51.8	51.6	50.9
Percentage divorced:											
Male	2.0	2.5	2.5	3.5	3.7	4.0	4.5	4.7	4.8	5.2	5.7
White	2.0	2.4	2.4	3.3	3.6	3.8	4.4	4.5	4.5	5.0	5.5
Black and other	2.2	3.4	3.4	4.8	4.6	5.5	5.0	6.3	6.6	6.4	7.0
Female	2.9	3.3	3.9	4.9	5.3	5.7	6.2	6.6	6.6	7.1	7.6
White	2.7	3.1	3.8	4.7	5.0	5.5	6.0	6.3	6.4	6.8	7.2
Black and other	4.8	4.5	4.8	6.3	7.1	7.4	8.2	8.8	8.3	8.8	9.6

Source: *Statistical Abstract of the United States, 1982–83*, p. 41.

TABLE 1.5. BIRTHRATES BY RACE, 1915–1979; ESTIMATED NUMBER AND RATES OF ILLEGITIMATE BIRTHS, 1950–1979

Total births declined after 1960 and rose modestly in the late 1970s. Nonwhite birthrates remained higher than white rates but fell after 1960; nonwhite nonmarried birthrates are several times the rate among whites.

	Live Births				Births to Unmarried Women			
	Total[a] (thousands)	Rate per 1,000 Population			Total (thousands)	Rate per 1,000 Live Births[b]		
Year		Total	White	Black and Other		Total	White	Black and Other
1910	2,777	30.1	—	—	—	—	—	—
1915	2,965	29.5	—	—	—	—	—	—
1920	2,950	27.7	—	—	—	—	—	—
1925	2,909	25.1	—	—	—	—	—	—
1930	2,618	21.3	—	—	—	—	—	—
1935	2,377	18.7	—	—	—	—	—	—
1940	2,559	19.4	—	—	—	—	—	—
1945	2,858	20.4	—	—	—	—	—	—
1950	3,632	24.1	23.0	33.3	141.6	14.1	6.1	71.2
1955	4,097	25.0	23.8	34.5	183.3	19.3	7.9	87.2
1960	4,258	23.7	22.7	32.1	224.3	21.6	9.2	98.3
1965	3,760	19.4	18.3	27.6	291.2	23.5	11.6	97.6
1970	3,731	18.4	17.4	25.1[c]	398.7	26.4	13.8	89.9
1975	3,144	14.8	13.8	21.2	447.9	24.8	12.6	80.4
1976	3,168	14.8	13.8	21.1	468.1	24.7	12.7	78.1
1977	3,327	15.4	14.4	21.9	515.7	26.0	13.7	79.4
1978	3,333	15.3	14.2	22.1	543.9	26.2	13.9	78.7
1979	3,494	15.9	14.8	22.8	597.8	27.8	15.1	80.9

[a]Through 1955, adjusted for underregistration.
[b]Rate per 1,000 unmarried women (never married, widowed, and divorced).
[c]1971.
Source: *Statistical Abstract of the United States, 1982–1983*, pp. 60, 61, and 66.

TABLE 1.6. LIFETIME BIRTHS EXPECTED BY WIVES 18-34 YEARS OLD; PERCENTAGE DISTRIBUTION, 1967-1980[a]

The number of children married women expect to bear has declined markedly since 1967; the trend is strongest among white women, but black women also show the same expectation; working women expect to bear fewer children than nonworkers.

1967[b]

Number of Births Expected	Race		Age		
	White	Black	18-24	25-29	30-34
None	2.2	3.0	1.3	2.5	6.1
One	5.5	8.1	6.1	5.1	5.5
Two	31.4	24.9	37.1	29.3	18.8
Three	30.3	25.1	29.8	33.5	14.9
Four or more	30.6	39.0	25.7	29.9	55.3

1975[b]

Number of Births Expected	Race			Age		
	Spanish Origin	Black	White	18-24	25-29	30-34
None	3.2	3.0	4.9	4.1	4.9	5.2
One	10.6	10.7	10.8	11.2	11.7	9.8
Two	40.4	40.0	49.8	58.2	50.4	38.3
Three	25.2	22.4	23.3	19.4	23.3	26.8
Four or more	20.5	24.0	11.1	7.0	9.8	19.8

1980[b]

Numbers of Births Expected	Race			Age			Education			Labor Force	
	White	Black	Spanish Origin	18-24	25-29	30-34	Not High School Graduate	High School, 4 Years	College, 1 Year or More	In Labor Force	Not in Labor Force
None	6.0	4.0	2.8	4.9	5.5	7.0	2.6	5.6	7.7	8.3	2.5
One	13.2	14.4	9.4	12.8	13.2	13.6	11.7	14.4	12.4	15.8	9.8
Two	51.5	45.3	44.3	56.0	52.8	45.7	39.7	52.6	54.4	52.1	49.8
Three	20.4	22.2	24.2	19.1	20.3	21.8	26.7	19.7	18.8	17.5	24.5
Four or more	8.8	14.2	19.4	7.2	8.3	11.9	19.4	7.7	6.8	6.3	13.4

[a]Refers to currently married women in civilian, noninstitutional population.
[b]Data reported as of February-March 1967 and as of June in 1975 and 1980.
Source: *Statistical Abstract of the United States, 1982-83*, p. 64.

TABLE 1.7. SOCIAL AND ECONOMIC CHARACTERISTICS OF WOMEN IN THE UNITED STATES, 18–44 YEARS OLD, WHO HAD A CHILD IN THE YEAR 1980

Women bearing children as widowed, divorced, single, or married with a spouse absent accounted for 18 percent of the births.

Category	Total Number of Women (thousands)	Women Who Had a Child in 1980	
		Number (thousands)	Per 1,000 Women
Total women, 18–44 years[a]	45,652	3,247	71.1
18–24 years old	14,456	1,396	96.6
25–29 years old	9,419	1,081	114.8
30–34 years old	8,651	519	60.0
35–39 years old	7,144	192	26.9
40–44 years old	5,983	59	9.9
White	38,989	2,670	68.5
Black	5,610	471	84.0
Spanish origin[b]	3,003	320	106.6
Married, spouse present	27,381	2,660	97.2
Married, spouse absent[c]	1,934	126	65.2
Widowed or divorced	4,069	112	27.5
Single	12,270	348	28.4
Labor force status:			
In labor force	30,179	1,233	40.9
Employed	27,403	1,025	37.4
Unemployed	2,775	208	75.0
Not in labor force	15,474	2,013	130.1
Family income:			
Under $5,000	3,721	351	94.3
$5,000–$9,999	6,132	532	86.8
$10,000–$14,999	7,877	661	83.9
$15,000–$19,999	6,663	514	77.1
$20,000–$24,999	6,803	475	69.8
$25,000 and over	11,947	579	48.5
Years of school completed:			
Not a high school graduate	8,617	792	91.9
High school, 4 years	20,643	1,475	71.5
College, 1–3 years	9,276	542	58.4
College, 4 years	4,794	316	65.9
College, 5 or more years	2,322	121	52.1

[a]Includes women of other races and women with family income not reported, not shown separately.
[b]Persons of Spanish origin may be of any race.
[c]Includes separated women.
Source: *Statistical Abstract of the United States, 1982–83,* p. 64.

TABLE 1.8. INFANT MORTALITY RATES BY RACE, 1967–1979

Rates fell substantially, but significant differences persisted: black infant mortality
rates between 1977 and 1979 exceeded those for whites ten years earlier.

	Deaths per Thousand Live Births		
Race	1967–69	1972–74	1977–79
White	19.1	15.7	11.9
Black	36.1	28.2	22.8

Source: Public Health Service, *Health—United States, 1982*, p. 55.

TABLE 1.9. LEGAL ABORTIONS—ESTIMATED NUMBER, RATE, AND RATIO BY RACE, 1972–1980[a]

The number of abortions rose to more than 1.5 million in 1980. Rates among blacks
and others were three times those of whites in 1976 but declined to 2.3 times the
white rate in 1980.

	White		Black and Other		
Year	Number of Abortions (thousands)	Abortion Rate per 1,000 Women	Number of Abortions (thousands)	Abortion Rate per 1,000 Women	Ratio of Rate Among Blacks and Others to White Rate
1972	455.3	11.8	131.5	21.7	1.8
1975	701.2	17.2	333.0	49.3	2.9
1976	784.9	18.8	394.4	56.3	3.0
1977	888.8	20.9	427.9	59.0	2.8
1978	969.4	22.3	440.2	58.7	2.6
1979	1,062.4	24.0	435.3	56.2	2.3
1980	1,093.6	24.3	460.3	56.8	2.3

[a]Refers to women 15–44 years old.
Sources: The Alan Guttmacher Institute, New York, N.Y., unpublished data reported in *Statistical Abstract of the United States, 1982-83*, p. 69.

TABLE 1.10. IMMIGRANTS ADMITTED TO THE UNITED STATES, 1930–1982

Immigration increased substantially in the late 1970s.

Year	Number Admitted
1930	241,700
1940	70,756
1950	249,187
1960	265,398
1970	373,326
1975	386,194
1976	398,613
1977	462,315
1978	601,442
1979	460,348
1981[a]	600,000
1982[a]	610,000

[a]Preliminary.

Sources: *Statistical Abstract of the United States, 1982–83,* p. 88; and the U.S. Immigration and Naturalization Service.

TABLE 1.11. IMMIGRATION BY AREA, 1951–1979

America and Asia dominated immigration in the period 1971–1979; Asian immigration more than doubled in the same period.

Area	1951–1960		1961–1970		1971–1979	
	Number (thousands)	Percentage	Number (thousands)	Percentage	Number (thousands)	Percentage
Europe	1,325.6	52.7	1,123.4	33.8	728.2	18.4
Asia	153.3	6.1	427.8	12.9	1,352.1	34.1
America	996.9	39.6	1,716.4	51.7	1,778.3	44.9
All other	39.6	1.6	54.3	1.6	104.1	2.6
Total	2,515.5	—	3,321.7	—	3,962.5	—

Source: *Statistical Abstract of the United States, 1982–83,* p. 89.

SECTION 2

The Economy, Wealth, and Income

TABLE 2.1. GROSS NATIONAL PRODUCT (GNP) IN CURRENT AND CONSTANT (1972) DOLLARS, 1960–1981

Real rates of growth were lower than nominal rates and on occasion were negative.

	Current Dollars		Constant Dollars	
Year	GNP (billions)	Percentage Change[a]	GNP (billions)	Percentage Change[a]
1960	$ 507	4.9	$ 737	2.3
1965	691	6.4	929	4.7
1970	993	7.5	1,086	3.2
1975	1,549	8.0	1,232	−1.2
1980	2,633	8.9	1,474	−0.4
1981	2,938	11.6	1,503	1.9

[a]From prior year.
Source: *Statistical Abstract of the United States, 1982–83*, p. 419.

TABLE 2.2. ANNUAL CONSUMER PRICE CHANGES, SELECTED YEARS, 1960–1982

Inflation rates in the 1970s were higher than previously and maintained consistent double-digit levels from 1979 to 1981.

Year	Percentage Change
1960	1.6
1965	1.7
1970	5.9
1971	4.3
1972	3.3
1973	6.2
1974	11.0
1975	9.1
1976	5.8
1977	6.5
1978	7.7
1979	11.3
1980	13.5
1981	10.4
1982	6.0

Sources: *Statistical Abstract of the United States, 1982–83*, p. 453; and U.S. Bureau of Labor Statistics, *Monthly Labor Review* (September 1983), p. 64.

TABLE 2.3. SHARE OF WEALTH AND ASSETS CONCENTRATED WITH TOP ONE PERCENT OF
WEALTH HOLDERS, 1949–1972

*Wealth holdings, particularly securities, are concentrated; real estate and insurance are
more widely dispersed.*

Category	1949	1958	1962	1972
Percentage share of top one percent of wealth holders age 21 or over	20.8	23.8	22.0	20.7
Percentage share of assets held by top one percent of all persons:				
Total	—	25.5	26.2	24.1
Corporate stocks	—	75.4	62.0	56.5
Bonds	—	41.4	40.6	60.0
Real estate	—	15.1	15.3	15.1
Life insurance	—	14.1	11.4	7.0

Source: *Statistical Abstract of the United States, 1982–83*, p. 449.

TABLE 2.4. FAMILY INCOME IN CONSTANT (1982) DOLLARS, 1960–1982

*Median income rose little between 1970 and 1980, then fell between 1980 and 1982.
The proportion of families with incomes below $15,000 fell between 1960 and 1970,
but rose thereafter.*

	Percentage			
Income	1960	1970	1980	1982
Over $50,000	—	9.0	11.0	10.9
$25,000–$50,000[a]	28.1	39.6	37.8	35.5
$15,000–$25,000	34.0	26.2	24.1	24.4
$10,000–$15,000	15.4	11.2	11.7	12.4
$ 5,000–$10,000	13.3	9.4	10.1	10.6
Under $5,000	9.2	4.6	5.3	6.0
Median Income	$18,317	$24,528	$24,626	$23,433

[a]$25,000 and over for 1960.
Source: *Money Income and Poverty Status of Families and Persons in the United States, 1982*, Current
Population Survey, Series P-60 (Washington, D.C.: U.S. Bureau of the Census, 1983), p. 10.

TABLE 2.5. FAMILIES' SHARES OF AGGREGATE INCOME, 1968 AND 1982

Income shares remain highly skewed.

Group	Share of Total Income Received (percentage)	
	1968	1982
Lowest fifth of families	5	5
Second fifth	11	11
Third fifth	18	17
Fourth fifth	23	24
Highest fifth	43	43
Top 5 percent	—	16

Source: Herman P. Miller, *Rich Man Poor Man* (New York: Thomas Y. Crowell Co., 1971), p. 16; and *Money Income and Poverty Status of Families and Persons in the United States, 1982*, p. 11.

TABLE 2.6. PERCENTAGE SHARE OF HOUSEHOLD AGGREGATE INCOME,
BEFORE AND AFTER TAXES, 1983

Taxes modestly reduce income inequality.

Group	Percentage Before Taxes	Percentage After Taxes
Lowest fifth	4.1	4.9
Second fifth	10.2	11.6
Third fifth	16.8	17.9
Fourth fifth	24.8	25.1
Highest fifth	44.2	40.6
Top 5 percent	16.5	14.1

Source: *Estimating After-Tax Money Income Distributions Using Data from the March Current Population Survey* (Washington, D.C.: U.S. Bureau of the Census, 1983).

TABLE 2.7. PER CAPITA PERSONAL AND DISPOSABLE INCOME IN CURRENT AND CONSTANT (1972) DOLLARS, 1960–1981

Growth of personal disposable income in real terms slowed in the late seventies and declined slightly from 1979 to 1980.

	Personal Income	Disposable Income	
Year	Current Dollars	Current Dollars	Constant Dollars
1960	$ 2,226	$ 1,947	$ 2,709
1965	2,782	2,448	3,171
1970	3,955	3,390	3,665
1975	5,857	5,075	4,051
1979	8,668	7,331	4,512
1980	9,490	8,012	4,472
1981	10,510	8,827	4,538

Source: *Statistical Abstract of the United States, 1982–83,* p. 421.

TABLE 2.8. DISTRIBUTION OF FAMILY INCOME BY PLACE OF RESIDENCE AND BY RACE AND SPANISH ORIGIN, 1980

Suburban family income exceeds central city and nonmetropolitan income for all groups; blacks are substantially below whites in all areas; Hispanic income falls between white and black.

		Percentage of Families				
Category	Median Income	Under $10,000	$10,000–19,999	$20,000–29,999	$30,000–49,999	Over $50,000
Central cities:						
White	$21,293	17.7	28.7	24.8	21.6	7.2
Black	12,865	40.8	29.0	17.0	11.3	1.9
Spanish origin	13,357	37.4	33.0	17.7	10.1	2.1
Metropolitan areas outside central cities:						
White	25,138	11.7	23.6	27.1	27.7	9.8
Black	16,242	30.4	28.7	20.8	17.4	2.8
Spanish origin	16,975	25.6	32.0	22.0	16.8	3.6
Outside metropolitan areas:						
White	18,794	20.8	32.9	25.2	17.0	4.2
Black	10,257	48.9	31.8	12.9	6.2	0.3
Spanish origin	13,866	32.7	38.6	19.8	7.5	1.5

Source: *Statistical Abstract of the United States, 1982–83,* 433.

TABLE 2.9. DISTRIBUTION OF HOUSEHOLD MONEY INCOME IN CONSTANT (1981) DOLLARS BY RACE AND SPANISH ORIGIN, 1967–1981

Real incomes declined for all groups; black incomes were heavily skewed to lower levels compared to white; Hispanic families fell in between.

		Percentage of Households			
Category	Median Income	Under $10,000	$10,000–19,999	$20,000–34,999	$35,000 and Over
All households					
1977	$20,369	23.7	25.4	31.0	19.8
1981	19,074	25.4	26.7	28.6	19.3
White					
1967	20,291	22.6	30.4	32.4	14.5
1977	21,420	21.7	25.0	32.2	21.2
1981	20,153	23.1	26.6	29.8	20.6
Black					
1967	11,781	43.9	33.3	18.5	4.4
1977	12,640	41.1	29.1	21.8	8.2
1981	11,309	45.0	27.8	19.1	8.0
Spanish origin					
1977	15,979	29.3	33.0	27.3	10.4
1981	15,300	31.8	31.5	25.0	11.6

Source: *Statistical Abstract of the United States, 1982–83*, p. 429.

TABLE 2.10. FEDERAL INCOME TAXES PAID, BY INCOME GROUP, 1981

The federal income tax is modestly progressive across income classes.

Adjusted Gross Income	No. of Returns (thousands)	Income Tax as Percentage of Income
No Income	8	—
Under $5,000	4,694	3.0
$5,000–under $10,000	14,411	7.1
$10,000–under $15,000	13,914	9.9
$15,000–under $20,000	10,961	11.9
$20,000–under $30,000	15,850	13.7
$30,000–under $50,000	10,954	17.2
$50,000–under $100,000	2,554	24.1
$100,000–under $200,000	442	33.2
$200,000 or more	117	42.5
Total	73,906	16.1

Source: Internal Revenue Service, *Statistical Income, Individual Income Tax Returns, 1981*, p. 83.

TABLE 2.11. WEIGHTED AVERAGE POVERTY THRESHOLDS FOR NONFARM FAMILIES, 1960–1982[a]

Criteria of poverty measurement changed only to adjust for changes in Consumer Price Index.

Year	Unrelated Individuals (Under Age 65)	Two-Person Families (Head Under Age 65)	Four-Person Families
1960	$1,526	$1,982	$3,022
1970	2,010	2,604	3,968
1980	4,290	5,537	8,414
1981	4,729	6,111	9,287
1982	5,019	6,487	9,862

[a]Poverty thresholds are derived from the 1964 index devised by the Social Security Administration, adjusted annually for price change.

Sources: Annual statistical supplement to the *Social Security Bulletin*, 1981, p. 59; and *Money Income and Poverty Status of Families and Persons in the United States, 1982*, p. 30.

TABLE 2.12. POVERTY IN AMERICA, 1970–1982

In 1981 and 1982, poor people increased in numbers and as a percentage of the population among all categories except over age 65; nonwhite female-headed families remain at greatest risk.

Categories	1970	1975	1979	1981	1982
Total number of poor persons (in millions)	25.3	25.9	25.3	31.8	34.4
Poor as percentage of population	12.6	12.3	11.6	14.0	15.0
Black poor as percentage of black population	33.5	31.3	31.0	34.2	35.6
Hispanic poor as percentage of Hispanic population	—	26.9	21.8	26.5	29.9
White poor as percentage of white population	9.9	9.7	8.9	11.1	12.0
Poverty rate among families headed by women:					
All	38.1	37.5	34.9	34.6	36.3
Black	58.7	54.3	53.2	52.9	56.2
Hispanic	—	57.2	51.2	53.2	55.4
White	28.4	29.4	25.2	27.4	27.9
Number of poor children under 18 (in millions)	10.2	10.9	10.0	12.1	13.1
Poor children as percentage of all children	14.9	16.8	16.0	19.5	21.3
Poor children as percentage of all black children	41.5	41.4	42.8	44.9	47.3
Poor over 65 as percentage of all over 65	48.0	36.3	36.2	39.0	38.2

Sources: Annual statistical supplement to the *Social Security Bulletin*, 1981, pp. 60–62; *Money Income and Poverty Status of Families and Persons in the United States, 1982*, pp. 4, 20, and 21; and *Characteristics of the Population below the Poverty Level, 1981*, pp. 7, 8, and 72.

TABLE 2.13. PART-TIME WORK AND POVERTY STATUS OF PERSONS AGED 22–64, MARCH 1980

Part-time work shields only partially from poverty; unemployment directly affects poverty status; women in all categories are more vulnerable to poverty than men.

Categories	Percentage Poor		
	Total	Men	Women
Total	11	6	24
Worked part year or part time	18	14	27
Did not work at all	46	30	60

Source: Annual statistical supplement to the *Social Security Bulletin*, 1981, p. 63.

TABLE 2.14. POVERTY STATUS OF PERSONS 65 AND OLDER, 1979

Women in poverty over 65 outnumber men. The poor are a larger share among older people than in the population as a whole. Older individuals living alone are disproportionately poor, both men and women.

Categories	Total (thousands)	Percentage poor
Total number of people	23,743	15.1
Unrelated individuals	7,656	29.3
Living in families	16,076	8.3
Male—total	9,783	11.0
Unrelated individuals	1,666	25.3
Living in families	8,117	8.1
Female—total	13,960	14.9
Unrelated individuals	5,990	30.5
Living in families	7,961	8.6

Source: Annual statistical supplement to the *Social Security Bulletin*, 1981, p. 62.

SECTION 3

Employment, Unemployment, and Underemployment

TABLE 3.1. CIVILIAN NONINSTITUTIONAL POPULATION, ANNUAL LABOR FORCE PARTICIPATION RATES FOR SELECTED DEMOGRAPHIC GROUPS, 1951–1981

Male participation rates declined for all age groups, sharply for those age 55–64 and over 65; female participation rates rose consistently for all age groups except those over 65.

Demographic Groups	Participation Rates (Percentage)			
	1951	1961	1971	1981
Total	59.3	59.3	60.2	63.9
Teenagers, 16 to 19 years, both sexes	52.2	46.9	49.7	55.4
Men, 20 years and over	88.2	85.7	82.1	79.0
20 to 24 years	88.4	87.8	83.0	85.5
25 to 34 years	96.9	97.5	95.9	94.9
35 to 54 years	96.8	96.6	95.2	93.5
55 to 64 years	87.2	87.3	82.1	70.6
65 years and over	44.9	31.7	25.5	18.4
Women, 20 years and over	34.0	38.0	43.3	52.1
20 to 24 years	46.5	47.0	57.7	69.6
25 to 34 years	35.4	36.4	45.6	66.7
35 to 54 years	39.7	46.8	52.9	64.2
55 to 64 years	27.6	37.9	42.9	41.4
65 years and over	8.9	10.7	9.5	8.0

Source: *Employment and Training Report of the President* (Washington, D.C.: U.S. Department of Labor, 1982), p. 4.

TABLE 3.2. MALES AND FEMALES IN THE LABOR FORCE, 1950–1982

The number of women in the labor force increased faster than men in absolute and relative terms throughout this thirty-year period; by 1980 women were 42 percent of the total.

	Male		Female	
Year	Number in Civilian Labor Force (thousands)	Average Unemployment Rate (percentage)	Number in Civilian Labor Force (thousands)	Average Unemployment Rate (percentage)
1950	41,578	5.1	17,340	5.7
1960	43,904	5.4	21,874	5.9
1970	48,990	4.4	29,688	5.9
1975	51,857	7.9	33,989	9.3
1980	56,455	5.9	41,106	6.4
1981	57,197	6.3	42,485	6.8
1982	57,980	8.8	43,699	8.3

Sources: *Employment and Training Report of the President, 1982*, pp. 147 and 148; and U.S. Bureau of Labor Statistics, *Monthly Labor Review,* September 1983, p. 51.

TABLE 3.3. LABOR FORCE PARTICIPATION BY RACE AND SEX, 1960–1981

Black male rates declined more rapidly than white; white female rates rose more rapidly than black.

	Males		Females	
Year	White	Black	White	Black
1960	83.4	83.0	36.5	48.2
1970	80.0	76.5	42.6	49.5
1980	78.2	71.5	51.2	53.6
1981	77.9	70.6	51.9	53.6

Source: *Employment and Training Report of the President, 1982*, pp. 156-157.

TABLE 3.4. OCCUPATIONAL DISTRIBUTION OF EMPLOYED PERSONS, 1961–1981 (PERCENTAGE)

There is a growing white-collar and service economy, with women and blacks securing some of the better jobs and whites and males representing significant shares of the jobs in the professional, technical, managerial, and craft sectors.

Category	1961	1966	1971	1976	1981
White-collar workers—total	43.9	45.4	48.3	50.0	52.7
Professional, technical, managerial	22.5	23.0	25.0	25.8	27.9
Sales and clerical	21.4	22.4	23.4	24.1	24.9
White-collar workers—males	38.1	38.6	40.9	41.1	42.9
Professional, technical, managerial	25.0	25.7	28.3	28.8	30.5
Sales and clerical	12.9	12.8	12.6	12.3	12.4
White-collar workers—females	55.6	57.6	60.6	63.1	65.9
Professional, technical, managerial	17.5	17.9	19.5	21.5	24.4
Sales and clerical	38.1	39.8	41.1	41.6	41.5
White-collar workers—whites	47.1	48.3	50.6	51.8	54.3
Professional, technical, managerial	24.3	24.6	26.4	27.1	29.0
Sales and clerical	22.8	23.8	24.3	24.7	25.3
White-collar workers—blacks and others	16.3	20.9	29.1	34.6	41.1
Professional, technical, managerial	7.2	9.6	13.1	16.1	19.7
Sales and clerical	9.1	11.3	16.0	18.6	21.4
Blue-collar workers—total	36.0	37.0	34.4	33.1	31.1
Craft and kindred	13.1	13.2	12.9	12.9	12.6
Operatives and laborers	22.9	23.8	21.5	20.2	18.6
Blue-collar workers—males	46.0	48.0	45.9	45.5	44.3
Craft and kindred	19.2	19.9	19.9	20.5	20.7
Operatives and laborers	26.7	28.1	26.0	25.1	23.7
Blue-collar workers—females	16.4	17.1	15.4	14.5	13.6
Craft and kindred	1.0	1.0	1.3	1.6	1.9
Operatives and laborers	15.3	16.1	14.1	12.9	11.7
Blue-collar workers—whites	35.6	36.4	33.7	32.6	30.7
Craft and kindred	13.9	13.8	13.5	13.4	13.1
Operatives and laborers	21.7	22.5	20.3	19.1	17.6
Blue-collar workers—blacks and others	39.4	41.9	39.9	37.6	34.8
Craft and kindred	6.2	7.6	7.9	8.7	9.2
Operatives and laborers	33.2	34.3	32.0	28.9	25.7

(Continued)

TABLE 3.4 *Continued*

Category	1961	1966	1971	1976	1981
Service workers—total	12.6	12.6	13.5	13.7	13.4
Private household	3.1	2.6	1.9	1.3	1.0
Other	9.5	10.0	11.6	12.4	12.3
Service workers—males	6.7	7.1	8.2	8.8	8.9
Private household	0.1	0.1	0.1	0.1	0.1
Other	6.6	7.0	8.1	8.8	8.8
Service workers—females	24.2	22.7	22.2	21.0	19.4
Private household	9.0	7.2	4.9	3.1	2.3
Other	15.2	15.5	17.4	17.9	17.1
Service workers—whites	10.2	10.4	11.8	12.3	12.2
Private household	1.8	1.5	1.2	0.9	0.8
Other	8.4	8.9	10.6	11.4	11.4
Service workers—blacks and others	32.8	31.4	27.6	25.4	22.4
Private household	14.5	11.8	7.3	4.4	2.9
Other	18.3	19.6	20.3	21.0	19.6
Farm workers—total	7.5	5.0	3.8	3.2	2.7
Males	9.3	7.1	5.1	4.5	3.9
Females	3.9	2.6	1.7	1.3	1.1
Whites	7.0	4.9	3.9	3.3	2.9
Blacks and others	11.4	5.8	3.4	2.3	1.6

Source: *Employment and Training Report of the President, 1982,* pp. 178–180.

TABLE 3.5. LABOR FORCE, EMPLOYMENT, UNEMPLOYMENT, ANNUAL AVERAGES, 1948–1982
(IN THOUSANDS)

Unemployment rates were relatively low in 1970, substantially higher thereafter; high rates of growth in the labor force exceeded increases in employment.

Year	Civilian Labor Force	Employed	Unemployed	Unemployment Rate
1948	60,621	58,343	2,276	3.8
1950	62,208	58,918	3,288	5.3
1955	65,023	62,170	2,852	4.4
1960	69,628	65,778	3,852	5.5
1965	74,455	71,088	3,366	4.5
1970	82,771	78,678	4,093	4.9
1975	93,775	85,846	7,929	8.5
1980	106,940	99,303	7,637	7.1
1981	108,670	100,397	8,273	7.6
1982	110,204	99,526	10,678	9.7

Sources: *Employment and Training Report of the President, 1982,* p. 147; and U.S. Bureau of Labor Statistics, *State Unemployment in 1982,* March 15, 1983.

TABLE 3.6. SHORT-TERM AND LONG-TERM UNEMPLOYMENT, 1948–1981: PERCENTAGE OF ALL UNEMPLOYED OUT OF WORK LESS THAN FIVE WEEKS, FIFTEEN TO TWENTY-SIX WEEKS, AND TWENTY-SIX WEEKS AND OVER

After 1975 fewer than half of the unemployed stayed out of work for less than five weeks. Many remained unemployed for fifteen weeks or more.

Year	Less Than 5 Weeks	15–26 Weeks	27 Weeks and Over
1948	57.1	8.5	5.1
1952	60.2	7.9	4.5
1957	49.3	11.2	8.4
1962	42.4	13.6	15.0
1967	54.9	9.1	5.9
1972	45.9	12.3	11.6
1977	41.7	13.1	14.8
1980	43.1	13.8	10.8
1981	41.7	13.6	14.0

Source: *Employment and Training Report of the President, 1982*, p. 201.

TABLE 3.7. ANNUAL UNEMPLOYMENT RATES BY SEX, RACE, AND ETHNIC CATEGORY, 1947–1981

Moderate differences in unemployment rates between men and women become sharply differentiated when race is taken into account; the differences remain great over two decades.

Year	Total	Males				Females			
		All	White	Black and Other	Hispanic Origin	All	White	Black and Other	Hispanic Origin
1947	3.9	4.0	—	—	—	3.7	—	—	—
1952	3.0	2.8	2.5	5.2	—	3.6	3.3	5.7	—
1957	4.3	4.1	3.6	8.3	—	4.7	4.3	7.3	—
1962	5.5	5.2	4.6	10.9	—	6.2	5.5	11.0	—
1967	3.8	3.1	2.7	6.0	—	5.2	4.6	9.1	—
1972	5.6	5.0	4.5	8.9	—	6.6	5.9	11.4	—
1977	7.1	6.3	5.5	12.3	9.0	8.2	7.3	13.9	11.9
1978	6.1	5.3	4.6	11.0	7.7	7.2	6.2	13.0	11.3
1979	5.8	5.1	4.5	10.4	7.0	6.8	5.9	12.3	10.3
1980	7.1	6.9	6.1	13.2	9.7	7.4	6.5	13.1	10.7
1981	7.6	7.4	6.5	14.1	10.2	7.9	6.9	14.3	10.8

Source: *Employment and Training Report of the President, 1982*, pp. 190 and 197.

TABLE 3.8. UNEMPLOYMENT RATES OF YOUNG WORKERS BY AGE, 1948–1982

Youth unemployment rose relative to adult rates in the 1960s; the relationship stabilized in the 1970s; nonwhite youth unemployment deteriorated sharply after 1970.

| Year | All Workers | | | Nonwhite Workers |
	16–19	20–24	16–24	16–19
1948	9.2	6.2	7.3	—
1950	12.2	7.7	9.3	—
1955	11.0	7.0	8.7	15.8
1960	14.7	8.7	11.2	24.4
1965	14.8	6.7	10.1	26.2
1970	15.3	8.2	11.0	19.1
1975	19.9	13.6	16.1	36.7
1980	17.8	11.5	13.8	35.4
1981	19.6	12.3	14.9	41.4
1982	23.2	14.9	17.8	48.0

Sources: *Employment and Training Report of the President, 1982,* pp. 159 and 161; and U.S. Bureau of Labor Statistics, *Monthly Labor Review,* September 1983, pp. 53–54.

TABLE 3.9. UNEMPLOYMENT RATES FOR GROUPS IN THE LABOR FORCE, JULY 1982

Teenagers, younger workers, blue-collar workers, and minorities in all categories are at greatest risk; government, white-collar, service, and mature workers are least vulnerable to unemployment.

Group	Percentage Unemployed	Times the Overall Unemployment Rate
Total labor force	9.8	—
Black teenagers	49.7	5.07
White teenagers	21.0	2.14
All black persons	18.5	1.89
Young men aged 20–24	15.9	1.62
Blue-collar workers	14.4	1.49
Persons of Hispanic origin	13.9	1.42
Young women aged 20–24	12.9	1.32
Women heads of households	12.0	1.22
Part-time workers	11.4	1.16
Service workers	10.5	1.07
Workers in private industry	10.2	1.04
Full-time workers	9.5	0.98
All white persons	8.7	0.89
Men aged 25 and over	7.5	0.77
Married women	7.4	0.76
Women aged 25 and over	7.4	0.76
Married men	6.6	0.67
Farm workers	6.1	0.62
White-collar workers	4.9	0.50
Government workers	4.6	0.47

Source: U.S. Bureau of Labor Statistics, *Monthly Labor Review,* September 1982.

TABLE 3.10. UNEMPLOYMENT RATES BY OCCUPATIONAL GROUP, 1960–1981

Blue-collar workers show the greatest vulnerability to unemployment, white-collar workers the least.

Group	1960	1965	1970	1975	1980	1981
White collar	2.7	2.3	2.8	4.7	3.7	4.0
Blue collar	7.8	5.3	6.2	11.7	10.0	10.3
Service	5.8	5.3	5.3	8.6	7.9	8.9

Source: *Employment and Training Report of the President, 1982,* p. 199.

TABLE 3.11. UNEMPLOYMENT RATES IN MAJOR METROPOLITAN AREAS, JUNE 1983 (PERCENTAGE)

Unemployment rates vary widely; many cities are well above the overall rate of unemployment.

City	Rate
Baltimore	7.5
Boston	6.5
Chicago	11.7
Cleveland	12.2
Columbus (Ohio)	9.7
Dallas	5.7
Detroit	15.4
Houston	10.1
Indianapolis	8.7
Jacksonville	8.2
Los Angeles–Long Beach	10.2
Memphis	9.4
Milwaukee	10.1
New Orleans	11.5
New York	8.9
Philadelphia	9.4
San Antonio	6.3
San Diego	9.0
San Francisco–Oakland	8.4
San Jose	8.1
Washington, D.C.	5.1

Source: *State and Metropolitan Area Employment and Unemployment, July, 1983* (Washington, D.C.: U.S. Bureau of Labor Statistics, 1983).

TABLE 3.12. UNEMPLOYMENT BY STATE, 1982 AND 1983 (PERCENTAGE)

Sharp contrasts exist among states and regions.

State	1982	1983	State	1982	1983
Ala.	14.5	12.7	Mont.	8.7	8.2
Alaska	9.9	9.9	Neb.	6.3	5.7
Ariz.	10.4	10.3	Nev.	9.9	9.0
Ark.	9.2	9.1	N.M.	9.6	10.8
Calif.	9.4	10.1	N.H.	7.0	4.7
Colo.	7.8	7.3	N.C.	9.3	8.5
Conn.	6.8	6.4	N.D.	5.5	4.7
Del.	8.7	7.7	N.J.	8.6	8.5
D.C.	10.5	11.0	N.Y.	8.5	9.1
Fla.	7.7	8.8	Ohio	12.3	12.8
Ga.	7.9	6.8	Okla.	5.5	9.0
Hawaii	7.1	7.2	Ore.	11.2	9.1
Idaho	9.3	9.7	Pa.	10.3	12.9
Ill.	11.7	12.7	R.I.	10.3	8.3
Ind.	11.5	9.8	S.C.	11.5	9.8
Iowa	8.4	7.7	S.D.	5.7	5.2
Kan.	6.3	6.2	Tenn.	11.7	11.1
Ky.	10.2	10.8	Texas	7.7	8.5
La.	10.7	12.8	Utah	7.4	9.4
Me.	8.1	8.6	Vt.	6.6	7.0
Md.	8.4	6.5	Va.	7.8	5.8
Mass.	9.0	7.5	Wash.	11.8	10.9
Mich.	14.3	14.6	W.Va.	13.2	17.5
Minn.	7.8	8.1	Wis.	10.5	9.5
Miss.	11.2	13.6	Wyo.	5.5	9.5
Mo.	9.4	9.2			

Source: U.S. Department of Labor, as reported in the *New York Times*, August 17, 1983.

TABLE 3.13. STATES AND TERRITORIES WITH HIGH AND LOW RATES OF UNEMPLOYMENT, 1976–1981

Differences among states had become even stronger by 1981.

State or Territory	1976	1977	1978	1979	1980	1981
National rate	7.7	7.1	6.1	5.8	7.1	7.6
Puerto Rico	19.5	19.9	18.1	17.0	17.1	19.9
Michigan	9.4	8.2	6.9	7.8	12.4	12.3
West Virginia	7.5	7.1	6.3	6.7	9.4	10.7
Alabama	6.8	7.4	6.3	7.1	8.8	10.7
Indiana	6.1	5.7	5.7	6.4	9.6	10.1
Oklahoma	5.6	5.0	3.9	3.4	4.8	3.6
Nebraska	3.3	3.7	2.9	3.2	4.1	4.1
Wyoming	4.1	3.6	3.3	2.8	4.0	4.1
Kansas	4.2	4.1	3.1	3.4	4.5	4.2
New Hampshire	6.4	5.9	3.8	3.1	4.7	5.0
North Dakota	3.6	4.8	4.6	3.7	5.0	5.0

Source: *Employment and Training Report of the President, 1982,* pp. 159 and 260.

TABLE 3.14. AVERAGE WEEKLY HOURS OF WORKERS BY INDUSTRY, 1947–1981

The shortened work week in retail trade and services reflects the increase of part-time work in those sectors, which employ many women.

Industry	1947	1957	1967	1977	1981
Manufacturing	40.4	39.8	40.6	40.3	39.8
Mining	40.8	40.1	42.6	43.4	43.6
Construction	38.2	37.0	37.7	36.5	36.8
Wholesale trade	41.1	40.3	40.3	38.8	38.6
Retail trade	40.3	38.1	35.3	31.6	30.1
Finance, insurance, real estate	37.9	36.7	37.1	36.4	36.3
Services	—	—	35.1	33.0	32.6

Source: *Employment and Training Report of the President, 1982,* p. 242.

TABLE 3.15. MEDIAN WEEKLY EARNINGS OF MALE AND FEMALE FULL-TIME WAGE AND SALARY WORKERS BY AGE, EDUCATION, AND OCCUPATION, 1981

Sex-based earnings differentials are present at all age and educational levels, and in all occupational groups.

Category	Men	Women
Age:		
16–19	$225	$184
20–24	241	193
25–34	346	242
35–44	406	241
45–54	408	231
55–64	386	227
65 and over	270	190
Years of school completed:		
8 or less	259	169
1–3 years of high school	314	187
4 years of high school	363	222
1–3 years of college	398	259
4 or more years of college	482	325
Occupation:		
Professional and technical	439	316
Managerial and administrative	466	283
Sales	366	190
Clerical	328	220
Craft	360	239
Operative	298	187
Transport operative	307	237
Nonfarm labor	244	193
Service	238	165
Farmwork	183	148

Source: U.S. Bureau of Labor Statistics, *Monthly Labor Review,* April 1982, p. 16.

TABLE 3.16. MEDIAN WEEKLY EARNINGS BY INDUSTRY, 1982 ANNUAL AVERAGES

Earnings of white workers exceed those of others in all branches except agriculture; blacks fall below Hispanics except in manufacturing, trade, and government.

Industry	White	Black	Hispanic
All workers	$317	$247	$242
Agriculture	207	148	209
Mining	465	323	432
Construction	365	271	298
Manufacturing	336	260	236
Durable goods	356	289	—
Nondurable goods	304	233	—
Transportation/public utilities	419	339	352
Trade	254	210	209
Finance, insurance, real estate	292	241	246
Services	278	217	226
Government	346	284	302

Source: U.S. Bureau of Labor Statistics, "Employment in Perspective: Minority Workers," Report 699, 1983.

TABLE 3.17. FEMALE-TO-MALE EARNINGS RATIOS BY OCCUPATION, 1981 (DOLLARS EARNED BY WOMEN PER $1,000 EARNED BY MEN)

Sex differences are pervasive; women are most disadvantaged in banks and advertising agencies.

Occupation	Earnings Ratio	Occupation	Earnings Ratio
Postal clerks	$939	Waiters and waitresses	$720
Cashiers	920	Accountants	712
Security guards	907	Lawyers	710
Packers and wrappers	854	Real estate agents	709
Editors and reporters	850	School administrators	699
Bartenders	844	Bookkeepers	694
High school teachers	829	Manufacturing assemblers	690
Elementary school teachers	822	Office machine operators	688
Nursing aides and orderlies	822	Engineers	678
Textile operatives	821	Sales clerks	674
Stock handlers	812	Insurance agents	671
Physicians and dentists	809	Health administrators	655
College teachers	803	Office managers	655
Social workers	799	Personnel workers	643
Cleaning service workers	756	Blue-collar supervisors	642
Social scientists	749	Buyers	623
Computer programmers	736	Advertising workers	617
Cooks	734	Bank officers and financial managers	602

Source: U.S. Bureau of Labor Statistics, *Monthly Labor Review,* April 1982.

TABLE 3.18. OCCUPATIONS AND RELATIVE EARNINGS OF MEN AND WOMEN 18 YEARS OLD OR OVER, WORKING FULL TIME, 1980

Differences are significant, including the sectors in which most women work.

Sector	Number (thousands)		Ratio of Female-to-Male Average Earnings (percentage)
	Male	Female	
White-collar	20,506	17,003	52.8
Blue-collar	16,933	3,225	61.2
Service	2,804	2,997	58.2
Farm	1,432	107	37.0
Total	41,675	23,332	—

Source: *Money Income of Households, Families, and Persons in the United States, 1980,* Current Population Survey, Series P-60 (Washington, D.C.: U.S. Bureau of the Census, 1980), p. 184.

TABLE 3.19. WORKERS' SPENDABLE WEEKLY EARNINGS IN CONSTANT (1977) DOLLARS, 1948–1981

Stagnation and decline of real earnings occurred in all sectors in the 1970s and continued through 1981, often to levels at or below those of fifteen to twenty years earlier.

Industry	1948	1958	1968	1973	1978	1981
Total	$122.19	$144.88	$165.99	$173.78	$167.95	$147.05
Mining	158.21	180.71	213.45	232.95	256.98	235.76
Construction	157.58	193.94	243.87	271.90	247.49	215.79
Manufacturing	131.69	157.04	185.98	195.77	199.69	178.24
Transportation and public utilities	—	—	208.26	234.98	236.86	209.88
Wholesale and retail trades	101.74	122.60	137.58	137.87	132.04	114.10
Finance, insurance, real estate	113.43	136.58	157.94	156.58	149.71	133.69
Services	—	—	133.33	143.85	139.33	123.57

Source: *Employment and Training Report of the President, 1982,* pp. 253.

TABLE 3.20. YEARS OF SCHOOL COMPLETED BY CIVILIAN LABOR FORCE, BY RACE AND ETHNIC ORIGIN, 1962 AND 1981

Racial differences in education narrowed over this period; Hispanics have the lowest levels of education.

| | Percentage of Group | | | | | | | |
| | All | | White | | Black and Other | | Hispanic Origin | |
Education	1962	1981	1962	1981	1962	1981	1962	1981
College:								
4 years or more	11.0	18.3	11.8	19.1	4.8	9.3	5.7	7.6
1-3 years	10.7	17.9	11.3	18.0	5.7	16.9	10.6	13.4
High school:								
4 years	32.1	40.9	33.5	41.3	21.0	39.6	28.4	30.6
1-3 years	19.3	14.9	18.8	14.1	23.2	22.4	20.6	19.3
Elementary school:								
5-8 years	22.4	6.7	21.4	6.4	29.8	9.5	23.0	20.4
Less than 5 years	4.6	1.2	3.3	1.0	15.4	2.3	11.8	8.6

Source: *Employment and Training Report of the President, 1982*, pp. 227-230.

TABLE 3.21. OCCUPATIONAL INJURY AND ILLNESS INCIDENCE, 1973-1978[a]

Total cases declined, lost workdays and lost workday cases rose virtually across the board in this period.

| | Total Cases | | Lost Workday Cases | | Lost Workdays | |
Sector	1973	1978	1973	1978	1973	1978
Agriculture, forestry, and fishing	11.6	11.6	4.6	5.4	68.0	80.7
Mining	12.5	11.5	5.8	6.4	119.6	143.2
Construction	19.8	16.0	6.1	6.4	98.1	109.4
Manufacturing	15.3	13.2	4.5	5.6	68.2	84.9
Transportation and public utilities	10.3	10.1	4.4	5.7	82.5	102.3
Wholesale and retail trade	8.6	7.9	2.7	3.2	37.6	44.9
Finance, insurance, and real estate	2.4	2.1	0.8	0.8	10.2	12.5
Services	6.2	5.5	1.9	2.4	27.5	36.2

[a]Rates per one hundred full-time workers.
Source: *Handbook of Labor Statistics* (Washington, D.C.: U.S. Bureau of Labor Statistics, December 1980), pp. 443-444.

TABLE 3.22. UNION MEMBERSHIP BY OCCUPATION AND SECTOR, SEPTEMBER 1981

Total union membership is less than one quarter of the work force and is concentrated among men, blue-collar workers, and the manufacturing, construction, transport, and local government sectors.

Category	Union Membership (percentage)
All workers	23.0
White-collar workers	15.3
Blue-collar workers	39.1
Service workers	16.2
Men	28.4
Women	15.9
White	22.2
Nonwhite	29.0
Sectors	
Railroads	81.8
U.S. Postal Service	73.7
Automobile manufacturing	61.2
Primary metals	58.4
Paper manufacturing	49.1
Aircraft manufacturing	42.4
Food processing	37.5
Local governments	36.9
Fabricated metals	36.1
Education	34.3
Petroleum processing	34.1
Mining	32.1
Construction industry	31.6
Rubber and plastics	29.6
Furniture manufacturing	27.0
Electrical equipment	26.9
State governments	26.0
Chemicals processing	25.8
Apparel	25.1
Printing	20.2
Federal government	19.3
Hospitals	17.7
Textiles	14.9
Insurance and real estate	5.5
Eating and drinking places	4.9
Agriculture	3.5
Banking and finance	1.6
Private employment	21.7
Government employment	43.4

Source: U.S. Bureau of Labor Statistics, "Earnings and Other Characteristics of Organized Workers," Bulletin 2105 (September 1981), pp. 9-10, 20-21, and 28.

SECTION 4

Government Revenues and Expenditures

TABLE 4.1. FEDERAL TAX EXPENDITURES BY MAJOR CATEGORY, 1982

Substantial tax benefits flow to corporations, securities owners, home owners, recipients of public benefits, and recipients of employer-supported pension and health benefits.

Major Categories[a]	Amount (millions)
Total tax expenditures	$253,505
Capital gains	28,760
Employer pension contributions	25,765
Mortgage interest	23,030
State and local tax exemption	20,395
Investment credit	19,985
Employer contributions to medical insurance and medical care	15,330
Social security benefits	12,810
Charitable contributions	10,600
State and local bond interest exemption	10,590
Accelerated depreciation	8,595
Nonmortgage interest in excess of investment income	7,585
Corporate deduction on first $100,000 of income	6,605
Oil and gas expensing and depletion	5,670
Dividend and interest exclusion	4,935
Medical care deduction	3,925
Workers' compensation	3,100
Exemption for the elderly	2,490
Research and development	2,430
Unemployment compensation	2,060
Employer group life insurance contributions	2,000
Armed forces benefits and allowances	1,885
Veterans' benefits	1,620
Domestic international sales corporation (DISC) deferral	1,560
Safe harbor leasing investment credit	1,365
Child care and dependent care expenses	1,350
Self employment pension contributions	1,005
Employee stock option (ESOP) credit	1,005

[a]Items totaling $1 billion or more.

Source: Congressional Budget Office, *Tax Expenditures: Budget Control Options and Five-Year Budget Projections for Fiscal Years 1982–1987,* November 1982, table A-1.

TABLE 4.2. REVENUES AND EXPENDITURES BY LEVEL OF GOVERNMENT, 1950–1980

Federal share of the total fell steadily but in 1980 accounted for 60.5 percent of revenues and 54.8 percent of spending.

	Revenue				Spending			
	Federal		State and Local		Federal		State and Local	
Year	Total (billions)	Share (percentage)	Total (billions)	Share (percentage)	Total (billions)	Share (percentage)	Total (billions)	Share (percentage)
1950	$ 44	65.3	$ 23	34.7	$ 42	60.3	$ 28	39.7
1960	100	65.2	53	34.8	90	59.7	61	40.3
1970	206	61.6	128	38.4	185	55.5	148	44.5
1980	564	60.5	369	39.5	526	54.8	432	45.2

Source: *Statistical Abstract of the United States, 1982–83*, p. 273.

TABLE 4.3. DISTRIBUTION OF TAX EXPENDITURES FOR INDIVIDUALS BY INCOME CLASS, 1982

Most benefits accrue to groups with incomes of $50,000 or more.

	Amount of Tax Benefit (millions)					
Income Group (Adjusted Gross Income)	Mortgage Interest	Property Tax	Capital Gains	State/Local Tax	Charitable Contributions	Medical Expense
Less than $10,000	$220	$109	$428	$118	$36	$85
$10,000–$15,000	343	198	384	230	129	190
$15,000–$20,000	892	374	308	497	249	299
$20,000–$30,000	3,633	1,429	1,140	2,276	985	827
$30,000–$50,000	8,639	3,252	2,564	6,289	2,550	1,201
$50,000–$100,000	4,672	2,291	3,179	5,050	2,109	614
$100,000–$200,000	979	725	2,148	2,032	1,126	150
$200,000 and over	225	302	3,081	1,352	1,652	56

Source: Congressional Budget Office, *Tax Expenditures: Budget Control Options and Five-Year Budget Projections for Fiscal Years 1982–1987*, November 1982, pp. 96-97.

TABLE 4.4. CHANGES IN LOCAL GOVERNMENT UNITS, 1952 AND 1982

Consolidation of school districts was the most common change during this period.
Local government remains highly local and fragmented.

Type of Unit	Number	
	1952	1982
Counties	3,049	3,041
Municipalities	16,778	19,083
Townships and towns	17,202	16,748
School districts	67,346	15,032
Special districts	12,319	28,733

Source: *Statistical Abstract of the United States, 1982–83*, p. 273.

SECTION 5

Social Welfare Expenditures, Programs, and Recipients

TABLE 5.1. PUBLIC SOCIAL WELFARE EXPENDITURES, 1950–1979 (IN BILLIONS)

Overall expenditures continued to grow rapidly; social insurance grew almost fourfold between 1970 and 1979, as did public aid.

Category	1950	1960	1970	1975	1979
Total	$23.5	$52.3	$145.9	$290.0	$428.3
Social insurance	4.9	19.3	54.7	123.0	193.6
OASDHI[a]	0.8	11.0	36.8	78.4	131.8
Medicare	—	—	7.1	14.8	29.2
Public employee retirement	0.8	2.6	8.7	20.1	33.8
Unemployment insurance-employment service	2.2	2.8	3.8	13.8	11.3
Workers' compensation	0.6	1.3	3.0	6.5	11.1
Other	0.5	1.6	4.7	4.1	5.6
Public aid	2.5	4.1	16.5	41.3	64.6
Public assistance[b]	2.5	4.0	14.4	27.4	40.7
Supplemental Security Income	—	—	—	6.1	7.5
Food stamps	—	—	0.6	4.7	6.5
Other	—	0.1	1.5	3.2	9.9
Health and medical programs	2.1	4.5	9.9	17.7	24.5
Veterans' programs	6.9	5.5	9.1	17.0	20.5
Education	6.7	17.6	50.8	80.9	108.3
Housing	0.0	0.2	0.7	5.2	6.2

[a]Called OASDI prior to 1966.
[b]Cash and medical payments under the Social Security Act and state and local general assistance.
Source: Annual statistical supplement to the *Social Security Bulletin,* 1981, p. 54.

TABLE 5.2. PRIVATE PHILANTHROPY: ESTIMATED FUNDS BY SOURCE AND ALLOCATION, 1955-1982 (IN MILLIONS)[a]

Individuals remain the major source of private philanthropy. Overall giving outpaced inflation in 1981 and 1982. The rate of increase slowed in 1982 as it did during the economic turndown in the mid-1970s. Contributors gave more than half their gifts to religious organizations, and in 1982 an increased share of the philanthropic dollar went to social service agencies and to education.

Category	1955	1960	1965	1970	1975	1980	1981	1982
Total	$6,660	$9,390	$13,290	$20,750	$29,680	$47,740	$53,620	$60,390
Source								
Individuals	5,710	7,630	10,360	15,920	24,240	39,930	44,510	48,690
Foundations	300	710	1,130	1,900	2,010	2,400	2,620	3,150
Business corporations	415	482	785	797	1,202	2,550	3,000	3,100
Charitable bequests	237	574	1,020	2,130	2,230	2,860	3,490	4,450
Allocation								
Religion	3,330	4,790	6,510	9,300	12,910	22,150	24,850	28,060
Education	733	1,500	2,260	3,240	3,950	6,680	7,490	8,590
Social Welfare	1,530	1,410	1,860	2,880	3,140	4,730	5,320	6,330
Health and hospitals	596	1,130	1,460	3,400	4,420	6,490	7,360	8,410
Arts and humanities	199	188	226	623	1,720	2,960	3,350	4,960
Civic and public	75	94	173	415	890	1,360	1,540	1,670
Other	197	282	797	892	2,650	3,370	3,710	2,370

[a]Estimates for sources of funds are based largely on reports of the Internal Revenue Service (IRS) for itemized deductions, corporate profits, and bequests. Data are adjusted for nonitemized IRS deductions and after comparison with levels of gross national product, personal income, population, and publicly reported large bequests. For bases of allocation of funds, see source.
Source: *Giving USA, 1983*, annual report (New York: American Association of Fund-Raising Counsel, 1983) and earlier annual reports.

TABLE 5.3. SOCIAL WELFARE EXPENDITURES AS PERCENTAGE OF GROSS NATIONAL PRODUCT (GNP), 1950-1979

Social welfare spending increased until 1975 and declined thereafter. About seven-tenths of these expenditures are represented by social insurance and education.

Category	1950	1960	1970	1975	1979
GNP (billions)	$264.8	$498.3	$960.2	$1,452.3	$2,313.4
Total social welfare expenditures— percentage of GNP	8.9	10.5	15.2	20.0	18.5
Social insurance	1.9	3.9	5.7	8.5	8.4
Public aid	0.9	0.8	1.7	2.8	2.8
Health and medical programs	0.8	0.9	1.0	1.2	1.1
Veterans' programs	2.6	1.1	0.9	1.2	0.9
Education	2.5	3.5	5.3	5.6	4.7
Other social welfare	0.2	0.2	0.4	0.5	0.4

Source: Annual statistical supplement to the *Social Security Bulletin,* 1981, p. 53.

TABLE 5.4. OLD AGE AND SURVIVORS INSURANCE TRUST FUND, 1970-1982

Assets peaked in 1974-1975; declined, often sharply, in succeeding years; and rose slightly in 1982.

Year	Receipts (billions)	Expenditures (billions)	Total Assets, End of Year (billions)
1970	$32.2	$29.8	$32.5
1975	59.9	60.4	37.0
1977	72.4	75.6	32.5
1979	90.3	93.1	24.7
1980	105.9	107.6	22.8
1981	125.4	126.7	21.5
1982	125.2	142.1	22.1

Source: *Social Security Bulletin* (May 1983), p. 25.

TABLE 5.5. HOSPITAL INSURANCE TRUST FUND, 1970-1981

The Hospital Insurance Trust Fund grew steadily during this period.

Year	Receipts (billions)	Expenditures (billions)	Total Assets, End of Year (billions)
1970	$ 6.0	$ 5.1	$ 3.2
1975	13.0	11.3	10.5
1981	35.7	30.3	18.7

Source: Annual statistical supplement to the *Social Security Bulletin,* 1981, p. 82.

TABLE 5.6. COVERAGE AND BENEFITS UNDER FEDERAL BENEFIT PROGRAMS, 1950–1979
(NUMBER IN THOUSANDS; BENEFITS IN DOLLARS PER MONTH)

Retired women now outnumber retired men among the widowed or nonmarried cohort; benefits to retired or disabled women lag substantially behind those to men.

| | Retired Worker Families | | | | | | Survivors | | Disabled Workers | | | |
| | Men (Worker Only) | | Women (Worker Only) | | Worker and Wife | | Aged Widow Only | | Men (Worker Only) | | Women (Worker Only) | |
Year	Number	Average Benefits	Number	Average Benefits	Number	Average Benefits	Number	Average Benefits	Number	Average Benefits	Number	Average Benefits
1950	939	$ 44.60	301	$ 34.80	498	$ 71.70	314	$ 36.50	—	—	—	—
1960	2,922	79.90	2,820	59.60	2,122	123.90	1,527	57.70	261	$ 91.90	96	$ 76.90
1970	4,904	128.70	5,629	101.60	2,457	198.90	3,080	102.40	680	136.30	374	113.10
1975	6,134	225.50	7,385	181.80	2,618	343.90	3,606	195.90	1,080	240.00	671	185.00
1979	7,044	324.00	8,704	257.10	2,710	488.60	3,964	270.30	1,248	343.60	802	254.80

Source: Annual statistical supplement to the *Social Security Bulletin*, 1981, pp. 102 and 103.

TABLE 5.7. PUBLIC SOCIAL INSURANCE BENEFICIARIES AND BENEFITS, 1950–1979

Old Age, Survivors, Disability, and Health Insurance (OASDHI) beneficiaries account for 87 percent of the total and 79 percent of benefit payments.

| Year | OASDHI[a] | | Other Programs | | | |
| | | | Federal | | State and Local | |
	Beneficiaries (thousands)	Benefits (billions)	Beneficiaries (thousands)	Benefits (billions)	Beneficiaries (thousands)	Benefits (billions)
1950	1,918	$ 1.0	0.3	$222.0	0.3	—
1960	10,310	11.2	442.2	1.1	535.0	$ 0.8
1970	16,870	31.9	1,119.4	4.5	1,085.0	2.7
1975	20,014	66.9	1,644.2	11.3	1,480.0	6.1
1979	22,421	104.6	2,051.0	18.1	1,097.7	10.0

[a]Called OASDI prior to 1966.
Source: Annual statistical supplement to the *Social Security Bulletin,* 1981, pp. 66–67.

TABLE 5.8. WORKERS AND TAXABLE EARNINGS UNDER SOCIAL SECURITY, 1937–1982

Coverage and earnings grew consistently, earnings more rapidly as a result of inflation and increases in maximum taxable earnings.

Year	Number of Workers (thousands)	Taxable Earnings (billions)
1937	32,900	$29.6
1950	48,280	87.5
1960	72,530	207.0
1970	93,090	415.6
1975	100,200	664.7
1978	110,600	915.8
1982[a]	114,990	1,358.0

[a]Estimated.
Source: Annual statistical supplement to the *Social Security Bulletin,* 1981, p. 84.

TABLE 5.9. STATES WITH ONE MILLION OR MORE SOCIAL SECURITY BENEFICIARIES, JUNE 1980

Half of all beneficiaries live in nine states, several with large and aging industrial economies.

State	Number of Beneficiaries (millions)
California	3.179
New York	2.862
Pennsylvania	2.053
Florida	2.039
Texas	1.799
Illinois	1.620
Ohio	1.611
Michigan	1.349
New Jersey	1.152
Nine-state total	17,664
U.S. total	35.220

Source: Annual statistical supplement to the *Social Security Bulletin,* 1981, p. 192.

TABLE 5.10. AVERAGE MONTHLY PAYMENTS, SELECTED PUBLIC ASSISTANCE PROGRAMS, 1960–1981[a]

Significant differences exist and persist among different categories of beneficiaries: Old Age, Survivors, Disability, and Health Insurance (OASDHI) beneficiaries received rising real incomes; those of the aged, disabled, and Aid to Families with Dependent Children (AFDC) clients fell.

Program	1960	1970	1975	1981
OASDHI,[b] all retired workers	$233.40	$279.14	$350.70	$385.97
OASDHI,[b] widowed mother with two children	592.63	688.03	795.41	858.00
Old Age Assistance (until 1970)	185.67	183.53	—	—
Supplemental Security Income (after 1974)	—	—	153.87	137.81
Aid to Families with Dependent Children	89.37	118.89	121.20	107.47[c]

[a]All figures for December of the year cited and in real (1981) dollars.
[b]Called OASDI prior to 1966.
[c]This figure for 1980.
Source: Annual statistical supplement to the *Social Security Bulletin,* 1981, p. 70.

TABLE 5.11. STATE CASELOADS AND BENEFIT PAYMENTS, AID TO FAMILIES WITH
DEPENDENT CHILDREN, 1980

*Major differences prevail in benefit payments by state. Three states with the largest
caseloads are among the four highest paying states. The lowest payments
are in southern states.*

State	Number of Recipients	Average Monthly Payment for Family
States paying $300 or more:		
California	1,420,037	$398.68
Hawaii	60,478	385.57
Michigan	711,277	379.44
New York	1,102,390	371.13
Wisconsin	218,571	365.58
Washington	161,084	365.26
Alaska	15,361	358.86
Connecticut	140,018	357.91
Massachusetts	349,529	340.64
Vermont	23,349	339.86
Minnesota	138,894	336.32
Rhode Island	53,321	324.90
Oregon	101,949	317.90
Utah	39,853	313.68
New Jersey	462,940	311.19
Iowa	107,345	307.33
States paying $150–$300:		
Pennsylvania	632,339	$296.71
Illinois	678,274	277.28
North Dakota	13,084	276.57
Nebraska	36,058	273.88
Kansas	69,733	271.23
New Hampshire	22,786	271.03
Wyoming	6,964	262.28
Idaho	20,950	258.02
Ohio	532,980	249.94
Oklahoma	90,356	249.53
Colorado	78,448	238.60
Maine	59,776	232.84
Montana	19,885	228.22
Maryland	214,837	227.86
Delaware	32,607	226.98
South Dakota	19,969	217.63
Missouri	205,038	216.93
Virginia	168,771	214.24
Nevada	12,411	206.98
Indiana	161,597	203.28
New Mexico	54,452	185.27
West Virginia	77,817	182.36
Kentucky	169,839	176.91
Florida	264,085	174.98
North Carolina	200,015	163.61

(Continued)

TABLE 5.11 *Continued*

State	Number of Recipients	Average Monthly Payment for Family
States paying less than $150:		
Louisiana	214,959	$147.69
Arkansas	84,886	144.50
Georgia	225,748	132.81
Tennessee	165,563	113.41
Alabama	179,723	110.50
Texas	311,987	108.76
South Carolina	154,405	107.29
Mississippi	174,147	87.53

Source: Annual Statistical Supplement to the *Social Security Bulletin,* 1981, p. 250.

TABLE 5.12. DISABILITY BENEFICIARIES AND BENEFITS, 1960–1979[a]

Expenditures (mostly federal) under federal disability programs consistently are the major source of disability benefits, and expenditures rose more rapidly than the number of beneficiaries.

Year	Disability Payments		Workers' Compensation
	Beneficiaries (thousands)	Benefits (billions)	Benefits (billions)
1960	4,258.7	$4.9	$0.8
1970	6,683.4	11.0	1.7
1975	9,045.1	21.9	3.2
1979	9,962.2	39.2	6.1

[a]Excluding payments for remedial care.
Source: Annual statistical supplement to the *Social Security Bulletin,* 1981, pp. 66 and 67.

TABLE 5.13. SUPPLEMENTAL SECURITY INCOME (SSI), BENEFICIARIES AND BENEFITS, 1974–1981[a]

SSI coverage declined steadily; benefits rose modestly, then declined after 1980.

Year	Beneficiaries (thousands)			Average Monthly Benefit
	Federal SSI	Supplementation	Total[b]	
1974	—	—	4,027.6	$114.76
1975	3,893.4	1,987.4	4,359.6	116.36
1976	3,799.1	1,912.6	4,285.3	121.53
1977	3,777.9	1,927.3	4,287.0	126.39
1978	3,754.7	1,946.8	4,265.5	131.79
1979	3,687.1	1,941.6	4,202.7	157.87
1980	3,682.4	1,934.3	4,194.3	170.42
1981	3,590.1	1,874.9	4,496.0	167.80

[a]All figures are for December of each year.
[b]Figures include double counting.
Source: Annual statistical supplement to the *Social Security Bulletin*, 1981, pp. 224 and 226.

TABLE 5.14. SUPPLEMENTAL SECURITY INCOME (SSI), BENEFICIARIES BY CATEGORY, 1974 AND 1981

Disability accounted for virtually all growth over this period.

Category	December 1974 (thousands)	December 1981 (thousands)
Aged	2,307.7	1,955.3
Blind	75.5	88.5
Disabled	1,644.3	2,451.7
Total	4,027.6	4,496.0

Source: Annual statistical supplement to the *Social Security Bulletin*, 1981, p. 224.

TABLE 5.15. FOOD STAMP PROGRAM, 1965–1981

Program participants, coupon values, and total expenditures rose steadily.

Year	Number of Persons Participating (thousands)	Average Monthly Bonus per Person	Annual Bonus Value of Coupons (millions)
1965	424	$6.39	$32.5
1970	4,340	10.58	550.8
1975	17,063	21.42	4,386.2
1981	22,430	39.44	10,616.0

Source: Annual statistical supplement to the *Social Security Bulletin*, 1981, p. 78.

SECTION 6

Social Indicators

TABLE 6.1. NEW HOUSING UNITS STARTED, 1960–1982

Housing starts peaked in 1972; they have been below 2 million since 1979.

Year	Total (thousands)	Publicly Owned (thousands)
1960	1,296	44
1961	1,365	52
1962	1,492	30
1963	1,635	32
1964	1,561	32
1965	1,510	37
1966	1,196	31
1967	1,322	30
1968	1,545	38
1969	1,500	33
1970	1,469	35
1971	2,085	32
1972	2,379	22
1973	2,057	12
1974	1,353	15
1975	1,171	11
1976	1,548	10
1977	2,002	15
1978	2,036	16
1979	1,760	15
1980	1,313	20
1981	1,100	16
1982	1,072	10

Sources: *Statistical Abstract of the United States, 1982–83*, p. 747; and U.S. Department of Commerce, *Survey of Current Business*, August 1983, pp. 5–7.

TABLE 6.2. HOME OWNERSHIP BY RACE, 1960–1980

Significant differences in home ownership by race persist.

Race	1960	1970	1980
White	64.4	65.4	68.7
Nonwhite	38.4	41.6	43.9

Source: *Statistical Abstract of the United States, 1982–83*, p. 752.

TABLE 6.3. AGE OF OCCUPANT-OWNED HOUSING BY RACE, 1980

Nonwhite owners live in older housing.

When Built	Percentage Black Owners	Percentage White or Other Owners
1970 or later	15.3	24.6
1960–1969	18.5	21.6
1950–1959	18.2	19.4
1950 or before	<u>47.9</u>	<u>34.4</u>
	100.0	100.0

Source: U.S. Bureau of the Census, *Annual Housing Survey, 1980; Part A, General Housing Characteristics.*

TABLE 6.4 WORK DISABILITY, 1978

Disability is highest among older, less educated, nonwhite persons; income of the disabled is low.

Category	Rate per Thousand Population		
	Severely Disabled	Occupationally Disabled	Secondary Work Limitations
By age			
20–34	26	21	34
35–44	64	37	44
45–55	113	60	64
55–64	248	58	59
By race		Partially Disabled	
White	8	8	—
Black	13	8	—
Other	6	9	—
Spanish origin	13	8	—
By educational level		Partially Disabled	
College or more	13	26	—
4 years high school	30	37	—
1–3 years high school	23	20	—
8 years or less elementary school	34	15	—
By income level			
Under $5,000	28	—	—
$5,000–$9,999	25	—	—
$10,000–$14,999	18	—	—
$15,000–$19,999	13	—	—
$20,000 and over	14	—	—

Source: *Work Disability in the United States: A Chartbook* (Washington, D.C.: U.S. Department of Health and Human Services, Social Security Administration, 1980).

TABLE 6.5. FEMALE FAMILY HOUSEHOLDERS WITH NO SPOUSE PRESENT BY RACE AND PRESENCE OF CHILDREN, 1960-1981[a]

The number of female-headed households rose during this period among whites and blacks. The ratio of black to white proportions of such households was 2.6 to 1 in 1960, 3.1 to 1 in 1970, and 3.5 to 1 in 1980 when more than four of every ten black families were headed by a woman.

Category	1960	1965	1970	1975	1980[b]	1981	With One or More Own Children, Under 18			
							1960	1970	1980[b]	1981
Total families[c] (thousands)	45,128	47,956[d]	51,586	55,712	59,550	60,309	25,661	28,812	31,022	31,227
Female family householders (thousands)	4,194	5,026[d]	5,591	7,242	8,705	9,082	1,891	2,926	5,445	5,634
Percentage of all families	9.3	10.5	10.8	13.0	14.6	15.1	7.4	10.2	17.6	18.0
Percentage under 35 years old	17.7	19.1	24.4	32.5	34.6	34.9	35.0	43.1	52.4	52.9
White families (thousands)	40,872	43,081	46,261	49,451	52,243	52,710	23,264	25,543	26,474	26,523
Female family householders (thousands)	3,305	3,882	4,165	5,212	6,052	6,266	1,394	1,995	3,558	3,694
Percentage of white families	8.1	9.0	9.0	10.5	11.6	11.9	6.0	7.8	13.4	13.9
Percentage under 35 years old	14.7	—	20.8	19.0	30.8	31.7	30.7	39.8	49.2	49.8
Black families (thousands)[e]	4,256	4,752	4,887	5,498	6,184	6,317	2,397	2,984	3,820	3,873
Female family householders (thousands)	889	1,125	1,382	1,940	2,495	2,634	497	912	1,793	1,823
Percentage of black families	20.9	23.7	28.3	35.3	40.3	41.7	20.7	30.6	46.9	47.1
Percentage under 35 years old	28.7	—	35.2	42.4	44.0	42.3	47.1	50.0	59.1	59.3

[a]Figures for 1960 to 1975 cover persons 14 years old and over; beginning with 1980, figures cover persons 15 years old and over. Census data for 1960 as of April; thereafter, data based on Current Population Survey compiled each March.
[b]Population controls based on 1980 census.
[c]Beginning 1970, totals include other races not shown separately.
[d]Revised figures; revisions not available by race.
[e]All figures for 1960 and 1965 grouped blacks with other races.
Source: *Statistical Abstract of the United States, 1982-83*, p. 51.

TABLE 6.6. ENROLLMENT IN PUBLIC AND PRIVATE ELEMENTARY AND SECONDARY SCHOOLS, 1960–1980; PROJECTIONS, 1985 AND 1990

The number of children in elementary and secondary schools is expected to continue to decline from the highpoint of 1970.

Pupils Enrolled[a]	1960	1965	1970	1975	1978	1979	1980	1985	1990
Total (thousands)	42,181	48,473	51,272	49,791	47,636	46,679	46,095	44,166	46,667
Annual percentage change	3.6	2.8	1.1	-.6	-1.5	-2.0	-1.3	-.9	1.1
Elementary	29,150	31,570	31,553	29,340	28,749	28,551	27,987	27,338	31,022
Secondary	13,031	16,904	19,719	20,451	18,887	18,128	18,108	16,828	15,645
Public (thousands)	36,281	42,173	45,909	44,791	42,550	41,579	40,995	39,166	41,267
Elementary	24,350	26,670	27,501	25,640	25,017	24,851	24,287	23,738	27,022
Secondary	11,931	15,504	18,408	19,151	17,534	16,728	16,708	15,428	14,245
Private (thousands)	5,900	6,300	5,363	5,000	5,085	5,100	5,100	5,000	5,400
Elementary	4,800	4,900	4,052	3,700	3,732	3,700	3,700	3,600	4,000
Secondary	1,100	1,400	1,311	1,300	1,353	1,400	1,400	1,400	1,400

[a]Enrollments as of fall of year. Schools are classified by type of organization, rather than by grade group: elementary includes kindergarten; secondary includes junior high school. Minus sign (−) denotes decrease.
Source: *Statistical Abstract of the United States, 1982–83*, p. 153.

TABLE 6.7. COLLEGE ENROLLMENT OF PERSONS 18–24 YEARS OLD AND PERCENTAGE OF HIGH SCHOOL GRADUATES BY SEX AND RACE, 1960–1981

After a steady rise in the proportion of high school graduates enrolling in college in the 1960s, enrollment remained relatively static during the next decade; however, sex and race differences diminished.

Year	All Persons			Male			Female		
	Total[a]	White	Black and Other Races	Total[a]	White	Black and Other Races	Total[a]	White	Black and Other Races
College enrollment (thousands)									
1960	2,215	2,081	134	1,334	1,269	65	880	811	69
1970	5,805	5,305	416	3,331	3,096	192	2,474	2,209	225
1975	6,935	6,116	665	3,693	3,326	294	3,243	2,790	372
1980	7,226	6,334	688	3,604	3,224	278	3,625	3,110	410
1981	7,575	6,549	750	3,833	3,340	325	3,741	3,208	424
Percentage of high school graduates enrolled:									
1960	23.7	24.2	18.4	30.3	31.1	20.8	17.8	17.9	16.5
1970	32.7	33.2	26.0	41.2	42.3	28.7	25.6	25.6	24.1
1975	32.5	32.4	32.0	36.2	36.4	32.8	29.2	28.6	31.5
1980	31.8	32.0	27.8	33.5	34.0	26.4	30.3	30.2	28.8
1981	32.5	32.5	28.0	34.7	34.7	28.2	30.4	30.5	27.8

[a]Includes other races not shown separately.
Source: *Statistical Abstract of the United States, 1982–83*, p. 159.

TABLE 6.8. ENROLLMENT IN INSTITUTIONS OF HIGHER EDUCATION BY SPECIFIED MINORITY GROUPS, 1968–1980

The presence of black students as a percentage of total enrollment in institutions of higher education has risen by about 4 percent since 1968; other minority students have shown a 3 percent rise.

Year	Number of Institutions	Black Enrollment			Other Minority Groups				
		Total Enrollment (thousands)	Number (thousands)	Percentage	Total (thousands)	Percentage	American Indian (thousands)	Asian American (thousands)	Spanish-Surnamed American (thousands)
1968	2,054	4,820	287	6.0	169	3.5	29	48	91
1970	2,516	4,966	345	6.9	181	3.7	27	52	103
1972	2,665	5,531	459	8.3	219	4.0	32	57	130
1974	2,808	5,639	508	9.0	255	4.5	33	64	158
1976	2,821	5,755	605	10.5	331	5.8	38	101	191
1978	2,897	5,664	601	10.6	346	6.1	36	114	196
1980	2,979	5,993	625	10.4	396	6.6	39	136	221

Source: *Statistical Abstract of the United States, 1982–83*, p. 162.

TABLE 6.9. CRIME RATES BY TYPE, 1972–1981[a]

Property crime constitutes 90 percent of all crime; the incidence of both violent crime and property crime rose at similar rates during this period.

Year	Violent Crime					Property Crime			
	Total	Murder[b]	Forcible Rape	Robbery	Aggravated Assault	Total	Burglary	Larceny Theft	Motor Vehicle Theft
Rate per 100,000 inhabitants									
1972	401	9.0	22.5	181	189	3,560	1,141	1,994	426
1973	417	9.4	24.5	183	201	3,737	1,223	2,072	443
1974	461	9.8	26.2	209	216	4,389	1,438	2,490	462
1975	482	9.6	26.3	218	227	4,800	1,526	2,805	469
1976	460	8.8	26.4	196	229	4,807	1,439	2,921	446
1977	467	8.8	29.1	187	242	4,588	1,411	2,730	448
1978	487	9.0	30.8	191	256	4,622	1,424	2,744	455
1979	535	9.7	34.5	212	279	4,986	1,499	2,988	495
1980	581	10.2	36.4	244	291	5,319	1,668	3,156	495
1981	577	9.8	35.6	251	281	5,223	1,632	3,122	469
Average annual percentage of change									
1972–1976	3.7	-.5	4.3	2.1	5.3	8.8	6.5	11.6	1.2
1977–1981	5.9	2.8	.8	7.6	4.1	3.5	3.9	3.6	1.2
1980–1981	-.7	-3.9	-2.2	2.9	-3.3	-1.8	-2.2	-1.1	-5.2

[a]Data refers to offenses known to the police. Rates are based on Bureau of the Census estimated resident population as of July 1, except 1980, enumerated as of April 1. Minus sign (–) denotes decrease.
[b]Includes nonnegligent manslaughter.
Source: *Statistical Abstract of the United States, 1982–83*, p. 174.

SECTION 7

Health Status and Medical Care

TABLE 7.1. PUBLIC EXPENDITURES FOR HEALTH CARE, 1950–1981

The public share has exceeded 40 percent of the total since 1974.

Year	All Expenditures (billions)	Public Expenditures as Percentage of Total
1950	$12.7	27.2
1960	26.9	24.7
1970	74.7	37.2
1980	249.0	42.3
1981	286.6	42.7

Source: Public Health Service, *Health—United States, 1982,* p. 137.

TABLE 7.2. HEALTH CARE EXPENDITURES IN DOLLARS PER CAPITA AND AS PERCENTAGE OF GROSS NATIONAL PRODUCT (GNP), 1950–1980

Inflation raised the per capita cost more rapidly than the share of GNP; both grew without interruption in this period.

Year	Dollars per Capita	Percentage of GNP
1950	$82	4.4
1960	146	5.3
1970	358	7.5
1980	1,075	9.5

Source: Public Health Service, *Health—United States, 1982,* p. 130.

TABLE 7.3. HEALTH EXPENDITURES BY TYPE, 1950–1981 (PERCENTAGE)

Hospital and nursing home care costs grew to almost half of all health expenditures.

Type	1950	1960	1970	1981
Hospital care	30.4	33.8	37.2	41.2
Physician services	21.7	21.1	19.2	19.1
Nursing home care	1.5	2.0	6.3	8.4
Drugs and drug sundries	13.6	13.6	10.7	7.5
Dentist services	7.6	7.4	6.4	6.0
Other services	7.6	15.7	13.0	13.2
Research and construction	7.6	6.4	7.2	4.6

Source: Public Health Service, *Health—United States, 1982,* p. 140.

TABLE 7.4. SOURCES OF PAYMENT FOR PERSONAL HEALTH CARE, 1950–1981 (PERCENTAGE)

Government now pays the largest share of costs; direct payment is larger than insurance.

Year	Third Party		Government	Direct Payment
	Private Health Insurance	Philanthropy and Industry		
1950	9.1	2.9	22.4	65.5
1960	21.1	2.3	21.8	54.9
1970	24.0	1.6	34.5	39.9
1981	26.2	1.4	40.4	32.1

Source: Public Health Service, *Health—United States, 1982*, p. 139.

TABLE 7.5. ENROLLMENTS IN MEDICARE PARTS A (HOSPITAL INSURANCE) AND B (SUPPLEMENTARY MEDICAL INSURANCE), 1966–1980

Women enrollees outnumber men; most Medicare enrollees purchase part B.

Year	Hospital Insurance			Supplementary Medical Insurance		
	Men	Women	Total	Men	Women	Total
	(thousands)			(thousands)		
1966	8,133	10,950	19,082	7,534	10,202	17,736
1970	8,507	11,855	20,361	8,132	11,452	19,584
1975	9,168	13,304	22,472	8,873	13,073	21,945
1980	10,156	14,948	25,104	9,868	14,813	24,680

Source: Annual statistical supplement to the *Social Security Bulletin*, 1981, p. 205.

TABLE 7.6. HOSPITAL CHARGES UNDER MEDICARE, 1966–1981

Reimbursements rose rapidly, then began to decline: rising daily charges were somewhat offset by decline in length of stay and in the share of total charges covered by Medicare.

Year	Reimbursements (millions)	Charges per Day	Number of Days Covered	Reimbursements as Percentage of Total Charges
1966	$799.5	$44	12.5	79.7
1970	4,500.8	76	12.4	77.2
1975	9,835.7	145	10.6	75.1
1981	19,436.1	342	9.7	68.7

Source: Annual statistical supplement to the *Social Security Bulletin*, 1981, p. 209.

TABLE 7.7. MEDICARE REIMBURSEMENTS, 1967–1981

Physicians and hospitals account for the preponderance of payments.

Category	1967	1970	1975	1980	1981
			(millions)		
Hospital insurance:					
Hospital inpatient	$2,864.0	$4,578.1	$10,006.2	$22,153.7	$19,683.8
Home health	23.3	46.9	145.6	472.2	469.4
Skilled nursing facilities	240.6	230.2	262.4	347.7	282.7
Total	3,134.9	4,855.2	10,414.2	22,973.6	20,435.9
Supplementary medical insurance:					
Physicians services	999.9	1,572.7	3,010.1	6,724.2	—
Home health services	—	22.7	56.8	164.4	—
Outpatient hospital services	—	84.5	315.2	1,006.1	—
Independent laboratory services	—	9.4	36.7	105.0	—
All other	—	61.1	178.1	589.3—	
Total	1,079.6	1,750.5	3,605.0	8,609.0	—

Source: Annual statistical supplement to the *Social Security Bulletin,* 1981, pp. 208 and 211.

TABLE 7.8. UNDUPLICATED MEDICAID RECIPIENTS AND VENDOR PAYMENTS, 1972–1980

Enrollment peaked in 1977 and then fell; disbursements continued to increase steadily.

Year	Number (thousands)	Payments (millions)
Ending June		
1972	17,606	$6,299
1973	19,622	8,650
1974	21,462	9,983
1975	22,013	12,292
1976	22,891	14,135
Ending September		
1977	22,929	$16,276
1978	22,207	17,975
1979	21,250	20,462
1980	21,604	23,301

Source: Annual statistical supplement to the *Social Security Bulletin,* 1981, p. 220.

TABLE 7.9. MEDICAID RECIPIENTS BY CATEGORY, 1972–1980 (IN THOUSANDS)

Under Aid to Families with Dependent Children (AFDC), families are the largest eligible group; they account for the post-1977 decline in beneficiaries.

Year	Total	Age 65 or Older	Blindness	Total Disability	Families with Dependent Children		
					Adults	Children	Other
Ending June							
1972	17,606	3,318	108	1,625	3,137	7,841	1,576
1973	19,622	3,496	101	1,804	4,066	8,659	1,495
1974	21,462	3,732	135	2,222	4,392	9,478	1,502
1975	22,013	3,643	106	2,265	4,573	9,602	1,824
1976	22,891	3,644	94	2,497	4,810	9,939	1,906
Ending September							
1977	22,929	3,611	91	2,683	4,795	9,715	2,036
1978	22,207	3,379	83	2,637	4,703	9,500	1,905
1979	21,250	3,296	80	2,633	4,498	9,022	1,721
1980	21,604	3,416	92	2,724	4,774	9,285	1,507

Source: Annual statistical supplement to the *Social Security Bulletin*, 1981, p. 221.

TABLE 7.10. HEALTH INSURANCE COVERAGE, MULTIPLE-PERSON FAMILIES WITH HEAD UNDER
65 YEARS OF AGE, 1980

*Significant numbers of lower-income families lack health coverage; income is
inversely related to the burden of payment on the family.*

Income Level, 1979	Number of Families (thousands)	Public and/or Private Coverage (percentage)	Public Coverage Only	Family Pays All or Part of Premium (percentage)
Less than $10,000	8,524	77.7	35.6	75.3
$10,000–$19,999	14,797	87.5	7.2	62.4
$20,000–$34,999	15,418	91.0	2.1	55.0
$35,000 or more	5,929	92.2	1.1	57.3

Source: *Health Care Coverage and Insurance Premiums of Families: United States, 1980,* Preliminary
Data Report No. 3 (Washington, D.C.: U.S. Department of Health and Human Services, Health Care
Financing Agency, 1983).

TABLE 7.11. PHYSICIANS PER 100,000 POPULATION BY REGION, 1970 AND 1980

*All regions showed an increase in the physician-population ratio; the Northeast and
the West maintained higher ratios than the North Central and South regions.*

Region	1970	1980
Northeast	185.0	233.6
North Central	127.5	175.0
South	114.8	163.7
West	158.2	212.3
United States total	142.7	191.4

Source: Public Health Service, *Health—United States, 1982,* p. 115.

TABLE 7.12. METROPOLITAN-NONMETROPOLITAN DISTRIBUTION OF HEALTH CARE
RESOURCES AND POPULATION, 1979

*Nonmetropolitan areas have more poor families, fewer hospitals, and
many fewer physicians.*

Category	Metropolitan (percentage)	Nonmetropolitan (percentage)
Population	72.8	27.2
Incomes below $10,000	65.5	34.5
General hospitals	74.6	25.4
Physicians	86.6	13.4

Source: *Health Status of Minorities and Low-Income Groups, 1979* (Washington, D.C.: U.S. Department
of Health and Human Services), p. 26.

TABLE 7.13. AVERAGE OF INDIVIDUALS' VISITS TO PHYSICIANS PER YEAR BY RACE AND INCOME, 1964 AND 1980 (NUMBER PER PERSON)

Differences of access by race and income were narrowed substantially, and access by the poor greatly increased after the introduction of Medicaid and Medicare.

Category	1964	1980
White	4.7	4.8
Black	3.6	4.6
Income level:		
Less than $7,000	3.9	5.5
$7,000–$9,999	4.2	4.4
$10,000–$14,999	4.7	4.9
$15,000–$24,999	4.8	4.7
$25,000 or more	5.2	4.6

Source: Public Health Service, *Health—United States, 1982,* p. 90.

TABLE 7.14. SOURCE OF PHYSICIAN CARE BY RACE AND INCOME, 1980

Lower-income and nonwhite patients use hospital outpatient departments more and doctors' offices or the telephone less than whites and higher-income patients.

Category	Percentage of Visits		
	Doctors' Offices, Clinics, or Group Practices	Hospital Outpatient Departments	Telephone
White	68.4	11.3	13.8
Black	57.0	26.2	5.5
Income level:			
Less than $7,000	58.8	20.7	9.1
$7,000–9,999	61.7	16.0	13.8
$10,000–$14,999	66.1	14.0	13.2
$15,000–$24,999	70.5	10.8	12.9
$25,000 or more	70.6	9.0	14.5

Source: Public Health Service, *Health—United States, 1982,* p. 90.

TABLE 7.15. EMPLOYMENT IN HEALTH CARE, 1970 AND 1980

Substantial growth occurred over the decade, with more employed in hospitals than in all other categories combined.

Employment	1970	1980
Physicians and others in physicians' offices	477	756
Dentists' offices	222	407
Hospitals	2,690	3,947
Convalescent institutions	509	1,185
Other	349	931
Total	4,245	7,226

Source: Public Health Service, *Health—United States, 1982,* p. 112.

TABLE 7.16. INFANTS WEIGHING 2,500 GRAMS OR LESS AT BIRTH BY RACE AND REGION, 1977–1979

Rates of low-weight births among blacks are more than double those of whites in all regions but one.

Region	Total	White	Black
		(number per 100 live births)	
United States total	7.0	5.9	12.7
New England (Maine, New Hampshire, Vermont, Massachusetts, Rhode Island, Connecticut)	6.4	5.9	12.5
Middle Atlantic (New York, New Jersey, Pennsylvania)	7.4	6.1	13.2
East North Central (Ohio, Indiana, Illinois, Michigan, Wisconsin)	6.9	5.7	13.3
West North Central (Minnesota, Iowa, Missouri, North Dakota, South Dakota, Nebraska, Kansas)	5.9	5.3	12.8
South Atlantic (Delaware, Maryland, District of Columbia, Virginia, West Virginia, North Carolina, South Carolina, Georgia, Florida)	8.1	6.1	12.6
East South Central (Kentucky, Tennessee, Alabama, Mississippi)	7.9	6.3	12.2
West South Central (Arkansas, Louisiana, Oklahoma, Texas)	7.5	6.2	12.8
Mountain (Montana, Idaho, Wyoming, Colorado, New Mexico, Arizona, Utah, Nevada)	6.8	6.6	13.3
Pacific (Washington, Oregon, California, Alaska, Hawaii)	6.0	5.3	11.4

Source: Public Health Service, *Health—United States, 1982,* pp. 75–76.

SECTION 8

The Emotionally Disturbed, Mentally Retarded, and Other Institutionalized Groups

TABLE 8.1. RESIDENTIAL FACILITIES FOR THE MENTALLY RETARDED, 1960–1980

The use of institutions for the mentally retarded has declined since 1970.

Year	Number of Institutions	Resident Patients at End of Year	Total Admissions[a]	Net Releases
1960	108	163,730	14,701	6,451
1965	143	187,273	17,300	7,993
1970	190	186,743	14,985	14,702
1975	210	159,041	13,424	18,320
1978	398	152,476	14,286	19,665
1979	391	147,729	17,308	21,406
1980	393	141,203	5,642	16,258
Community Facilities, 1977	4,290	76,250	17,398	9,297

[a]Includes readmissions and excludes transfers.
Source: *Statistical Abstract of the United States, 1982–83.* p. 117.

TABLE 8.2. INPATIENT AND OUTPATIENT MENTAL HEALTH SERVICES, 1955–1979

Outpatient services grew substantially between 1955 and 1975, a reflection of deinstitutionalization.

Year	Episodes per 1,000 Population	
	Inpatient Services	Outpatient Services
1955	8.0	2.3
1965	8.2	5.6
1975	8.5	21.9
1979[a]	8.1	20.6

[a]Provisional data.
Source: Public Health Service, *Health—United States, 1982,* p. 110.

TABLE 8.3. INPATIENT DAYS OF CARE IN MENTAL HEALTH FACILITIES, 1971 AND 1979

*State and county mental hospital deinstitutionalization drastically lowered total
inpatient mental health services.*

Mental Health Facility	1971	1979
		(thousands)
Nonfederal psychiatric hospitals	123,420	55,184
State and county hospitals	119,200	50,110
Veterans Administration	14,277	10,628[a]
Other[b]	19,627	22,753
Total	153,104	83,491

[a]1977 data.

[b]Private hospitals, nonfederal hospital psychiatric units, residential treatment centers for emotionally disturbed children, and community mental health centers.

Source: Public Health Service, *Health—United States, 1982,* p. 111.

TABLE 8.4. NURSING AND PERSONAL CARE HOMES, SELECTED CHARACTERISTICS OF HOMES AND RESIDENTS, 1964 TO 1977

*Total residents increased between 1964 and 1977 by 135 percent. The share of those
below age 75 fell slightly over this period. The number of beds per thousand persons
65 and older rose by 78 percent.*

Characteristic	Number (In thousands, except as indicated)			
	1964	1969	1973–1974	1977
Total residents	554	815	1,076	1,303
White	—	779	318	1,201
Black and other	—	37	758	102
Male	194	252	318	375
Female	360	563	758	928
Under 65 years	66	93	114	177
65 years and over	488	722	962	1,126
65–74 years	104	137	163	211
75–84 years	231	323	385	465
85 years and over	152	262	413	450
Total beds	660	881	1,175	1,402
Per 1,000 persons 65 and older	33.6	45.2	55.2	59.7
Estimated number of homes	17.3	18.4	15.7	18.9
By type of ownership				
Proprietary	14.2	14.2	11.9	14.5
Nonprofit	2.2	2.8	2.7	3.4
Government	1.0	1.4	1.2	1.0

Source: *Statistical Abstract of the United States, 1982–83,* p. 116.

TABLE 8.5. FEDERAL AND STATE PRISONERS, 1950–1981

The proportion of the nation's population imprisoned and under maximum sentence of more than one year rose by 39 percent over a thirty-year period; most of this increase occurred in state prison populations.

	Present at End of Year						Received from Courts					
	All Institutions		Federal		State		All Institutions		Federal		State	
Year	Number	Rate[a]	Number	Rate[a]	Number	Rate[a]	Number	Rate[a]	Number	Rate[a]	Number	Rate[a]
1950	166,123	110.3	17,134	11.4	148,989	98.9	69,473	46.1	14,237	9.5	55,236	36.7
1960	212,953	118.6	23,218	12.9	189,735	105.7	88,575	49.3	13,723	7.6	74,852	41.7
1965	210,895	109.5	21,040	10.9	189,855	98.6	87,505	45.4	12,781	6.6	74,724	38.8
1970	196,429	96.7	20,038	9.8	176,391	86.8	79,351	39.1	12,047	5.9	67,304	33.1
1975	240,593	113.3	24,131	11.4	216,462	102.0	129,573	61.0	16,770	7.9	112,803	53.1
1979	301,470	137.3	22,588	10.3	278,882	127.0	131,047	59.7	12,619	5.7	118,428	53.9
1980	315,974	139.2	20,611	9.1	295,363	130.1	142,122	62.7	10,907	4.8	131,215	57.9
1981	353,167	153.2	22,169	9.6	330,998	143.6	160,272	69.5	11,106	4.8	149,186	64.7

[a]Per hundred thousand estimated population.
Source: *Statistical Abstract of the United States, 1982–83*, p. 191.

TABLE 8.6. CHILDREN'S CASES DISPOSED OF BY JUVENILE COURTS, 1960–1979

The proportion of children involved in cases disposed of by juvenile courts climbed by 138 percent over a twenty-year period.

Item	1960	1965	1970	1975	1978	1979
Population 10–17 years old (thousands)	25,368	29,536	32,614	33,045	29,423	28,713
Delinquency cases excluding traffic (thousands)	510	697	1,052	1,317	1,359	1,374
Delinquency cases per 1,000 population 10–17 years old	20.1	23.6	32.3	39.9	46.2	47.8
Male (thousands)	415	555	800	1,002	1,055	1,058
Female (thousands)	99	142	252	315	304	316
Percentage of total cases	19.3	20.4	24.0	23.9	22.4	23.0
Population under 18 years old (thousands)	64,516	69,699	69,669	66,251	64,359	63,494
Dependency and neglect cases (thousands)	131	157	133	143	158	157
Dependency and neglect cases per 1,000 population under 18 years old	2.0	2.3	1.9	2.2	2.5	2.6

Source: *Statistical Abstract of the United States, 1982–83*, p. 190.

SECTION 9

International Comparative Data

TABLE 9.1. CONSUMER PRICE INDEX IN 1981 (1970 = 100), SELECTED COUNTRIES

Substantial inflation occurred in all major industrial countries in the 1970–1981 period; the United States ranked eighth among thirteen countries.

Country	Consumer Price Index, 1981
United States	234.0
Australia	295.1
Austria	196.4
Belgium	218.9
Canada	243.3
Denmark	285.5
Federal Republic of Germany	174.2
France	283.0
Japan	247.2
Netherlands	215.9
Sweden	271.2
Switzerland	172.4
United Kingdom	404.0

Source: *Social Security Bulletin* (March 1983), p. 54.

TABLE 9.2. TAXATION AS PERCENTAGE OF NATIONAL INCOME FOR SELECTED COUNTRIES, 1978[a]

Most industrial countries tax at higher rates than the United States.

Country	Taxation
United States	35.0
Austria	43.4
Canada	36.0
Denmark	37.4
Federal Republic of Germany	45.2
France	43.5
Italy (1977)	38.1
Japan	31.5
Switzerland	34.0
United Kingdom	39.0

[a]Direct and indirect taxes, compulsory fees, and social security contributions.
Source: United Nations, *1979/80 Statistical Yearbook;* and United Nations, *Yearbook of National Accounts, 1980 Statistics,* Vol. 1.

TABLE 9.3. ANNUAL GROWTH RATES (PERCENTAGE) OF GROSS DOMESTIC PRODUCT, SELECTED COUNTRIES, 1950–1980

U.S. and U.K. growth rates were often below those of other major industrial economies; growth rates generally fell in the decade, 1970–1980.

Country	1950–1960	1960–1970	1970–1980	1950–1980
United States				
Total	3.1	3.9	3.0	3.3
Per capita	1.3	2.6	2.0	2.0
Canada				
Total	4.6	5.2	4.0	4.6
Per capita	1.9	3.4	2.8	2.7
Federal Republic of Germany				
Total	8.0	4.7	2.8	5.1
Per capita	6.4	3.8	2.7	4.3
France				
Total	4.6	5.6	3.6	4.5
Per capita	6.4	3.8	2.7	4.3
Italy[a]				
Total	5.5	5.7	3.1	4.8
Per capita	4.8	5.0	2.5	4.1
Japan[b]				
Total	8.0	10.6	4.9	7.8
Per capita	6.9	9.5	3.6	6.6
United Kingdom				
Total	2.8	2.8	1.9	2.5
Per capita	2.4	2.3	1.8	2.1

[a]Initial year 1957.
[b]Initial year 1952.
Source: *Statistical Abstract of the United States, 1982–83*, p. 421.

TABLE 9.4. UNEMPLOYMENT RATES, SELECTED COUNTRIES, 1970–1981

In 1981, unemployment rates were high in many but not all industrial countries, with the U.S. rate among the highest in this entire period.

Country	1970	1975	1977	1979	1981
United States	4.9	8.5	7.1	5.8	7.6
Australia	1.6	4.9	5.6	6.2	5.8
Canada	5.7	6.9	8.1	7.5	7.6
Federal Republic of Germany	0.5	3.5	3.5	3.0	4.2[a]
France	2.4	4.2	5.0	6.1	7.7[a]
Great Britain	3.1	4.6	6.4	5.7	11.3[a]
Italy	3.1	3.2	3.6	3.9	4.2[a]
Japan	1.2	1.9	2.0	2.1	2.2

[a]Preliminary estimate based on incomplete data.
Source: *Statistical Abstract of the United States, 1982–83*, p. 873.

TABLE 9.5. FEMALE-TO-MALE WAGE RATIOS AS PERCENTAGE BY SECTOR, SELECTED COUNTRIES, 1979

The United States ranks lowest of these countries in each sector, except for manufacturing in Japan.

Country	Manufacturing	Nonmanufacturing
United States	61.2[a]	52.8[b]
Federal Republic of Germany	72.8	72.6
France	76.8	87.4
Japan	44.9	54.9
Netherlands (1978)	80.4	—
Norway	80.2	—
Sweden	88.7	—
Switzerland	64.9	66.6
United Kingdom	69.1	70.7

[a]Blue-collar workers, 1980.
[b]White-collar workers, 1980.
Sources: *Year Book of Labor Statistics* (Geneva: International Labor Organization, 1980); and *Current Population Reports, Consumer Income,* Series P-60, No. 137 (Washington, D.C.: U.S. Bureau of the Census, 1980), p. 184.

TABLE 9.6. LIFE EXPECTANCY AT BIRTH IN SELECTED COUNTRIES, 1973 AND 1978

In all major industrial countries, life expectancies are rising and expectancies are higher for females than for males.

Country	Male		Female	
	1973	1978	1973	1978
United States	67.6	69.5	75.3	77.2
Australia	68.3	70.0[e]	75.3	77.0[e]
Austria	67.4	68.4	74.7	75.7
Canada	69.5	70.5[e]	77.0	78.2[e]
Denmark	71.1	71.7	76.6	77.7
England and Wales	69.2	70.2[e]	75.5	76.3[e]
Federal Republic of Germany	67.8	69.2	74.4	76.0
France	69.5	69.9[d]	77.3	77.9[d]
German Democratic Republic	68.9[a]	68.9[d]	74.2[a]	74.5[d]
Ireland	68.5[b]	69.0[c]	73.4[b]	74.3[c]
Israel	70.2	71.6	73.2	75.1
Japan	70.9	73.2	76.3	78.6
Netherlands	71.2	72.0	77.2	78.7
Sweden	72.1	72.5	77.7	79.0
Switzerland	71.1	72.0	77.2	78.9

[a]1969–1970.
[b]1972.
[c]1975.
[d]1976.
[e]1977.
Source: Public Health Service, *Health—United States, 1982,* p. 58.

TABLE 9.7. INFANT MORTALITY RATES IN SELECTED COUNTRIES, 1973 AND 1978

Four countries out of fourteen reported higher death rates than the U.S. in both years.

Country	Rate per 1,000 Live Births	
	1973	1978
United States	17.7	13.8
Australia	16.5	12.5[a]
Austria	23.8	15.0
Canada	15.5	12.4[a]
Denmark	11.5	8.9[b]
England and Wales	16.9	13.1
Federal Republic of Germany	22.7	14.7
France	15.5	10.6[b]
German Democratic Republic	15.6	13.2
Ireland	18.0	15.6[a]
Israel	22.8	17.2
Japan	11.3	8.4
Netherlands	11.5	9.6
Sweden	9.9	7.8
Switzerland	13.2	8.6

[a]1977 data.
[b]Provisional data.
Source: Public Health Service, *Health—United States, 1982*, p. 57.

TABLE 9.8. MATERNITY OR PARENTAL LEAVES IN SIX COUNTRIES, 1975

The countries cited have pioneered in a benefit still not provided under U.S. law.

	Sweden	German Democratic Republic	Federal Republic of Germany	Hungary	France	United States
Number of days	270	182	224	140	112	None
Replacement rate[a]	100	100	77[b]	100	100	—

[a]Percentage of wages.
[b]Plus a supplement from the employer.
Source: Sheila B. Kamerman and Alfred J. Kahn, *Child Care, Family Benefits, and Working Parents: A Study in Comparative Policy* (New York: Columbia University Press, 1981), p. 208.

TABLE 9.9. FUNDING OF SOCIAL SECURITY PROGRAMS, SELECTED COUNTRIES, 1981 (PERCENTAGE OF EARNINGS OR PAYROLL)

Some countries exclude workers' earnings from tax or tax employees at a lower rate than employers. Government frequently supplements direct contributions.

Country	Old Age, Invalidism, and Death			Sickness and Maternity			Work Injury			Unemployment		
	Worker	Employer	Govt.	Worker	Employer	Govt.	Worker	Employer	Govt.	Worker	Employer	Govt.
Federal Republic of Germany	9.25	9.25	Subsidy	3.5–7.5	3.5–7.5	Subsidy	—	1.5	Subsidy	1.5	1.5	Subsidy
France	4.8	8.2	—	4.5	8.95	Misc. charges	—	4.0	—	0.84	2.76	—
German Democratic Republic				......Government covers all programs......								
Hungary	3.0–10.0	10.0	ca. 40% of cost	......Government covers all programs......								
Israel	2.7	4.2	15% Supplement	0.7	0.7	—	—	0.7–4.0	—	0.2	0.4	—
Japan	5.3(M)[a] 4.5(F)	5.3(M) 4.5(F)	20% of benefits	4.2	4.2	16.4% of cost	—	0.5–12.9	Deficit	0.55	0.9	25% of cost
Sweden	—	8.4	ca. 30% of cost	—	10.5	ca. 15% of cost	—	0.6	—	1.5–4.0	0.4	ca. 46% of cost
U.S.S.R.	—	4.4–9.0	ca. 50% of cost	......Government covers all programs......								

[a] Rates differ for males (M) and females (F).

Source: *Social Security Programs throughout the World, 1981.*

TABLE 9.10. SOCIAL SECURITY PAYROLL CONTRIBUTION RATES AS PERCENTAGE OF WAGE,
SELECTED COUNTRIES, JANUARY 1981

*Many countries tax employers more heavily than employees;
in only two instances—the Netherlands and Switzerland—are employees levied more
heavily than employers in one or more programs.*

Country	All Programs		Old-Age, Disability, and Survivors Insurance Program		Health Insurance	
	Employer	Employee	Employer	Employee	Employer	Employee
United States	11.45	6.65	5.35	5.35	1.30	1.30
Austria	26.10	14.20	11.35	9.75	6.95	3.15
Belgium	26.82	10.10	8.86	6.25	5.59	2.95
Federal Republic of Germany	17.75	16.25	9.25	9.25	5.5	5.5
France	37.41	11.14	8.20	4.80	13.45	5.50
Japan	12.80	10.05	5.30[a]	5.30[a]	4.20	4.20
Netherlands	29.225	25.625	12.90	19.55	13.65	5.30
Sweden	32.65	.11	21.15	0	10.5	0
Switzerland	6.45[b]	9.15	4.20	4.20	0	0
United Kingdom	13.70	7.75	13.70	7.75	—	—

Country	Work Injury		Unemployment		Family Allowance	
	Employer	Employee	Employer	Employee	Employer	Employee
United States	1.90	0	2.90	0	—	—
Austria	1.50	0	1.30	1.30	5.00	0
Belgium	3.85	0	1.27	.90	7.25	0
Federal Republic of Germany	1.50	0	1.50	1.50	0	0
France	4.00	0	2.76	.84	9.00	0
Japan	2.30	0	.90	.55	.10	0
Netherlands	—	—	.775	.775	1.90	0
Sweden	.60	0	.40	.11	0	0
Switzerland	—[b]	0	.25	.25	2.00	0
United Kingdom	—	—	—	—	0	0

[a]Rates for men; rate for women is 4.5.
[b]Employer pays whole cost of work injury.
Source: *Social Security Programs throughout the World, 1981.*

TABLE 9.11. REPLACEMENT RATES OF SOCIAL SECURITY OLD-AGE PENSIONS FOR WORKERS WITH AVERAGE WAGES IN MANUFACTURING AND FOR COUPLES, SELECTED COUNTRIES, 1969–1980

The United States is among the countries that increased replacement rates after 1969; it ranked in the middle of the twelve countries.

	Pension as Percentage of Earnings in Year before Retirement											
	Single Worker						Aged Couple					
Country	1969	1975	1977	1978	1979	1980	1969	1975	1977	1978	1979	1980
Austria	67	63	64	65	67	68	67	63	64	65	67	68
Canada	24	33	33	32	33	34	41	47	47	47	48	49
Denmark	31	29	27	28	30	29	45	44	44	48	54	52
Federal Republic of Germany	55	51	54	54	50	49	55	51	54	54	50	59
France	41	60	64	67	67	66	56	74	78	79	77	75
Italy	62	61	64	66	66	69	62	61	64	66	66	69
Japan	26	37	45	44	44	54	27	39	57	57	57	61
Netherlands	43	43	45	44	44	44	61	61	65	65	65	63
Sweden	42	57	59	63	68	68	56	73	73	79	79	83
Switzerland	28	40	39	38	37	37	45	60	59	58	56	55
United Kingdom	27	31	28	29	29	31	43	47	43	45	45	47
United States	30	38	40	41	41	44	44	58	60	61	62	66

Source: *Social Security Bulletin* (November 1982), p. 5.

SECTION 10

Social Work Education

TABLE 10.1. SCHOOLS OFFERING ADVANCED PROGRAMS IN SOCIAL WORK AND DOCTORAL
DEGREES IN SOCIAL WORK AWARDED, 1949–1982

Doctoral programs have shown steady growth.

Year	Number of Schools	Number of Degrees Awarded
1949	9	6
1951	10	10
1953	12	8
1955	14	12
1957	15	20
1959	15	26
1961	16	31
1963	16	35
1965	16	39
1967	18	54
1969	20	89
1971	24	129
1973	27	112
1975	31	155
1976	33	179
1977	34	179
1978	35	178
1979	38	174
1980	38	213
1981	41	226
1982	42	284

Source: Council on Social Work Education, annual statistical reports.

TABLE 10.2. FULL-TIME STUDENT ENROLLMENT IN MASTER'S DEGREE PROGRAMS IN ACCREDITED SCHOOLS OF SOCIAL WORK AND NUMBER OF ACCREDITED SCHOOLS IN THE UNITED STATES AND CANADA, 1929–1982

There has been a 25 percent increase in the number of schools since 1970; full-time student enrollment climbed by 38 percent from that time until 1978, but declined significantly after that.

Year[a]	Number of Schools	Full-Time Student Enrollment
1929	25	1,306
1932	24	948
1935	31	1,837
1938	35	2,150
1941	36	2,421
1944	42	2,283
1947	44	3,737
1950	49	4,336
1953	52	3,694
1956	52	3,811
1959	56	4,934
1962	56	6,039
1965	67	8,989
1968	72	11,700
1970[b]	70	12,821
1971	76	13,986
1972	78	15,031
1973	79	16,099
1974	79	16,590
1975	81	16,676
1976	82	16,869
1977	84	17,533
1978	84	17,672
1979	84	17,397
1980	84	17,122
1981	87	16,552
1982	87	15,131

[a]As of November 1.

[b]From 1970, when the Canadian schools established a separate accreditation system, data are for the United States only.

Source: Council on Social Work Education, annual statistical reports.

TABLE 10.3. STUDENTS IN ACCREDITED BACCALAUREATE SOCIAL WORK PROGRAMS BY TYPE OF
ENROLLMENT, 1974–1981

*Over an eight-year period, the number of full-time degree students declined by 11
percent; that of part-time students increased by 60 percent.*

Year[a]	Full-Time Degree Students	Part-Time Degree Students	Other Students Taking Social Work Courses
1974	29,909	1,946	14,176
1975	22,966	1,879	10,372
1976	25,281	2,433	12,184
1977	29,173	3,715	12,537
1978	29,350	4,037	13,595
1979	27,996	3,770	12,181
1980	27,051	3,059	11,686
1981	26,602	3,107	10,961

[a]As of November 1.
Source: Council on Social Work Education, annual statistical reports.

TABLE 10.4. MASTER'S DEGREES AWARDED TO GRADUATES OF SCHOOLS OF SOCIAL WORK IN THE
UNITED STATES BY SEX, 1944–1945 TO 1981–1982

The steady climb in the number of degrees awarded came to an end in 1979.

Academic Year	Total	Men	Women
1944–1945	839	43	796
1947–1948	1,765	496	1,269
1950–1951	1,923	744	1,179
1953–1954	1,651	566	1,085
1956–1957	1,612	601	1,011
1959–1960	2,087	836	1,251
1962–1963	2,505	1,025	1,480
1965–1966	3,693	1,482	2,210
1968–1969	5,060	2,029	3,031
1970–1971	6,909	2,630	4,269
1974–1975	8,824	3,037[a]	5,730[a]
1975–1976	9,080	2,832	6,138
1976–1977	9,254	2,832	6,422
1977–1978	9,476	2,644	6,832
1978–1979[b]	10,080	2,772	7,308
1979–1980	9,850	2,615	7,235
1980–1981[c]	9,750	2,374	7,045
1981–1982	9,556	2,041	7,515

[a]Breakdown by sex not reported for 57 students.
[b]One school did not respond in time to be included in 1979 totals.
[c]Breakdown by sex not reported for 331 students.
Source: Council on Social Work Education, annual statistical reports.

Appendix

NASW CODE OF ETHICS, 1980

The Code of Ethics that follows was adopted by the Delegate Assembly of the National Association of Social Workers in 1979 and took effect July 1, 1980.

Preamble

This code is intended to serve as a guide to the everyday conduct of members of the social work profession and as a basis for the adjudication of issues in ethics when the conduct of social workers is alleged to deviate from the standards expressed or implied in this code. It represents standards of ethical behavior for social workers in professional relationships with those served, with colleagues, with employers, with other individuals and professions, and with the community and society as a whole. It also embodies standards of ethical behavior governing individual conduct to the extent that such conduct is associated with an individual's status and identity as a social worker.

This code is based on the fundamental values of the social work profession that include the worth, dignity, and uniqueness of all persons as well as their rights and opportunities. It is also based on the nature of social work, which fosters conditions that promote these values.

In subscribing to and abiding by this code, the social worker is expected to view ethical responsibility in as inclusive a context as each situation demands and within which ethical judgment is required. The social worker is expected to take into consideration all the principles in this code that have a bearing upon any situation in which ethical judgment is to be exercised and professional intervention or conduct is planned. The course of action that the social worker chooses is expected to be consistent with the spirit as well as the letter of this code.

In itself, this code does not represent a set of rules that will prescribe all the behaviors of social workers in all the com-plexities of professional life. Rather, it offers general principles to guide conduct, and the judicious appraisal of conduct, in situations that have ethical implications. It provides the basis for making judgments about ethical actions before and after they occur. Frequently, the particular situation determines the ethical principles that apply and the manner of their application. In such cases, not only the particular ethical principles are taken into immediate consideration, but also the entire code and its spirit. Specific applications of ethical principles must be judged within the context in which they are being considered. Ethical behavior in a given situation must satisfy not only the judgment of the individual social worker, but also the judgment of an unbiased jury of professional peers.

This code should not be used as an instrument to deprive any social worker of the opportunity or freedom to practice with complete professional integrity; nor should any disciplinary action be taken on the basis of this code without maximum provision for safeguarding the rights of the social worker affected.

The ethical behavior of social workers results not from edict, but from a personal commitment of the individual. This code is offered to affirm the will and zeal of all social workers to be ethical and to act ethically in all that they do as social workers.

The following codified ethical principles should guide social workers in the various roles and relationships and at the various levels of responsibility in which they function professionally. These principles also serve as a basis for the adjudication by the National Association of Social Workers of issues in ethics.

In subscribing to this code, social workers are required to cooperate in its implementation and abide by any disciplinary rulings based on it. They should also take adequate measures to discourage, prevent, expose, and correct the unethical conduct of colleagues. Finally, social workers should be equally ready to defend and assist colleagues unjustly charged with unethical conduct.

Summary of Major Principles

I. The Social Worker's Conduct and Comportment as a Social Worker

A. Propriety. The social worker should maintain high standards of personal conduct in the capacity or identity as social worker.

B. Competence and Professional Development. The social worker should strive to become and remain proficient in professional practice and the performance of professional functions.

C. Service. The social worker should regard as primary the service obligation of the social work profession.

D. Integrity. The social worker should act in accordance with the highest standards of professional integrity.

E. Scholarship and Research. The social worker engaged in study and research should be guided by the conventions of scholarly inquiry.

II. The Social Worker's Ethical Responsibility to Clients

F. Primacy of Clients' Interests. The social worker's primary responsibility is to clients.

G. Rights and Prerogatives of Clients. The social worker should make every effort to foster maximum self-determination on the part of clients.

H. Confidentiality and Privacy. The social worker should respect the privacy of clients and hold in confidence all information obtained in the course of professional service.

I. Fees. When setting fees, the social worker should ensure that they are fair, reasonable, considerate, and commensurate with the service performed and with due regard for the clients' ability to pay.

III. The Social Worker's Ethical Responsibility to Colleagues

J. Respect, Fairness, and Courtesy. The social worker should treat colleagues with respect, courtesy, fairness, and good faith.

K. Dealing with Colleagues' Clients. The social worker has the responsibility to relate to the clients of colleagues with full professional consideration.

IV. The Social Worker's Ethical Responsibility to Employers and Employing Organizations

L. Commitments to Employing Organizations. The social worker should adhere to commitments made to the employing organizations.

V. The Social Worker's Ethical Responsibility to the Social Work Profession

M. Maintaining the Integrity of the Profession. The social worker should uphold and advance the values, ethics, knowledge, and mission of the profession.

N. Community Service. The social worker should assist the profession in making social services available to the general public.

O. Development of Knowledge. The social worker should take responsibility for identifying, developing, and fully utilizing knowledge for professional practice.

VI. The Social Worker's Ethical Responsibility to Society

P. Promoting the General Welfare. The social worker should promote the general welfare of society.

The NASW Code of Ethics

I. The Social Worker's Conduct and Comportment as a Social Worker

A. Propriety—The social worker should maintain high standards of personal conduct in the capacity or identity as social worker.

1. The private conduct of the social worker is a personal matter to the same degree as is any other person's, except when such conduct compromises the fulfillment of professional responsibilities.

2. The social worker should not participate in, condone, or be associated with dishonesty, fraud, deceit, or misrepresentation.

3. The social worker should distinguish clearly between statements and actions made as a private individual and as a representative of the social work profession or an organization or group.

B. Competence and Professional Development—The social worker should strive to become and remain proficient in professional practice and the performance of professional functions.

1. The social worker should accept responsibility or employment only on the basis of existing competence or the intention to acquire the necessary competence.

2. The social worker should not misrepresent professional qualifications, education, experience, or affiliations.

C. Service—The social worker should regard as primary the service obligation of the social work profession.

1. The social worker should retain ultimate responsibility for the quality and extent of the service that individual assumes, assigns, or performs.

2. The social worker should act to prevent practices that are inhumane or discriminatory against any person or group of persons.

D. Integrity—The social worker should act in accordance with the highest standards of professional integrity and impartiality.

1. The social worker should be alert to and resist the influences and pressures that interfere with the exercise of professional discretion and impartial judgment required for the performance of professional functions.

2. The social worker should not exploit professional relationships for personal gain.

E. Scholarship and Research—The social worker engaged in study and research should be guided by the conventions of scholarly inquiry.

1. The social worker engaged in research should consider carefully its possible consequences for human beings.

2. The social worker engaged in research should ascertain that the consent of participants in the research is voluntary and informed, without any implied deprivation or penalty for refusal to participate, and with due regard for participants' privacy and dignity.

3. The social worker engaged in research should protect participants from unwarranted physical or mental discomfort, distress, harm, danger, or deprivation.

4. The social worker who engages in the evaluation of services or cases should discuss them only for the professional purposes and only with persons directly and professionally concerned with them.

5. Information obtained about participants in research should be treated as confidential.

6. The social worker should take credit only for work actually done in connection with scholarly and research endeavors and credit contributions made by others.

II. The Social Worker's Ethical Responsibility to Clients

F. Primacy of Clients' Interests—The social worker's primary responsibility is to clients.

1. The social worker should serve clients with devotion, loyalty, determination, and the maximum application of professional skill and competence.

2. The social worker should not exploit relationships with clients for personal advantage, or solicit the clients of one's agency for private practice.

3. The social worker should not prac-

tice, condone, facilitate, or collaborate with any form of discrimination on the basis of race, color, sex, sexual orientation, age, religion, national origin, marital status, political belief, mental or physical handicap, or any other preference or personal characteristic, condition, or status.

4. The social worker should avoid relationships or commitments that conflict with the interests of clients.

5. The social worker should under no circumstances engage in sexual activities with clients.

6. The social worker should provide clients with accurate and complete information regarding the extent and nature of the services available to them.

7. The social worker should apprise clients of their risks, rights, opportunities, and obligations associated with social service to them.

8. The social worker should seek advice and counsel of colleagues and supervisors whenever such consultation is in the best interest of clients.

9. The social worker should terminate service to clients, and professional relationships with them, when such service and relationships are no longer required or no longer serve the clients' needs or interests.

10. The social worker should withdraw services precipitously only under unusual circumstances, giving careful consideration to all factors in the situation and taking care to minimize possible adverse effects.

11. The social worker who anticipates the termination or interruption of service to clients should notify clients promptly and seek the transfer, referral, or continuation of service in relation to the clients' needs and preferences.

G. Rights and Prerogatives of Clients—The social worker should make every effort to foster maximum self-determination on the part of clients.

1. When the social worker must act on behalf of a client who has been adjudged legally incompetent, the social worker should safeguard the interests and rights of that client.

2. When another individual has been legally authorized to act in behalf of a client, the social worker should deal with that person always with the client's best interest in mind.

3. The social worker should not engage in any action that violates or diminishes the civil or legal rights of clients.

H. Confidentiality and Privacy—The social worker should respect the privacy of clients and hold in confidence all information obtained in the course of professional service.

1. The social worker should share with others confidences revealed by clients, without their consent, only for compelling professional reasons.

2. The social worker should inform clients fully about the limits of confidentiality in a given situation, the purposes for which information is obtained, and how it may be used.

3. The social worker should afford clients reasonable access to any official social work records concerning them.

4. When providing clients with access to records, the social worker should take due care to protect the confidences of others contained in those records.

5. The social worker should obtain informed consent of clients before taping, recording, or permitting third party observation of their activities.

I. Fees—When setting fees, the social worker should ensure that they are fair, reasonable, considerate, and commensurate with the service performed and with due regard for the clients' ability to pay.

1. The social worker should not divide a fee or accept or give anything of value for receiving or making a referral.

III. The Social Worker's Ethical Responsibility to Colleagues

J. Respect, Fairness, and Courtesy—The social worker should treat colleagues with respect, courtesy, fairness, and good faith.

1. The social worker should cooperate with colleagues to promote professional interests and concerns.

2. The social worker should respect confidences shared by colleagues in the course of their professional relationships and transactions.

3. The social worker should create and maintain conditions of practice that facilitate ethical and competent professional performance by colleagues.

4. The social worker should treat with respect, and represent accurately and fairly, the qualifications, views, and findings of colleagues and use appropriate channels to express judgments on these matters.

5. The social worker who replaces or is replaced by a colleague in professional practice should act with consideration for the interest, character, and reputation of that colleague.

6. The social worker should not exploit a dispute between a colleague and employers to obtain a position or otherwise advance the social worker's interest.

7. The social worker should seek arbitration or mediation when conflicts with colleagues require resolution for compelling professional reasons.

8. The social worker should extend to colleagues of other professions the same respect and cooperation that is extended to social work colleagues.

9. The social worker who serves as an employer, supervisor, or mentor to colleagues should make orderly and explicit arrangements regarding the conditions of their continuing professional relationship.

10. The social worker who has the responsibility for employing and evaluating the performance of other staff members, should fulfill such responsibility in a fair, considerate, and equitable manner, on the basis of clearly enunciated criteria.

11. The social worker who has the responsibility for evaluating the performance of employees, supervisees, or students should share evaluations with them.

K. Dealing with Colleagues' Clients—The social worker has the responsibility to relate to the clients of colleagues with full professional consideration.

1. The social worker should not solicit the clients of colleagues.

2. The social worker should not assume professional responsibility for the clients of another agency or a colleague without appropriate communication with that agency or colleague.

3. The social worker who serves the clients of colleagues, during a temporary absence or emergency, should serve those clients with the same consideration as that afforded any client.

IV. The Social Worker's Ethical Responsibility to Employers and Employing Organizations

L. Commitments to Employing Organization—The social worker should adhere to commitments made to the employing organization.

1. The social worker should work to improve the employing agency's policies and procedures, and the efficiency and effectiveness of its services.

2. The social worker should not accept employment or arrange student field placements in an organization which is currently under public sanction by NASW for violating personnel standards, or imposing limitations on or penalties for professional actions on behalf of clients.

3. The social worker should act to prevent and eliminate discrimination in the employing organization's work assignments and in its employment policies and practices.

4. The social worker should use with scrupulous regard, and only for the purpose for which they are intended, the resources of the employing organization.

V. The Social Worker's Ethical Responsibility to the Social Work Profession

M. Maintaining the Integrity of the Profession—The social worker should

uphold and advance the values, ethics, knowledge, and mission of the profession.

1. The social worker should protect and enhance the dignity and integrity of the profession and should be responsible and vigorous in discussion and criticism of the profession.

2. The social worker should take action through appropriate channels against unethical conduct by any other member of the profession.

3. The social worker should act to prevent the unauthorized and unqualified practice of social work.

4. The social worker should make no misrepresentation in advertising as to qualifications, competence, service, or results to be achieved.

N. Community Service—The social worker should assist the profession in making social services available to the general public.

1. The social worker should contribute time and professional expertise to activities that promote respect for the utility, the integrity, and the competence of the social work profession.

2. The social worker should support the formulation, development, enactment, and implementation of social policies of concern to the profession.

O. Development of Knowledge—The social worker should take responsibility for identifying, developing, and fully utilizing knowledge for professional practice.

1. The social worker should base practice upon recognized knowledge relevant to social work.

2. The social worker should critically examine, and keep current with, emerging knowledge relevant to social work.

3. The social worker should contribute to the knowledge base of social work and share research knowledge and practice wisdom with colleagues.

VI. The Social Worker's Ethical Responsibility to Society

P. Promoting the General Welfare—The social worker should promote the general welfare of society.

1. The social worker should act to prevent and eliminate discrimination against any person or group on the basis of race, color, sex, sexual orientation, age, religion, national origin, marital status, political belief, mental or physical handicap, or any other preference or personal characteristic, condition, or status.

2. The social worker should act to ensure that all persons have access to the resources, services, and opportunities which they require.

3. The social worker should act to expand choice and opportunity for all persons, with special regard for disadvantaged or oppressed groups and persons.

4. The social worker should promote conditions that encourage respect for the diversity of cultures which constitute American society.

5. The social worker should provide appropriate professional services in public emergencies.

6. The social worker should advocate changes in policy and legislation to improve social conditions and to promote social justice.

7. The social worker should encourage informed participation by the public in shaping social policies and institutions.

Index